Case Studies in Contemporary Criticism

Case Studies in Contemporary Criticism
SERIES EDITOR: Ross C Murfin

Case Studies in Contemporary Criticism

SERIES EDITOR: Ross C Murfin, *Southern Methodist University*

SAMUEL TAYLOR COLERIDGE
The Rime of the Ancient Mariner

Complete, Authoritative Texts of
the 1798 and 1817 Versions with
Biographical and Historical Contexts,
Critical History, and Essays from
Contemporary Critical Perspectives

EDITED BY

Paul H. Fry

Yale University

Bedford/St. Martin's
BOSTON • NEW YORK

Dedicated to the students of Ezra Stiles College.

For Bedford/St. Martin's

Executive Editor: Stephen A. Scipione
Associate Editor: Maura E. Shea
Production Supervisor: Dennis Conroy
Project Management: Stratford Publishing Services, Inc.
Marketing Manager: Charles Cavaliere
Text Design: Sandra Rigney, The Book Department
Cover Design: Donna Lee Dennison
Cover Photo: Waves by Darrell Gulin/AllStock/PNI.
Composition: Stratford Publishing Services, Inc.
Printing and Binding: Haddon Craftsmen, an
R. R. Donnelley & Sons Company

President: Charles H. Christensen
Editorial Director: Joan E. Feinberg
Director of Editing, Design, and Production: Marcia Cohen
Manager, Publishing Services: Emily Berleth

Library of Congress Catalog Card Number: 98-87524

8   7   6
g   f   e

For information, write: Bedford/St. Martin's
75 Arlington Street, Boston, MA 02116 (617-399-4000)

ISBN-10: 0-312-11223-8 (paperback)
          0-312-21917-2 (hardcover)
ISBN-13: 978-0-312-11223-3

Published and distributed outside North America by:

MACMILLAN PRESS LTD.
Houndmills, Basingstoke, Hampshire RG21 2XS and London
Companies and representatives throughout the world.

ISBN: 0-333-76450-1

A catalogue record for this book is available from the British Library.

Acknowledgments

*Acknowledgments and copyrights can be found at the back of the book on page 358, which
constitutes an extension of the copyright page.*

About the Series

Volumes in the Case Studies in Contemporary Criticism series introduce college students to the current critical and theoretical ferment in literary studies. Each volume reprints the complete text of a significant literary work, together with critical essays that approach the work from different theoretical perspectives and editors' introductions to both the literary work and the critics' theoretical perspectives.

The volume editor of each Case Study has selected and prepared an authoritative text of the literary work, written an introduction to the work's biographical and historical contexts, and surveyed the critical responses to the work since its original publication. Thus situated biographically, historically, and critically, the work is subsequently examined in several critical essays that have been prepared especially for students. The essays show theory in practice; whether written by established scholars or exceptional young critics, they demonstrate how current theoretical approaches can generate compelling readings of great literature.

As series editor, I have prepared introductions to the critical essays and to the theoretical approaches they entail. The introductions explain and historicize the principal concepts, major figures, and key works of particular theoretical approaches as a prelude to discussing how they pertain to the critical essays that follow. Each introduction also includes a bibliography to which students can refer if they wish to augment their knowledge of the various critical theories represented in the volume. It is my hope that the introductions will reveal to students that effective criticism — including their own — is informed by a set of coherent assumptions that can be not only articulated but also modified and extended through comparison of different theoretical approaches. Finally, I have included a glossary of key terms that recur in these volumes and in the discourse of contemporary theory and criticism. I hope that the Case Studies in Contemporary Criticism series will reaffirm the richness of its literary works, even as it presents invigorating new ways to mine their apparently inexhaustible wealth.

I would like to thank Supryia M. Ray, with whom I wrote *The Bedford Glossary of Critical and Literary Terms,* for her invaluable help in revising the introductions to the critical approaches represented in this volume.

Ross C Murfin
Provost, Southern Methodist University
Series Editor

About This Volume

Probably no British Romantic poem is more familiar to the general reader than "The Rime of the Ancient Mariner." One overhears the most unlikely people engrossed in some chore and muttering to themselves, "Water, water every where, / Nor any drop to drink" (1817 ll. 121–22). It is difficult to say why this should be. The "Rime" is not a perfect poem, but it has outlasted even fully considered changes in curricular choice and remains a favorite in those introduction-to-methods courses in which the teacher's aim is to show how diverse approaches can transform a single text.

Perhaps in this last fact there is a clue to the endurance of the "Rime." There appears to be something in it for everyone, from the fascination of oceanic quests both literal and symbolic to the more clinical interest we have found lately in testimonies that are conditioned by trauma and survivor guilt. But in addition to what is demonstrably present in the poem, the complexity of its structure and organization — already in 1798 when it first appeared but then increasingly in later revisions — allows the interpretive imagination a tremendous range of responses that find little or no discouragement from the poem itself. Nothing in Coleridge's suggestive narrative allows us positively to deny, for example (and various details seem to confirm), the argument set forth by more than one able critic that the "Rime" is about the guilt and anxiety attendant upon maritime expansion throughout the age of Magellan and the ensuing slave trade. As the account given later in this volume of the copious and varied existing "Rime" commentary will show — together with the six critical essays in this volume that illustrate contemporary approaches — Coleridge's great literary ballad, like the soliloquies of Hamlet, is a poem that rewards nearly endless speculation.

To help students begin their own speculations, this volume reprints two key versions of the "Rime"— the 1798, with its enigmatically archaic tone, and the 1817, with the famous marginal gloss added — together with notes indicating variants in other versions. Five of the exemplary speculations presented in Part Two reflect recent trends in reader-response, Marxist, new historical, psychoanalytic, and deconstructive criticism, respectively; the sixth, drawing eclectically from several of those approaches (among others), suggests the fluid, combinatorial character of much recent criticism. While it is important for students to see that particular theoretical approaches can generate powerful critical readings, it is no less important for them to understand that effective criticism need not be constrained by theoretical categories.

Acknowledgments

I am indebted first and last to my friend, series editor Ross Murfin, for patience and good humor in equal measure and for contributions well beyond the ordinary in recent months. My colleagues Leslie Brisman and Geoffrey Hartman are genii, whether they know it or not, who have kept "Porlock" from the door these many years. My wife Brigitte Peucker and son Spencer Fry have been as saintly as always. With equal gratitude I thank the splendid contributors to this volume and the executive editor at Bedford/St. Martin's, Steve Scipione, for their forbearance and flexibility. Others at the publisher whose help has been indispensable are Elizabeth Schaaf, Emily Berleth, and Maura Shea, as well as the staff at Stratford Publishing Services.

Paul H. Fry
Yale University

Contents

PART ONE

"The Rime
of the Ancient Mariner":
The 1798 and 1817 Texts

Biographical and Historical Contexts

Samuel Taylor Coleridge was born on October 21, 1772 at Ottery St. Mary, Devonshire. He was the youngest of ten children and had four additional siblings by the previous marriage of his father, the Reverend John Coleridge, a genial and intelligent man who was vicar of Ottery and master of the local grammar school, King's School, which Coleridge began to attend at age six. After his father died three years later, the new vicar-schoolmaster proved only half-literate, and the promising young "STC," whose charming, erudite conversation already dazzled children and adults in all stations of life, was enrolled as a scholarship student at Christ's Hospital, London, under the mastership of James Boyer, an irascible but passionately clear-minded man who made a lasting impression on the intellectually impressionable Coleridge. At this school Coleridge numbered among his friends the essayist-to-be Charles Lamb and Tom Evans, whose family stood proxy for his own (which Coleridge rarely revisited for reasons that are not entirely clear). Coleridge remained romantically attached to Tom Evans's sister Mary until — and perhaps beyond — the time of his marriage.

In 1791 Coleridge entered Jesus College, Cambridge, on scholarship. There he continued to read his way through whole libraries while leading a convivial life among his friends and sliding by degrees into debt. In his second year he won the Browne Medal for a Greek sapphic "Ode on the Slave Trade" in which his republican and socially liberal sentiments were on full display. (When six years later he wrote the "Rime of the Ancient Mariner"— a poem in which many readers have found an allegory of imperial expansion and the slave trade — the groundswell begun in 1787 by the younger Pitt for the abolition of the slave trade within the British Empire was increasing, and efforts to this end by the great reform minister Charles James Fox finally succeeded in 1807.) The following year, which saw Coleridge's first poem published in the *Morning Chronicle,* likewise saw his departure from Cambridge under a burden of debt, which he absurdly hoped to evade by enlisting in the Fifteenth Light Dragoons. A terrible horseman in every way unfit for this mode of life, Coleridge managed to have his commission cancelled (with the help of friends and of his then-favorite brother, the Reverend George Coleridge, an archconservative who wanted less and less to do with the eccentric STC as the years passed) and returned to Cambridge, which he soon left without a degree. He had already begun to make a living of sorts by publishing miscellaneous political and other pamphlets and preaching in Unitarian pulpits. On a visit to Oxford, he met Robert Southey, soon to be a well-known poet and man of letters, with whom he hatched a scheme to emigrate to the shores of the Susquehanna River in the United States to live in an ideal society, or "pantisocracy." In pursuit of this vision, Coleridge allowed himself to be drawn into an engagement with Sara Fricker, the sister of the Bristol woman Southey was soon to marry. In this year (1794), with Southey and another friend, Coleridge composed a play, *The Fall of Robespierre.* Written when the events it chronicles were scarcely over, this play reflects the consternation British radicals were feeling in the immediate aftermath of the 1793 Terror (a bloodbath by guillotine of revisionists and alleged timeservers carried out by Robespierre in the name of "reason" and political purity), which had dashed or at the least severely curtailed their populist hopes for the antiaristocratic, eventually anti-monarchic French Revolution of 1789.

Living much of the time in Bristol the next year, Coleridge met William Wordsworth in August — marking the start of the celebrated friendship to which we shall return in describing the composition of the "Rime" below — and married Sara Fricker in October. The couple moved to a cottage in nearby Clevedon, where Coleridge wrote "The Eolian Harp," the first of a group of blank verse poems written over the next three years in a meditative, conversational style, including "Lines on Leaving a Place of Retirement," "This Lime-Tree Bower My Prison," "Frost at Midnight," and "The Nightingale." These poems comprise an important part of his poetic accomplishment. ("To William

Wordsworth" [1807] and the strophic "Dejection: An Ode" [1802] are later poems in a related mode.) Seventeen ninety-six witnessed Coleridge's persistent drifting, marked by his first continued use of laudanum as a painkiller (a common practice of the time that in Coleridge's case led to opium addiction), the publication of a periodical miscellany called *The Watchman,* and the birth of a son, Hartley. At the end of the year the family moved to a drafty, smoky, mice-infested cottage in Nether Stowey, Somersetshire, not far from the Bristol Channel, largely in order to be neighbors of Coleridge's friend and advisor, Thomas Poole.

Here blossomed Coleridge's friendship with Wordsworth and his sister Dorothy, and the ensuing period was perhaps the happiest — and certainly the most productive poetically — of Coleridge's adult life. The so-called mystery poems — the "Rime," the unfinished "Christabel," and "Kubla Khan" (also a fragment according to Coleridge) — were composed in rapid succession. These and the Conversation Poems reflect not so much the influence of Wordsworth (in 1796 and 1797 Coleridge was actually the more productive of the two, and his conversational style of writing influenced Wordsworth rather than the other way around) as the sheer inspiration of continued contact with the person Coleridge more or less instinctively believed to be the supreme poetical talent of the age. It is important to remember that Coleridge never considered himself to be first and foremost a poet. Even at this period, his highest aim was to produce a major work of moral and religious philosophy; and at later periods, apart from this continued ambition, he was chiefly devoted to the exploration of aesthetics, literary criticism, and political philosophy. It is often said that by 1802 or so the gigantic shadow of Wordsworth had withered and destroyed his hopes as a poet; and while it is true that, as Coleridge himself said, Wordsworth's example had brought him to believe that his own talents were inferior, there is really no evidence that Coleridge had ever viewed poetry as his chief vocation.

I shall return below to the crucial period spanning 1797 and early 1798 that witnessed the joint venture called *Lyrical Ballads,* in which the "Rime" appeared. Here it need only be added that, as Poole knew, Coleridge's reputation for radicalism had preceded him to the village and made his sojourn there, complicated further by the bohemian, seemingly incestuous ménage of the Wordsworths, somewhat uncomfortable. Matters worsened when the more militant radical John Thelwall, a convicted seditionist against the government of William Pitt, came for a long visit and expressed his wish to settle in Nether Stowey.

Coleridge was contemplating the composition of a long allegorical poem to be called *The Brook,* and to that end the band of friends took frequent walks, taking notes on the local waterways. Fearing an imminent naval invasion by the French, the Pitt ministry perhaps naturally concluded that Coleridge and his cronies were helping to plan the attack, and accordingly dispatched its own spy to keep track of their doings. The notes taken by the hapless "Spy Nosy"— as Coleridge dubbed him in allusion to the philosopher Spinoza — concerning conversations utterly beyond his grasp are among the more comical documents in the annals of literature; but they should not lead us to underestimate the atmosphere of repression (it was to deepen in the coming years as Napoleon gained in strength) and the genuine threat to freedom of expression that pervaded England at the time the "Rime" was composed. The everyday influence of massive historical forces was then clearly hard to ignore, as those recent critics who have emphasized political and historical issues in Coleridge's poetry insist. It should also be pointed out, however, that Wordsworth had never been in any sense an activist and that at this time Coleridge's radicalism was already diminishing. His view of the social order and its relation to the Christian life (concerning which he was coming to form more conservative views) was already inflected by the traditionalism that more deeply colored his later thinking.

Coleridge's affairs appeared to become more settled when in January of 1798 he accepted a £150 annuity from the famous pottery manufacturer Josiah Wedgwood. Coleridge and the Wordsworths now determined to go to Germany, where Coleridge hoped to gain more firsthand knowledge of philosophical materials needed for his magnum opus. Having seen *Lyrical Ballads* through the press and marked the birth of Coleridge's second son, Berkeley, the travelers left Coleridge's family under the protection of Poole and set sail. It was perhaps not as unheard-of then as it is now for a husband and father to absent himself indefinitely from his family in quest of personal betterment, but Coleridge did experience plenty of guilt on the subject, as he did on most subjects (albatrosses were everywhere in his life). His wife at times viewed this adventure as a desertion or dereliction of family duty, and the whole interlude, during which Sara endured in solitude the death of the infant Berkeley, did much to assure their eventual estrangement. In Germany, the Wordsworths spent a freezing winter in the village of Goslar (where Wordsworth wrote much of the finest poetry of his life), while Coleridge caroused and studied by turns in the university atmosphere of Göttingen.

On returning from Germany in 1799, Coleridge met Sara Hutchinson, the sister of Wordsworth's future wife Mary. Coleridge soon fell deeply in love with Sara, and suffered much from the platonic nature of their relationship, which was partly self-imposed, as Coleridge held strong views on the importance of marital fidelity. In this year Coleridge took a position on the *Morning Post* and began to spend more time in London. In 1800, however, he followed Wordsworth into the Lake District, where he settled with his family in Greta Hall, Keswick. There his third son, Derwent, was born. For the next two years he moved back and forth between Keswick and London. Although relations between Coleridge and his wife continued to deteriorate, his daughter Sara was born in December of 1802. This child, like her brother Hartley, was to have an occasionally brilliant but more often troubled adult life, much engaged with literature and prone to severe depression. It was Sara who, after her father's death, first defended him against the charge — largely true though subject to various sorts of extenuation — of extensive plagiarism from the German philosophers.

In 1803 a walking tour of the Highlands with William and Dorothy accentuated Coleridge's growing estrangement from them. William had become more openly intolerant of Coleridge's irregular behavior, and during the course of this tour Coleridge parted with the Wordsworths, feigning illness in order to be free to increase his daily intake of opium. In the following year Coleridge sailed out to Malta, where he was appointed Acting Public Secretary to the British High Commissioner, in the hope of improving his health and getting the better of his addiction. Two years later, having visited Rome, he returned to England in worse condition than ever. He briefly revisited the Lake District, but relations with the Wordsworths were evermore strained, and, in addition, he decided to separate from his wife. By the end of 1808 Coleridge was back in London, where he lived, not counting sojourns on country estates with patrons, for the remaining twenty-seven years of his life. He lived first with Basil Montagu, who relayed some remarks of Wordsworth's that damaged the Coleridge-Wordsworth friendship almost beyond mending. He soon joined the household of John Morgan, a wealthy wine merchant, and over the next few years intermittently delivered his famous lectures on Shakespeare. He continued the effort to cope with his illness and addiction, sometimes placing himself under medical care and more often entrusting his benefactor of the moment with the impossible task of preventing him from taking opium. By 1815 he had launched plans for the publication both of a collection of his poems, to be called *Sibylline Leaves,* and his "literary life," the

Biographia Literaria, which featured a careful, profound, but somewhat vindictive critique of Wordsworth. Owing to numerous delays,
these important volumes did not appear until 1817.

In the meantime, Coleridge had finally found a patron, head of
household, and doctor in James Gillman, who would succeed to some
extent in imposing regularity on Coleridge's life. While furtive visits to
the apothecary were still not infrequent, Dr. Gillman's watchful and
benevolent eye proved sufficient to smooth the path of Coleridge's
remaining eighteen years from the time that Coleridge moved into his
home in Highgate, north of Hampstead. Coleridge was soon known as
"the Sage of Highgate" and attracted visitors both distinguished and
curious to the Gillmans' house, especially on what came to be known as
his "Thursday evenings," for the rest of his life. He continued to write
and publish in every genre. In 1827 the first signs appeared of the con-
gestive heart failure that was to erode Coleridge's health steadily, but
his life continued peacefully enough, with visits from Carlyle, Fenimore
Cooper, Emerson, Wordsworth (for the last time in 1831), and many
others. In 1828 he toured the Rhine with the Wordsworths — father
and daughter — and saw through the publication of his *Poetical Works*
in three volumes. In 1829 his daughter Sara married her cousin Henry
Nelson Coleridge. The couple settled near Highgate, and Henry Coleridge helped his uncle revise the 1828 edition during the year of
Coleridge's death. When death finally came, on July 25, 1834, Dr. Gillman, who was Coleridge's first biographer, reports that in the presence
of the body still lying in place a flowering plant in the window burst
into bloom.

COMPOSITION AND PUBLICATION HISTORY OF THE POEM

In 1797, the friendship and mutual admiration of Coleridge,
William Wordsworth, and Wordsworth's sister Dorothy developed into
an almost constant intellectual companionship. Coleridge was living
with his wife and their infant son in the small Nether Stowey cottage;
the Wordsworths meanwhile had sublet a nearby country estate called
Alfoxden that Coleridge and Thomas Poole had found for them. Coleridge and the two Wordsworths frequently walked out across the Quan-
tock Hills in the vicinity, talking of poetry, and sometimes their
excursions took them as far as Bristol or along the Channel, past such
places as the Valley of Rocks in Linton (where they could often see the

sun shining through the rigging of ships as it does through the spectre ship in the "Rime"), Kilve (where they may have seen the weathercock mentioned both in the "Rime" and in Wordsworth's "Anecdote for Fathers"), or across the channel to Llyswyn Farm in Wales (also mentioned in "Anecdote for Fathers") where their radical friend John Thelwall had settled. On November 13, Coleridge and Wordsworth set off on one of their long walks through the region, this one to Dulverton, according to Dorothy in a letter written a week later (geographically conflicting accounts of the walk will be found in Coleridge's note to the poem in *Sibylline Leaves* [1817] and Wordsworth's note to "We Are Seven" dictated to Isabella Fenwick in 1843). On the way, having decided that they needed to produce a saleable poem to defray expenses for an upcoming outing (probably a trek through Wales), they began to compose "The Rime of the Ancient Mariner" as a joint venture.

"I soon found," remarked Wordsworth in 1835, "that the style of myself and Coleridge would not assimilate"; and so Coleridge fared forward alone with the project, not however before Wordsworth had contributed several lines and suggested both the shooting of an albatross (an incident he had just found in Captain George Shelvocke's *Voyages*) and "the reanimation of the dead bodies, to work the ship." Wordsworth also testified in his old age that the poem had been based on a nightmare of Coleridge's friend John Cruikshank concerning a ghost ship; and in addition to these main sources there is evidence that Coleridge adapted to the "Rime" many of the materials he was using for projected "Hymns to the Sun, Moon, and Elements," together with an epic on the "Origin of Evil"— all projects left characteristically undone or incomplete, yet just as characteristically fruitful in oblique and unpredictable ways.

Even on this first day the poem evidently grew so fast that it seemed no longer suitable either for the *Monthly Magazine* or for the modest five pounds the two poets had had in view. By the end of November there was a draft of three hundred lines, and Dorothy Wordsworth's journal shows that on March 23, 1798, Coleridge brought the completed "Rime" to read at Alfoxden. The two friends had begun at some point to speak of producing a joint volume consisting, as Wordsworth said to Fenwick, of "poems chiefly on supernatural subjects taken from common life, but looked at, as much as might be, through an imaginative medium." Wordsworth speaks here as though both poets had agreed all along to produce the same kind of poem, but readers have always ascribed a great deal more authority to the account given by Coleridge in the *Biographia Literaria* (1817), if only because it seems

to accord more closely to the actual differences between the poets'
eventual contributions:

> The thought suggested itself (to which of us I do not recollect)
> that a series of poems might be composed of two sorts. In the
> one, the incidents and agents were to be, in part at least, supernat-
> ural; and the excellence aimed at was to consist in the interesting
> of the affections by the dramatic truths of such emotions as would
> naturally accompany such situations, supposing them real. And
> real in this sense they have been to every human being who, from
> whatever source of delusion, has at any time believed himself
> under supernatural agency. For the second class, subjects were to
> be chosen from ordinary life; the characters and incidents were
> to be such as will be found in every village and its vicinity where
> there is a meditative and feeling mind to seek after them, or notice
> them when they present themselves.

The plan began to take shape, alongside other plans for joint publication that actually appeared closer to realization in the next months.
(There was talk in particular of publishing their two plays — Coleridge's
Osorio and Wordsworth's *The Borderers* — together.) At the end of
May, Coleridge took the "Rime" to Bristol, where he and Wordsworth
began to enlist the counsel and support of their acquaintance the Bristol bookseller and printer Joseph Cottle. Wordsworth had proven to be
by far the more prolific contributor — surprisingly, in that hitherto
during the course of their friendship Coleridge had been the more productive. In pursuing his version of their joint venture (articulated most
fully in his famous "Preface" of 1800), Wordsworth appears finally to
have found what he wanted to say. Balladic poems "on ordinary life,"
spoken by narrators seemingly only at a slight remove from the world
they describe, poured forth from his hand in the spring of 1798, and
to these were added a variety of important poems in more sustained
reflective forms, only one of which, "Lines left upon a Seat in a Yew-
tree," was an earlier composition. But in addition to the "Rime," meanwhile, Coleridge could only supply two fragments from his tragedy,
Osorio, together with a rewritten Wordsworth poem that Coleridge
entitled "Lewti: Or, The Circassian Love Chant." After a publisher had
been found and *Lyrical Ballads* was printed by Biggs and Cottle late in
1798, "Lewti" was quickly replaced — when the first few copies had
been produced — by Coleridge's "conversational poem" called "The
Nightingale," probably because Wordsworth's "Tintern Abbey," completed just days before the volume had been put to press, now autho-

rized the inclusion of poems in this mode. In part wishing to reduce the imbalance of their output, Coleridge had begun composing "Christabel," but Wordsworth appears never to have liked the poem, or in any case not to have seen its relevance to the project in hand, and Coleridge's famous fragment never appeared in any edition of *Lyrical Ballads*.

For reasons that cannot be discussed at length here, the 1798 *Lyrical Ballads*, published anonymously with the "Rime" its leadoff poem and with a brief "Advertisement" by Wordsworth, is considered one of the most important turning points in English literary history. It was a challenge to conventional tastes both in politics and literature: the focus on rustic persons and themes, together with the implicit attack on the artificial poetic diction of most eighteenth-century poetry through the example of Wordsworth's seemingly artless narrators, presented the reading public with fare that seemed starkly new — although just how new in fact has been subject to scholarly dispute. From the beginning the volume had its admirers, but it was judged by adherents to the traditions it attacks to be puerile and imbecilic, and inspired both condescending reviews and drawing-room ridicule, some of which reached the authors' ears.

Coleridge, whose name was better known than Wordsworth's at the time, was rumored in some quarters to be the sole author, but he seems never to have paid much attention to the jibes of the critics, being indeed his own severest critic. Wordsworth, on the other hand, whose vocation and career ambition had obviously strengthened in the preceding months and who came to identify closely with the fortunes of the volume, almost from the beginning began to chafe under the burden of joint authorship. Endeavoring to ignore the widespread jokes about the fatuousness of "The Thorn" and the idiocy of *The Idiot Boy*, Wordsworth expressed his belief in a letter to Cottle of early 1799 that it was the "Rime" that had "done an injury to the volume," evidently thinking that the "old style" in which his "Advertisement" had said it was written suited neither the taste of the public nor the purpose of his announced literary experiment. Coleridge appears to have been meekly submissive in response to this criticism — if he was aware of it — although he was evidently studying Cottle's ledgers and claimed many years later that the 1798 edition had sold briskly among seafarers.

Wordsworth's subsequent behavior toward the "Rime" comprised the earliest offense given in what became a difficult and eventually estranged friendship. In preparing the two-volume edition of 1800, which had only his name on the title page, Wordsworth convinced

Coleridge that he should eliminate nearly all his archaic spellings and many of his quainter turns of phrase. He wanted to stress the dramatic qualities of the poem, distancing the reader from any unwary identification of the Mariner with the author, by insisting on a new title: "The Ancient Mariner. A Poet's Reverie." (The subtitle was dropped in 1802 and 1805. It should be mentioned perhaps that this same anxiety lest the speaker be confused with the author led to the headnote Wordsworth added to his own poem "The Thorn.") He demoted the poem to a penultimate position in the volume. And, finally, he wrote an unforgivable "Note" (deleted owing to the remonstrance of Charles Lamb and others in 1802 and thenceforth), in which he says that Coleridge had wanted the "Rime" suppressed and that it was well worthy of suppression, having neither characterization nor proper agency nor skill in the handling of imagery nor a wise choice of meter; but that because its high passion "gave to the poem a value that is not often possessed by better poems," he, Wordsworth, had prevailed on Coleridge to republish it.

Wordsworth quietly continued to modernize spellings for the editions of 1802 and 1805, and there Coleridge's poem rested for some time. At some point, though, between 1805 and 1817, when Coleridge prepared the "Rime" for his own collected volume *Sibylline Leaves*, he composed the marginal prose Gloss, which makes the poem seem like a rare manuscript and thus has the effect of reintroducing much of the archaic atmosphere that Wordsworth had wished to dispel. In the *Biographia*, which appeared together with *Sibylline Leaves*, Coleridge announced that in future the "Rime" would be prefaced by an "Essay on the Supernatural," but regrettably this essay never materialized. With a few more minor revisions, completed in 1828, the poem appeared in Coleridge's collected edition of 1834, the year of his death. Editors, anthologists, and readers have since had to choose among editions (typically 1798 or 1817, both printed in the present volume on facing pages), often printing their rejected version in an appendix. The present editor is anticipated in the practice of giving facing texts by Royal Gettman in his edition of 1961 (1798 and 1834) and by the "experimental" edition of Martin Wallen (1993), which prints three-tiered pages with blocks of verse from 1798, 1800, and 1817 on each page. Consensus in standard collections has leaned toward the 1817 edition as incorporating nearly everything of value from earlier versions, but strong dissenting voices have been those of David Pirie and William Empson, who collaborated on a selection of Coleridge's poems in 1972 and felt that the High Church Coleridge of 1817 had hedged around the literal, direct impression given by a mariner who was happily not too different from Coleridge the political and religious radical of the early 1790s.

PLOT

Anyone who has read the "Rime" knows how difficult it is to keep the order and multiplicity of events clearly in mind, and how many interpretive mistakes can be avoided by readers who succeed in doing so. It is not inappropriate, then, to begin a consideration of the poem with a plot summary.

The narrator introduces the characters, beginning abruptly with the speaker to come: "IT is an ancient Mariner" (1817 1.1). This personage stands before one of three young men about to participate in a marriage feast, and gradually, over protest, subdues both Wedding Guest and reader into entranced audition. Like the narrator, the Mariner begins abruptly: "There was a ship" (1817 1.10). (The events he describes in the past tense for most of the rest of the poem are here recounted, as they tend to be experienced, in the present tense.) The Mariner's ship, the story goes, departs from the harbor and sails south across the equator (here the Wedding Guest hears the "loud bassoon" at the feast [1817 1.32]) until a storm drives the ship, "for days and weeks" (1798 1.47), into the Antarctic region. The ship becomes ice-bound. An Albatross appears in the fog and is greeted by the crew. The ice splits and the ship begins to move northward, followed by the friendly Albatross. At this point the Wedding Guest sees the tormented expression on the Mariner's face and asks the reason. The Mariner blurts out that after nine days and nights he "shot the ALBATROSS" (1817 1.82).

As the second part of the poem opens, the south wind and sunshine continue. The crew first blames the Mariner for shooting the Albatross, then praises him, as the good weather persists, because it has replaced the fog and frost. The ship arrives in the uncharted territory of the Pacific Ocean. The breeze drops, and at this point the supernatural begins to make itself felt. A long, sweltering drought ensues, and phosphorescent shiny creatures with legs appear in the sea. Some among the crew report dreaming of a spirit that has followed them from the polar region, "Nine fathom deep" (1817 1.133). Eventually no one can speak for thirst. The entire crew glares at the Mariner and hangs the Albatross around his neck.

A speck appears on the horizon at the start of the third part of the poem. It soon stands revealed as an approaching ship, tacking and veering as it nears. The Mariner bites his arm, sucks the blood, and cries, "A sail! A sail!" (1817 l.161). The ship comes nearer, now in a straight line, despite the calm that has left the Mariner's ship motionless. The setting sun glows through the visitant's ribbed sails and the "naked ribs" of its hull (1798 l.177). Of the two who are aboard, the male figure is a skeleton with bits of charnel crust attached, while the garishly painted female is an image of syphilitic prostitution. (These figures are not yet called Death and Life-in-Death, respectively, in the original edition of 1798.) They play at dice, and the female cries out that she has won. As it turns out, she has won the life of the Mariner from her companion, Death, who claims all the others. The specter ship suddenly departs. The crescent moon rises, and by moonlight all two hundred crew members curse the Mariner with their eyes and fall dead. The soul of each rushes past him, "Like the whiz of my Cross-bow" (1798 l.225).

At the beginning of the fourth part, the Wedding Guest professes to "fear" the Mariner, thinking him a ghost (1798 l.226–32). The Mariner reassures him that he "dropt not down" and resumes his tale (1817 l.235). "Alone on a wide wide sea" (1817 l.237), he regards the "men, so beautiful" (1817 l.240) and regrets the survival of the "slimy things" (1817 l.242) and of himself. He tries and fails to pray. The dead do not decompose, but go on cursing him with their glaring eyes for seven days. The Mariner observes the "moving Moon" (1817 l.267), and then, by its light, he becomes fascinated by the hitherto ghastly seeming sea creatures and "bless[es] them unaware" (1817 l.289). Then he can pray, and the Albatross falls from his neck into the sea.

The Mariner falls into a deep sleep at the start of the fifth part, dreams of moisture, and awakens to find it raining. A loud wind is heard, and a storm comes on. The dead men arise and start manning the ship when the storm reaches it. The Mariner works next to the body of his nephew. All are silent until morning, when all the dead gather around the mast and give forth "Sweet sounds" that recall life on land (1817 l.356). All hands then return to work, and the ship goes forward now without the help of wind. The subaqueous Polar Spirit slips away at this point, and the ship again stands still. With the sun at zenith, the ship lurches forward and the Mariner falls in a swoon. Before awaking, he hears two voices in the air, discussing his crime.

As the sixth part begins, the First Voice asks what makes the ship move. The Second Voice speaks of the harmony subsisting between ocean and moon. The First Voice still wants an answer to the question, and the Second Voice replies that the air is "cut away" in front of the ship and closes behind it (1817 l.428). The Mariner awakens, sailing in gentle weather. He is at first mesmerized by the crew, which still stands glaring at him, and then "this spell [is] snapt" (1817 l.446). The ship sails into the harbor, where illuminated dark-red shadows rise out of the calm water. The ship advances, the body of each crew member lies prone on the deck, and a glowing seraph stands above each of them. A boat appears, and its Pilot shouts. The lights vanish and the bodies resume their stations. The Mariner hears the Pilot and Pilot's boy approaching, then sees a Hermit aboard and hears him singing hymns.

In the concluding part of the poem, there is first a description of the Hermit as a woodland dweller. Now within earshot, the approaching threesome wonders what became of the strange lights. The Hermit marvels at the decrepit appearance of the Mariner's ship, and the Pilot thinks it looks "fiendish." A sound is heard underwater, the waters part, and the ship sinks — as did the Albatross —"like lead" (1817 l.553), spewing the Mariner up to the surface of the whirlpool. Having been pulled safely into the Pilot's boat, the Mariner moves his lips to speak, causing the Pilot to have a fit and the Hermit to pray. The Mariner takes the oars, and the Pilot's boy goes crazy, thinking himself in the company of the Devil. The Mariner asks the Hermit for absolution, and the Hermit asks, "What manner of man art thou?" (1817 l.581). The Mariner's frame is painfully wrenched at this, and for the first time he tells his story. He explains to the Wedding Guest that from that time forth, traveling from place to place, he has been seized with "strange power of speech" (1817 l.591) and tells his story whenever he finds, by divination, a destined auditor. The wedding party is again heard, and the Mariner says he would rather go to church in pious company than to a wedding. He bids farewell, with the parting declaration (the famous "moral") that persons who love all creatures are those who can pray "best"— that is, most easily and efficaciously. The Wedding Guest turns away from the festivities, and the next day awakens "A sadder and a wiser man" (1817 l.628).

SOME INTERPRETIVE ISSUES

Without anticipating the survey of commentaries to be found in Part Two of this volume, it may be helpful here to review some of the issues that readers have found at once frustrating and fascinating in their attempt to account for the poem as a whole. To begin with, there is the question begged by the previous sentence: Is the poem, in fact, a fully coherent composition of the "organic" kind that Coleridge so often celebrated in his critical and philosophical prose, with the "whole" implicit in its every detail, or is it rather an inspired fragment, or sequence of fragments, of the sort that so many of his other poems, especially "Christabel" and "Kubla Khan," might lead us to expect? Finding satisfactory ways of accounting for difficulties apart from this one may carry the reader some way toward deciding the question, but perhaps it is best simply to admit in advance that too much critical and aesthetic presupposition goes into the very terms in which the question is posed. Two or three generations ago, critics much influenced by the literary philosophy of Coleridge himself looked for, and therefore tended to find, artistic unity in poems; but since that time disunity and the aesthetics of fragmentation have been preferred. The "Rime" seems not to be a perfect poem. Apart from local infelicities, Parts IV through VI, in the opinion of most readers, could be much compressed. These latter parts of the poem contain passages of great beauty, but they inexplicably prolong the mariner's penance for his arbitrary act of shooting the albatross while complicating the process with successive installments of supernatural machinery that seem finally to thwart each other's purpose. If, however, as connoisseurs of disorder, we discover in repetition itself — necessary in miniature for the rhythm of a ballad but problematic at the level of plot — the signal of the authentic disjointedness we are looking for, then the poem's structural flaccidity is also its oceanic depth.

Not unrelated to this perhaps unprofitable concern is the question whether the poem is dogmatic or indecisive in outlook. Much depends here on whether one thinks the moral equal to its occasion or whether one can assign a coherent purpose to the varieties of supernatural machinery, and to these matters we shall return below. A broader issue surfaces when one reflects, with a recent critic, that the confidence with which the Gloss in many places explains away the strangeness of the poem, the confidence perhaps of a slightly pedantic antiquarian, is sharply at odds with the epigraph from Thomas Burnet that Coleridge added at the same stage of composition. This is a wonderfully urbane text in which we are told that no one has ever convincingly sorted out the ranks and family relations among invisible beings, and that, while it is best to wean ourselves from trivial things by imagining an ideal world, we should maintain a sense of proportion — a healthy skepticism, that is — in doing so (Ferguson 124). And even in the 1798 and 1800 versions of the poem, as another critic points out, the brief "Arguments" affixed perform the same positive, rationalizing function as the later Gloss (Wolfson 29).

The fact is, though, that despite these stabilizing tendencies even in its earliest versions the poem is an amalgam of voices in subtle discord. The hypnotic cadences of the Mariner predominate, of course, but there is in his language a great deal of pre-Reformation religiosity (with "Jesu," the saints, and Mariolatry at every turn), which the Church of England reader of Coleridge's time can scarcely be expected to share. In other words, even in ignorance of the fact that in 1797 the anonymous author had not yet given up his Unitarianism, the first readers would have seen that the views of the main speaker are not contemporary with their own. The Mariner is not the person, in other words, on whom we can rely to explain the supernatural, however much he may succeed in evoking its agency. The Wedding Guest for his part speaks at first with the immature petulance of one deprived of his fun, and we must assume that if his conversion to sober wisdom in the end were not a good thing his having heard the story can hardly matter. Yet it takes a certain amount of what Coleridge famously called "the willing suspension of disbelief" to accord this young man the measure of disapproval that the logic of the poem seems to demand. He speaks sensibly enough, much as we would speak having first been prevented from attending a wedding at which we were "next of kin" and then grudgingly rendered helpless to resist hearing a crazed monologue. After all, the festive rural pomp from which the Wedding Guest finds himself barred appears in most literary contexts as the pure essence of Merrie England. How comprehensive can that wisdom be, we are entitled to ask, that stands apart from the sacrament of marriage and indeed from all the forms of rooted community?

The Hermit also speaks, and in his voice we hear the accents of religion modulated and enriched by admiration of the natural world. He is distinguished from the abject superstition of the Pilot and Pilot's boy — but can we blame even them in the circumstances? — by his superior reflectiveness and honorable willingness to perform his ministry even in peril. But the Hermit is the first who apparently needs to hear the Mariner's story, just as the Wedding Guest is the most recent. What do these two have in common, and how do they divide the condition of landlocked unknowing between them? Finally there is the narrator, who seems determined to remain faceless: he refuses all comment, withholding any hint of judgment or even description. For this very reason, though, we can suspect him of endorsing both the Mariner's account and its purport: he scrupulously avoids the creation of critical distance throughout the poem until, at the very end, he confirms the Mariner's prediction that the Wedding Guest will be sadder and wiser after he has heard the story.

It may be that in effacing his narrator Coleridge means to profit from Aristotle's argument that Homer comes as close to being a dramatic poet as epic narrative allows because he lets his characters do as much of the speaking as possible; but whatever the reason, Coleridge's narrator, with his taciturn "It is" (1817 l.1) for an opening gambit, is interesting because he so relentlessly deflects interest away from himself. He certainly is not "Coleridge," the contemporary virtuoso of genres who would not spontaneously use archaic language or fall into the ballad cadences of the anonymous minstrels. Even within the poem Coleridge, or "the author," as we may call him, makes himself felt as yet another separate voice through the literary variations — the stretched stanzas of five or six lines and more — that he imposes on the regularity of an oral poet's ballad quatrain, and through such methodical symmetries as the circling back of each narrative unit except the seventh to the theme of the Albatross. The subtlety that allows the poem to seem at once both literary and oral is reflected in the very word "ancyent" (1798 l.1): the Mariner is very old in the eyes of a witness telling the story, but his adventure took place long ago, making him ancient as someone long dead is ancient; and yet, if we understand Life-in-Death's victory to be permanent, making the Mariner a Tiresias or Wandering Jew, then he is ancient in both senses of the word after all, so that the oral and the literary-historical viewpoints merge with each other. The word itself thus spelled is also ancient, and it is interesting that when all of Wordsworth's modernizations are accomplished as late as 1815, the word "ancyent" creeps back into the text at line 77.

And finally, in the later editions, there are the voices of Burnet, the naturalist pondering the frontiers of knowledge, and of the learned marginal commentator (the Gloss). For the Gloss, the solution to every mystery seems rather too transparent (as for the Renaissance humanists whose outlook Coleridge may be imitating, citing the authority of ancient authors confers at least momentary certainty) — until suddenly, in unexpectedly lyrical prose, the Gloss improves on the poem by meditating expansively on the "moving Moon" and surrounding stars of the fourth part (1817 l.267). But how this voice within a voice, which describes the homecoming of a beloved feudal lord, furthers our understanding of the Mariner's homecoming, apart perhaps from enhancing our sense of the fitness of all things in their station, has never been fully explained.

The very confusions of the poem, then, must also be considered finally indistinguishable from its intriguing complexities. Coleridge's is a *literary* ballad par excellence, fraught with all the syncretic learning, intricacy of composition, and multiple perspective that we must after all expect in retrospect from such a self-conscious, overburdened mind. In reflecting on Wordsworth's rough treatment of the poem, we must remember, indeed, that a literary ballad is a very different sort of thing from a "lyrical ballad," which is what the two poets had undertaken to produce. Even if one takes into account the division of labor Coleridge outlines in the *Biographia,* their joint enterprise did not encompass the antiquarian literariness of the "Rime"; and this may indeed be part of what Wordsworth meant in saying that their styles would not assimilate. The subjective cast implied in the notion of "lyric" comes to seem like one perspective among many in the distance imposed by Coleridge's tricks of pastiche and palimpsest. It has been suggested, for example, that the successive layers of intellectual complexity imposed by Coleridge's revisions of the poem accomplish a quasi-Hegelian history of the gradually more and more philosophical phases of Christianity, all to be considered from the syncretistic and symbolizing overview of the then-emergent Higher Criticism (McGann 144–48). Something like this intent may explain why saints, medieval bogies, Flying Dutchmen, spirits of the middle air, regional spirits or genii, troops of angels, and the Christian deity can jostle with one another for retributive authority. What instantly pleases the God to whom the Mariner can pray upon having his aesthetic epiphany in the presence of the sea creatures by no means suffices to appease the Polar Spirit who "loved the bird" (1817 1.408) and perhaps does not care a great deal whether the Mariner finds a school of bloated eels and phosphorescent worms beautiful or not. And so the mariner is buffeted about between these and other expiatory agendas, with an effect not dissimilar to the equally literary eschatological quarrels of Virgil's gods in the *Aeneid.*

No one is quite happy with the neatness of saying, in the tradition of Robert Penn Warren, that the "Rime" is the Christian story of sacrificial trespass and redemption revisited as the Romantic theme of the redemption of nature by the shaping spirit of imagination. Perhaps the strongest objection to this view is that if the Mariner is truly the protagonist of this sort of story then he ought somehow to benefit from it. He should seem transfigured, dignified, holy — and not the "grey-beard loon" traumatized by survivor guilt, suffering through periodic fits of compulsive speech, whose supplementary punishment of this kind (we would call it being sentenced to community service) will be everlasting. An acknowledged model for the *poète maudit* of the French Symbolists, Coleridge's Mariner has also been viewed as a figure of Coleridge himself torn between the exultant visions of imaginative power and the despairing hallucinations of opium addiction. Not yet completely in the thrall of the drug late in 1797, Coleridge had nevertheless already known periods of dependency, and one may well surmise that the poem's more lurid features are not to be found wholly in the pages of the seafaring memoirs that are known likewise to have contributed.

The shooting of the Albatross, for example, taken from the *Voyages* of Captain Shelvocke, Wordsworth claims somewhat surprisingly to have recommended to his far more learned friend as the sort of incident around which the poem could be plotted. But how did this bird come to be draped around the Mariner's shoulders "Instead of the cross" (1817 1.141)? As is often said, it must have been one of the smaller, grayish-black albatrosses mentioned in fact by Shelvocke and other travel writers rather than one of the majestic white ones with a fifteen-foot wingspan. Reflecting in this scientific vein, one can even agree with William Empson that because among other things the Albatross "ne'er had eat" (1817 1.67) the crew gave it "biscuit-worms" (1798 1.65), the ship's provisions must have been spoiled and the Mariner therefore probably shot the bird for food. The darker albatross, writes Empson in his best deadpan, "would make a tolerable soup which would help to keep off scurvy," and then later "only the externals" need be hung around the Mariner's neck (300). This approach to things is actually much closer to the spirit of the ships' logs Coleridge was reading, as Empson points out, than the symbolic approach; and yet it is pretty clearly a willful reduction. Coleridge forces us to note the repeated rhyme with "cross," and, again, the bird is hung "Instead of the cross" (1817 1.141) around the Mariner's shoulders. In the most primitive terms, the bird becomes the Mariner's totem, and the Mariner would then appear feathered in that totem like the faraway North American Indians, as he called them, about whom Coleridge had also been reading. In Christian terms, the Mariner's cross is that of Everyman cast adrift in an unredeemed natural world. And even from the ultra-low-church standpoint that would challenge the divinity of Christ (and it is again Empson who reminds us that in 1797 Coleridge the Unitarian preacher was still refusing to administer the Lord's Supper [298]), the albatross is nevertheless, in the sort of culturally resonant epithet that

Coleridge delighted to reflect on in his notebooks, "a cross to bear." At the very least, then, the Mariner must be said to have violated the spirit, the nature, of something that is larger than it appears to be: a dove appearing to the ark with the olive branch of its friendship typologically looking forward to the doctrine of the Holy Ghost; an image of imaginative flight beckoning to the mind through the fog and frigidity of ordinary perception, then forcing the mind in denial of this calling to wear lifeless wings in mockery of the totemistic identity it has rejected; or a bird, simply, whose apparently tutelary presence implies the bond among all living things that the Mariner violates simply in holding life cheap.

The bewilderingly diverse responses one can have to just one element of the poem — to say nothing of sun and moon, ship, sea creatures, and the ocean itself — show that among other accretive elements Coleridge keeps in play there is the diversity of its possible interpretive frameworks. Quite apart from deciding what the crossbow "means," for example, one must decide whether the kind of meaning one seeks is literal, symbolic, or allegorical. Of course it is a crossbow, we say: that is simply the weapon that one of the earliest maritime explorers ("We were the first" [1817 1.105]) would have used. Or: the crossbow, having both the name and the shape of a crucifix and also the shape and rhyme-likeness of an albatross with wings outspread, is a symbol of the Mariner's unacknowledged kinship, his mirror relationship, with his victim. Or again: the crossbow is an allegorical means of showing the swiftness and apparent arbitrariness of the great sea changes in our lives. Hence the souls of the dead whizzing past the Mariner remind him of his crossbow, and when first the albatross and later the ship plummet into the sea "like lead" (1817 1.553), he is in the presence yet again of comparable forces moving with an abrupt speed that surpasses the scope or strength of human agency. "Cross-bow," in this latter account, becomes the name for the whole range of agencies, from human irrationality to divine grace, that are not deliberative. Or — all of the above. Coleridge would have found the ingenious literal-mindedness of an Empson amusing and rather bracing; we must infer, though, from the evidently obscure tendency of his remarks about the poem to Clement Carlyon, one of his Göttingen cronies, that he did have some kind of metaphysical symbolism in mind. And then again, we find Coleridge conceding in a letter of 1819 that the "Rime" must have been an allegory of his own state of mind as a man and poet.

There are two other issues of persisting interest, not wholly unrelated to one another, that are thrown into confusion by the multiplicity of viewpoints the poem seems to encourage: the theme of marriage and the role played by the "moral." Their problematic interrelation can be stated as follows: If it is good to love all things, great and small things, if that is the Mariner's final and sufficient seal of approval, then how is it that the clear metaphysical implications of marriage, as embodied in what Wordsworth was to call the "great spousal verse" that weds the poetic imagination to the natural world, must here encounter the Mariner's openly stated disapproval? Not only does he keep the Wedding Guest from his destination, he also declares that he himself would rather go to church with pious companions than go to a wedding. Coleridge had already written an openly metaphysical epithalamium on the occasion of his honeymoon in "The Eolian Harp" (1796), and soon enough he would write, concerning the necessary galvanism of the natural world by the imagination, "Ours is her wedding garment, ours her shroud" ("Dejection: An Ode" 1802, l.49) — a passage he later frequently quoted in illustration of his theory of poetry.

The essay that I have contributed to this volume implies an answer to the question one is moved to raise about the status of marriage in the "Rime." I argue there, without dwelling at length on this aspect of the question, that marriage is in a sense a casualty of the need Coleridge felt, in writing the "Rime," to issue a corrective to Wordsworth's too-great immersion in what Coleridge called "natural religion." Coleridge's position, I argue, over against what he understood to be that of Wordsworth, is that one can embrace nature only as a consequence of having first turned one's back on it, initially through a gratuitous act of betrayal, malign yet liberating, and then through one's ensuing confrontation with the world that exists above and beyond the natural communion one has violated. The Mariner's moral, in other words, only makes sense as the outcome of a complex rite of passage that the conventionally landlocked imagination never undergoes.

This justification of the moral is in some ways defensible, I believe, but undoubtedly it leaves unanswered a number of important questions. Anna Letitia Barbauld, in a famous exchange recorded in Coleridge's *Table Talk*, complained that the "Rime" "has no moral"; and while it is hard to understand what she could have meant, being herself the author of hymns for children very similar to the Mariner's valedictory injunction, we usually take her to mean that there is no moral in any way commensurate with the profundity of experience the Mariner has endured, and with this position we are broadly in agreement. I do not pretend that the solution I propose above in any degree disposes of the problem that attaches to the triviality and puerility of tone one finds in these stanzas. ("Don't pull poor pussy's tail" is the inimitable Empson's gloss [301].) Coleridge's snappy response to Mrs. Barbauld was that there was too much moral, and then he compared his poem unfavorably in this respect with the tale from the *Arabian Nights* in which a merchant is subjected to an excruciating penance for having thrown a date pit over a wall and accidentally killed the son of a genie. In order to make sense of this exchange, posterity has tended to accord to Coleridge the same benefit of the doubt it has given Barbauld. Just as she really meant that the moral should have been more profound, so Coleridge for his part really meant, tacitly in agreement with her, that if there was to have been any moral at all it should have been more appropriate.

In other words, Coleridge was admitting on that occasion that he should have given the Mariner a better script for his parting words. One needs to acknowledge, perhaps, that here finally the constraints of the ballad genre, even loosely handled, let Coleridge down. After all, ballads speak for themselves. There is nearly always something a little gnomic about the best ballads known to Coleridge, largely because both the authentic ones (in Thomas Percy's *Reliques of Ancient English Poetry*) and the literary ones indebted to them (Thomas Chatterton's forgeries, or Gottfried Bürger's *Lenore* and *The Wild Huntsman* translated by Walter Scott, for example) tend to give the impression of stanzas left out, of transitional matter left to the imagination. And certainly, in addition to this sort of titillating reticence, ballads never point morals. Coleridge's speaker is more garrulous, after all, than any traditional ballad speaker one can think of, and it would be just like him, finally (if only as a kind of protest at having being possessed by "strange power of speech" [1817 l.591]), to spell out what had better have been left implied. It is hard to imagine what sort of moral conclusion could have been drawn, in the meter and accents chosen, that would satisfy an exacting reader; but we must remember, at the same time, how bewildered a young rustic spark like the Wedding Guest would naturally feel upon being read an ethical or theological lesson of any real subtlety. It is in handling the moral, in sum, that Coleridge's astonishing ability to harmonize the literary and the oral devices of his poem, sustaining the identification of the reader with the Wedding Guest, necessarily falls short at last. How touching it is, though, even edifying in an entirely different register, that when forced to choose between conflicting educational missions he remains loyal to the community of his imagined world. He had not yet ceased to think himself a poet.

                                                        Paul H. Fry

WORKS CITED

Empson, William. "The Ancient Mariner." 1964. *Argufying: Essays on Literature and Culture*. Ed. John Haffenden. Iowa City: U of Iowa P, 1987. 297–319.

Ferguson, Frances. "Coleridge and the Deluded Reader: 'The Rime of the Ancient Mariner.'" *Georgia Review* 31 (1977): 617–35. Reprinted in this book on pages 113–30.

McGann, Jerome J. "'The Ancient Mariner': The Meaning of Meanings." *The Beauty of Inflections: Literary Investigations in Historical Method and Theory*. Oxford: Clarendon, 1988. 135–72.

Wolfson, Susan. "The Language of Interpretation in Romantic Poetry: 'A Strong Working of the Mind.'" *Romanticism and Language*. Ed. Arden Reed. Ithaca: Cornell UP, 1984. 22–49.

"The Rime of the Ancient Mariner":
The 1798 and 1817 Texts

The Rime of the Ancyent Marinere, In Seven Parts.[1]

ARGUMENT.

How a Ship having passed the Line was driven by Storms to the cold Country towards the South Pole; and how from thence she made her course to the Tropical Latitude of the Great Pacific Ocean; and of the strange things that befell; and in what manner the Ancyent Marinere came back to his own Country.[2]

I.

It is an ancyent Marinere,
    And he stoppeth one of three:
"By thy long grey beard and thy glittering eye
    "Now wherefore stoppest me?

5 "The Bridegroom's doors are open'd wide,
    "And I am next of kin;
"The Guests are met, the Feast is set, —
    "May'st hear the merry din.

---

[1]In *LB* 1800, the title is: *"The Ancient Mariner:* A Poet's Reverie."
[2]In *LB* 1800, the Argument reads: "How a Ship, having first sailed to the Equator was driven by Storms to the cold Country towards the South Pole; how the Ancient Mariner cruelly, and in contempt of the laws of hospitality, killed a Seabird; and how he was followed by many and strange Judgements: and in what manner he came back to his own Country."

The Rime of the Ancient Mariner
In Seven Parts

Facile credo, plures esse Naturas invisibiles quam visibiles in rerum universitate. Sed horum omnium familiam quis nobis enarrabit? et gradus et cognationes et discrimina et singulorum munera? Quid agunt? quæ loca habitant? Harum rerum notitiam semper ambivit ingenium humanum, nunquam attigit. Juvat, interea, non diffiteor, quandoque in animo, tanquam in tabulâ, majoris et melioris mundi imaginem contemplari: ne mens assuefecta hodiernæ vitæ minutiis se contrahat nimis, & tota subsidat in pusillas cogitationes. Sed veritati interea invigilandum est, modusque servandus, ut certa ab incertis, diem a nocte, distinguamus. — T. Burnet: *Archæol. Phil.* (68).[1]

IT is an ancient Mariner,
And he stoppeth one of three.
"By thy long grey beard and glittering eye,
"Now wherefore stopp'st thou me?

An ancient Mariner meeteth three
Gallants bidden to a wedding-feast,
and detaineth one.

5 "The Bridegroom's doors are opened wide,
"And I am next of kin;
"The guests are met, the feast is set:
"May'st hear the merry din."

---

[1]The motto is adapted from the *Archaeologiae philosophicae* of Thomas Burnet (1635?–1715): "I can easily believe that there are more invisible natures than visible ones among the entities in the universe. But who will explain for us the family of all these beings? And the ranks and relationships and distinguishing features and qualities of each? What they do? What places they inhabit? The human intellect has always tried to approach knowledge of these matters, but has never touched it. Meanwhile, I do not deny that it is sometimes better to represent in the spirit as on a tablet, the image of a greater and better world, lest the mind, used to the daily occurrences of life, contract itself and subside completely into petty thoughts. But at the same time we must be vigilant for the truth and keep due proportion, so that we may distinguish the certain from the uncertain, day from night."

But still he holds the wedding-guest —
10   There was a Ship, quoth he —
"Nay, if thou'st got a laughsome tale,
   "Marinere! come with me."

He holds him with his skinny hand,
   Quoth he, there was a Ship —
15 "Now get thee hence, thou grey-beard Loon!
   "Or my Staff shall make thee skip.

He holds him with his glittering eye —
   The wedding guest stood still
And listens like a three year's child;
20   The Marinere hath his will.°

The wedding-guest sate on a stone,
   He cannot chuse but hear:
And thus spake on that ancyent man,
   The bright-eyed Marinere.

25 The Ship was cheer'd, the Harbour clear'd —
   Marrily did we drop
Below the Kirk,° below the Hill,
   Below the Light-house top.

The Sun came up upon the left,
30   Out of the Sea came he:
And he shone bright, and on the right
   Went down into the Sea.°

Higher and higher every day,
   Till over the mast at noon —°
35 The wedding-guest here beat his breast,
   For he heard the loud bassoon.°

20. Wordsworth claims to have composed lines 19–20.
27. Kirk: Church (Scots and Northern dialect).
32. The ship sails south.
34. They have reached the Equator.
36. bassoon: A slightly anachronistic word, as the instrument was introduced in the sixteenth century. Coleridge's neighbor Thomas Poole had recently bought a bassoon for the church in Nether Stowey.

He holds him with his skinny hand,
10 "There was a ship," quoth he,
"Hold off! unhand me, grey-beard loon!"
Eftsoons° his hand dropt he.

He holds him with his glittering eye —   *The wedding-guest is spellbound by*
The wedding-guest stood still,   *the eye of the old sea faring man,*
15 And listens like a three years child: *and constrained to hear his tale.*
The Mariner hath his will.

The wedding-guest sat on a stone:
He can not chuse but hear;
And thus spake on that ancient man,
20 The bright-eyed mariner.

"The ship was cheered, the harbour cleared,
Merrily did we drop
Below the kirk, below the hill,
Below the light-house top.

25 The Sun came up upon the left,   *The Mariner tells how the ship sailed*
Out of the sea came he!   *southward with a good wind and*
And he shone bright, and on the right   *fair weather, till it reached the line.*
Went down into the sea.

Higher and higher every day,
30 Till over the mast at noon —
The Wedding-Guest here beat his breast,
For he heard the loud bassoon.

12. Eftsoons: Immediately.

The Bride hath pac'd into the Hall,
   Red as a rose is she;
Nodding their heads before her goes
40   The merry Minstralsy.

The wedding-guest he beat his breast,
   Yet he cannot chuse but hear:
And thus spake on that ancyent Man,
   The bright-eyed Marinere.

45 Listen, Stranger! Storm and Wind,
   A Wind and Tempest strong!
For days and weeks it play'd us freaks —°
   Like Chaff we drove along.

   Listen, Stranger! Mist and Snow,
50   And it grew wond'rous cauld:
And Ice mast-high came floating by
   As green as Emerauld.

And thro' the drifts the snowy clifts°
   Did send a dismal sheen;
55 Ne shapes of men ne beasts we ken° —
   The Ice was all between.

The Ice was here, the Ice was there,
   The Ice was all around:
It crack'd and growl'd, and roar'd and howl'd —
60   Like noises of a swound.°

---

47. In *LB* 1800, lines 45–47 read: "But now the Northwind came more fierce, /
There came a Tempest strong! / And Southward still for days and weeks."
   53. clifts: Archaic for "cliffs," with a play on "clefts."
   55. ken: Discern.
   60. swound: Swoon. In *LB* 1800, line 60 reads: "A wild and ceaseless sound."

The bride hath paced into the hall,
Red as a rose is she:
35 Nodding their heads before her goes
The merry minstrelsy.

The wedding-guest heareth the bridal music; but the mariner continueth his tale.

The Wedding-Guest he beat his breast,
Yet he can not chuse but hear;
And thus spake on that ancient man,
40 The bright-eyed Mariner.

And now the STORM-BLAST came, and he
Was tyrannous and strong:
He struck with his o'ertaking wings,
And chased us south along.

The ship drawn by a storm toward the south pole.

45 With sloping masts and dipping prow,
As who pursued with yell and blow
Still treads the shadow of his foe
And forward bends his head,
The ship drove fast, loud roared the blast,
50 And southward aye° we fled.

And now there came both mist and snow,
And it grew wondrous cold:
And ice, mast-high, came floating by,
As green as emerald.

55 And through the drifts the snowy clifts
Did send a dismal sheen:
Nor shapes of men nor beasts we ken —
The ice was all between.

The land of ice, and of fearful sounds, where no living thing was to be seen.

The ice was here, the ice was there,
60 The ice was all around:
It cracked and growled, and roared and howled,
Like noises in a swound!

50. aye: Continuously.

At length did cross an Albatross,
  Thorough° the Fog it came;
And an° it were a Christian Soul,
  We hail'd it in God's name.

65 The Marineres gave it biscuit-worms,
    And round and round it flew:
The Ice did split with a Thunder-fit;°
  The Helmsman steer'd us thro'.

And a good south wind sprung up behind,°
70   The Albatross did follow;
And every day for food or play
  Came to the Marinere's hollo!

In mist or cloud on mast or shroud°
  It perch'd for vespers nine,°
75 Whiles all the night thro' fog smoke-white,
  Glimmer'd the white moon-shine.

"God save thee, ancyent Marinere!
  "From the fiends that plague thee thus —
"Why look'st thou so?"— with my cross bow
80   I shot the Albatross.

II.

The Sun came up upon the right,°
  Out of the Sea came he;
And broad as a weft° upon the left
  Went down into the Sea.

85 And the good south wind still blew behind,
    But no sweet Bird did follow
Ne any day for food or play
  Came to the Marinere's hollo!

> **62. Thorough:** Through.
> **63. And an:** As if.
> **67. Thunder-fit:** Thunder-clap.
> **69.** The ship is now sailing north.
> **73. shroud:** Heavy rope to fix the mast in place.
> **74. vespers nine:** Nine evenings.
> **81.** The ship sails north, having passed Cape Horn, South America.
> **83. weft:** Threads carried by a shuttle across the warp.

At length did cross an Albatross:
Thorough the fog it came;
65 As if it had been a Christian soul,
We hailed it in God's name.

Till a great sea-bird, called the
Albatross, came through the snow-fog,
and was received with great joy and
hospitality.

It ate the food it ne'er had eat,
And round and round it flew.
The ice did split with a thunder-fit;
70 The helmsman steered us through!

And a good south wind sprung up behind;
The Albatross did follow,
And every day, for food or play,
Came to the Mariner's hollo!

And lo! the Albatross proveth a bird
of good omen, and followeth the ship
as it returned northward, through
fog and floating ice.

75 In mist or cloud, on mast or shroud,
It perched for vespers nine;
Whiles all the night, through fog-smoke white,
Glimmered the white Moon-shine.

"God save thee, ancient Mariner!
80 From the fiends, that plague thee thus! —
Why look'st thou so?"— With my cross-bow
I shot the ALBATROSS!

The ancient Mariner inhospitably
killeth the pious bird of good omen.

PART THE SECOND.

THE Sun now rose upon the right:
Out of the sea came he,
85 Still hid in mist, and on the left
Went down into the sea.

And the good south wind still blew behind,
But no sweet bird did follow,
Nor any day for food or play
90 Came to the mariners' hollo!

And I had done an hellish thing
90   And it would work 'em woe:
For all averr'd, I had kill'd the Bird
That made the Breeze to blow.

Ne dim ne red, like God's own head,°
The glorious Sun uprist:
95 Then all averr'd, I had kill'd the Bird
That brought the fog and mist.
'Twas right, said they, such birds to slay
That bring the fog and mist.

The breezes blew, the white foam flew,
100   The furrow follow'd free:
We were the first that ever burst
Into that silent Sea.

Down dropt the breeze, the Sails dropt down,
'Twas sad as sad could be
105 And we did speak only to break
The silence of the Sea.

All in a hot and copper sky
The bloody sun at noon,
Right up above the mast did stand,°
110   No bigger than the moon.

Day after day, day after day,
We stuck, ne breath ne motion,
As idle as a painted Ship
Upon a painted Ocean.

115 Water, water, every where
And all the boards did shrink;
Water, water, every where,
Ne any drop to drink.

93. *LB* 1800 reads: "like an Angel's head."
109. Now in the Pacific Ocean, the ship is at the Equator.

And I had done an hellish thing,
And it would work 'em woe:
For all averred, I had killed the bird
That made the breeze to blow.
95 Ah wretch! said they, the bird to slay,
That made the breeze to blow!

His shipmates cry out against the
ancient Mariner, for killing the bird
of good luck.

Nor dim nor red, like God's own head,
The glorious Sun uprist:
Then all averred, I had killed the bird
100 That brought the fog and mist.
'Twas right, said they, such birds to slay,
That bring the fog and mist.

But when the fog cleared off, they jus-
tify the same, and thus make them-
selves accomplices in the crime.

The fair breeze blew, the white foam flew,
The furrow stream'd off free:°
105 We were the first that ever burst
Into that silent sea.

The fair breeze continues; the ship
enters the Pacific Ocean and sails
northward, even till it reaches the
Line.

Down dropt the breeze, the sails dropt down,
'Twas sad as sad could be;
And we did speak only to break
110 The silence of the sea!

The ship hath been suddenly
becalmed.

All in a hot and copper sky,
The bloody Sun, at noon,
Right up above the mast did stand,
No bigger than the Moon.

115 Day after day, day after day,
We stuck, nor breath nor motion,
As idle as a painted ship
Upon a painted ocean.

Water, water, every where,
120 And all the boards did shrink;
Water water, every where,
Nor any drop to drink.

And the Albatross begins to be
avenged.

104. 1828: "The furrow followed free." Sailing to Malta in 1804, his first time ever
on shipboard in an open sea, Coleridge quickly saw how a wake looks from the deck. The
adjustment eventually made its way into the poem.

The very deeps did rot: O Christ!
120   That ever this should be!
Yea, slimy things did crawl with legs
    Upon the slimy Sea.

About, about, in reel and rout
    The Death-fires° danc'd at night;
125 The water, like a witch's oils,
    Burnt green and blue and white.°

And some in dreams assured were
    Of the Spirit that plagued us so:°
Nine fathom deep he had follow'd us
130   From the Land of Mist and Snow.

And every tongue thro' utter drouth
    Was wither'd at the root;
We could not speak no more than if
    We had been choked with soot.

135 Ah wel-a-day! what evil looks
    Had I from old and young;
Instead of the Cross the Albatross
    About my neck was hung.

---

124. Death-fires: St. Elmo's fire, an electrostatic glow on a ship's mast or rigging, thought to portend disaster.

126. This stanza alludes to the Witches' scene in *Macbeth* (I, iii, 32–24): "The weird sisters, hand in hand, / Posters of the sea and land, / Thus do go about, about." One of the witches has just cursed a mariner with drought, insomnia, and shipwreck.

128. This is one of the spirits of the middle air, neither angelic nor demonic, common in writers — especially Neoplatonic — like those mentioned in the 1817 gloss.

The very deep did rot: O Christ!
That ever this should be!
125 Yea, slimy things did crawl with legs
Upon the slimy sea.

About, about, in reel and rout
The death-fires danced at night;
The water, like a witch's oils,
130 Burnt green, and blue and white.

And some in dreams assured were
Of the spirit that plagued us so:
Nine fathom deep he had followed us
From the land of mist and snow.

A spirit had followed them; one of the invisible inhabitants of this planet, neither departed souls nor angels; concerning whom the learned Jew, Josephus, and the Platonic Constantinopolitan, Michael Psellus, may be consulted. They are very numerous, and there is no climate or element without one or more.

135 And every tongue, through utter drought,
Was withered at the root;
We could not speak, no more than if
We had been choak'd with soot.

Ah! well a-day! What evil looks
140 Had I from old and young!
Instead of the cross, the Albatross
About my neck was hung.

The Shipmates, in their sore distress, would fain throw the whole guilt on the ancient mariner: in sign whereof they hang the dead sea-bird round his neck.

III.

I saw a something in the Sky°
140   No bigger than my fist;
At first it seem'd a little speck
And then it seem'd a mist:
It mov'd and mov'd, and took at last
A certain shape, I wist.°

145 A speck, a mist, a shape, I wist!
And still it ner'd and ner'd;
And, an° it dodg'd a water-sprite,
It plung'd and tack'd and veer'd.

With throat unslack'd, with black lips bak'd
150   Ne could we laugh, ne wail:
Then while thro' drouth all dumb they stood
I bit my arm and suck'd the blood°
And cry'd, A sail! a sail!

With throat unslack'd, with black lips bak'd
155   Agape they hear'd me call:
Gramercy!° they for joy did grin
And all at once their breath drew in
As° they were drinking all.

139. Corresponding to lines 139–44, two separate stanzas appear as follows in *LB* 1800:

So past a weary Time; each Throat
Was parched, and glazed each eye,
When, looking westward, I beheld
A something in the Sky.

At first it seemed a little speck
And then it seemed a mist:
It moved and moved, and took at last,
A certain shape, I wist.

144. wist: Knew, became aware.
147. an: As if.
152. In *LB* 1800 these lines read: "Through utter drouth all dumb we stood / Till I bit my arm and sucked the blood."
156. Gramercy: OF *grand-merci,* great thanks. "Mercy on us!" in Samuel Johnson's 1775 *Dictionary.*
158. As: As if.

PART THE THIRD.

THERE passed a weary time. Each throat
Was parched, and glazed each eye.
145 A weary time! a weary time!
How glazed each weary eye!
When looking westward, I beheld
A something in the sky.

The ancient Mariner beholdeth a
sign in the element afar off.

At first it seemed a little speck,
150 And then it seemed a mist:
It moved and moved, and took at last
A certain shape, I wist.

A speck, a mist, a shape, I wist!
And still it neared and neared;
155   As if it dodged a water-sprite,
It plunged and tacked and veered.

With throat unslacked,° with black lips baked,
We could nor laugh nor wail;
Through utter drought all dumb we stood!
160 I bit my arm, I sucked the blood,
And cried, A sail! a sail!

At its nearer approach, it seemeth
him to be a ship; and at a dear ran-
som he freeth his speech from the
bonds of thirst.

With throat unslacked, with black lips baked,
Agape they heard me call:
Gramercy! they for joy did grin,
165 And all at once their breath drew in,
As they were drinking all.

A flash of joy.

157. unslacked: Changed to "unslaked" in 1828.

She doth not tack from side to side —
160   Hither to work us weal°
Withouten wind, withouten tide
    She steddies with upright keel.

The western wave was all a flame,
    The day was well nigh done!
165 Almost upon the western wave
    Rested the broad bright Sun;
When that strange shape drove suddenly
    Betwixt us and the Sun.

And strait the Sun was fleck'd with bars
170   (Heaven's mother send us grace)
As if thro' a dungeon grate he peer'd
    With broad and burning face.

Alas! (thought I, and my heart beat loud)
    How fast she neres and neres!
175 Are those *her* Sails that glance in the Sun
    Like restless gossameres?°

Are those *her* naked ribs, which fleck'd°
    The sun that did behind them peer?
And are those two all, all the crew,
180   That woman and her fleshless Pheere?°

        Are those her ribs, which fleck'd the Sun,
           Like the bars of a dungeon grate?
        And are these two all, all the crew
           That woman and her Mate?

160. weal: Benefit.
176. gossameres: Cobwebs that float in air.
177. For the three stanzas comprising lines 177–90, *LB* 1800 has only:
      Are those *her* Ribs through which the sun
         Did peer, as through a grate?
      Are those two all, all her crew,
         That Woman, and her Mate?
180. Pheere: Companion or mate.

See! see! (I cried) she tacks no more!
Hither to work us weal;
Without a breeze, without a tide,
170 She steddies with upright keel!

And horror follows. For can it be a ship that comes onward without wind or tide?

The western wave was all a-flame.
The day was well nigh done!
Almost upon the western wave
Rested the broad bright Sun;
175 When that strange shape drove suddenly
Betwixt us and the Sun.

And straight the Sun was flecked with bars,
(Heaven's Mother send us grace!)
As if through a dungeon-grate he peered,
180 With broad and burning face.

It seemeth him but the skeleton of a ship.

Alas! (thought I, and my heart beat loud)
How fast she nears and nears!
Are those *her*° sails that glance in the Sun,
Like restless gossameres?

185 Are those *her* ribs through which the Sun
Did peer, as through a grate?
And is that Woman all her crew?
Is that a DEATH?° and are there two?
Is DEATH that woman's mate?°

And its ribs are seen as bars on the face of the setting Sun. The spectre-woman and her death-mate, and no other on board the skeleton-ship.

183, 185. *her:* Italics dropped in 1834.
188. a DEATH?: A skeleton.
189, 193. Note that until 1817 neither Death nor Life-in-Death were named outright.

185   This Ship, it was a plankless Thing,°
                   A rare Anatomy!
                A plankless Spectre — and it mov'd
                   Like a Being of the Sea!
                The Woman and a fleshless Man
190   Therein sate merrily.

His bones were black with many a crack,
    All black and bare, I ween;
Jet-black and bare, save where with rust
Of mouldy damps and charnel crust
195   They're patch'd with purple and green.

Her lips are red, *her* looks are free,°
    Her locks are yellow as gold:
Her skin is as white as leprosy,
And she is far liker Death than he;
200   Her flesh makes the still air cold.

The naked Hulk alongside came
    And the Twain were playing dice;
"The Game is done! I've won, I've won!"
    Quoth she, and whistled thrice.

205 A gust of wind sterte up behind
    And whistled thro' his bones;
Thro' the holes of his eyes and the hole of his mouth
    Half-whistles and half-groans.

With never a whisper in the Sea
210   Oft darts the Spectre-ship;
While clombe above the Eastern bar°
The horned Moon,° with one bright Star
    Almost atween the tips.°

185. Lines 185–90 were first published in 1912, but Coleridge had wanted them inserted in *LB* 1800.
196. free: Bold, licentious.
211. bar: Horizon.
212. horned Moon: "It is a common superstition among sailors that something evil is about to happen whenever a star dogs the moon" (Coleridge's manuscript note).
213. After line 213, Coleridge composed — sometime between 1806 and 1811 — roughly the lines that are added in 1817, but beginning in manuscript: "And stifled words & groans of pain / Mix'd on each murmuring lip."

190   *Her* lips were red, *her* looks were free,
      Her locks were yellow as gold:
      Her skin was as white as leprosy,   *Like vessel, like crew!*
      The Night-Mair° LIFE-IN-DEATH was she,
      Who thicks man's blood with cold.

195   The naked hulk alongside came,   DEATH, *and* LIFE-IN-DEATH *have*
      And the twain were casting dice;   *diced for the ship's crew, and she (the*
      "The game is done, I've, I've won"   *latter) winneth the ancient Mariner.*
      Quoth she, and whistles thrice.

      A gust of wind sterte up behind°
200   And whistled through his bones;
      Through the holes of his eyes and the hole of his mouth,
      Half whistles and half groans.

---

193. Night-Mair: "Night-mare" in 1828. A night-mare was literally a female monster or spirit that bestrode the chests of sleepers.
199. Coleridge had wanted lines 199–202 omitted from 1817. They were omitted in 1828 and thereafter.

One after one by the horned Moon
215   (Listen, O Stranger! to me)
Each turn'd his face with a ghastly pang
And curs'd me with his ee.°

Four times fifty living men,
    With never a sigh or groan,
220 With heavy thump, a lifeless lump
    They dropp'd down one by one.

Their souls did from their bodies fly, —
    They fled to bliss or woe;
And every soul it pass'd me by,
225   Like the whiz of my Cross-bow.

217. Ee: Eye.

The Sun's rim dips; the stars rush out: *No twilight within the courts of the*
At one stride comes the dark;   *sun.*°
205 With far-heard whisper, o'er the sea,
Off shot the spectre-bark.

We listened and looked sideways up!
Fear at my heart, as at a cup,
My life-blood seemed to sip!
210 The stars were dim, and thick the night,
The steersman's face by his lamp gleamed white;

From the sails the dews did drip —
Till clombe above the eastern bar   *At the rising of the Moon,*
The horned Moon, with one bright star
215 Within the nether tip.

One after one, by the star-dogged Moon,   *One after another,*
Too quick for groan or sight,
Each turned his face with a ghastly pang,
And cursed me with his eye.

220 Four times fifty living men,   *His shipmates drop down dead;*
(And I heard nor sigh nor groan)
With heavy thump, a lifeless lump,
They dropped down one by one.

The souls did from their bodies fly, —   *But* LIFE-IN-DEATH *begins her work*
225 They fled to bliss or woe!   *on the ancient Mariner.*
And every soul, it passed me by,
Like the whiz of my CROSS-BOW!

203. Although there is no gloss to lines 203–06 in 1817, Coleridge had wanted one, and wrote the following variants in various copies of the *Sibylline Leaves* edition: "Within the tropics there is no twilight. As the sun sinks, the Evening Gun is fired, and the Starry Heaven is at once overall, like men in ambush that have been listening for the signal — [?] blare!=(Row)[?]"; "Within the Tropics there is no Twilight. At the moment, the second, that the Sun sinks, the Stars appear all at once as if at the word of a command announced by the evening Gun, in our W. India Islands"; "Between the Tropics there is no twilight. As the Sun's last segment dips down and the evening gun is fired the constellations appear arrayed"; "No twilight where there is no latitude nor yet on either side within the Park and Race-course of the Sun. —" In 1828, he printed the gloss that stands here.

IV.

"I fear thee, ancyent Marinere!
    "I fear thy skinny hand;
"And thou art long and lank and brown°
    "As is the ribb'd Sea-sand.

230 "I fear thee and thy glittering eye
    "And thy skinny hand so brown —
Fear not, fear not, thou wedding guest!
    This body dropt not down.

Alone, alone, all all alone
235   Alone on the wide wide Sea;
And Christ would take no pity on
    My soul in agony.

The many men so beautiful,
    And they all dead did lie!
240 And a million million slimy things
    Liv'd on — and so did I.

I look'd upon the rotting Sea,
    And drew my eyes away;
I look'd upon the eldritch° deck,
245   And there the dead men lay.

I look'd to Heaven, and try'd to pray;
    But or° ever a prayer had gusht,
A wicked whisper came and made
    My heart as dry as dust.

250 I clos'd my lids and kept them close,
    Till the balls like pulses beat;
For the sky and the sea, and the sea and the sky
Lay like a load on my weary eye,
    And the dead were at my feet.

228. In 1817, Coleridge acknowledges Wordsworth for these lines. The beach along the Bristol Channel at Kilve, where Wordsworth and Coleridge walked, is "ribbed" with dark shale.
244. eldritch: Spooky. Changed to "ghastly" in *LB* 1800.
247. or: Before.

PART THE FOURTH.

"I FEAR thee, ancient Mariner!
I fear thy skinny hand!
230 And thou art long, and lank, and brown,
As is the ribbed sea-sand.

The wedding-guest feareth that a
spirit is talking to him;

I fear thee and thy glittering eye,
And thy skinny hand, so brown."—
Fear not, fear not, thou Wedding-Guest!
235 This body dropt not down.

But the ancient Mariner assureth
him of his bodily life, and proceedeth
to relate his horrible penance.

Alone, alone, all, all alone,
Alone on a wide wide sea!
And never a saint took pity on
My soul in agony.

240 The many men, so beautiful!
And they all dead did lie:
And a thousand thousand slimy things
Lived on; and so did I.

He despiseth the creatures of the calm,

I looked upon the rotting sea,
245 And drew my eyes away;
I look'd upon the rotting deck,
And there the dead men lay.

And envieth that they should live,
and so many lie dead.

I looked to Heaven, and tried to pray;
But or ever a prayer had gusht,
250 A wicked whisper came, and made
My heart as dry as dust.

I closed my lids, and kept them close,
And the balls like pulses beat;
For the sky and the sea, and the sea and the sky
255 Lay, like a cloud,° on my weary eye,
And the dead were at my feet.

255. cloud: Printed in 1817, corrected to "load" in the errata.

255 The cold sweat melted from their limbs,
      Ne rot, ne reek did they;
    The look with which they look'd on me,
      Had never pass'd away.

    An orphan's curse would drag to Hell
260   A spirit from on high:
    But O! more horrible than that
      Is the curse in a dead man's eye!
    Seven days, seven nights I saw that curse,
      And yet I could not die.

265 The moving Moon went up the sky
      And no where did abide:
    Softly she was going up
      And a star or two beside —

    Her beams bemock'd the sultry main°
270   Like morning frosts yspread;°
    But where the ship's huge shadow lay,
    The charmed water burnt alway
      A still and awful red.

    Beyond the shadow of the ship
275   I watch'd the water-snakes:°
    They mov'd in tracks of shining white;
    And when they rear'd, the elfish light
      Fell off in hoary flakes.

    Within the shadow of the ship
280   I watch'd their rich attire:
    Blue, glossy green, and velvet black
    They coil'd and swam; and every track
      Was a flash of golden fire.

---

269. bemock'd the sultry main: Offset (with the impression of coolness) the tropically warm sea.

270. yspread: Overspread.

275. water-snakes: There do exist marine worms that look like luminous ribbons, some up to twenty-five yards long. Outside the shadow they would gleam white ("hoary flakes") in the moonlight; inside the shadow their colors would glow.

The cold sweat melted from their limbs,
Nor rot nor reek did they:
The look with which they looked on me
260 Had never passed away.

*But the curse liveth for him in the eye
of the dead men.*

An orphan's curse would drag to Hell
A spirit from on high;
But oh! more horrible than that
Is the curse in a dead man's eye!
265 Seven days, seven nights, I saw that curse,
And yet I could not die.

The moving Moon went up the sky,
And no where did abide:
Softly she was going up,
270 And a star or two beside —

*In his loneliness and fixedness he
yearneth towards the journeying
Moon and the stars that still sojourn,
yet still move onward; and every
where the blue sky belongs to them,
and is their appointed rest, and their
native country and their own natural homes, which they enter unan-
nounced as lords that are certainly
expected and yet there is a silent joy
at their arrival.*

Her beams bemocked the sultry main,
Like April hoar-frost° spread;
But where the ship's huge shadow lay,
The charmed water burnt alway
275 A still and awful red.

Beyond the shadow of the ship,
I watched the water-snakes:
They moved in tracks of shining white,
And when they reared, the elfish light
280 Fell off in hoary flakes.

*By the light of the Moon he beholdeth
God's creatures of the great calm.*

Within the shadow of the ship
I watched their rich attire:
Blue, glossy green, and velvet black,
They coiled and swam; and every track
285 Was a flash of golden fire.

272. hoar-frost: White, frozen dew.

O happy living things! no tongue
285   Their beauty might declare:
A spring of love gusht from my heart,
    And I bless'd them unaware!
Sure my kind saint look pity on me,
    And I bless'd them unaware.

290 The self-same moment I could pray;
    And from my neck so free°
The Albatross fell off, and sank
    Like lead into the sea.

V.

O sleep, it is a gentle thing
295   Belov'd from pole to pole!
To Mary-queen the praise be yeven°
She sent the gentle sleep from heaven
    That slid into my soul.

The silly° buckets on the deck
300   That had so long remain'd,
I dreamt that they were fill'd with dew
    And when I awoke it rain'd.

My lips were wet, my throat was cold,
    My garments all were dank;
305 Sure I had drunken in my dreams
    And still my body drank.

I mov'd and could not feel my limbs,
    I was so light, almost
I thought that I had died in sleep,
310   And was a blessed Ghost.

---

291. so free: Thus freed, that is, by the falling away of the Albatross.

296. yeven: Given.

299. silly: There is no consensus about this word. It may just mean "simple" or rough-hewn. It may mean "holy," as it did in even more archaic English, suggesting that the buckets are bathed, as water bearers, in the blessing of the water snakes. The modern sense of "ridiculous," implying that they have so long lacked a function that they have come to seem incongruous, is unlikely.

O happy living things! no tongue
Their beauty might declare:
A spring of love gusht from my heart,
And I blessed them unaware!
290 Sure my kind saint took pity on me,
And I blessed them unaware.

Their beauty and their happiness.

He blesseth them in his heart.

The self same moment I could pray;
And from my neck so free
The Albatross fell off, and sank
295 Like lead into the sea.

The spell begins to break.

PART THE FIFTH.

O, SLEEP, it is a gentle thing!
Beloved from pole to pole!
To Mary Queen the praise be given!
She sent the gentle sleep from Heaven,
300 That slid into my soul.

The silly buckets on the deck,
That had so long remained,
I dreamt that they were filled with dew;
And when I awoke, it rained.

By grace of the holy Mother, the ancient Mariner is refreshed with rain.°

305 My lips were wet, my throat was cold,
My garments all were dank;
Sure I had drunken in my dreams,
And still my body drank.

I moved, and could not feel my limbs:
310 I was so light — almost
I thought that I had died in sleep,
And was a blessed ghost.

He heareth sounds, and seeth strange sights and commotions in the sky and the element.

302. Note the pre-Reformation piety of this sentiment — curious in that the gloss is commonly thought to simulate the scholia of a seventeenth-century archivist. (Other signs of Catholicism in the gloss can be explained, unlike this one, as dispassionate scholarly clarifications.)

The roaring wind! it roar'd far off,
    It did not come anear;
But with its sound it shook the sails
    That were so thin and sere.°

315 The upper air bursts into life,
    And a hundred fire-flags sheen°
To and fro they are hurried about;
And to and fro, and in and out
    The stars dance on between.

320 The coming wind doth roar more loud;
    The sails do sigh, like sedge:°
The rain pours down from one black cloud
    And the Moon is at its edge.

Hark! hark! the thick black cloud is cleft,
325   And the Moon is at its side:
Like waters shot from some high crag,
The lightning falls with never a jag
    A river steep and wide.

The strong wind reach'd the ship: it roar'd
330   And dropp'd down, like a stone!
Beneath the lightning and the moon
    The dead men gave a groan.

They groan'd, they stirr'd, they all uprose,
    Ne spake, ne mov'd their eyes:
335 It had been strange, even in a dream
    To have seen those dead men rise.

314. sere: Withered, brittle, nearly in shreds.
316. fire-flags sheen: Shining streaks of light, either lightning (likelier, as the wind is increasing) or from the aurora australis or southern lights (mysteriously appearing in the equatorial sky). The word "sheen" probably means "bright" or "shining," but it could also be a verb meaning "shone." If the latter, the absence of punctuation or conjunction until 1817 (where the comma still leaves the matter unclear) would make the passage even more awkwardly ungrammatical. If "sheen" is an adjective, the reader need only supply an imaginary dash after the word, anticipating the comma of 1817.
321. sedge: A kind of marsh grass.

And soon I heard a roaring wind:
It did not come anear;
315 But with its sound it shook the sails,
That were so thin and sere.

The upper air burst into life!
And a hundred fire-flags sheen,
To and fro they were hurried about!
320 And to and fro, and in and out,
The wan stars danced between.

And the coming wind did roar more loud,
And the sails did sigh like sedge;
And the rain poured down from one black cloud;
325 The Moon was at its edge.

The thick black cloud was cleft, and still
The Moon was at its side:
Like waters shot from some high crag,
The lightning fell with never a jag,
330 A river steep and wide.

The loud wind never reached the ship,   *The bodies of the ship's crew are*
Yet now the ship moved on!   *inspirited,° and the ship moves on.*
Beneath the lightning and the Moon,
The dead men gave a groan.°

335 They groaned, they stirred, they all uprose,
Nor spake, nor moved their eyes;
It had been strange, even in a dream,
To have seen those dead men rise.

331. inspirited: 1828 prints "inspired." Both words mean "animated with breath," as if from the nearby wind.

334. Note that this version of lines 331–32, introduced in 1800, contradicts the account of 1798.

The helmsman steerd, the ship mov'd on;
    Yet never a breeze up-blew;
The Marineres all 'gan° work the ropes,
340   Where they were wont° to do:
They rais'd their limbs like lifeless tools —
    We were a ghastly crew.

The body of my brother's son
    Stood by me knee to knee:
345 The body and I pull'd at one rope,
    But he said nought to me —
And I quak'd to think of my own voice
    How frightful it would be!

The day-light dawn'd — they dropp'd their arms,
350   And cluster'd round the mast:
Sweet sounds rose slowly thro' their mouths
    And from their bodies pass'd.

Around, around, flew each sweet sound,
    Then darted to the sun:
355 Slowly the sounds came back again
    Now mix'd, now one by one.

Sometimes a dropping from the sky
    I heard the Lavrock° sing;
Sometimes all little birds that are
360 How they seem'd to fill the sea and air
    With their sweet jargoning.°

And now 'twas like all instruments,
    Now like a lonely flute;
And now it is an angel's song
365   That makes the heavens be mute.

339. 'gan: Began.
340. wont: Accustomed.
358. Lavrock: Skylark.
361. jargoning: Twittering.

The helmsman steered, the ship moved on;
340 Yet never a breeze up blew;
The mariners all 'gan work the ropes,
Where they were wont to do:
They raised their limbs like lifeless tools —
We were a ghastly crew.

345 The body of my brother's son
Stood by me, knee to knee:
The body and I pulled at one rope,
But he said nought to me.

"I fear thee, ancient Mariner!"°
350 Be calm, thou Wedding-Guest!
'Twas not those souls that fled in pain,
Which to their corses° came again,
But a troop of spirits blest:

But not by the souls of the men, nor by dæmons of earth or middle air, but by a blessed troop of angelic spirits, sent down by the invocation of the guardian saint.

For when it dawned — they dropped their arms,
355 And clustered round the mast;
Sweet sounds rose slowly through their mouths,
And from their bodies passed.

Around, around, flew each sweet sound,
Then darted to the Sun;
360 Slowly the sounds came back again,
Now mixed, now one by one.

Sometimes a-dropping from the sky
I heard the sky-lark sing;
Sometimes all little birds that are,
365 How they seemed to fill the sea and air
With their sweet jargoning!

And now 'twas like all instruments,
Now like a lonely flute;
And now it is an angel's song,
370 That makes the Heavens be mute.

349. Next to this stanza, which was added in 1800, a manuscript of *LB* 1800 contains the following gloss: "By the interception of his kind saint a choir of angels desc[ended] from Heaven, & entered into the dead bod[ies] using the bodies a[s] material Instrum[ents]."
352. **corses:** Corpses.

It ceas'd: yet still the sails made on
  A pleasant noise till noon,
A noise like of a hidden brook
  In the leafy month of June,
370 That to the sleeping woods all night
  Singeth a quiet tune.

Listen, O listen, thou Wedding-guest!
  "Marinere! thou hast thy will:
"For that, which comes out of thine eye, doth make
375   "My body and soul to be still."

Never sadder tale was told
  To a man of woman born:
Sadder and wiser thou wedding-guest!
  Thou'lt rise to-morrow morn.

380 Never sadder tale was heard
  By a man of woman born:
The Marineres all return'd to work
  As silent as beforne.

The Marineres all 'gan pull the ropes,
385   But look at me they n'old:°
Thought I, I am as thin as air —
  They cannot me behold.

Till noon we silently sail'd on
  Yet never a breeze did breathe:
390 Slowly and smoothly went the ship
  Mov'd onward from beneath.

Under the keel nine fathom deep
  From the land of mist and snow
The spirit slid: and it was He
395   That made the Ship to go.
The sails at noon left off their tune
  And the Ship stood still also.

385. n'old: Would not.

It ceased; yet still the sails made on
A pleasant noise till noon,
A noise like of a hidden brook
In the leafy month of June,
375 That to the sleeping woods all night
Singeth a quiet tune.

Till noon we quietly sailed on,
Yet never a breeze did breathe:
Slowly and smoothly went the ship,
380 Moved onward from beneath.

Under the keel nine fathom deep,
From the land of mist and snow,
The spirit slid: and it was he
That made the ship to go.
385 The sails at noon left off their tune,
And the ship stood still also.

*The lonesome spirit from the south-
pole carries on the ship as far as the
line, in obedience to the angelic troop,
but still requireth vengeance.*

The sun right up above the mast
　　Had fix'd her to the ocean:
400 But in a minute she 'gan stir
　　With a short uneasy motion —
Backwards and forwards half her length
　　With a short uneasy motion.

Then, like a pawing horse let go,
405　　She made a sudden bound:
It flung the blood into my head,
　　And I fell into a swound.°

How long in that same fit I lay,
　　I have not° to declare;
410 But ere my living life return'd,
I heard and in my soul discern'd
　　Two voices in the air,

"Is it he? quoth one, "Is this the man?"
　　"By him who died on cross,
415 "With his cruel bow he lay'd full low
　　"The harmless Albatross.

"The spirit who 'bideth by himself
　　"In the land of mist and snow,
"He lov'd the bird that lov'd the man
420　　"Who shot him with his bow.

The other was a softer voice,
　　As soft as honey-dew:°
Quoth he the man hath penance done,
　　And penance more will do.

407. swound: Blackout.
409. have not: Am unable.
422. honey-dew: Manna-like substance.

The Sun, right up above the mast,
Had fixt her to the ocean;
But in a minute she 'gan stir,
390 With a short uneasy motion —
Backwards and forwards half her length,
With a short uneasy motion.

Then like a pawing horse let go,
She made a sudden bound:
395 It flung the blood into my head,
And I fell down in a swound.

How long in that same fit I lay,   *The Polar Spirit's fellow-dæmons, the*
I have not to declare;   *invisible inhabitants of the element,*
                                          take part in the wrong; and two of
But ere my living life returned,   *them relate, one to the other, that*
400 I heard and in my soul discerned   *penance long and heavy for the*
Two VOICES in the air.   *ancient Mariner hath been accorded*
                                          to the Polar Spirit, who returneth
                                          southward.

"Is it he?" quoth one, "Is this the man?
By him who died on cross,
With his cruel bow he laid full low,
405 The harmless Albatross.

The spirit who bideth by himself
In the land of mist and snow,
He loved the bird that loved the man
Who shot him with his bow."

410 The other was a softer voice,
As soft as honey-dew:
Quoth he, "The man hath penance done,
And penance more will do."

VI.

First Voice.

425 "But tell me, tell me! speak again,
       "Thy soft response renewing —
     "What makes that ship drive on so fast?
       "What is the Ocean doing?

Second Voice.

     "Still as a Slave before his Lord,
430   "The Ocean hath no blast:°
     "His great bright eye most silently
       "Up to the moon is cast —

     "If he may know which way to go,
       "For she guides him smooth or grim.
435 "See, brother, see! how graciously
       "She looketh down on him.

First Voice.

     "But why drives on that ship so fast
       "Withouten wave or wind?

Second Voice.

     "The air is cut away before,
440 "And closes from behind.

     "Fly, brother, fly! more high, more high,
       "Or we shall be belated:
     "For slow and slow that ship will go,
       "When the Marinere's trance is abated."

445 I woke, and we were sailing on
       As in a gentle weather:
     'Twas night, calm night, the moon was high;
       The dead men stood together.

430. blast: Wind.

PART THE SIXTH.

First Voice.

"But tell me, tell me! speak again,
415 Thy soft response renewing —
What makes that ship drive on so fast?
What is the ocean doing?"

Second Voice.

"Still as a slave before his lord,
The ocean hath no blast;
420 His great bright eye most silently
Up to the Moon is cast —

If he may know which way to go;
For she guides him smooth or grim.
See, brother, see! how graciously
425 She looketh down on him."

First Voice.

But why drives on that ship so fast,
Without or wave or wind?

*The Mariner hath been cast into a
trance; for the angelic power causeth
the vessel to drive northward, faster
than human life could endure.*

Second Voice.

The air is cut away before,
And closes from behind.

430 Fly, brother, fly! more high, more high!
Or we shall be belated:
For slow and slow that ship will go,
When the Mariner's trance is abated.

I woke, and we were sailing on
435 As in a gentle weather:
'Twas night, calm night, the Moon was high;
The dead men stood together.

*The supernatural motion is retarded;
the Mariner awakes, and his penance
begins anew.*

All stood together on the deck,
450   For a charnel-dungeon° fitter:
All fix'd on me their stony eyes
    That in the moon did glitter.

The pang, the curse, with which they died,
    Had never pass'd away:
455 I could not draw my een° from theirs
    Ne turn them up to pray.

And in its time the spell was snapt,
    And I could move my een:
I look'd far-forth, but little saw
460   Of what might else be seen.

Like one, that on a lonely road
    Doth walk in fear and dread,
And having once turn'd round, walks on
    And turns no more his head:
465 Because he knows, a frightful fiend
    Doth close behind him tread.

But soon there breath'd a wind on me,
    Ne sound ne motion made:
Its path was not upon the sea
470   In ripple or in shade.

It rais'd my hair, it fann'd my cheek,
    Like a meadow-gale of spring —
It mingled strangely with my fears,
    Yet it felt like a welcoming.

475 Swiftly, swiftly flew the ship,
    Yet she sail'd softly too:
Sweetly, sweetly blew the breeze —
    On me alone it blew.

O dream of joy! is this indeed
480   The light-house top I see?
Is this the Hill? Is this the Kirk?
    Is this mine own countrée?

450. charnel-dungeon: Vault where bodies were placed before burial.
455. een: Eyes.

All stood together on the deck,
For a charnel-dungeon fitter:
440 All fixed on me their stony eyes,
That in the Moon did glitter.

The pang, the curse, with which they died,
Had never passed away:
I could not draw my eyes from theirs,
445 Nor turn them up to pray.

And now this spell was snapt: once more   *The curse is finally expiated.*
I viewed the ocean green,
And looked far forth, yet little saw
Of what had else been seen —

450 Like one, that on a lonesome road
Doth walk in fear and dread,
And having once turned round, walks on,
And turns no more his head;
Because he knows, a frightful fiend
455 Doth close behind him tread.

But soon there breathed a wind on me,
Nor sound nor motion made:
Its path was not upon the sea,
In ripple or in shade.

460 It raised my hair, it fanned my cheek
Like a meadow-gale of spring —
It mingled strangely with my fears,
Yet it felt like a welcoming.

Swiftly, swiftly flew the ship,
465 Yet she sailed softly too:
Sweetly, sweetly blew the breeze —
On me alone it blew.

O! dream of joy! is this indeed   *And the ancient Mariner beholdeth*
The light-house top I see?   *his native country.*
470 Is this the hill? is this the kirk?
Is this mine own countrée?

We drifted o'er the Harbour-bar,°
   And I with sobs did pray —
485 "O let me be awake, my God!
   "Or let me sleep alway!"

The harbour-bay was clear as glass,
   So smoothly it was strewn!
And on the bay the moon light lay,
490   And the shadow° of the moon.

The moonlight bay was white all o'er,
   Till rising from the same,
Full many shapes, that shadows were,
   Like as of torches came.

495 A little distance from the prow
   Those dark-red shadows were;
But soon I saw that my own flesh
   Was red as in a glare.

I turn'd my head in fear and dread,
500   And by the holy rood,°
The bodies had advanc'd, and now
   Before the mast they stood.

They lifted up their stiff right arms,
   They held them strait and tight;
505 And each right-arm burnt like a torch,
   A torch that's borne upright.
Their stony eye-balls glitter'd on
   In the red and smoky light.

I pray'd and turn'd my head away
510   Forth looking as before.
There was no breeze upon the bay,
   No wave against the shore.

483. Harbour-bar: Sand reef across the mouth of a harbor.
490. shadow: Reflected image (cf. lines 492, 519).
500. rood: Cross.

We drifted o'er the harbour-bar,
And I with sobs did pray —
O let me be awake, my God!
475 Or let me sleep alway.

The harbour-bay was clear as glass,
So smoothly it was strewn!
And on the bay the moonlight lay,
And the shadow of the moon.

480 The rock shone bright, the kirk no less,
That stands above the rock:
The moonlight steeped in silentness
The steady weathercock.

And the bay was white with silent light,
485 Till rising from the same,
Full many shapes, that shadows were,
In crimson colours came.

A little distance from the prow
Those crimson shadows were:
490 I turned my eyes upon the deck —
Oh! Christ! what saw I there!

And appear in their own forms of light.

Each corse lay flat, lifeless and flat,
And, by the holy rood!
A man all light, a seraph-man,
495 On every corse there stood.

The rock shone bright, the kirk no less
   That stands above the rock:
515 The moonlight steep'd in silentness
   The steady weathercock.

And the bay was white with silent light,
   Till rising from the same
Full many shapes, that shadows° were,
520   In crimson colours came.

A little distance from the prow
   Those crimson shadows were:
I turn'd my eyes upon the deck —
   O Christ! what saw I there?

525 Each corse lay flat, lifeless and flat;
   And by the Holy rood
A man all light, a seraph-man,°
   On every corse there stood.

This seraph-band, each wav'd his hand:
530   It was a heavenly sight:
They stood as signals to the land,
   Each one a lovely light:

This seraph-band, each wav'd his hand,
   No voice did they impart —
535 No voice; but O! the silence sank,
   Like music on my heart.

Eftsones I heard the dash of oars,
   I heard the pilot's cheer:°
My head was turn'd perforce away
540   And I saw a boat appear.

    519. shadows: Technically a viewer on shipboard would not see anything on the deck (see line 527) reflected in the water.
    527. seraph-man: The seraphim, tinged red in medieval iconography, were the highest order of angels, noted for the intensity of their love for God and the creation.
    538. pilot's cheer: Pilots are assigned to guide craft in the harbor to their mooring. They "cheer" (halloo, verbally signal) approaching ships.

This seraph-band, each waved his hand:
It was a heavenly sight!
They stood as signals to the land,
Each one a lovely light;

500 This seraph-band, each waved his hand,
No voice did they impart —
No voice; but oh! the silence sank
Like music on my heart.

But soon I heard the dash of oars,
505 I heard the Pilots's cheer;
My head was turned perforce away,
And I saw a boat appear.

Then vanish'd all the lovely lights;°
     The bodies rose anew:
With silent pace, each to his place,
     Came back the ghastly crew.
545 The wind, that shade nor motion made,
     On me alone it blew.

               Then vanish'd all the lovely lights,
                    The spirits of the air;
               No souls of mortal men were they,
550   But spirits bright and fair.

The pilot, and the pilot's boy
     I heard them coming fast:
Dear Lord in Heaven! it was a joy,
     The dead men could not blast.°

555 I saw a third — I heard his voice:
     It is the Hermit good!
He singeth loud his godly hymns
     That he makes in the wood.
He'll shrieve° my soul, he'll wash away
560   The Albatross's blood.

VII.

This Hermit good lives in that wood
     Which slopes down to the Sea.
How loudly his sweet voice he rears!
He loves to talk with Marineres
565   That come from a far Countrée.

He kneels at morn and noon and eve —
     He hath a cushion plump:
It is the moss, that wholly hides
     The rotted old Oak-stump.

541. In a copy of *LB* 1798, Coleridge penciled in the following revision of lines 541–46: "Then vanish'd all the lovely ligh[ts,] / The spirits of the air; / No souls of mortal men we[re] they[,] / But spirits bright and fair."
554. blast: Destroy.
559. shrieve: Absolve by hearing confession.

The Pilot, and the Pilot's boy,
I heard them coming fast:
510 Dear Lord in Heaven! it was a joy
The dead men could not blast.

I saw a third — I heard his voice:
It is the Hermit good!
He singeth loud his godly hymns
515 That he makes in the wood.
He'll shrieve my soul, he'll wash away
The Albatross's blood.

PART THE SEVENTH.

THIS Hermit good lives in that wood   *The Hermit of the Wood,*
Which slopes down to the sea.
520 How loudly his sweet voice he rears!
He loves to talk with marineres°
That come from a far countrée.

He kneels at morn, and noon and eve —
He hath a cushion plump:
525 It is the moss that wholly hides
The rotted old oak-stump.

521. The archaic spelling "marineres" is here retained to rhyme with "rears."

570 The Skiff-boat ne'rd: I heard them talk,
      "Why, this is strange, I trow!°
   "Where are those lights so many and fair
      "That signal made but now?

   "Strange, by my faith! the Hermit said —
575   "And they answer'd not our cheer.
   "The planks look warp'd, and see those sails
      "How thin they are and sere!
   "I never saw aught like to them
      "Unless perchance it were

580 "The skeletons of leaves that lag
      "My forest-brook along:
   "When the Ivy-tod° is heavy with snow,
   "And the Owlet whoops to the wolf below
      "That eats the she-wolf's young.

585 "Dear Lord! it has a fiendish look —
      (The Pilot made reply)
   "I am a-fear'd. —"Push on, push on!
      "Said the Hermit cheerily.

   The Boat came closer to the Ship,
590   But I ne spake ne stirr'd!
   The Boat came close beneath the Ship,
      And strait a sound was heard!

   Under the water it rumbled on,
      Still louder and more dread:
595 It reach'd the Ship, it split the bay;
      The Ship went down like lead.

   Stunn'd by that loud and dreadful sound,
      Which sky and ocean smote:
   Like one that had been seven days drown'd
600   My body lay afloat:°
   But, swift as dreams, myself I found
      Within the Pilot's boat.

571. trow: Believe.
582. Ivy-tod: Ivy clump or bush.
600. Drowned bodies rise to the surface after seven days.

The Skiff-boat neared: I heard them talk,
"Why, this is strange, I trow!
Where are those lights so many and fair,
530 That signal made but now?"

"Strange, by my faith!" the Hermit said —   *Approacheth the ship with wonder.*
"And they answered not our cheer!
The planks looked warped! and see those sails,
How thin they are and sere!
535 I never saw aught like to them,
Unless perchance it were

The° skeletons of leaves that lag
My forest-brook along;
When the ivy-tod is heavy with snow,
540 And the owlet whoops to the wolf below,
That eats the she-wolf's young."

"Dear Lord! it hath a fiendish look —
(The Pilot made reply)
I am a-feared"—"Push on, push on!"
545 Said the Hermit cheerily.

The boat came closer to the ship,
But I nor spake nor stirred;
The boat came close beneath the ship,
And straight a sound was heard.

550 Under the water it rumbled on,   *The ship suddenly sinketh.*
Still louder and more dread:
It reach[e]d the ship, it split the bay;
The ship went down like lead.

Stunned by that loud and dreadful sound,   *The ancient Mariner is saved in the*
555 Which sky and ocean smote,   *Pilot's boat.°*
Like one that hath been seven days drowned,
My body lay afloat;
But swift as dreams, myself I found
Within the Pilot's boat.

---

537. The: Changed to "Brown" in the errata for 1817 and so printed in 1828.
   554. This gloss suggests — without quite establishing clearly — that the Mariner is
helped into the boat (that is, what is thought to be his dead body is hauled into the boat),
not spewed into it by the whirlpool.

Upon the whirl, where sank the Ship,
   The boat spun round and round:
605 And all was still, save that the hill
   Was telling of the sound.

I mov'd my lips: the Pilot shriek'd
   And fell down in a fit.
The Holy Hermit rais'd his eyes
610   And pray'd where he did sit.

I took the oars: the Pilot's boy,
   Who now doth crazy go,
Laugh'd loud and long, and all the while
   His eyes went to and fro,
615 "Ha! ha!" quoth he —"full plain I see,
   "The devil knows how to row."

And now all in mine own Countrée
   I stood on the firm land!
The Hermit stepp'd forth from the boat,
620   And scarcely he could stand.

"O shrieve me, shrieve me, holy Man!
   The Hermit cross'd his brow° —
"Say quick," quoth he, "I bid thee say
   "What manner man art thou?

625 Forthwith this frame of mine was wrench'd
   With a woeful agony,
Which forc'd me to begin my tale
   And then it left me free.

Since then at an uncertain hour,
630   Now oftimes and now fewer,
That anguish comes and makes me tell
   My ghastly aventure.

I pass, like night, from land to land;
   I have strange power of speech;
635 The moment that his face I see
I know the man that must hear me;
   To him my tale I teach.

---

622. cross'd his brow: Made the sign of the cross on his forehead.

560 Upon the whirl, where sank the ship,
    The boat spun round and round;
    And all was still, save that the hill
    Was telling of the sound.

    I moved my lips — the Pilot shrieked
565 And fell down in a fit;
    The holy Hermit raised his eyes,
    And prayed where he did sit.

    I took the oars: the Pilot's boy,
    Who now doth crazy go,
570 Laughed loud and long, and all the while
    His eyes went to and fro.
    "Ha! ha!" quoth he, "full plain I see,
    The Devil knows how to row."

    And now, all in my own countrée,
575 I stood on the firm land!
    The Hermit stepped forth from the boat,
    And scarcely he could stand.

    "O shrieve me, shrieve me, holy man!"   *The ancient Mariner earnestly*
    The Hermit crossed his brow.   *entreateth the Hermit to shrieve him;*
                                                   and the penance of life falls on him.
580 "Say quick," quoth he, "I bid thee say —
    What manner of man art thou?"

    Forthwith this frame of mine was wrenched
    With a woeful agony,
    Which forced me to begin my tale;
585 And then it left me free.

    Since then, at an uncertain hour,   *And ever and anon throughout his*
    That agony returns;°   *future life an agony constraineth*
    And till my ghastly tale is told,   *him to travel from land to land,*
    This heart within me burns.

590 I pass, like night, from land to land;
    I have strange power of speech;
    That moment that his face I see,
    I know the man that must hear me:
    To him my tale I teach.

587. In some copies of *LB* 1800, the version in which lines 587–89 were altered to their 1817 form, "agony" appeared as "agency."

What loud uproar bursts from that door!
    The Wedding-guests are there;
640 But in the Garden-bower the Bride
    And Bride-maids singing are:
And hark the little Vesper-bell°
    Which biddeth me to prayer.

O Wedding-guest! this soul hath been
645   Alone on a wide wide sea:
So lonely 'twas, that God himself
    Scarce seemed there to be.

O sweeter than the Marriage-feast,
    'Tis sweeter far to me
650 To walk together to the Kirk
    With a goodly company.

To walk together to the Kirk
    And all together pray,
While each to his great Father bends,
655 Old men, and babes, and loving friends,
    And Youths, and Maidens gay.

Farewell, farewell! but this I tell
    To thee, thou wedding-guest!
He prayeth well who loveth well,
660   Both man and bird and beast.

He prayeth best who loveth best,
    All things both great and small:
For the dear God, who loveth us,
    He made and loveth all.

665 The Marinere, whose eye is bright,
    Whose beard with age is hoar,
Is gone; and now the wedding-guest
    Turn'd from the bridegroom's door.

He went, like one that hath been stunn'd
670   And is of sense forlorn:°
A sadder and a wiser man
    He rose the morrow morn.

642. Vesper-bell: Church bell announcing evening service.
670. forlorn: Deprived.

595 What loud uproar bursts from that door!
The wedding-guests are there:
But in the garden-bower the bride
And bride-maids singing are;
And hark the little vesper bell,
600 Which biddeth me to prayer!

O Wedding-Guest! this soul hath been
Alone on a wide wide sea:
So lonely 'twas, that God himself
Scarce seemed there to be.

605 O sweeter than the marriage-feast,
'Tis sweeter far to me,
To walk together to the kirk
With a goodly company! —

To walk together to the kirk,
610 And all together pray,
While each to his great Father bends,
Old men, and babes, and loving friends,
And youths and maidens gay!

Farewell, farewell! but this I tell   *And to teach by his own example, love*
615 To thee, thou Wedding-Guest!   *and reverence to all things that God*
He prayeth well, who loveth well   *made and loveth.*
Both man and bird and beast.

He prayeth best, who loveth best
All things both great and small;
620 For the dear God who loveth us,
He made and loveth all."

The Mariner, whose eye is bright,
Whose beard with age is hoar,
Is gone: and now the Wedding-Guest
625 Turned from the bridegroom's door.

He went like one that hath been stunned,
And is of sense forlorn:
A sadder and a wiser man,
He rose the morrow morn.

PART TWO

"The Rime
of the Ancient Mariner":
A Case Study in
Contemporary Criticism

A Critical History of
"The Rime of the Ancient Mariner"

Throughout the nineteenth century, readers considered the "Rime" to be an obscurely mysterious poem, and this view leant itself with equal readiness, not surprisingly, to expressions of strong approval or disapproval. The memorable appreciations begin with scattered remarks by Charles Lamb (the more satisfying because they come in letters chiding Wordsworth and Robert Southey, respectively, for their ungenerous reactions) and with positive notices in the *Literary Gazette* (1828, unsigned) and the *Westminster Review* (1829, by Charles Bowring). J. G. Lockhart in *Blackwood's* (1819) and Leigh Hunt in *The Examiner* (1821) both express praise as well (see Jones and Tydeman 76, 80). The best-known Victorian encomia can be found in essays on Coleridge by A. C. Swinburne and Walter Pater. Displeasure surfaces first in the dismissive "Dutch attempt at German sublimity" notice written by Southey (who knew that the unsigned poem was by his fellow Pantisocrat and brother-in-law) in the *Critical Review* (1798; Jackson 53), and the well-known music historian Charles Burney's Shandean pronouncement, in the *Monthly Review* for June 1799, that the "Rime" "is the strangest story of a cock and a bull we ever saw on paper" (Jackson 56).

It is perhaps a little more surprising that the *Monthly Review* as late as 1819, noticing the appearance of the poem with its new gloss in

Sibylline Leaves, still confidently derides the man then commonly
revered as the Sage of Highgate for his vices of style and opinion without any apparent need to boast of flouting literary fashion. At the time
of Coleridge's death in 1834, in any case, the *Literary Gazette* with
equal confidence could call the "Rime" "the finest instance of the
supernatural sustained in narrative that we have in our language" (Jackson 610). Among the negative opinions, the one that surely rankled
most and also set the table for the most modern discussions (unless the
exchange with Mrs. Barbauld about the moral be said to have done so)
is the disclaimer Wordsworth affixed to the 1800 *Lyrical Ballads.* The
Mariner has no character, said Wordsworth, and he never acts but is
acted upon; the events do not follow from one another; and the sur-
plusage of imagery does not arise naturally. Not only these early views,
though, but issues raised by others mentioned here anticipate modern
attitudes more closely, as Richard Haven has shown (1972), than we
commonly realize.

The floodgates of modern "Rime" criticism did not open, however,
until the publication of *The Road to Xanadu* by John Livingston Lowes
in 1927. This is an immense tome interspersing dozens of sources from
Coleridge's readings in travel literature and occult philosophy (for
Christabel and "Kubla Khan" as well as for the "Rime") with exuberant
prose excurses generating just as many dozen metaphors for the workings of the poet's imagination. Amazingly, for all its bulk Lowes's book
is almost wholly devoid of interpretation (the poems for him are works
of "pure" imagination); and this stubborn literalism, although it came
near the end of a period when colorful evaluation was considered the
whole task of criticism, has had its more plainspoken adherents in more
recent times. Apart from R. C. Bald in 1940, who contributed a number of important additional sources, E. E. Stoll in 1948 (who had
launched the same sort of attack against what he considered wilful distortions of Shakespeare's plain sense), and Elisabeth Schneider in 1953
(who was soon to write a learned book in which everything not plainly
intelligible in Coleridge is attributed to opium) were late adherents to
the notion, in itself perhaps not fully intelligible, that a poem must
mean just what it says — and that this literal sense is also what the
author intended it to mean. Also harking back to the strictly evaluative
norm was the neo-humanist critic Irving Babbitt in *On Being Creative*
(1929), who no doubt saw that Lowes's book would start a vogue for
Coleridge and hastened to launch an attack, reminiscent of Burney and
Southey, in which the plain sense of the moral (be kind to animals, con-

firmed in the death of two hundred men in atonement for the death of one bird) is an absurd outrage to traditional human values.

Interpretation, however, or at least the imputation of a present fact to an absent cause, fast became the norm of academic criticism after the time of Lowes, and almost immediately hermeneutic exercises began to appear. Newton Stallknecht in 1932 saw that the redemptive force of the poem is "esthetic" (the beauty of the water snakes), and was the first to hint, therefore, that the poem may be about poetry among other things. Dorothy Waples in 1936 believed that the poem was an allegory of the six levels of human sympathy in the work of the Associationist psychologist David Hartley — after whom Coleridge had named his first son — despite evidence that Coleridge had become critical of Hartley as early as 1796. Two critics, finally, B. R. McElderry (1932) and Huntington Brown (1945), seized upon the gloss as a means of referring stable meaning back into the poem — an undoubted temptation that Brown to some extent resists in recognizing (the first to anticipate a recent trend) that the Reformation-period gloss is one of several historical layerings that imposes relativity on meanings to be adduced from any one layer. Brown's argument, the importance of which is acknowledged by Jerome McGann (see below), is largely recapitulated in an elegant recent essay on literary glosses in general (1977) by Lawrence Lipking.

The first critics emphasizing "symbols" in the poem were indeed among the wildest: Maud Bodkin in a famous book of 1934 (*Archetypal Patterns in Poetry*) argued quite movingly in Jungian terms, with frequent recourse to personal experience that anticipates certain trends in criticism today, that the poem evokes a return from the womblike depths of a night-sea journey, or "Rebirth archetype." In the previous year, George Herbert Clarke had been the first to fix definite symbols in place to make sense of the poem: the Mariner is humanity, the sun is the god of law, the moon is the god of love. G. Wilson Knight in 1941 (*The Starlit Dome*) applied his patented mixture of psychoanalysis and Christian mysticism to a lively reading of Coleridge's imagery, concluding that the "Rime," midway between the hell of *Christabel* and the paradise of "Kubla Khan," was Coleridge's *Purgatorio*. Other important approaches emphasizing symbolism are those of Elder Olson, "A Symbolic Reading of the *Ancient Mariner*" (1948), and Richard Harter Fogle, "The Genre of *The Ancient Mariner*" (1957).

Psychological approaches dominate this period of what might be called paradigmatic instability in interpreting the poem. D. W. Harding in 1941 evokes symptoms of depression and loneliness in largely Freudian terms, anticipating the important essay of George Whalley in 1946, which attends more closely to the dramatic character and situation of the Mariner. The wildest but also the most thought-provoking of all these readings was that of Kenneth Burke in *The Philosophy of Literary Form* (1941), which can only be travestied in summary: the Albatross is Coleridge's wife Sarah, the water snakes are his attraction to opium (not unmixed with elements of forbidden sexuality), the Pilot's boy driven mad is a scapegoat draining off the excess of the Mariner's punishment, and the sun is the stern father. Freud also stands behind strong later essays by David Beres (1951) and Joseph Sitterson (1982); and Freud aided by Harold Bloom still governs the colorful reading of the Mariner as "heroine" in Camille Paglia's *Sexual Personae* (1987). Other studies of psychological projection in the poem will be found in Richard Haven, *Patterns of Consciousness*, 1969, and Anya Taylor, *Magic and English Romanticism*, 1979. Also interesting in this untrammeled vein is the passing observation by W. H. Auden in *The Enchafèd Flood* (1950) that a ship (as opposed to a city or a garden) is a symbol of society in an uneasy political and moral state, both escaping itself and exploring new states. Two years before, E. M. W. Tillyard had incautiously remarked upon "the total lack of politics" in the "Rime," and we shall see what withering contempt a certain strain of more recent criticism, invoking and amplifying Auden's suggestion, has had for that opinion.

In 1946 there appeared by far the most ambitious and important reading of the poem to date and for many years to come, Robert Penn Warren's "A Poem of Pure Imagination." This was a benchmark performance by one of the New Critics then just coming to prominence (though much more dependent on biographical and secondary materials than most such work), and the open or covert awareness of Warren's methodological agenda has colored and tended to polarize critical response, both to him and to the poem, to this day. Believing that through the agency of the shaping imagination the "Rime" fuses the theme of the One Life in the form of a sacramental narrative (the eucharistic bird eating the food it ne'er did eat only to be crucified, then redeemed by the blessing of nature's bounty) together with a self-referentially redemptive emphasis on the imagination itself, with the retributive sun offset throughout by the visionary moon, Warren argued for the unity of the poem, as composition and as organic whole, by way of celebrating its achievement. It is this faith in the self-justifying value of hard-earned unity (Coleridge's "multëity in unity"), underwritten as a struggle to achieve harmony through the central paradoxes of Christianity, that sets the stage for subsequent criticism of the poem.

Critics have either acceded in some measure to these New Critical premises, as when Lionel Stevenson argued in 1949 that the inconsistencies of the Mariner's story should be understood as part of his unified character in a Browningesque dramatic monologue, or they have turned against them, claiming that the poem is un-Christian or anti-Christian and frequently claiming also that its genius (or defect, or inevitable form) is fragmentary rather than unitary. It must be admitted by anyone who actually reads through this criticism that Warren's argument is far more often attacked than confirmed, and that changing times do partly account for this; but scholarly reputations are rarely made except by disagreement, and throughout the history of Warren-bashing, at least until a variety of attempts at a metacritical stance appear in the 1970s, critics are for the most part candid in agreeing that the strong outlines of what he said have organized and conditioned — in some degree enabled — their own thinking.

Before turning to some of these, I should mention the partly confirmatory voices, especially that of the revered Coleridge scholar Humphry House in the Clark Lectures of 1953, whose measured qualifications Warren attempts respectfully to rebut in footnotes added later, but whose evident admiration may have helped the legion of dissenters to believe that there indeed existed a status quo ante to overturn. Perhaps here one should also mention John Beer's *Coleridge the Visionary* (1959), which, in addition to stressing the mystical and redemptive aspects of the poem, suggests the most important additional sources since Bald: Jakob Boehme's writings, Bishop Berkeley's *Siris*, Scott's translations of Bürger's ballads, Richard Hole's commentary on *The Arabian Nights*, and above all the neoplatonic allegorizations of Ulysses' homecoming in the writings of Proclus and Thomas Taylor — which point toward the emphasis on "epic" and "epic symbol" in the commentaries of James D. Boulger (1965, 1969) and Warren Stevenson (1976). More than one critic has complained that Beer's Coleridge is too easily confused with Blake, but he is influential nonetheless. Also within the Christianizing pale are James Boulger abovementioned, whose notion of "Christian skepticism" is a persuasive way of reconciling irrational elements that cannot be argued away with the undeniable evidence of a Christian framework in the narrative. Stressing the sacramental aspect of "the marriage metaphor," finally, Milton Teichman (1969) argues that the Mariner's vision transforms rather than negates the wedding that frames the poem.

Two recent critiques of Warren by Homer Obed Brown and Jonathan Arac, stressing his investment in the values of the New Criticism, will be found in a single volume, *The Question of Textuality* (1982). Commentaries antithetical to Warren's were pioneered, however, by E. E. Bostetter's "The Nightmare World of *The Ancient Mariner*" (1962), which it is now conventional to credit with having fixed the poles of debate in place. Placing special emphasis on the game of dice between Death and Life-in-Death, Bostetter insists that the Mariner is adrift in a completely arbitrary and malign cosmos, from which he is redeemed only by the settling of derangement into numbness, only to transmit his infectious compulsion from listener to listener. Insofar as Christianity can be discerned at all, Bostetter infers a kind of Calvinism, bred of the poet's private torments. Elaborating on this position while retreating from its aggressive gloom is an article by A. M. Buchan (1964) that emphasizes the smothering of the Mariner by the sheer excess of the sense impressions to which he is susceptible (perhaps there is an echo of Wordsworth on Coleridge's supernumerary imagery here) — an interesting antidote to readings that lift the Mariner out of the material world altogether — together with the later book by Paul Magnuson, *Coleridge's Nightmare Poetry* (1974), in which the technical and poetological implications of "Night-mair" are rigorously explored. For other views emphasizing the atmosphere of demonological compulsion in the poem, see essays by Ward Pafford (1963), Gayle Smith (1963), and Arnold Davidson (1981). James Twitchell's lively article on the importance of vampirism in the poem (1977) — for which indeed there is much evidence — belongs here as well.

Two years after Bostetter, the brilliant maverick William Empson, having become interested in the "Rime" while helping David Pirie put together an anthology of Coleridge's poems, delivered perhaps the most telling blow to the Warren position simply by pointing out that in 1797 Coleridge was still a Unitarian, fresh from having preached two sermons explaining why he could not in conscience administer any of the Anglican sacraments. Empson's obsession in later years was the barbarism of blood sacrifice — the Crucifixion — in Christianity and its influence on Anglo-American literary commentary (Warren and his legions climb "a steep but direct path to the wild heights of Pecksniffery which are their spiritual home" ["The Ancient Mariner"]), and this obsession he cheerfully bestowed on Coleridge; yet the underlying point still has force, and to this point Empson adds a fascinating elaboration of Auden's passing remarks in *The Enchafèd Flood* on the ship as a metaphor for discontented exploration (evoking the evils of empire and the slave traffic), with the Mariner a kind of crazed Magellan issuing forth from the known boundaries of Europe and enduring the trials of historical transformation. This approach, anticipated in some ways by Malcolm Ware's 1961 essay suggesting that the spectre-bark is a slave ship, established a tradition more clearly identifiable, though sometimes less generously acknowledged, than Bostetter's. Empson's most candid follower is J. R. Ebbatson in his essay on Coleridge and "the Rights of Man" (1972), the most thorough of the essays that find the Terror and other aspects of the French Revolution lurking in the poem. To other more recent politicizing revisionists I shall return below.

This brings me to what I shall crudely but I hope uncondescendingly call the threshold of critical awareness (or better, the domain of received information) that will be found in the essays printed in the present volume. The "contemporary" in Coleridge criticism was launched by two essays in particular, Frances Ferguson's "Coleridge and the Deluded Reader" (1977 — an annus mirabilis for "Rime" criticism), and Jerome McGann's "The Meaning of the Ancient Mariner" (1981), both powerful arguments that mark their own historical moment by attempting to achieve a metacritical position with respect to other criticism, reconsidering all the critics who in some measure naively set forth unmediated interpretations of the poem against the backdrop of their intellectual preconditioning. A neopragmatist drawing tacitly upon Stanley Fish's notion of "interpretive communities," Ferguson argues that Coleridge establishes within the structure of the "Rime" the ways in which readers of whatever persuasion will inevitably read the poem they were destined in advance to read. Neopragmatism shares with most progressive criticism the determinist premise that certain forms of discourse predetermine the thinking of critics and even poets, hence sheds a kind of influence on much of what follows. McGann's essay further develops his influential thesis that most commentary on the Romantic period remains firmly within the "romantic ideology" it purports to comment upon — an ideology that is Christian, privatizing, and, at its most sophisticated, Hegelian. Drawing not on Hegel's great machine for evolving consciousness, McGann argues, but on the comparable historicizing approach to Biblical authorship adopted by avatars of the Higher Criticism, Coleridge in the successive revisions of the poem (envisioned to some extent in advance) creates a layered text that reflects the evolution of religious consciousness from early superstitions (the crew, the primitive nature of the narrative elements) to medieval Christianity (the consciousness of the Mariner), to Reformation exegesis (the learned Gloss), to the relativist perspective concerning the exact details of Christian revelation embodied in the "poet" who brings all these accretions together. Anyone who reads the poem either as Christian symbolism (not the literal account of the Bible but its equivalent) or as Christian skepticism (the text is uncertain, but its framework of faith is unshaken), or even as anti-Christian pessimism (trapped in a hated theological framework) is simply the reader that Coleridge constituted in the first place, and the only way to take an independent view of the poem is to stand wholly outside its Christian ideology.

This account even more than Ferguson's, with which it shares the notion of the preconstituted reader, reverberates through several of the selections of recent criticism printed in the present volume. McGann draws on elements of Marxism, like David Simpson, of the not unrelated new historicism, like Raimonda Modiano, and of reader-response criticism, though of a very different kind from that embodied in Ferguson's and my own contributions. Taking up these threads in turn: there is a recent and in some ways convincing essay by Daniel P. Watkins, "History as Demon in Coleridge's *The Rime of the Ancient Mariner*" (1988), which turns on the Marxist concept (developed by Fredric Jameson, Pierre Macherey, and others) of "contradiction" in soon-to-be-supplanted social orders that manifests itself in the characteristic texts of their time. The contradiction here is between the communal moral (loving all things, great and small things, in a goodly company) and the crazed individuality and isolation of the Mariner's experience, which subverts not just the wedding feast but every possible enactment of community. In this regard see also essays by Peter Kitson (1989) and Chris Rubinstein (1990), together with a book by Patrick Keane, *Coleridge's Submerged Politics: The Ancient Mariner and Robinson Crusoe* (1994). Modiano considers these contributions at length in the essay published below, and in the *Modern Language Quarterly* for 1998 there is a critique of such readings by David Perkins. As to the New Historicism, which renders literary texts as a dialogue reflecting and responding to cultural and social texts of other kinds, one may cite Modiano's 1989 essay on the poetics of gift exchange in Coleridge (which also belongs below, as the exchange takes place with Wordsworth), together with Warren Stevenson's eclectic but interestingly detailed essay on the "Power Politics" of the "Rime" (1995), which revives the Empsonian theme of European expansion in examining the fact that the Mariner's ship, unlike the spectre-bark and the Pilot's boat, seems not to have a captain.

Reader-Response criticism is always present in approaches that see the poem as in any way dialogic. Thus Susan Wolfson's 1984 essay on the role of interpretive language and persistent questioning in the "Rime" supposes an implied hermeneutic engagement in the very act of composing the poem. Modiano's essay of 1977 on the way in which the inadequacy of language to authentic experience is made a theme in the poem perforce entails a frustrated interlocutor seeking to make sense of "languageless" experience. An essay by Jean-Pierre Mileur (1982) pursues a similar argument. Richard Payne (1978) studies the poem as a learned amalgam of sixteenth- and seventeenth-century idioms. Unique among essays that can be classified here is Leslie Brisman's incisive chapter on the "Rime" in his *Romantic Origins,* which in part concerns the struggle to inherit the voice of Milton that takes place between the visionary Mariner and the rather bovine embodiment of ordinary, "natural" consciousness that Brisman dubs "Porlock" — the town from which the man who allegedly interrupted the composition of "Kubla Khan" allegedly came. Brisman's Porlock reminds me in many ways of the "Wordsworth" as Coleridge imagined him that the reader will find portrayed in my own essay, and that leads me to say that by far the most extensive recent work on reader interactions in the "Rime" concerns the "symbiosis," as Thomas McFarland calls it, of Wordsworth and Coleridge during the gestation of the *Lyrical Ballads.* For a list of these readings, consult the first two footnotes of my essay below, here reduced to a roll call: Mark L. Reed, Mary Jacobus, McFarland, Jonathan Wordsworth, Modiano, Stephen Parrish, Lucy Newlyn, Magnuson, Gordon Thomas, Richard Gravil, and James Holt McGavran have all made important contributions to our understanding of this extraordinarily complex literary relationship.

Anne Williams, together with the authors she cites, has kept the psychoanalytic tradition of commentary on the poem current by infusing it with post-Freudian and feminist elements, drawing especially on Julia Kristeva's concept of the "semiotic," which in some measure finds its antecedent in the Jungian role of the oceanic in Maud Bodkin. Also contemporary, but not represented as a genre in the format of this anthology, is the gay and lesbian studies framework, which has its voice, linked to that of Williams through its focus on psychoanalysis and gender issues, in the foreword written by Donald Ault for the new edition of the "Rime" compiled under the influence of McGann's essay (with the 1798, 1800, and 1817 versions to be read simultaneously across each page) by Martin Wallen (1993). Ault is especially interested in the fact that in the 1798 version the gender of Death on the spectre ship is not disclosed, and for him a good deal follows from that. One should also mention here the argument of Wayne Koestenbaum in *Double Talk: The Erotics of Male Literary Collaboration* (1989), which sheds interesting light, too, on the Wordsworth-Coleridge interchange.

Deconstruction, represented here by Susan Eilenberg's essay (which also contributes, needless to say, to our understanding of the Wordsworth-Coleridge relationship) has not focused as assiduously on Coleridge as it has on Wordsworth, if only because Coleridge himself seems at times an avatar of deconstruction, as of so many other strange seas of thought, whose self-consciousness precludes the disclosure on our part of anything that we cannot suspect him of having put there for us to find. Eilenberg acknowledges an essay by Lawrence Kramer (1979) as the strongest anticipation of her emphasis on usurpations of voice, but there are two essays apart from Eilenberg's that belong more squarely under the heading of "deconstruction." The more recent, by William Galperin (1991), is largely a reprise of the metacritical gesture made by Ferguson and McGann, shifting the language in which one speaks of critics read by the poem rather than the other way around more fully to entail the notion of entering a linguistic stream, with final homage paid to Jacques Derrida. The earlier of the two, "The Mariner Rimed" by Arden Reed (1984), expatiates in fascinating ways on what is surely the most inexplicably overlooked datum in the whole history of commentary on the poem — namely, the fact that after all the modernizations of spelling "Rime" is still spelled the same in the 1817 edition. It is clearly an important pun waiting to be explicated, and Reed very carefully shows how rhyming, discoursing, and being frosted (all clearly relevant senses of the word) work both to unify and to fragment the senses that can be drawn from the whole poem. It is an important reading, to which Eilenberg's essay on Coleridge's "ventriloquism" — harking back perhaps in some ways to Max L. Schulz on the "voice" of the Mariner (1963) — is a worthy successor.

It remains only to speak of a neglected approach to the poem, of which indeed there are few distinguished exemplars. Despite the impressive work that has been done over the years on Coleridge's heavy investment in the metaphysical tradition of philosophy (research on his plagiarisms apart, there is major work by René Wellek, G. N. G. Orsini, McFarland, and James Engell), very little has been said about philosophy in the "Rime," perhaps because critics dread being accused of thinking allegorically. However, Irene Chayes in 1965 did venture to argue that the "Rime" is an allegory of epistemological categories. There is also a philosopher who has been hindered by no such fear of allegory, Stanley Cavell in *In Quest of the Ordinary* (1988). Cavell speaks eloquently about Coleridge's poetic version of the effort in Kant to overcome the skepticism for which he himself is responsible, a task that is best given to poetry because of its superior capacity to evoke the actual: "the calling of poetry is to give the world back, to bring it back, as to life." Allegorical or not, this sentence marvelously evokes the plot of the "Rime," and one henceforth listens spellbound as Cavell lets us think that the Polar Spirits are polarities of thought and that the equatorial "Line" is the line one draws, in Kantian thought, around the thing-in-itself — to know it negatively, to escape from it, and to recover it, as the Mariner at last recovers his "own countrée": — no doubt a diminished thing, but a thing nonetheless.

A CRITICAL HISTORY:
A SELECTED BIBLIOGRAPHY

Primary Works

Coleridge, Samuel Taylor. *The Annotated Ancient Mariner*. Ed. Martin Gardner. New York: Potter, 1965.

———. *Biographia Literaria*. Ed. James Engell and Walter Jackson Bate. 2 vols. Vol. 7 of *The Collected Works of Samuel Taylor Coleridge*. Princeton: Princeton UP, 1983.

———. *Coleridge's "Ancient Mariner." An Experimental Edition of Texts and Revisions 1798–1828*. Ed. Martin Wallen. Barrytown: Station Hill, 1993.

———. *Coleridge's Miscellaneous Criticism*. Ed. Thomas M. Raysor. Cambridge: Harvard UP, 1936.

———. *Coleridge's Shakespearean Criticism*. Ed. Thomas M. Raysor. 2 vols. Cambridge: Harvard UP, 1930.

———. *Collected Letters of Samuel Taylor Coleridge*. Ed. Earl Leslie Griggs. 6 vols. Oxford: Clarendon, 1956–71.

———. *The Complete Poetical Works of Samuel Taylor Coleridge*. Ed. Ernest Hartley Coleridge. 2 vols. Oxford: Clarendon, 1975.

———. *Essays on His Times*. Ed. David V. Erdman. 3 vols. Vol. 3 of *The Collected Works of Samuel Taylor Coleridge*. Princeton: Princeton UP, 1978.

———. *Lay Sermons* (incl. *The Statesman's Manual*). Ed. R. J. White.

Vol. 6 of *The Collected Works of Samuel Taylor Coleridge*. Princeton: Princeton UP, 1972.

———. *Lectures 1795 on Politics and Religion*. Ed. Lewis Patton and Peter Mann. Vol. 1 of *The Collected Works of Samuel Taylor Coleridge*. Princeton: Princeton UP, 1971.

———. *Marginalia*. Ed. George Whalley. 5 vols. Vol. 12 of *The Collected Works of Samuel Taylor Coleridge*. Princeton: Princeton UP, 1980.

———. *The Notebooks of Samuel Taylor Coleridge*. Ed. Kathleen Coburn. 3 vols. Princeton: Princeton UP, 1957.

———. *"The Rime of the Ancient Mariner": A Handbook*. Ed. Royal Gettman. San Francisco: Wadsworth, 1961.

———. *Table Talk*. Ed. Carl Woodring. Vol. 14 of *The Collected Works of Samuel Taylor Coleridge*. Princeton: Princeton UP, 1990.

Wordsworth, Dorothy. *The Journals of Dorothy Wordsworth*. Ed. Ernest de Selincourt. 2 vols. Oxford: Clarendon, 1941.

Wordsworth, William. *"Lyrical Ballads," and Other Poems, 1797–1800*. Ed. James Butler and Karen Green. Ithaca: Cornell UP, 1992.

Wordsworth, William, and Dorothy Wordsworth. *The Letters of William and Dorothy Wordsworth*. Ed. Ernest de Selincourt. *The Early Years, 1787–1805*. Rev. Ed. C. L. Shaver. Oxford: Clarendon, 1967.

Secondary Works

Alcorn, Marshall. "Coleridge's Literary Use of Narcissism." *Wordsworth Circle* 16 (1985): 13–21.

Arac, Jonathan. "Repetition and Exclusion: Coleridge and the New Criticism Reconsidered." *The Question of Textuality: Strategies of Reading in Contemporary American Criticism*. Ed. William V. Spanos, Paul A. Bové, and Daniel O'Hara. Bloomington: Indiana UP, 1982.

Auden, Wystan Hugh. *The Enchafèd Flood, or the Romantic Iconography of the Sea*. London: Faber, 1950.

Babbitt, Irving. *On Being Creative*. Boston: Houghton, 1929.

Bald, R. C. "Coleridge and *The Ancient Mariner*: Addenda to *The Road to Xanadu*." *Nineteenth Century Studies in Honor of C. S. Northup*. Ed. H. Davis, William Clyde DeVane, and R. C. Bald. Ithaca: Cornell UP, 1940. 1–45.

Bate, Walter Jackson. *Coleridge*. Masters of World Literature Ser. New York: Macmillan, 1968.

Beer, John. *Coleridge the Visionary.* London: Chatto, 1959.

Beres, David. "A Dream, A Vision and a Poem: A Psycho-Analytic Study of the Origins of the Rime of the Ancient Mariner." *The Question of Textuality: Strategies of Reading in Contemporary American Criticism.* Ed. William V. Spano, Paul A. Bové, and Daniel O'Hara. Bloomington: Indiana UP, 1982.

Bloom, Harold, ed. *Samuel Taylor Coleridge's The Rime of the Ancient Mariner.* Modern Critical Interpretations. New York: Chelsea, 1986.

Bodkin, Maud. "A Study of 'The Ancient Mariner' and of the Rebirth Archetype." *Archetypal Patterns in Poetry: Psychological Studies of Imagination.* 1934. New York: Vintage, 1958. 25–85.

Bostetter, Edward E. "The Nightmare World of *The Ancient Mariner.*" *Studies in Romanticism* 1–3 (1962): 241–54.

Boulger, James. "Christian Skepticism in *The Rime of the Ancient Mariner.*" *From Sensibility to Romanticism: Essays Presented to Frederick A. Pottle.* Ed. Frederick W. Hilles and Harold Bloom. London: Oxford UP, 1965.

———, ed. *Twentieth Century Interpretations of the Rime of the Ancient Mariner.* Englewood Cliffs: Prentice, 1969.

Brisman, Leslie. "Coleridge and the Supernatural." *Studies in Romanticism* 21 (1982): 123–59.

———. "Coleridge and the Ancestral Voices." *Romantic Origins.* Ithaca: Cornell UP, 1978. 21–54.

Brown, Homer Obed. "The Art of Theology and the Theology of Art: Robert Penn Warren's Reading of Coleridge's Rime of the Ancient Mariner." *Boundary 2* 8 (1979): 237–60.

Brown, Huntington. "The Gloss to the Ancient Mariner." *Modern Language Quarterly* 6 (1945).

Buchan, A. M. "The Sad Wisdom of the Mariner." *Studies in Philology* 61 (1964): 669–88.

Burke, Kenneth. *The Philosophy of Literary Form.* 1941. Rev. ed. New York: Vintage, 1957.

Cavell, Stanley. *In Quest of the Ordinary: Lines of Skepticism and Romanticism.* Chicago: U of Chicago P, 1988.

Chayes, Irene. "A Coleridgean Reading of the Ancient Mariner." *Studies in Romanticism* 4 (1965): 81–103.

Christensen, Jerome. *Coleridge's Blessed Machine of Language.* Ithaca: Cornell UP, 1981.

Clarke, George Herbert. "Certain Symbols in *The Rime of the Ancient Mariner.*" *Queens Quarterly* 40 (1933): 27–45.

D'Avanzo, Mario. "Coleridge's Wedding Guest and Marriage Feast: The Biblical Context." *University of Windsor Review* 8 (1972): 62–65.

Davidson, Arnold. "The Concluding Moral in Coleridge's *The Rime of the Ancient Mariner.*" *Philological Quarterly* 60 (1981): 87–94.

Ebbatson, J. R. "Coleridge and the Rights of Man." *Studies in Romanticism* 11 (1972): 171–206.

Empson, William. "The Ancient Mariner." *Critical Quarterly* 6 (1964): 298–319.

———. "The Ancient Mariner: An Answer to Warren." *Kenyon Review* 15 (1993): 155–77.

———. Introduction. *Coleridge's Verse: A Selection.* Ed. David Pirie. New York: Schocken, 1973.

Ferguson, Frances. "Coleridge and the Deluded Reader: *The Rime of the Ancient Mariner.*" *Georgia Review* 31 (1977): 617–35.

Fogle, Richard Harter. "The Genre of *The Ancient Mariner.*" *Texas Studies in English Literature* 7 (1957): 111–24.

Galperin, William. "Coleridge and Critical Intervention." *Wordsworth Circle* 22 (1991): 56–64.

Gill, Stephen. *William Wordsworth: A Life.* Oxford: Clarendon, 1989.

Gose, Elliott, Jr. "Coleridge and the Luminous Gloom: An Analysis of the Symbolical Language in the *Rime of the Ancient Mariner.*" *Publications of the Modern Language Association* 75 (1960): 238–44.

Gravil, Richard. "Coleridge's Wordsworth." *Wordsworth Circle* 14–15 (1983–84): 38–46.

———. "The Whale and the Albatross." *Wordsworth Circle* 28 (1997): 2–10.

Hall, Wendy. "Interpreting Poetic Shadows: The Gloss of 'The Rime of the Ancient Mariner.'" *Criticism* 29 (1987): 179–95.

Harding, Davis W. "The Theme of 'The Ancient Mariner.'" *Scrutiny* 9 (1941): 334–42.

Hartman, Geoffrey. "On Traumatic Knowledge and Literary Studies." *New Literary History* 26 (1995): 537–63.

Haven, Richard. "The Ancient Mariner in the Nineteenth Century." *Studies in Romanticism* 11 (1972): 360–74.

———. *Patterns of Consciousness: An Essay on Coleridge.* Amherst: U of Massachusetts P, 1969.

Hoeveler, Diane Long. "Glossing the Feminine in the Rime of the Ancient Mariner." *European Romantic Review* 2 (1992): 145–62.

Holmes, Richard. *Coleridge: Early Visions.* New York: Viking, 1990.

House, Humphry. "The Ancient Mariner." *Coleridge: The Clark Lectures, 1951–1952*. London: Hart, 1953. 84–113.

Jackson, J. R. de J., ed. *Coleridge: The Critical Heritage*. The Critical Heritage Series. London: Routledge, 1970.

Jones, Alun R., and William Tydeman, ed. *The Ancient Mariner and Other Poems*. Casebook Series. London: Macmillan, 1973.

Jost-Frey, Hans. "Überlegungen an der Textgrenze." *Modern Language Notes* 109 (1994): 356–71.

Keane, Patrick J. *Coleridge's Submerged Politics: The Ancient Mariner and Robinson Crusoe*. Columbia: U of Missouri P, 1994.

Kitson, Peter. "Coleridge, the French Revolution, and 'The Ancient Mariner': Collective Guilt and Individual Salvation." *Yearbook of English Studies* 19 (1989): 197–207.

Knight, G. Wilson. *The Starlit Dome: Studies in the Poetry of Vision*. 1941. London: Oxford, 1971.

Koestenbaum, Wayne. *Double Talk: The Erotics of Male Collaboration*. New York: Routledge, 1989.

Kramer, Lawrence. "The Other Will: The Daemonic in Coleridge and Wordsworth." *Philological Quarterly* 58 (1979): 298–320.

Lefebure, Molly. "A Mystic Peregrination — The Ancient Mariner." *Charles Lamb Bulletin* 65 (1989): 8–26.

Lipking, Lawrence. "The Marginal Gloss: Notes and Asides on Poe, Valéry, 'The Ancient Mariner,' the Ordeal of the Margin, Storiella as She Is Sung, Versions of Leonardo, and the Plight of Modern Criticism." *Critical Inquiry* 3 (1977): 609–55.

Lowes, John Livingston. *The Road to Xanadu: A Study in the Ways of the Imagination*. Boston: Houghton, 1927.

Lukits, Stephen. "Wordsworth Unawares: The Boy of Winander, the Poet, and the Mariner." *Wordsworth Circle* 19 (1988): 156-60.

Magnuson, Paul. *Coleridge and Wordsworth: A Lyrical Dialogue*. Princeton: Princeton UP, 1988.

———. *Coleridge's Nightmare Poetry*. Charlottesville: UP of Virginia, 1974.

Matlak, Richard. "Forty Questions to Ask of the Ancient Mariner." *Approaches to Teaching Coleridge's Poetry*. Ed. Matlak. New York: MLA, 1991. 102–09.

McElderry, Bruce R., Jr. "Coleridge's Revision of *The Ancient Mariner*." *Studies in Philology* 29 (1932): 68–94.

McFarland, Thomas. *Romanticism and the Forms of Ruin: Wordsworth, Coleridge, and the Modalities of Fragmentation*. Princeton: Princeton UP, 1981.

McGann, Jerome J. "The Ancient Mariner. The Meaning of the Meanings." *The Beauty of Inflections: Literary Investigations in Historical Method and Theory.* Oxford: Clarendon, 1988. 135–72.

McKusick, James. "Coleridge and the Economy of Nature." *Studies in Romanticism* 35 (1996): 375–93.

Miall, David S. "Guilt and Death: The Predicament of the Ancient Mariner." *Studies in English Literature* 24 (1984): 633–53.

Mileur, Jean-Pierre. *Vision and Revision: Coleridge's Art of Immanence.* Berkeley: U of California P, 1982.

Modiano, Raimonda. "Coleridge and Wordsworth: The Ethics of Gift Exchange." *Wordsworth Circle* 20 (1989): 113–20.

———. "Words and 'Languageless' Meanings: Limits of Expression in *The Rime of the Ancient Mariner.*" *Modern Language Quarterly* 38 (1977): 40–61.

Newlyn, Lucy. *Coleridge, Wordsworth, and the Language of Allusion.* Oxford: Clarendon, 1986.

Olson, Elder. "A Symbolic Reading of the *Ancient Mariner.*" *Modern Philology* 45 (1948): 275–79.

Pafford, Ward. "Coleridge's Wedding Guest." *Studies in Philology* 60 (1963): 618–26.

Paglia, Camille. *Sexual Personae: Art and Decadence from Nefertiti to Emily Dickinson.* New Haven: Yale UP, 1990.

Parrish, Stephen Maxfield. "Coleridge's Lyrical Ballads." *Coleridge's Imagination: Essays in Memory of Peter Laver.* Ed. Richard Gravil, Lucy Newlyn, and Nicholas Roe. Cambridge: Cambridge UP, 1985. 102–16.

———. "The Wordsworth-Coleridge Controversy." *Publications of the Modern Language Association* 73 (1958): 367–74.

Payne, Richard. "'The Style and Spirit of the Elder Poets': The Ancient Mariner and the English Literary Tradition." *Modern Philology* 75 (1978): 368–84.

Perkins, David. "The 'Ancient Mariner' and Its Interpreters: Some Versions of Coleridge." *Modern Language Quarterly* 57 (1996): 425–48.

Pottle, Frederick. "Modern Criticism of *The Ancient Mariner.*" *Essays on the Teaching of English.* Ed. Edward J. Gordon and Edward Simpson Noyes. New York: Appleton, 1960.

Reed, Arden. "The Riming Mariner and the Mariner Rimed." *Romantic Weather: The Climates of Coleridge and Baudelaire.* Hanover: UP of New England, 1983. 147–81.

Reed, Mark L. "Wordsworth, Coleridge, and the 'Plan' of the Lyrical Ballads." *University of Toronto Quarterly* 34 (1965): 238–53.

Rubinstein, Chris. "A New Identity for the Mariner? A Further Exploration of 'The Rime of the Ancient Mariner.'" *The Coleridge Bulletin* 2 (1990): 16–29.

Schneider, Elisabeth. *Coleridge, Opium, and Kubla Khan.* Chicago: U of Chicago P, 1953.

Schulz, Max F. "The Ventriloquism Voice." *The Poetic Voices of Coleridge.* Detroit: Wayne State UP, 1963. 51–71.

Sitterson, Joseph. "'The Rime of the Ancient Mariner' and Freudian Dream Theory." *Papers on Language and Literature* 18 (1982): 17–35.

Smith, Gayle. "A Reappraisal of the Moral Stanzas in 'The Rime of the Ancient Mariner.'" *Studies in Romanticism* 3 (1963): 42–52.

Stallknecht, Newton P. "The Moral of *The Ancient Mariner.*" 1932. *Strange Seas of Thought: Studies in Wordsworth's Philosophy of Man and Nature.* Bloomington: U of Indiana P, 1958. 141–71.

Stevenson, Lionel. "*The Rime of the Ancient Mariner* as a Dramatic Monologue." *The Personalist* 30 (1949): 34–44.

Stevenson, Warren. *Nimbus of Glory: A Study of Coleridge's Three Great Poems.* Salzburg: Institut für Anglistik, 1983.

———. "The Case of the Missing Captain: Power Politics in 'The Rime of the Ancient Mariner.'" *Wordsworth Circle* 26 (1995): 12–18.

———. "The Rime of the Ancient Mariner as Epic Symbol." *Dalhousie Review* 56 (1976): 542–47.

Stillinger, Jack. *Coleridge and Textual Instability: The Multiple Versions of the Major Poems.* New York: Oxford, 1994.

Stoll, Elmer Edgar. "Symbolism in Coleridge." *Publications of the Modern Language Association* 63 (1948): 214–33.

Taylor, Anya. *Magic and English Romanticism.* Athens: U of Georgia P, 1979.

Teichman, Milton. "The Marriage Metaphor in *The Rime of the Ancient Mariner.*" *Bulletin of the New York Public Library* 73 (1969): 40–48.

Tillyard, Eustace M. W. *Five Poems 1470-1870.* London: Chatto, 1948.

Twitchell, James. "*The Rime of the Ancient Mariner* as a Vampire Poem," *College Literature* 4 (1977): 21–39.

Waples, Dorothy. "David Hartley in *The Ancient Mariner.*" *Journal of English and Germanic Philology* 35 (1936): 337–51.

Ware, Malcolm. "Coleridge's 'Spectre-Bark': A Slave Ship?" *Philological Quarterly* 40 (1961): 589–93.

Warren, Robert Penn. "A Poem of Pure Imagination: An Experiment in Reading." *New and Selected Essays*. New York: Random, 1989. 335–423.

Watkins, Daniel P. "History as Demon in Coleridge's *The Rime of the Ancient Mariner.*" *Papers on Language and Literature* 24 (1988): 23–33.

Whalley, George. "The Mariner and the Albatross." *University of Toronto Quarterly* 16 (1946): 381–98.

Wolfson, Susan. "The Language of Interpretation in Romantic Poetry: 'A Strong Working of the Mind.'" *Romanticism and Language*. Ed. Arden Reed. Ithaca: Cornell UP, 1984. 22–49.

Reader-Response Criticism and "The Rime of the Ancient Mariner"

WHAT IS READER-RESPONSE CRITICISM?

Students are routinely asked in English courses for their reactions to the texts they are reading. Sometimes there are so many different reactions that we may wonder whether everyone has read the same text. And some students respond so idiosyncratically to what they read that we say their responses are "totally off the wall." This variety of response interests reader-response critics, who raise theoretical questions about whether our responses to a work are the same as its meanings, whether a work can have as many meanings as we have responses to it, and whether some responses are more valid than others. They ask what determines what is and what isn't "off the wall." What, in other words, is the wall, and what standards help us define it?

In addition to posing provocative questions, reader-response criticism provides us with models that aid our understanding of texts and the reading process. Adena Rosmarin has suggested that a literary text may be likened to an incomplete work of sculpture: to see it fully, we must complete it imaginatively, taking care to do so in a way that responsibly takes into account what exists. Other reader-response critics have suggested other models, for reader-response criticism is not a monolithic school of thought but, rather, an umbrella term covering a variety of approaches to literature.

Nonetheless, as Steven Mailloux has shown, reader-response critics *do* share not only questions but also goals and strategies. Two of the basic goals are to show that a work gives readers something to do and to describe what the reader does by way of response. To achieve those goals, the critic may make any of a number of what Mailloux calls "moves." For instance, a reader-response critic might typically (1) cite direct references to reading in the text being analyzed, in order to justify the focus on reading and show that the world of the text is continuous with the one in which the reader reads; (2) show how other nonreading situations in the text nonetheless mirror the situation the reader is in ("Fish shows how in *Paradise Lost* Michael's teaching of Adam in Book XI resembles Milton's teaching of the reader throughout the poem"); and (3) show, therefore, that the reader's response is, or is analogous to, the story's action or conflict. For instance, Stephen Booth calls *Hamlet* the tragic story of "an audience that cannot make up its mind" (Mailloux, "Learning" 103).

Although reader-response criticism is often said to have emerged in the United States in the 1970s, it is in one respect as old as the foundations of Western culture. The ancient Greeks and Romans tended to view literature as rhetoric, a means of making an audience react in a certain way. Although their focus was more on rhetorical strategies and devices than on the reader's (or listener's) response to those methods, the ancients by no means left the audience out of the literary equation. Aristotle thought, for instance, that the greatness of tragedy lay in its "cathartic" power to cleanse or purify the emotions of audience members. Plato, by contrast, worried about the effects of artistic productions, so much so that he advocated evicting poets from the Republic on the grounds that their words "feed and water" the passions!

In our own century, long before 1970, there were critics whose concerns and attitudes anticipated those of reader-response critics. One of these, I. A. Richards, is usually associated with formalism, a supposedly objective, text-centered approach to literature that reader-response critics of the 1970s roundly attacked. And yet in 1929 Richards managed to sound surprisingly *like* a 1970s-vintage reader-response critic, writing in *Practical Criticism* that "the personal situation of the reader inevitably (and within limits rightly) affects his reading, and many more are drawn to poetry in quest of some reflection of their latest emotional crisis than would admit it" (575). Rather than deploring this fact, as many of his formalist contemporaries would have done, Richards argued that the reader's feelings and experiences provide a kind of reality check, a way of testing the authenticity of emotions and events represented in literary works.

Approximately a decade after Richards wrote *Practical Criticism,* an American named Louise M. Rosenblatt published *Literature as Exploration* (1938). In that seminal book, now in its fourth edition (1983), Rosenblatt began developing a theory of reading that blurs the boundary between reader and text, subject and object. In a 1969 article entitled "Towards a Transactional Theory of Reading," she sums up her position by writing that "a poem is what the reader lives through under the guidance of the text and experiences as relevant to the text" (127). Rosenblatt knew her definition would be difficult for many to accept: "The idea that a *poem* presupposes a *reader* actively involved with a *text*," she wrote, "is particularly shocking to those seeking to emphasize the objectivity of their interpretations" ("Transactional" 127).

Rosenblatt implicitly and generally refers to formalists (also called the "New Critics") when she speaks of supposedly objective interpreters shocked by the notion that a "poem" is something cooperatively produced by a "reader" and a "text." Formalists spoke of "the poem itself," the "concrete work of art," the "real poem." They had no interest in what a work of literature makes a reader "live through." In fact, in *The Verbal Icon* (1954), William K. Wimsatt and Monroe C. Beardsley defined as fallacious the very notion that a reader's response is relevant to the meaning of a literary work:

The Affective Fallacy is a confusion between the poem and its *results* (what it *is* and what it *does*). . . . It begins by trying to derive the standards of criticism from the psychological effects of a poem and ends in impressionism and relativism. The outcome . . . is that the poem itself, as an object of specifically critical judgment, tends to disappear. (21)

Reader-response critics have taken issue with their formalist predecessors. Particularly influential has been Stanley Fish, whose early work is seen by some as marking the true beginning of contemporary reader-response criticism. In "Literature in the Reader: Affective Stylistics" (1970), Fish took on the formalist hegemony, the New Critical establishment, by arguing that any school of criticism that would see a work of literature as an object, claiming to describe what it *is* and never what it *does,* is guilty of misconstruing the very essence of literature and reading. Literature exists when it is read, Fish suggests, and its force is an affective force. Furthermore, reading is a temporal process. Formalists assume it is a spatial one as they step back and survey the literary work as if it were an object spread out before them. They may find elegant patterns in the texts they examine and reexamine, but they fail to take into account that the work is quite different to a reader who is turning the pages and being moved, or affected, by lines that appear and disappear as the reader reads.

In discussing the effect that a sentence penned by the seventeenth-century physician Thomas Browne has on a reader reading, Fish pauses to say this about his analysis and also, by extension, about his critical strategy: "Whatever is persuasive and illuminating about [it] is the result of my substituting for one question — what does this sentence mean? — another, more operational question — what does this sentence do?" He then quotes a line from John Milton's *Paradise Lost*, a line that refers to Satan and the other fallen angels: "Nor did they not perceive their evil plight." Whereas more traditional critics might say that the "meaning" of the line is "They did perceive their evil plight," Fish relates the uncertain movement of the reader's mind *to* that half-satisfying interpretation. Furthermore, he declares that "the reader's inability to tell whether or not 'they' do perceive and his involuntary question . . . are part of the line's *meaning*, even though they take place in the mind, not on the page" (*Text* 26).

The stress on what pages *do* to minds (and what minds do in response) pervades the writings of most, if not all, reader-response critics. Stephen Booth, whose book *An Essay on Shakespeare's Sonnets* (1969) greatly influenced Fish, sets out to describe the "reading experience that results" from a "multiplicity of organizations" in a sonnet by Shakespeare (*Essay* ix). Sometimes these organizations don't make complete sense, Booth points out, and sometimes they even seem curiously contradictory. But that is precisely what interests reader-response critics, who, unlike formalists, are at least as interested in fragmentary, inconclusive, and even unfinished texts as in polished, unified works. For it is the reader's struggle to *make sense* of a challenging work that reader-response critics seek to describe.

The German critic Wolfgang Iser has described that sense-making struggle in his books *The Implied Reader* (1972) and *The Act of Reading: A Theory of Aesthetic Response* (1976). Iser argues that texts are full of "gaps" (or "blanks," as he sometimes calls them). These gaps powerfully affect the reader, who is forced to explain them, to connect what they separate, to create in his or her mind aspects of a poem or novel or play that aren't *in* the text but that the text incites. As Iser puts it in *The*

Implied Reader, the "unwritten aspects" of a story "draw the reader into the action" and "lead him to shade in the many outlines suggested by the given situations, so that these take on a reality of their own." These "outlines" that "the reader's imagination animates" in turn "influence" the way in which "the written part of the text" is subsequently read (276).

In *Self-Consuming Artifacts: The Experience of Seventeenth-Century Literature* (1972), Fish reveals his preference for literature that makes readers work at making meaning. He contrasts two kinds of literary presentation. By the phrase "rhetorical presentation," he describes literature that reflects and reinforces opinions that readers already hold; by "dialectical presentation," he refers to works that prod and provoke. A dialectical text, rather than presenting an opinion as if it were truth, challenges readers to discover truths on their own. Such a text may not even have the kind of symmetry that formalist critics seek. Instead of offering a "single, sustained argument," a dialectical text, or self-consuming artifact, may be "so arranged that to enter into the spirit and assumptions of any one of [its] . . . units is implicitly to reject the spirit and assumptions of the unit immediately preceding" (*Artifacts* 9). Whereas a critic of another school might try to force an explanation as to why the units are fundamentally coherent, the reader-response critic proceeds by describing how the reader deals with the sudden twists and turns that characterize the dialectical text, returning to earlier passages and seeing them in an entirely new light.

"The value of such a procedure," Fish has written, "is predicated on the idea of meaning as *an event,*" not as something "located (presumed to be embedded) *in* the utterance" or "verbal object as a thing in itself" (*Text* 28). By redefining meaning as an event rather than as something inherent in the text, the reader-response critic once again locates meaning in time: the reader's time. A text exists and signifies while it is being read, and what it signifies or means will depend, to no small extent, on *when* it is read. (*Paradise Lost* had some meanings for a seventeenth-century Puritan that it would not have for a twentieth-century atheist.)

With the redefinition of literature as something that exists meaningfully only in the mind of the reader, with the redefinition of the literary work as a catalyst of mental events, comes a concurrent redefinition of the reader. No longer is the reader the passive recipient of those ideas that an author has planted in a text. "The reader is *active,*" Rosenblatt insists ("Transactional" 123). Fish begins "Literature in the Reader" with a similar observation: "If at this moment someone were to ask, 'what are you doing,' you might reply, 'I am reading,' and thereby acknowledge that reading is . . . something *you do*" (*Text* 22). Iser, in focusing critical interest on the gaps in texts, on what is not expressed, similarly redefines the reader as an active maker.

Amid all this talk of "the reader," it is tempting and natural to ask, "Just who *is* the reader?" (Or, to place the emphasis differently, "Just who is *the* reader?") Are reader-response critics simply sharing their own idiosyncratic responses when they describe what a line from *Paradise Lost* does in and to the reader's mind? "What about my responses?" you may want to ask. "What if they're different? Would reader-response critics be willing to say that my responses are equally valid?"

Fish defines "the reader" in this way: "*the* reader is the *informed* reader." The informed reader (whom Fish sometimes calls "the *intended* reader") is someone who is "sufficiently experienced as a reader to have internalized the properties of literary discourses, including everything from the most local of devices (figures of speech, etc.) to whole genres." And, of course, the informed reader is in full possession of the "semantic knowledge" (knowledge of idioms, for instance) assumed by the text (*Artifacts* 406).

Other reader-response critics define "*the* reader" differently. Wayne C. Booth, in *A Rhetoric of Irony* (1974), uses the phrase "the implied reader" to mean the reader "created by the work." (Only "by agreeing to play the role of this created audience," Susan Suleiman explains, "can an actual reader correctly understand and appreciate the work" [8].) Gerard Genette and Gerald Prince prefer to speak of "the narratee, . . . the necessary counterpart of a given narrator, that is, the person or figure who receives a narrative" (Suleiman 13). Like Booth, Iser employs the term "the implied reader," but he also uses "the educated reader" when he refers to what Fish called the "informed reader."

Jonathan Culler, who in 1981 criticized Fish for his sketchy definition of the informed reader, set out in *Structuralist Poetics* (1975) to describe the educated or "competent" reader's education by elaborating those reading conventions that make possible the understanding of poems and novels. In retrospect, however, Culler's definitions seem sketchy as well. By "competent reader," Culler meant competent reader of "literature." By "literature," he meant what schools and colleges mean when they speak of literature as being part of the curriculum. Culler, like his contemporaries, was not concerned with the fact that curricular content is politically and economically motivated. And "he did not," in Mailloux's words, "emphasize how the literary competence he described was embedded within larger formations and traversed by political ideologies extending beyond the academy" ("Turns" 49). It remained for a later generation of reader-oriented critics to do those things.

The fact that Fish, following Rosenblatt's lead, defined reader-response criticism in terms of its difference from and opposition to the New Criticism or formalism should not obscure the fact that the formalism of the 1950s and early 1960s had a great deal in common with the reader-response criticism of the late 1960s and early 1970s. This has become increasingly obvious with the rise of subsequent critical approaches whose practitioners have proved less interested in the close reading of texts than in the way literature represents, reproduces, and/or resists prevailing ideologies concerning gender, class, and race. In a retrospective essay entitled "The Turns of Reader-Response Criticism" (1990), Mailloux has suggested that, from the perspective of hindsight, the "close reading" of formalists and "Fish's early 'affective stylistics' " seem surprisingly similar. Indeed, Mailloux argues, the early "reader talk of . . . Iser and Fish enabled the continuation of the formalist practice of close reading. Through a vocabulary focused on a text's manipulation of readers, Fish was especially effective in extending and diversifying the formalist practices that continued business as usual within literary criticism" (48).

Since the mid-1970s, however, reader-response criticism (once commonly referred to as the "School of Fish") has diversified and taken on a variety of new forms, some of which truly *are* incommensurate with formalism, with its considerable respect for the integrity and power of the text. For instance, "subjectivists" like David Bleich, Norman Holland, and Robert Crosman have assumed what Mailloux calls the "absolute priority of individual selves as creators of texts" (*Conventions* 31). In other words, these critics do not see the reader's response as one "guided" by the text but rather as one motivated by deep-seated, personal, psychological needs. What they find in texts is, in Holland's phrase, their own "identity theme." Holland has argued that as readers we use "the literal work to symbolize and finally to replicate ourselves. We work out through the text our own characteristic patterns of desire" ("UNITY" 816). Subjective critics, as you may already have guessed, often find themselves confronted with the following question: If all interpretation is a function of private, psychological identity, then why have so many readers interpreted, say, Shakespeare's *Hamlet* in the same way? Different subjective critics have answered the question differently. Holland simply has said that common identity themes exist, such as that involving an oedipal fantasy.

Meanwhile, Fish, who in the late 1970s moved away from reader-response criticism as he had initially helped define it, came up with a different answer to the question of why different readers tend to read the same works the same way. His answer, rather than involving common individual identity themes, involved common *cultural* identity. In "Interpreting the *Variorum*" (1976), he argues that the "stability of interpretation among readers" is a function of shared "interpretive strategies." These strategies, which "exist prior to the act of reading and therefore determine the shape of what is read," are held in common by "interpretive communities" such as the one constituted by American college students reading a novel as a class assignment (*Text* 167, 171). In developing the model of interpretive communities, Fish truly has made the break with formalist or New Critical predecessors, becoming in the process something of a social, structuralist, reader-response critic. Recently, he has been engaged in studying reading communities and their interpretive conventions in order to understand the conditions that give rise to a work's intelligibility.

Fish's shift in focus is in many ways typical of changes that have taken place within the field of reader-response criticism — a field that, because of those changes, is increasingly being referred to as "reader-oriented" criticism. Less and less common are critical analyses examining the transactional interface between the text and its individual reader. Increasingly, reader-oriented critics are investigating reading communities, as the reader-oriented cultural critic Janice A. Radway has done in her study of female readers of romance paperbacks (*Reading the Romance,* 1984). They are also studying the changing reception of literary works across time; see, for example, Mailloux in his "pragmatic readings" of American literature in *Interpretive Conventions* (1982) and *Rhetorical Power* (1989).

An important catalyst of this gradual change was the work of Hans Robert Jauss, a colleague of Iser's whose historically oriented reception theory (unlike Iser's theory of the implied reader) was not available in English book form until the early 1980s. Rather than focusing on the implied, informed, or intended reader, Jauss examined actual past readers. In *Toward an Aesthetics of Reception* (1982), he argued that the reception of a work or author tends to depend upon the reading public's "horizons of expectations." He noted that, in the morally conservative climate of mid-nineteenth-century France, *Madame Bovary* was literally put on trial, its author Flaubert accused of glorifying adultery in passages representing the protagonist's fevered delirium via free indirect discourse, a mode of narration in which a third-person narrator tells us in an unfiltered way what a character is thinking and feeling.

As readers have become more sophisticated and tolerant, the popularity and reputation of *Madame Bovary* have soared. Sometimes, of course, changes in a reading public's horizons of expectations cause a work to be *less* well received over time. As American reception theorists influenced by Jauss have shown, Mark Twain's *Adventures of Huckleberry Finn* has elicited an increasingly ambivalent reaction from a reading public increasingly sensitive to demeaning racial stereotypes and racist language. The rise of feminism has prompted a downward revaluation of everything from Andrew Marvell's "To His Coy Mistress" to D. H. Lawrence's *Women in Love.*

Some reader-oriented feminists, such as Judith Fetterley, Patrocinio Schweickart, and Monique Wittig, have challenged the reader to become what Fetterley calls "the resisting reader." Arguing that literature written by men tends, in Schweickart's terms, to "immasculate" women, they have advocated strategies of reading that involve substituting masculine for feminine pronouns and male for female characters in order to expose the sexism inscribed in patriarchal texts. Other feminists, such as Nancy K. Miller in *Subject to Change* (1988), have suggested that there may be essential differences between the way women and men read and write.

That suggestion, however, has prompted considerable disagreement. A number of gender critics whose work is oriented toward readers and reading have admitted that there is such a thing as "reading like a woman" (or man), but they have also tended to agree with Peggy Kamuf that such forms of reading, like gender itself, are cultural rather than natural constructs. Gay and lesbian critics, arguing that sexualities have been similarly constructed within and by social discourse, have argued that there is a homosexual way of reading; Wayne Koestenbaum has defined "the (male twentieth-century first world) gay reader" as one who "reads resistantly for inscriptions of his condition, for texts that will confirm a social and private identity founded on a desire for other men. . . . Reading becomes a hunt for histories that deliberately foreknow or unwittingly trace a desire felt not by author but by reader, who is most acute when searching for signs of himself" (in Boone and Cadden 176–77).

Given this kind of renewed interest in the reader and reading, some students of contemporary critical practice have been tempted to conclude that reader-oriented theory has been taken over by feminist, gender, gay, and lesbian theory. Others, like Elizabeth Freund, have suggested that it is deconstruction with which the reader-oriented approach has mixed and merged. Certainly, all of these approaches have informed and been informed by reader-response or reader-oriented theory. The case can be made, however, that there is in fact still a distinct reader-oriented approach to literature, one whose points of tangency are neither with deconstruction nor with feminist, gender, and so-called queer theory but, rather, with the new historicism and cultural criticism.

This relatively distinct form of reader theory is practiced by a number of critics, but is perhaps best exemplified by the work of scholars like Mailloux and Peter J. Rabinowitz. In *Before Reading: Narrative Conventions and the Politics of Interpretation* (1987), Rabinowitz sets forth four conventions or rules of reading, which he calls the rules of "notice," "signification," "configuration," and "coherence" — rules telling us which parts of a narrative are important, which details have a reliable secondary or special meaning, which fit into which familiar patterns, and how stories fit together as a whole. He then proceeds to analyze the misreadings and misjudgments of critics and to show that politics governs the way in which those rules are applied and broken ("The strategies employed by critics when they read [Raymond Chandler's] *The Big Sleep*," Rabinowitz writes, "can teach us something about the structure of misogyny, not the misogyny of the novel itself, but the misogyny of the world outside it" [195].) In subsequent critical essays, Rabinowitz proceeds similarly, showing how a society's ideological assumptions about gender, race, and class determine the way in which artistic works are perceived and evaluated.

Mailloux, who calls his approach "rhetorical reception theory" or "rhetorical hermeneutics," takes a similar tack, insofar as he describes the political contexts of (mis)interpretation. In a recent essay on "Misreading as a Historical Act" (1993), he shows that a mid-nineteenth-century review of Frederick Douglass's *Narrative* by proto-feminist Margaret Fuller seems to be a misreading until we situate it "within the cultural conversation of the 'Bible politics' of 1845" (Machor 9). Woven through Mailloux's essay on Douglass and Fuller are philosophical pauses in which we are reminded, in various subtle ways, that all reading (including Mailloux's and our own) is culturally situated and likely to seem like *mis*reading someday. One such reflective pause, however, accomplishes more; in it, Mailloux reads the map of where reader-oriented criticism is today, affords a rationale for its being there, and plots its likely future direction. "However we have arrived at our present juncture," Mailloux writes,

> the current talk about historical acts of reading provides a welcome opportunity for more explicit consideration of how reading is historically contingent, politically situated, institutionally embedded, and materially conditioned; of how reading any text, literary or nonliterary, relates to a larger cultural politics that goes well beyond some hypothetical private interaction between an autonomous reader and an independent text; and of how our particular views of reading relate to the liberatory potential of literacy and the transformative power of education. (5)

In the essay that follows, Frances Ferguson tells us that Coleridge's "Rime" has been faulted since its first appearance for inconsistency of character and plot and, more generally, for its overall strangeness. Critics have sought to explain how such a poem came into being (opium use? psychosis?) — and why it has been so persistently popular. Robert Penn Warren, who claimed that Coleridge meant the poem to convey a moral point of view, discovered in the "Rime" a poetic unity that supports the theme of "One Life" advanced in the poem's concluding lines. Ferguson, however, implies that Warren projected his own critical principles onto the poem ("since unity and coherence are poetry for Warren, this poem must be both unified and unifying"). For Ferguson, "the possibility of learning from the Mariner's experience depends upon sorting that experience into a more linear and complete pattern than the poem ever agrees to do" (116).

Citing numerous examples of the poem's confusing atemporality — the admixture of past and present tense that keeps the "action or progress" of the poem in "temporal limbo" — Ferguson argues that there is too little apparent relation between cause and effect in the "Rime" for the reader to develop a clear sense of the poem's implied moral values. ("The Albatross seems good, then bad, then good, because the death of the Albatross causes first fog and mist (bad), then clearing (good), and finally the failure of the breeze (bad). Our difficulty is that all the evidences of moral value are mutually contradictory" [117].) Warren, like most other critics, believes that the poem's marginal gloss clears up our difficulties, resolving such contradictions; indeed, he assumes that "Coleridge wrote the Gloss . . . because he was attempting to clarify and unify the poem after entertaining the legion of hostile comments upon its confusions." Even if this is so, however, that doesn't make the attempt successful. Arguing that "the Gloss provides a strange kind of clarity and unity," Ferguson proceeds by showing the gap between the "value judgments" (118) made in the Gloss and the lines they supposedly echo in condensed form.

At this point, midway through her essay, Ferguson discusses at some length a woman to whom she had briefly referred earlier, one Mrs. Anna Laetitia Barbauld, whose objection that the "Rime" had "no moral" prompted Coleridge to reply that it had "too much." Citing Mrs. Barbauld's book entitled *Lessons for Children of Three Years Old,* which contains a story about sad events that befell a boy who pulled the tail of a starving robin, Ferguson argues that "the moral causality that most critics discern in the *Rime*" is more typical of Mrs. Barbauld's book — and of Coleridge's domesticating, morally definitive gloss — than it is of the original poem proper, which in Ferguson's view is not about the wages of sin but, rather, the "difficulty . . . of recognizing the implications of an action before it is committed" (122). In making this argument, Ferguson does not contend that moral positions of the kind found in the Gloss, Glosslike critical readings of the "Rime," or even in Mrs. Barbauld's stories and poems are "wrong, and that uncertainty (or no position) is right" (125). But she does think that "the major issue" in the poem is "not the moral but the process of arriving at morals" (123). And that process is the process of reading, in the most general sense of the term.

To fully summarize the rest of Ferguson's argument would spoil its unfolding — or, rather, the pleasure you will take in the act of unfolding it. Suffice it to say that Ferguson makes many of the moves typical of reader-response criticism. She focuses on reading as a process of making meaning (and morals), making no bones about the fact that the process is often made difficult by what we, as readers, bring to the text as well as by gaps and inconsistencies within the text (which may itself contain inconsistent texts, such as Coleridge's narrative poem and prose gloss). Equally typical of reader-oriented criticism is Ferguson's reading of Coleridge's "Rime" as a story about or drama of reading (that is, she shows that the difficulty of knowing the implications of acts *within* the poem's world mirror *our* difficulty in knowing whether our interpretive acts will be justified by the text's unfolding). We read as the Mariner and his sailors act, and even as Coleridge writes, with incomplete understanding and often out of prejudice. Accordingly, the title of Ferguson's essay — "Coleridge and the Deluded Reader: 'The Rime of

the Ancient Mariner'" — may involve more than just the compound-
ing of two titles, one invented by Ferguson followed by another
invented by Coleridge. Although the title may simply imply that readers
of the poem are deluded readers, it may also imply that the "Rime" is
about its author and the deluded reader. If so, the category "deluded
reader" is broad enough to include Coleridge (whose writings, after all,
are "readings" of reality in the broadest sense), the Mariner (who, like a
reader, acts with incomplete understanding), his tale (which "reads"
experiences antecedent to it), and its audience (which includes the
Wedding Guest but also ourselves).

Ross C Murfin

READER-RESPONSE CRITICISM: A SELECTED BIBLIOGRAPHY

Some Introductions to Reader-Response Criticism

Beach, Richard. *A Teacher's Introduction to Reader-Response Theories.*
Urbana: NCTE, 1993.

Fish, Stanley E. "Literature in the Reader: Affective Stylistics." *New
Literary History* 2 (1970): 123–61. Rpt. in Fish, *Text* 21–67, and
in Primeau 154–79.

Freund, Elizabeth. *The Return of the Reader: Reader-Response
Criticism.* London: Methuen, 1987.

Holub, Robert C. *Reception Theory: A Critical Introduction.* New
York: Methuen, 1984.

Leitch, Vincent B. *American Literary Criticism from the Thirties to the
Eighties.* New York: Columbia UP, 1988.

Mailloux, Steven. "Learning to Read: Interpretation and Reader-
Response Criticism." *Studies in the Literary Imagination* 12
(1979): 93–108.

———. "Reader-Response Criticism?" *Genre* l0 (1977): 413–31.

———. "The Turns of Reader-Response Criticism." *Conversations:
Contemporary Critical Theory and the Teaching of Literature.* Ed.
Charles Moran and Elizabeth F. Penfield. Urbana: NCTE, 1990.
38–54.

Rabinowitz, Peter J. "Whirl Without End: Audience-Oriented
Criticism." *Contemporary Literary Theory.* Ed. G. Douglas Atkins
and Laura Morrow. Amherst: U of Massachusetts P, 1989. 81–100.

Rosenblatt, Louise M. "Towards a Transactional Theory of Reading." *Journal of Reading Behavior* 1 (1969): 31–47. Rpt. in Primeau 121–46.

Suleiman, Susan R. "Introduction: Varieties of Audience-Oriented Criticism." Suleiman and Crosman 3–45.

Tompkins, Jane P. "An Introduction to Reader-Response Criticism." Tompkins ix–xxiv.

Reader-Response Criticism in Anthologies and Collections

Flynn, Elizabeth A., and Patrocinio P. Schweickart, eds. *Gender and Reading: Essays on Readers, Texts, and Contexts.* Baltimore: Johns Hopkins UP, 1986.

Garvin, Harry R., ed. *Theories of Reading, Looking, and Listening.* Lewisburg: Bucknell UP, 1981. Essays by Cain and Rosenblatt.

Machor, James L., ed. *Readers in History: Nineteenth-Century American Literature and the Contexts of Response.* Baltimore: Johns Hopkins UP, 1993. Contains Mailloux essay "Misreading as a Historical Act: Cultural Rhetoric, Bible Politics, and Fuller's 1845 Review of Douglass's *Narrative.*"

Primeau, Ronald, ed. *Influx: Essays on Literary Influence.* Port Washington: Kennikat, 1977. Essays by Fish, Holland, and Rosenblatt.

Suleiman, Susan R., and Inge Crosman, eds. *The Reader in the Text: Essays on Audience and Interpretation.* Princeton: Princeton UP, 1980. See especially the essays by Culler, Iser, and Todorov.

Tompkins, Jane P., ed. *Reader-Response Criticism: From Formalism to Post-Structuralism.* Baltimore: Johns Hopkins UP, 1980. See especially the essays by Bleich, Fish, Holland, Prince, and Tompkins.

Reader-Response Criticism: Some Major Works

Bleich, David. *Subjective Criticism.* Baltimore: Johns Hopkins UP, 1978.

Booth, Stephen. *An Essay on Shakespeare's Sonnets.* New Haven: Yale UP, 1969.

Booth, Wayne C. *A Rhetoric of Irony.* Chicago: U of Chicago P, 1974.

Eco, Umberto. *The Role of the Reader: Explorations in the Semiotics of Texts.* Bloomington: Indiana UP, 1979.

Fish, Stanley Eugene. *Doing What Comes Naturally: Change, Rhetoric, and the Practice of Theory in Literary and Legal Studies.* Durham: Duke UP, 1989.

———. *Is There a Text in This Class? The Authority of Interpretive Communities.* Cambridge: Harvard UP, 1980. This volume contains most of Fish's most influential essays, including "Literature in the Reader: Affective Stylistics," "What It's Like to Read *L'Allegro* and *Il Penseroso,*" "Interpreting the *Variorum,*" "How to Recognize a Poem When You See One," "Is There a Text in This Class?" and "What Makes an Interpretation Acceptable?"

———. *Self-Consuming Artifact: The Experience of Seventeenth-Century Literature.* Berkeley: U of California P, 1972.

———. *Surprised by Sin: The Reader in "Paradise Lost."* 2nd ed. Berkeley: U of California P, 1971.

Holland, Norman N. *5 Readers Reading.* New Haven: Yale UP, 1975.

———. "UNITY IDENTITY TEXT SELF." *PMLA* 90 (1975): 813–22.

Iser, Wolfgang. *The Act of Reading: A Theory of Aesthetic Response.* Baltimore: Johns Hopkins UP, 1978.

———. *The Implied Reader: Patterns of Communication in Prose Fiction from Bunyan to Beckett.* Baltimore: Johns Hopkins UP, 1974.

Jauss, Hans Robert. *Toward an Aesthetics of Reception.* Trans. Timothy Bahti. Intro. Paul de Man. Brighton: Harvester, 1982.

Mailloux, Steven. *Interpretive Conventions: The Reader in the Study of American Fiction.* Ithaca: Cornell UP, 1982.

———. *Rhetorical Power.* Ithaca: Cornell UP, 1989.

Messent, Peter. *New Readings of the American Novel: Narrative Theory and Its Application.* New York: Macmillan, 1991.

Prince, Gerald. *Narratology.* New York: Mouton, 1982.

Rabinowitz, Peter J. *Before Reading: Narrative Conventions and the Politics of Interpretation.* Ithaca: Cornell UP, 1987.

Radway, Janice A. *Reading the Romance: Women, Patriarchy, and Popular Literature.* Chapel Hill: U of North Carolina P, 1984.

Rosenblatt, Louise M. *Literature as Exploration.* 4th ed. New York: MLA, 1983.

———. *The Reader the Text, the Poem: The Transactional Theory of the Literary Work.* Carbondale: Southern Illinois UP, 1978.

Slatoff, Walter J. *With Respect to Readers: Dimensions of Literary Response.* Ithaca: Cornell UP, 1970.

Steig, Michael. *Stories of Reading: Subjectivity and Literary Understanding.* Baltimore: Johns Hopkins UP, 1989.

Exemplary Short Readings of Major Texts

Anderson, Howard. "*Tristram Shandy* and the Reader's Imagination."
PMLA 86 (1971): 966–73.

Berger, Carole. "The Rake and the Reader in Jane Austen's
Novels." *Studies in English Literature, 1500–1900* 15 (1975):
531–44.

Booth, Stephen. "On the Value of *Hamlet.*" *Reinterpretations of
English Drama: Selected Papers from the English Institute.* Ed.
Norman Rabkin. New York: Columbia UP, 1969. 137–76.

Easson, Robert R. "William Blake and His Reader in *Jerusalem.*"
Blake's Sublime Allegory. Ed. Stuart Curran and Joseph A.
Wittreich. Madison: U of Wisconsin P, 1973. 309–28.

Kirk, Carey H. "*Moby-Dick:* The Challenge of Response." *Papers on
Language and Literature* 13 (1977): 383–90.

Leverenz, David. "Mrs. Hawthorne's Headache: Reading *The Scarlet
Letter.*" *Nathaniel Hawthorne, "The Scarlet Letter."* Ed. Ross C
Murfin. Case Studies in Contemporary Criticism. Boston:
Bedford, 1991. 263–74.

Lowe-Evans, Mary. "Reading with a 'Nicer Eye': Responding to
Frankenstein." *Mary Shelley, "Frankenstein."* Ed. Johanna M.
Smith. Case Studies in Contemporary Criticism. Boston: Bedford,
1992. 215–29.

Rabinowitz, Peter J. "'A Symbol of Something: Interpretive Vertigo
in 'The Dead.'" *James Joyce, "The Dead."* Ed. Daniel R. Schwarz.
Case Studies in Contemporary Criticism. Boston: Bedford, 1994.
137–49.

Treichler, Paula. "The Construction of Ambiguity in *The Awakening.*"
Kate Chopin, "The Awakening." Ed. Nancy A. Walker. Case
Studies in Contemporary Criticism. Boston: Bedford, 1993.
308–28.

Other Works Referred to
in "What Is Reader-Response Criticism?"

Culler, Jonathan. *Structural Poetics: Structuralism, Linguistics, and the
Study of Literature.* Ithaca: Cornell UP, 1975.

Koestenbaum, Wayne. "Wilde's Hard Labor and the Birth of Gay
Reading." *Engendering Men: The Question of Male Feminist
Criticism.* Ed. Joseph A. Boone and Michael Cadden. New York:
Routledge, 1990.

Richards, I. A. *Practical Criticism.* New York: Harcourt, 1929. Rpt.

in *Criticism: The Major Texts*. Ed. Walter Jackson Bate. Rev. ed. New York: Harcourt, 1970. 575.

Wimsatt William K., and Monroe C. Beardsley. *The Verbal Icon*. Lexington: U of Kentucky P, 1954. See especially the discussion of "The Affective Fallacy," with which reader-response critics have so sharply disagreed.

Other Reader-Oriented Approaches to the "Rime"

Brisman, Leslie. "Coleridge and the Ancestral Voices." *Romantic Origins*. Ithaca: Cornell UP, 1978. 21–54.

Mileur, Jean-Pierre. *Vision and Revision: Coleridge's Art of Immanence*. Berkeley: U of California P, 1982.

Modiano, Raimonda. "Words and 'Languageless' Meanings: Limits of Expression in *The Rime of the Ancient Mariner*." *Modern Language Quarterly* 38 (1977): 40–61.

Payne, Richard. " 'The Style and Spirit of the Elder Poets': The Ancient Mariner and the English Literary Tradition." *Modern Philology* 75 (1978): 368–84.

Wolfson, Susan. "The Language of Interpretation in Romantic Poetry: 'A Strong Working of the Mind.' " *Romanticism and Language*. Ed. Arden Reed. Ithaca: Cornell UP, 1984. 22–49.

FRANCES FERGUSON

Coleridge and the Deluded Reader: "The Rime of the Ancient Mariner"

The criticism of "The Rime of the Ancient Mariner" reflects a craving for causes. Opium, or Coleridge's guilt-obsessed personality, or (as Robert Penn Warren would have it) his convergent beliefs in the "One Life within us all" and in the Imagination caused the poem to come into being in its own peculiar form. A "teaching text" like *The Norton Anthology of English Literature* sets out to explicate the lines:

The Wedding-Guest stood still,
And listens like a three years' child:
The Mariner hath his will (ll.14–16)[1]

[1] All direct quotations from the "Rime" follow the text of *The Complete Poetical Works of Samuel Taylor Coleridge*, ed. Ernest Hartley Coleridge, Oxford, 1968.

— and sets up a nice causal connection by asserting that "the Mariner has gained control of the will of the Wedding Guest by hypnosis — or, as it was called in Coleridge's time — by 'mesmerism'" (2:331). There may be some form of hypnosis — or mesmerism — in the rather monotonous rhythms of the lines, but the annotation converts hypnosis into a misguidedly "scientific" explanation of why the Wedding Guest couldn't or didn't bother to get away.

This construction of causes — for the poem as a whole or for individual passages — is particularly striking because it appears as a series of belated rejoinders to the many complaints that greeted the poem's first public appearance. The "Rime" was quite widely censured for extravagance, unconnectedness, and improbability. Even Wordsworth in his Note to the "Rime" in the 1800 edition of *Lyrical Ballads* registered various objections that amounted to the assertion that the poem was deficient in connections and causes:

> The Poem of my Friend has indeed great defects; first, that the principal person has no distinct character, either in his profession of Mariner, or as a human being who having been long under the controul of supernatural impressions might be supposed himself to partake of something supernatural: secondly, that he does not act, but is continually acted upon: thirdly, that the events having no necessary connection do not produce each other; and lastly, that the imagery is somewhat too laboriously accumulated. (Wordsworth, pp. 270–710)

Wordsworth's account of the poem's "defects" in a note that is a manifesto for its being reprinted may well be of a piece with the simultaneously published Preface to *Lyrical Ballads,* in which he sought to avoid the appearance of "*reasoning* [the reader] into an approbation of these particular Poems" (Wordsworth, pp. 236–37). Everywhere in his account of defects Wordsworth cites formal features (albeit in the extended sense) — character, plot, motive, and imagery; and it is hard to believe that Wordsworth was doing anything more than repeating — and thereby acknowledging — the categories of poetic appreciation that he and Coleridge were explicitly attacking in *Lyrical Ballads.* But if the author of "The Thorn," "We are seven," and *The Prelude* seems improbable in the role of someone wedded to clearly delineated character, plot, motive, and imagery, Coleridge's own remarks about the poem are even more difficult to assimilate to the critical search for causes and consequences. For example, Coleridge's famous account of

Mrs. Barbauld's opinion of the "Rime" figures in almost every article on the poem, but to diverse ends:

> MRS. BARBAULD once told me that she admired the Ancient Mariner very much, but that there were two faults in it, — it was improbable, and had no moral. As for the probability, I owned that that might admit some question; but as to the want of a moral, I told her that in my own judgment the poem had too much; and that the only or chief fault, if I might say so, was the obtrusion of the moral sentiment so openly on the reader as a principle or cause of action in a work of such pure imagination. It ought to have had no more moral than the Arabian Nights' tale of the merchant's sitting down to eat dates by the side of a well, and throwing the shells aside, and lo! a geni starts up, and says he *must* kill the aforesaid merchant, *because* one of the date-shells had, it seems, put out the eye of the geni's son. (*Table Talk*, 2:100)

On the one hand, critics have harnessed this passage to an attempt to eschew interpretation; the poem as a "work of . . . pure imagination" has no discursively translatable meaning. (This is the "What-do-you-think-when-you-think-nothing?" school of criticism.) On the other hand, perhaps the most influential modern critic of the poem, Warren, confesses that he is "inclined to sympathize with the lady's desire that poetry have some significant relation to the world, some meaning" (p. 199). Thus, his reading of the passage from *Table Talk* about Mrs. Barbauld is this: "If the passage affirms anything, it affirms that Coleridge intended the poem to have a 'moral sentiment,' but felt that he had been a trifle unsubtle in fulfilling his intention" (p. 200).

The no-moral position seems patently unconvincing because it becomes an excuse for hanging in one's confusions; but even though Warren's essay remains the most provocative interpretation, it also seems progressively to overspecify the "moral sentiment." What Warren calls the sacramental vision, the theme of the "One Life" that is expressed in the poem's conclusion ("He prayeth best. . . .") and what he calls the imagination (the symbols of the poem) are both models of unity and fusion. And since unity and coherence are poetry for Warren, this poem must be both unified and unifying by definition; images must be symbols, and the symbols must speak of the Mariner's — and the reader's — "expressive integration" (p. 262) with the universe and "with other men, with society" (p. 255). Warren's interpretation suggests not merely that the sin of pride is involved in the "Rime" but also that the poem in some sense involves teaching one — all of us — to avoid that sin. But while I agree with Warren that morals are at issue in the poem, Coleridgean morality seems to me consistently more problematic than he suggests. For the difficulty of the poem is that the possibility of learning from the Mariner's experience depends upon sorting that experience into a more linear and complete pattern than the poem ever agrees to do. For the poem seems almost as thorough a work of backwardness — or hysteron proteron — as we have.

One aspect of this backwardness led a contemporary reviewer (Charles Burney) to fulminate in 1799 against *Lyrical Ballads* in general and against the "Rime" in particular:

> Though we have been extremely entertained with the fancy, the facility, and (in general) the sentiments, of these pieces, we cannot regard them as *poetry*, of a class to be cultivated at the expence of a higher species of versification, unknown in our language at the time when our elder writers, whom this author condescends to imitate, wrote their ballads. Would it not be degrading poetry, as well as the English language, to go back to the barbarous and uncouth numbers of Chaucer? . . . Should we be gainers by the retrogradation? . . . None but savages have submitted to eat acorns after corn was found. (Jackson, p. 55)

But the archaistic diction is only one aspect of the poem's "retrogradation." For Coleridge not only reverses linguistic and poetic *progress* in the "Rime," he so thoroughly compounds the past with the present tense that the action or progress of the poem hovers in a temporal limbo:

> The Wedding-Guest he beat his breast,
> Yet he cannot choose but hear;
> And thus spake on that ancient man,
> The bright-eyed Mariner. (ll.37–40)

And even such a basic question as that of the Mariner's motive for killing the bird is given a tardy (and insufficient) answer. The event of the killing is recounted in the first section of the poem; and the suggestion that the Mariner may have been trying to confute his shipmates' superstitious connections between the Albatross and the weather emerges only in the second section. The possibility that the Mariner may have hoped — scientifically — to disprove their superstition is the closest thing to an hypothesis we are offered, and it appears only when we desire a motive so strongly that we must mistrust our own efforts to reestablish a cause-and-effect sequence.

But how does any reader, any critic sort out the action that presumably points the moral of the poem? Or, in other words, how does one sort out the moral value of the agents of the poem? The Mariner concludes his story to the Wedding Guest with the following "good" words:

> He prayeth well, who loveth well
> Both man and bird and beast.

> He prayeth best, who loveth best
> All things both great and small;
> For the dear God who loveth us,
> He made and loveth all. (ll.616–21)

But the Mariner has a decidedly malignant effect on the persons who save his body after his spiritual redemption on the ship: the Pilot collapses in a fit, and the Pilot's boy goes mad. Likewise, the Albatross seems good, then bad, then good, because the death of the Albatross causes first fog and mist (bad), then clearing (good), and finally the failure of the breeze (bad). Our difficulty is that all the evidences of moral value are mutually contradictory.

There is, however, one element of the poem that leads us. In 1815–16 Coleridge added the Gloss along the left margin as he was readying his work for the 1817 edition of *Sibylline Leaves*. And the critical "advances" that have been made in the last century and a half pay tribute to Coleridge's sagacity in having supplied this helpful commentary. John Livingston Lowes notes the literary elegance of the Gloss's prose (pp. 297–98). B. R. McElderry, Jr., sees the Gloss as an "artistic restatement and ornament of what is obvious in the text," and as a chance for Coleridge to relive the pleasure of writing his "one completed masterpiece" (p. 91). And Robert Penn Warren peppers his long essay on the "Rime" with statements like this: "The Gloss here tells us all we need to know, defining the Mariner's relation to the moon" (p. 243). The almost universal opinion seems to be that Coleridge wrote the Gloss (either as Coleridge or in the role of a fictitious editor) because he was attempting to clarify and unify the poem after entertaining the legion of hostile comments upon its confusions and inconsequence.

But the Gloss provides a strange kind of clarity and unity. Consider some examples. As the Wedding Guest speaks for the first time about anything except the wedding he wishes he could attend, this is what the text offers:

"God save thee, ancient Mariner!
From the fiends, that plague thee thus! —
Why look'st thou so?" — With my cross-bow
I shot the ALBATROSS. (ll.79–82)

And the Gloss comments — "The ancient Mariner inhospitably killeth the pious bird of good omen." "Inhospitably," "pious," and "good omen" bespeak conclusions that do not echo the main text because the main text never reaches such value judgments.

The Argument that Coleridge deleted from the poem after 1800 recounted that "the Ancient Mariner cruelly and in contempt of the laws of hospitality killed a Sea-bird," but the Gloss here seems even stronger than the Argument had been. However forceful the ancient laws of hospitality, the notion of a man's hospitality toward a bird contains a rather anomalous and itself prideful assumption — that the bird is a visitor in the Mariner's domain. If the Mariner commits a sin of pride in killing the Albatross and thereby asserting his power over it, even the Mariner's refusal to kill the bird would in this context involve the pride-laden assurance that man's domain measures the universe. But the even more striking feature of the Gloss is the attribution of unambiguous moral qualities to the bird — "the pious bird of good omen." And while the text of the poem proper registers only the sailors' vacillations on the moral standing of the bird, the Gloss is conspicuously conclusive on that point. The main text offers the sailors' contradictory opinions:

And I had done a hellish thing,
And it would work 'em woe:
For all averred, I had killed the bird
That made the breeze to blow.
Ah wretch! said they, the bird to slay,
That made the breeze to blow!

Nor dim nor red, like God's own head,
The glorious Sun uprist:
Then all averred, I had killed the bird
That brought the fog and mist.

'Twas right, said they, such birds to slay,
That brought the fog and mist. (ll.91–102)

And the Gloss seems merely to scorn the sailors' confusions: first "His shipmates cry out against the ancient Mariner, for killing the bird of good luck"; then, "But when the fog cleared off, they justify the same, and thus make themselves accomplices in the crime."

When the ship is stalled, and everyone aboard is desperately searching the horizon in hope of rescue, the text recounts things this way:

A weary time! a weary time!
How glazed each weary eye,
When looking westward, I beheld
A something in the sky.

At first it seemed a little speck,
And then it seemed a mist;
It moved and moved, and took at last
A certain shape, I wist. (ll.145–52)

And the Gloss makes this remark: "The Ancient Mariner beholdeth a sign in the element afar off." Nothing is ever really "afar off" for the Gloss. What for the main text is merely "a something" and "a certain shape" is already categorized for the Gloss as a sign, a symbol. The Gloss, in assuming that things must be significant and interpretable, finds significance and interpretability, but only by reading ahead of — or beyond — the main text.

Now the only portion of the Gloss that has been cited as an editorializing incursion upon the main text is the scholarly comment that supports the dreams which some of the sailors have about an avenging spirit: "A Spirit had followed them; one of the invisible inhabitants of this planet, neither departed souls nor angels; concerning whom the learned Jew, Josephus, and the Platonic Constantinopolitan, Michael Psellus, may be consulted. They are very numerous, and there is no climate or element without one or more." But both the entire Gloss and the bulk of critical opinion of the poem may well be editorializing, in that they mold contradictory evidences into a cause-and-effect pattern that the main text never quite offers: the Albatross was a good bird, the Mariner killed it, the Mariner was punished for his crime, the Mariner learned to acknowledge the beauty of all natural creatures and was saved to proselytize for this eminently noble moral position.

But let us return to the remarks on the poem in the *Specimens of the Table Talk of the late Samuel Taylor Coleridge;* in Coleridge's account of the first tale from the *Arabian Nights* the geni "says he *must* kill the aforesaid merchant, *because* one of the date-shells had, it seems, put out the eye of the geni's son" (2:100, emphasis Coleridge's). If the poem should have had no more moral than this, we may ask, what kind of moral is it? The merchant, presumably, would not have thrown his date-shells into the well if he had dreamed that he would do harm to the geni's son; and by the same logic, the Mariner would, presumably, not have killed the Albatross if he had recognized its goodness and significance. As is common in Coleridge's work generally, intention and effect are absolutely discontinuous, and the moral is that morality appears to involve certainty only if you can already know the full outcome of every action before you commit it.

Coleridge's recounting his conversation with Mrs. Barbauld about the poem seems to me particularly striking in the context of this moral problem. A rather sizable collection of reviewers had complained about the poem's improbability and lack of moral, but Mrs. Barbauld became his most significant interlocutor on the poem's moral import. A brief excursus on Anna Laetitia Barbauld may suggest why she in particular would be an appropriate real or fictitious disputant of record. Mrs. Barbauld was firmly committed to the education of children, and she demonstrated her commitment by authoring *Lessons for Children* (1780) and *Hymns in Prose for Children* (1781). *Lessons for Children* was divided into four parts — *Lessons . . .* 1) For Children from Two to Three Years Old; 2) and 3) For Children of Three Years Old; and 4) For Children from Three to Four Years Old, so that the readings moved from simple to more complex in a gradual scale. As Mrs. Barbauld stated in her Preface to *Hymns in Prose,* this was her purpose:

> to impress devotional feelings as early as possible on the infant mind . . . to impress them by connecting religion with a variety of sensible objects; with all that he sees, all that he hears, all that affects his young mind with wonder or delight; and thus by deep, strong, and permanent associations to lay the best foundation for practical devotion in future life. (vi)

Reading was thus not merely a neutral exercise; reading and religion were to be taught simultaneously. Now in this respect Mrs. Barbauld's project was not exactly unheard of. Such a linkage was explicit in the practice of using the Bible as the textbook for reading; and from the sixteenth century, when people began to be concerned about the heretical interpretations of the Bible that neophyte readers produced, the primer had been seen as a temporary substitute for the Bible or as a preparation for the Bible itself. Additionally the primer was supposed to supply relevance; it would not merely link reading with religion, it would also prepare the child to recognize the moral dilemmas of his everyday life.

Thus, the child learning to read in the late eighteenth and early nineteenth centuries was given (by Mrs. Barbauld, Mrs. Trimmer, Thomas Day, Maria Edgeworth, and others) texts that endowed nature with particular significance for the child, and as a religious child, he was to behave with particular moral probity towards nature. In fact, the most frequently recurrent theme in primer literature of the time was the sinfulness of cruelty to animals — particularly birds. Mrs. Barbauld's *Lessons for Children of Three Years Old,* Part I, in fact, concludes with two short stories, the first of which enforces the moral of kindness to birds:

> A naughty boy will not feed a starving and freezing robin; in fact he even pulls the poor bird's tail! It dies. Shortly after that, the boy's parents leave him because he is cruel, and he is forced to beg for food. He goes into a forest, sits down and cries, and is never heard of again; it is believed that bears ate him. (Patterson, p. 44)

No wonder Wordsworth recounts in Book I of *The Prelude* (ll.333–50) that his childish act of stealing eggs from a bird's nest produced a major crisis of guilt.

Now I obviously don't mean to suggest either that Coleridge wrote "The Rime of the Ancient Mariner" or that Wordsworth wrote that passage from *The Prelude* as a direct attack on Mrs. Barbauld or primers generally. But I do want to suggest that the moral causality that most critics discern in the "Rime" sounds less appropriate to Coleridge's poem than to the conclusion of Mrs. Barbauld's "Epitaph on a Goldfinch":

> Reader,
> if suffering innocence can hope for retribution,
>   deny not to the gentle shade
>   of this unfortunate captive
>   the natural though uncertain hope
>   of animating some happier form,
>   or trying his new-fledged pinions
>   in some humble Elysium,
>   beyond the reach of Man,
>   the tyrant
>   of this lower universe. (*Works,* Vol. 2, p. 323)

The primary difference between Mrs. Barbauld's literary morals and Coleridge's seems to lie in her emphasis upon acts and his agonizing explorations of the difficulties of recognizing the full implications of an action before it is committed, put in the context of the full range of human history (particularly the context of the Bible), and interpreted. Mrs. Barbauld's story of the little boy who was cruel to the starving and freezing robin is, one might assert, no less improbable than the "Rime," no less committed to what we might see as excessive punishment for the crime perpetrated. But while the critics of the "Rime" almost invariably mock Mrs. Barbauld as an obtuse and simplistic moralist, they also subscribe to the moral line of the Gloss, which leads them to a Barbauldian moral.

We must return to a rather simple-minded question: How bad was the Mariner to kill the bird? The act was certainly one of "motiveless malignity," for the Albatross had done nothing to him. But the crucial point is that he "didn't know any better"; it's merely the kind of explanation that enlightened parents of our own century employ to exonerate a child who has just destroyed the drapes in order to "play dress-up" or who has pulled the cat's tail. And while Mrs. Barbauld could be said to regard the learning of reading and morals as *technical* skills, Coleridge recognizes reading as moral because one's *techné* can never suffice. One acts, Coleridge would say, on the basis of one's reading or interpretation, but if reading and interpretation are the genesis of moral action, they may be infinitely divorced for moral outcome — may, in fact, reverse one's interpretation of the moral value of the act. Reading as a *techné* and morals as techniques of behavior thus become suspect for Coleridge because they imply that experience — and one's interpretation of it — are both stable and repetitive — that one can learn what one needs to know.

In this context, Coleridge's Gloss to the "Rime" recalls not merely the archetypal glosses — those in the margins of early printed editions of the Bible; it also raises the question of the ways in which such glosses and the primer tradition made the Bible more accessible and comprehensible while also domesticating that main text. For if glosses and primers came to be felt necessary because readers "couldn't understand" the Bible properly, Coleridge's addition of his Gloss to the "Rime" seems to have answered the critics who called his poem incomprehensible, largely by a domestication. Think back to the main text of the poem. The Wedding Guest, in the first stanza, asks, "Now wherefore stopp'st thou me?" Nowhere in the poem is the Wedding Guest's question answered, not even at the end, although we know then:

He went like one that hath been stunned,
And is of sense forlorn:
A sadder and a wiser man,
He rose the morrow morn. (ll.626–29)

The Mariner's stopping the Wedding Guest is probably the most arbitrary event in a poem filled with arbitrary events, and any explanation
that asserts that he was chosen because his callowness needed correc-
tion seems farfetched. The main interest of the Wedding Guest is that
he has something to do. He has the intention of going to a wedding; in
Part I of the poem he alternately pays attention to the Mariner and to
the sounds of the wedding; but then, at the end of the poem he turns
"from the bridegroom's door." Most importantly, neither his personality nor his intentions matter; he becomes what he reads (or hears). But
if this account seems a fabulous escalation of the power of the word,
think of the fate of the other sailors on the Mariner's ship. Nothing
happens to them when they denounce the Mariner's act of murder, but
then they reverse themselves when the fog clears and the fair breeze
continues. The Gloss informs us that they thus become accomplices in
the Mariner's crime. But in Part III of the poem, the Mariner is
awarded to Life-in-Death while all the rest of the crew become the
property of Death. We never know whether this eventuality is a delayed
punishment for their first opinion or a more immediate punishment
for their second. Since the Mariner did the killing when they only
expressed opinions about it, their fate seems cruel indeed. But the
implication seems to be that every interpretation involves a moral commitment with consequences that are inevitably more far-reaching and
unpredictable than one could have imagined. And neither the sailors'
paucity of information (which necessarily produces a limited perspective) nor their intentions (to praise the good and denounce the bad) are
any exoneration for them (because most human interpretations are similarly limited, well-intentioned, and unexonerated).

    Some of the major revisions of the poem, at least in retrospect, seem
designed to make not the moral but the process of arriving at morals
the major issue. In 1798 the poem was published under the title, "The
Rime of the Ancient Mariner," and its Argument preceding the text
provided rather neutral information, primarily geographical — "How a
Ship having passed the Line was driven by storms to the Cold Country
towards the South Pole; . . . and of the strange things that befell. . . ."
But in keeping with Coleridge's rather persistent practice of giving with
one hand while taking away with the other, the 1800 version was titled

"The Ancient Mariner. A Poet's Reverie," as if to emphasize the unreality of the piece, while the Argument was far more morally directive — "how the Ancient Mariner cruelly and in contempt of the laws of hospitality killed a Sea-bird and how he was followed by many and strange Judgements." And a similar doubleness or confusion arises with the introduction of the Gloss in 1817. For while the Gloss sorts out a moral line for the poem, it is accompanied by an epigraph that Coleridge excerpted from Thomas Burnet:

> I believe easily that there are more invisible than visible beings in the universe. But of them all, who will tell us the race? and the ranks and relationships and differences and functions of each one? What do they do? What places do they inhabit? The human mind has always circled about the knowledge of these things but has never reached it. Still, it is undeniably desirable to contemplate in the mind, as it were in a picture, the image of a greater and better world: lest the mind, accustomed to the small details of daily life, become contracted and sink entirely into trivial thoughts. But meanwhile we must be watchful of truth and must keep within suitable limits, in order that we may distinguish the certain from the uncertain, day from night.
> (Translation of Burnet in Coleridge, *Selected Poetry and Prose,* ed. Schneider, pp. 634–35)

Although a number of critics have taken the epigraph as an ironic foil to the progress of the poem, its waverings between belief and self-cautionary gestures are closer to the pattern of the main text than has been acknowledged. For here an assertion of belief dissolves into a discourse on the lack of information, while an assertion of the necessity of belief even from limited information dwindles into the necessity of accepting limitation. But the most interesting feature of the epigraph is not primarily what it says but what it refuses to say. For the main text of the "Rime" is written in imitation of medieval ballads; and while the persona of the Gloss is that of a seventeenth-century editor who lays claim to sorting out the medieval tale, the author of the epigraph, his contemporary, merely provides us with a record of his lack of certainty. Thus, for the "Rime," a mini-epic of progress that moves largely by retrogradation, we have a Gloss of progress and an epigraph that sees the progress of knowledge only in terms of circling — or, perhaps, hanging on the line. Even Coleridge's revisions not only maintain but also intensify the contradictory interpretations that the main text keeps throwing up to us.

As Coleridge would (and did) say, "I would be understood." Although I have criticized (and perhaps even derided) the Gloss and Gloss-bound criticism, I do not mean to suggest simply that the position of the Gloss is wrong and that uncertainty (or no position) is right. That would be to plunge the poem back into the criticism that maintains that the poem doesn't mean anything because it is a "poem . . . of pure imagination." Coleridge vented his spleen against common schemes of the progress of knowledge — the "general conceit that states and governments might be and ought to be constructed as machines, every movement of which might be foreseen and taken into previous calculation" (*Lay Sermons*, p. 34) and against education infected by "the vile sophistications and mutilations of ignorant mountebanks" (*The Friend*, Essay XIV, 1:102). But he was equally virulent on the subject of indolence (especially his own) as an attempt to avoid commitment. Commitment — or belief — is inevitable for Coleridge, but it does not issue in certainty or as a guide to future action.

So what is "The Rime of the Ancient Mariner" then? Some have maintained that it is an attempt to befuddle the reader with a welter of strange evidence and contradictory interpretations, that it is an elaborate *tour de force* of mystification. This account of the poem casts Coleridge in the role of Milton's Satan, who continually changes shape to lure men to their doom. But it might be said that perhaps no other writer in English worries more concertedly than Coleridge about deluding his readers. One almost hears him saying, "My intentions are good, how can I be misunderstood?" And this discomfort at the possibility of being misunderstood perhaps accounts for the peculiar procedure of stratifying his lay sermons for preselected audiences (*The Statesman's Manual* was "addressed to the higher classes of society"; *A Lay Sermon* was to "the higher and middle classes"; and a projected third lay sermon was to have been directed to "the lower and labouring classes of society"). Even his critique (in *Biographia Literaria*, Chap. XVII) of the theories of poetic diction that Wordsworth expounded in the two Prefaces to *Lyrical Ballads* (and in the Appendix of 1802) involves primarily an argument against the confusions that might arise from importing a "natural" language that would appear strikingly "unnatural" to the audience for poetry. Wordsworth did not really mean what he said about imitating the language of the lower and rustic classes of society, Coleridge insists, because a rustic's language, "purified from all provincialism and grossness, and so far reconstructed as to be made consistent with the rules of grammar" is really a version of the philosophic and ideal language to which all poets and all readers of poetry are accustomed. Coleridge, as he says repeatedly, would be understood.

Why is it, then, that Coleridge is so monumentally difficult to understand? Not only poems like the "Rime," "Kubla Khan," and "Christabel," but also Coleridge's various prose works continually frustrate many readers who struggle to understand what, exactly, he is saying. And this is a particular problem because Coleridge is continually presented to us as important primarily because of his distinctions — between virtue and vice, symbol and allegory, imagination and fancy. Barbauld-like critics of the "Rime" separate good from evil, and I. A. Richards separates the good (the imagination) from the not-so-good (the fancy). What is it that they know that we don't know?

It may be useful here to turn to the *Biographia Literaria* because it provides the most explicit account of Coleridge's experience and views of reading (and of the ways in which reading involves one's entire set of beliefs about the world). Chapter XII is named "A Chapter of requests and premonitions concerning the perusal or omission of the chapter that follows." And Coleridge begins it with the following remarks on his reading:

> [In reading philosophical works, I have made the following resolve] *"until you understand a writer's ignorance, presume yourself ignorant of his understanding."* This *golden rule* of mine does, I own, resemble those of Pythagoras in its obscurity rather than its depth . . . [But the reader] will find its meaning fully explained by the following instances. I have now before me a treatise of a religious fanatic, full of dreams and supernatural *experiences*. I see clearly the writers grounds, and their hollowness. I have a complete insight into the causes, which through the medium of his body has [sic] acted on his mind; and by application of received and ascertained laws I can satisfactorily explain to my own reason all the strange incidents, which the writer records of himself. And this I can do without suspecting him of any intentional falsehood. . . . I UNDERSTAND HIS IGNORANCE.
>
> On the other hand, I have been re-perusing with the best energies of my mind the Timaeus of PLATO. Whatever I comprehend, impresses me with a reverential sense of the author's genius; but there is a considerable portion of the work, to which I can attach no consistent meaning. . . . I have no insight into the possibility of a man so eminently wise using words with such half-meanings to himself, as must perforce pass into no-meaning to his

readers. . . . Therefore, utterly baffled in all my attempts to understand the ignorance of Plato, I CONCLUDE MYSELF IGNORANT OF HIS
UNDERSTANDING. (Vol. I, pp. 160–61)

Although Coleridge later speaks of the "organic unity" of this chapter,
that "golden rule" of his turns the problem of reading from the text (or
the writer) to the reader. For Coleridge's "tolerance" for the ignorant
writer — in refusing to suspect him of "any intentional falsehood" —
exculpates that writer by turning the reader's own prejudices into a self-
reinforcing standard of judgment. No knowledge or virtue or imagination on the part of the author, from this perspective, is susceptible
of revealing itself to a reader who does not already believe that such
qualities inhere in the work. And the curiosity of the piece is that explanation is fullest (even including physiological causation) when Coleridge describes himself reading a book that he had dismissed before he
ever began to read. "Understanding ignorance" and being "ignorant of
an author's understanding" are merely techniques through which a
reader adjusts his demands to accord with his beliefs.

Such beliefs or prejudices are inevitable, unless, as Coleridge says,
we discover "the art of destroying the memory *a parte post,* without
injury to its future operations, and without detriment to the judge-
ment" (*Ibid.,* p. 162). Now Coleridge described his project in *Lyrical
Ballads* as that of writing on "supernatural" subjects "so as to transfer
from our inward nature a human interest and a semblance of truth sufficient to . . . [produce] that willing suspension of disbelief for the
moment, which constitutes poetic faith" (*Biographia Literaria,* Vol. II,
p. 6). But, after all that we have been saying Coleridge said, how is such
a "suspension of disbelief" possible? Disbelief is merely a subset of
belief, a kind of belief that a thing is not (to paraphrase Gulliver). And
the most famous chapter of the *Biographia Literaria,* Chapter XIII,
"On the imagination, or esemplastic power," reveals this process as well
as anything in Coleridge's work. Let us start from the end — the distinction between imagination and fancy — to which Coleridge has, he
says, been building through the entire book. The secondary imagination idealizes and unifies in its processes of *vital* understanding. The
fancy is merely a mechanical and associationist operation that can only
rearrange fixities and definites. At some moments Coleridge uses these
terms as classificatory (see *Shakespearean Criticism,* 1:203–20); and for
I. A. Richards they seem to be universally applicable categories.
Richards, for instance, quotes four lines of *Annus Mirabilis* and remarks,

"To attempt to read this in the mode of Imagination would be to experiment in mania. . . ." And then he generalizes that in "prose fiction, the detective novel is a type of Fancy, but any presentation of an integral view of life will take the structure of Imagination" (pp. 94–95).

But various other elements of Coleridge's chapter would seem to cast doubt on projects like Richards' *Coleridge on Imagination* and *Practical Criticism* and their assumption that one man's "imagination" is the same as another's. For the letter that Coleridge inserts immediately before the famous distinction is (fictitiously) a letter from a friend "whose practical judgment [Coleridge had] had ample reason to estimate and revere" (*Biographia Literaria,* Vol. I, pp. 198–99). And although the friend admits that he may not fully understand Coleridge's chapter on imagination, he continually suggests that Coleridge is guilty of breach of promise — for instance, he cites the *Biographia Literaria*'s subtitle, "Biographical Sketches of My Literary Life and Opinions," to argue that it does not lead the reader to anticipate Coleridge's arcane speculations in the *Biographia Literaria.* But the rather major difficulty here is that Coleridge's chapter must do battle with the accumulated expectations of the friend's lifetime: "Your opinions and method of argument were not only so new to me, but so directly the reverse of all I had ever been accustomed to consider as truth . . ." (*Ibid.,* p. 199). Once again, we are left with a question about the nature of the text (in this case, a deleted or unwritten text): Is the "deficiency" in the text or in the reader?

It seems that a reader can only read the texts that say what he already knows. Thus, the editor of the Gloss reads a text that he knows, while the no-moral critics read a text that they know. And the difficulty is that for Coleridge what you know and what you read are part of a moral dilemma, because one can only act on the basis of what one knows (i. e., believes) and vice is merely the result of incomplete information. Coleridge says in *The Friend* (Essay XIV, p. 104) that "virtue would not be virtue, could it be *given* by one fellow-creature to another" (italics his). In other words, a man must be virtuous to understand the understanding of anyone else's knowledge — and thus to be virtuous.

And if this situation seems to present us with an impasse, it may perhaps explain why Coleridge so desperately wanted to write a summa or *Omniana,* a book of universal knowledge. He continually quotes from an incredibly diverse collection of texts, makes one statement only to confound it with the next, and he even plagiarizes. Many readers feel imposed upon by what they take to be Coleridge's efforts to delude them with airy nothings and falsehoods; and Norman Fruman is merely the latest in the line of critics who "expose" the "scandal" of Coleridge's plagiarisms. But both the plagiarism and the voracious reading perhaps point to related ends: If you are what you read, plagiarism (in a more or less obvious form) becomes inevitable; and if insufficient knowledge or reading is the cause of moral inadequacy, then nothing less than all knowledge — everything — will suffice. Coleridge, like Leibnitz, would "explain and collect the fragments of truth scattered through systems apparently the most incongruous" (*Biographia Literaria*, Vol. I, p. 169). But like so many of Coleridge's projects, the summa was never completed because incomplete information (as Coleridge recognized) was not the problem. The problem, rather, was that he could sort information from knowledge, delusion from truth, with no more certainty than anyone else who has lived long enough to have a memory and, thus, prejudice. Robert Penn Warren aptly summarizes him as saying, in the *Aids to Reflection*, that "original sin is not hereditary sin; it is original with the sinner and is of his will" (p. 227). And for Coleridge this original sin was interpretation from a limited perspective that had disproportionate consequences, for the peril was that any apparent extension or reversal might, always, be merely a disguised entrenchment of that particular limitation or prejudice. The Ancient Mariner's redemption or conversion, we are told, occurs when he blesses the sea-snakes. But if it seems like a conversion for a man who killed a rather appealing bird to see beauty in snakes, there is also room for a different interpretation. The bird is spoken of in Part V of the poem as something of a Christ figure, and we all know about the spiritual connotations of snakes. The Mariner's conversion, then, may be a redemption, or, merely a deluded capitulation to the devil. For Coleridge, as for the Ancient Mariner, the problem is that one cannot know better even about whether or not one is knowing better.

WORKS CITED

Abrams, M. H., ed. *The Norton Anthology of English Literature*. 6th ed. Vol. 2. New York: Norton, 1996.

Barbauld, Mrs. (Anna Laetitia). Foreword. *Hymns in Prose for Children*. By Barbauld. London: Murray, 1866.

Barbauld, Anna Laetitia. *The Works of Anna Laetitia Barbauld*. (Memoir by Lucy Aikin). Vol. 2. New York: Carvill, 1826.

Coleridge, S. T. (Samuel Taylor). *Aids to Reflection*. Ed. Thomas Fenby. New York: Dutton, 1905.

————. *Biographia Literaria*. Ed. J. Shawcross. 2 Vols. Oxford: Clarendon, 1907.

————. *The Friend*. Ed. Barbara E. Rooke. 2 Vols. Bollingen Ser. 75: *The Collected Works of Samuel Taylor Coleridge*. 4. Princeton: Princeton UP, 1969.

————. *Lay Sermons*. Ed. R. J. White. Bollingen Ser. 75: *The Collected Works of Samuel Taylor Coleridge*. 6. Princeton: Princeton UP, 1972.

————. *Selected Poetry and Prose*. Ed. Elisabeth Schneider. San Francisco: Rinehart, 1971.

————. *Shakespearean Criticism*. Ed. Thomas Middleton Raysor. 2 Vols. London: Dent, 1960.

————. *Table Talk*. Ed. Carl Woodring. 2 Vols. Bollingen Ser. 75: *The Collected Works of Samuel Taylor Coleridge*. Princeton: Princeton UP, 1990.

Jackson, J. R. de J., ed., *Coleridge: The Critical Heritage*. Critical Heritage Ser. London: Routledge, 1970.

Lowes, John Livingston. *The Road to Xanadu: A Study in the Ways of the Imagination*. 1927. Boston: Houghton, 1955.

McElderry, B. R., Jr. "Coleridge's Revision of 'The Ancient Mariner.'" *Studies in Philology*, 29 (1932): 69–94.

Patterson, Sylvia W. *Rousseau's Emile and Early Children's Literature*. Metuchen: Scarecrow, 1971.

Richards, I. A. *Coleridge on Imagination*. 1934. 3rd Ed. London: Routledge, 1962.

Warren, Robert Penn. *Selected Essays*. New York: Random, 1958.

Wordsworth, William, and Samuel Taylor Coleridge. *Lyrical Ballads*. Ed. R. L. Brett and A. R. Jones. Cambridge: Cambridge UP, 1963.

Marxist Criticism and
"The Rime of the Ancient Mariner"

WHAT IS MARXIST CRITICISM?

To the question "What is Marxist criticism?" it may be tempting to respond with another question: "What does it matter?" In light of the rapid and largely unanticipated demise of Soviet-style communism in the former USSR and throughout Eastern Europe, it is understandable to suppose that Marxist literary analysis would disappear too, quickly becoming an anachronism in a world enamored with full-market capitalism.

In fact, however, there is no reason why Marxist criticism should weaken, let alone disappear. It is, after all, a phenomenon distinct from Soviet and Eastern European communism, having had its beginnings nearly eighty years before the Bolshevik revolution and having thrived since the 1940s, mainly in the West — not as a form of communist propaganda but rather as a form of critique, a discourse for interrogating *all* societies and their texts in terms of certain specific issues. Those issues — including race, class, and the attitudes shared within a given culture — are as much with us as ever, not only in contemporary Russia but also in the United States.

The argument could even be made that Marxist criticism has been strengthened by the collapse of Soviet-style communism. There was a time, after all, when few self-respecting Anglo-American journals would use Marxist terms or models, however illuminating, to analyze Western issues or problems. It smacked of sleeping with the enemy. With the collapse of the Kremlin, however, old taboos began to give way. Even the staid *Wall Street Journal* now seems comfortable using phrases like "worker alienation" to discuss the problems plaguing the American business world.

The assumption that Marxist criticism will die on the vine of a moribund political system rests in part on another mistaken assumption, namely, that Marxist literary analysis is practiced only by people who would like to see society transformed into a Marxist-communist state, one created through land reform, the redistribution of wealth, a tightly and centrally managed economy, the abolition of institutionalized religion, and so on. In fact, it has never been necessary to be a communist political revolutionary to be classified as a Marxist literary critic. (Many of the critics discussed in this introduction actually *fled* communist societies to live in the West.) Nor is it necessary to like only those literary works with a radical social vision or to dislike books that represent or even reinforce a middle-class, capitalist world-view. It is necessary, however, to adopt what most students of literature would consider a radical definition of the purpose and function of literary criticism.

More traditional forms of criticism, according to the Marxist critic Pierre Macherey, "set . . . out to deliver the text from its own silences by coaxing it into giving up its true, latent, or hidden meaning." Inevitably, however, non-Marxist criticism "intrude[s] its own discourse between the reader and the text" (qtd. in Bennett 107). Marxist critics, by contrast, do not attempt to discover hidden meanings in texts. Or if they do, they do so only after seeing the text, first and foremost, as a material product to be understood in broadly historical terms. That is to say, a literary work is first viewed as a product *of* work (and hence of the realm of production and consumption we call economics). Second, it may be looked upon as a work that *does* identifiable work of its own. At one level, that work is usually to enforce and reinforce the prevailing ideology, that is, the network of conventions, values, and opinions to which the majority of people uncritically subscribe.

This does not mean that Marxist critics merely describe the obvious. Quite the contrary: the relationship that the Marxist critic Terry Eagleton outlines in *Criticism and Ideology* (1978) among the soaring cost of books in the nineteenth century, the growth of lending libraries, the practice of publishing "three-decker" novels (so that three borrowers could be reading the same book at the same time), and the changing *content* of those novels is highly complex in its own way. But the complexity Eagleton finds is not that of the deeply buried meaning of the text. Rather, it is that of the complex web of social and economic relationships that were prerequisite to the work's production. Marxist criticism does not seek to be, in Eagleton's words, "a passage from text to reader." Indeed, "its task is to show the text as it cannot know itself, to manifest those conditions of its making (inscribed in its very letter) about which it is necessarily silent" (43).

As everyone knows, Marxism began with Karl Marx, the nineteenth-century German philosopher best known for writing *Das Kapital,* the seminal work of the communist movement. What everyone doesn't know is that Marx was also the first Marxist literary critic (much as Sigmund Freud, who psychoanalyzed E. T. A. Hoffmann's supernatural tale "The Sandman," was the first Freudian literary critic). During the 1830s Marx wrote critical essays on writers such as Goethe and Shakespeare (whose tragic vision of Elizabethan disintegration he praised).

The fact that Marxist literary criticism began with Marx himself is hardly surprising, given Marx's education and early interests. Trained in the classics at the University of Bonn, Marx wrote literary imitations, his own poetry, a failed novel, and a fragment of a tragic drama (*Oulanem*) before turning to contemplative and political philosophy. Even after he met Friedrich Engels in 1843 and began collaborating on works such as *The German Ideology* and *The Communist Manifesto,* Marx maintained a keen interest in literary writers and their works. He and Engels argued about the poetry of Heinrich Heine, admired Hermann Freiligrath (a poet critical of the German aristocracy), and faulted the playwright Ferdinand Lassalle for writing about a reactionary knight in the Peasants' War rather than about more progressive aspects of German history.

As these examples suggest, Marx and Engels would not — indeed, could not — think of aesthetic matters as being distinct and independent from such things as politics, economics, and history. Not surprisingly, they viewed the alienation of the worker in industrialized, capitalist societies as having grave consequences for the arts. How can people mechanically stamping out things that bear no mark of their producer's individuality (people thereby "reified," turned into things themselves) be expected to recognize, produce, or even consume things of beauty? And if there is no one to consume something, there will soon be no one to produce it, especially in an age in which production (even of something like literature) has come to mean *mass* (and therefore profitable) production.

In *The German Ideology* (1846), Marx and Engels expressed their sense of the relationship between the arts, politics, and basic economic reality in terms of a general social theory. Economics, they argued, provides the "base" or "infrastructure" of society, but from that base emerges a "superstructure" consisting of law, politics, philosophy, religion, and art.

Marx later admitted that the relationship between base and superstructure may be indirect and fluid: every change in economics may not be reflected by an immediate change in ethics or literature. In *The Eighteenth Brumaire of Louis Bonaparte* (1852), he came up with the word *homology* to describe the sometimes unbalanced, often delayed, and almost always loose correspondence between base and superstructure. And later in that same decade, while working on an introduction to his *Political Economy,* Marx further relaxed the base–superstructure relationship. Writing on the excellence of ancient Greek art (versus the primitive nature of ancient Greek economics), he conceded that a gap sometimes opens up between base and superstructure — between economic forms and those produced by the creative mind.

Nonetheless, *at* base the old formula was maintained. Economics remained basic and the connection between economics and superstructural elements of society was reaffirmed. Central to Marxism and Marxist literary criticism was and is the following "materialist" insight: consciousness, without which such things as art cannot be produced, is not the source of social forms and economic conditions. It is, rather, their most important product.

Marx and Engels, drawing upon the philosopher G. W. F. Hegel's theories about the dialectical synthesis of ideas out of theses and antitheses, believed that a revolutionary class war (pitting the capitalist class against a proletarian, antithetical class) would lead eventually to the synthesis of a new social and economic order. Placing their faith not in the idealist Hegelian dialectic but, rather, in what they called "dialectical materialism," they looked for a secular and material salvation of humanity — one in, not beyond, history — via revolution and not via divine intervention. And they believed that the communist society eventually established would be one capable of producing new forms of consciousness and belief and therefore, ultimately, great art.

The revolution anticipated by Marx and Engels did not occur in their century, let alone lifetime. When it finally did take place, it didn't happen in places where Marx and Engels had thought it might be successful: the United States, Great Britain, and Germany. It happened, rather, in 1917 Russia, a country long ruled by despotic czars but also enlightened by the works of powerful novelists and playwrights, including Chekhov, Pushkin, Tolstoy, and Dostoyevsky.

Perhaps because of its significant literary tradition, Russia produced revolutionaries like V.I. Lenin, who shared not only Marx's interest in literature but also his belief in literature's ultimate importance. But it was not without some hesitation that Lenin endorsed the significance of texts written during the reign of the czars. Well before 1917 he had questioned what the relationship should be between a society undergoing a revolution and the great old literature of its bourgeois past.

Lenin attempted to answer that question in a series of essays on Tolstoy that he wrote between 1908 and 1911. Tolstoy — the author of *War and Peace* and *Anna Karenina* — was an important nineteenth-century Russian writer whose views did not accord with all of those of young Marxist revolutionaries. Continuing interest in a writer like Tolstoy may be justified, Lenin reasoned, given the primitive and unenlightened economic order of the society that produced him. Since superstructure usually lags behind base (and is therefore usually *more* primitive), the attitudes of a Tolstoy were relatively progressive when viewed in light of the monarchical and precapitalist society out of which they arose.

Moreover, Lenin also reasoned, the writings of the great Russian realists would *have* to suffice, at least in the short run. Lenin looked forward, in essays like "Party Organization and Party Literature," to the day in which new artistic forms would be produced by progressive writers with revolutionary political views and agendas. But he also knew that a great proletarian literature was unlikely to evolve until a thoroughly literate proletariat had been produced by the educational system.

Lenin was hardly the only revolutionary leader involved in setting up the new Soviet state who took a strong interest in literary matters. In 1924 Leon Trotsky published a book called *Literature and Revolution,* which is still acknowledged as a classic of Marxist literary criticism.

Trotsky worried about the direction in which Marxist aesthetic theory seemed to be going. He responded skeptically to groups like Proletkult, which opposed tolerance toward pre- and nonrevolutionary writers, and which called for the establishment of a new, proletarian culture. Trotsky warned of the danger of cultural sterility and risked unpopularity by pointing out that there is no necessary connection between the quality of a literary work and the quality of its author's politics.

In 1927 Trotsky lost a power struggle with Josef Stalin, a man who
believed, among other things, that writers should be "engineers" of
"human souls." After Trotsky's expulsion from the Soviet Union, views
held by groups like Proletkult and the Left Front of Art (LEF), and by
theorists such as Nikolai Bukharin and A. A. Zhdanov, became more
prevalent. Speaking at the First Congress of the Union of Soviet Writers
in 1934, the Soviet author Maxim Gorky called for writing that would
"make labor the principal hero of our books." It was at the same writers' congress that "socialist realism," an art form glorifying workers and
the revolutionary State, was made Communist party policy and the official literary form of the USSR.

Of those critics active in the USSR after the expulsion of Trotsky
and the unfortunate triumph of Stalin, two critics stand out. One,
Mikhail Bakhtin, was a Russian, later a Soviet, critic who spent much of
his life in a kind of internal exile. Many of his essays were written in the
1930s and not published in the West or translated until the late 1960s.
His work comes out of an engagement with the Marxist intellectual tradition as well as out of an indirect, even hidden, resistance to the Soviet
government. It has been important to Marxist critics writing in the
West because his theories provide a means to decode submerged social
critique, especially in early modern texts. He viewed language — especially literary texts — in terms of discourses and dialogues. Within a
novel written in a society in flux, for instance, the narrative may include
an official, legitimate discourse, plus another infiltrated by challenging
comments and even retorts. In a 1929 book on Dostoyevsky and a
1940 study titled *Rabelais and His World*, Bakhtin examined what he
calls "polyphonic" novels, each characterized by a multiplicity of voices
or discourses. In Dostoyevsky the independent status of a given character is marked by the difference of his or her language from that of the
narrator. (The narrator's voice, too, can in fact be a dialogue.) In works
by Rabelais, Bakhtin finds that the (profane) language of the carnival
and of other popular festivals plays against and parodies the more official discourses, that is, of the king, church, or even socially powerful
intellectuals. Bakhtin influenced modern cultural criticism by showing,
in a sense, that the conflict between "high" and "low" culture takes
place not only between classic and popular texts but also between the
"dialogic" voices that exist within many books — whether "high" or
"low."

The other subtle Marxist critic who managed to survive Stalin's dic-
tatorship and his repressive policies was Georg Lukács. A Hungarian
who had begun his career as an "idealist" critic, Lukács had converted

to Marxism in 1919; renounced his earlier, Hegelian work shortly thereafter; visited Moscow in 1930–31; and finally emigrated to the USSR in 1933, just one year before the First Congress of the Union of Soviet Writers met. Lukács was far less narrow in his views than the most strident Stalinist Soviet critics of the 1930s and 1940s. He disliked much socialist realism and appreciated prerevolutionary, realistic novels that broadly reflected cultural "totalities" — and were populated with characters representing human "types" of the author's place and time. (Lukács was particularly fond of the historical canvasses painted by the early nineteenth-century novelist Sir Walter Scott.) But like his more rigid and censorious contemporaries, he drew the line at accepting nonrevolutionary, modernist works like James Joyce's *Ulysses*. He condemned movements like expressionism and symbolism, preferring works with "content" over more decadent, experimental works characterized mainly by "form."

With Lukács its most liberal and tolerant critic from the early 1930s until well into the 1960s, the Soviet literary scene degenerated to the point that the works of great writers like Franz Kafka were no longer read, either because they were viewed as decadent, formal experiments or because they "engineered souls" in "nonprogressive" directions. Officially sanctioned works were generally ones in which artistry lagged far behind the politics (no matter how bad the politics were).

Fortunately for the Marxist critical movement, politically radical critics *outside* the Soviet Union were free of its narrow, constricting policies and, consequently, able fruitfully to develop the thinking of Marx, Engels, and Trotsky. It was these non-Soviet Marxists who kept Marxist critical theory alive and useful in discussing all *kinds* of literature, written across the entire historical spectrum.

Perhaps because Lukács was the best of the Soviet communists writing Marxist criticism in the 1930s and 1940s, non-Soviet Marxists tended to develop their ideas by publicly opposing those of Lukács. German dramatist and critic Bertolt Brecht countered Lukács by arguing that art ought to be viewed as a field of production, not as a container of "content." Brecht also criticized Lukács for his attempt to enshrine realism at the expense not only of other "isms" but also of poetry and drama, both of which had been largely ignored by Lukács.

Even more outspoken was Brecht's critical champion Walter Benjamin, a German Marxist who, in the 1930s, attacked those conventional and traditional literary forms conveying a stultifying "aura" of culture. Benjamin praised dadaism and, more important, new forms of art ushered in by the age of mechanical reproduction. Those forms — including radio and film — offered hope, he felt, for liberation from capitalist culture, for they were too new to be part of its stultifyingly ritualistic traditions.

But of all the anti-Lukácsians outside the USSR who made a contribution to the development of Marxist literary criticism, the most important was probably Theodor Adorno. Leader since the early 1950s of the Frankfurt school of Marxist criticism, Adorno attacked Lukács for his dogmatic rejection of nonrealist modern literature and for his belief in the primacy of content over form. Art does not equal science, Adorno insisted. He went on to argue for art's autonomy from empirical forms of knowledge and to suggest that the interior monologues of modernist works (by Beckett and Proust) reflect the fact of modern alienation in a way that Marxist criticism ought to find compelling.

In addition to turning against Lukács and his overly constrictive canon, Marxists outside the Soviet Union were able to take advantage of insights generated by non-Marxist critical theories being developed in post–World War II Europe. One of the movements that came to be of interest to non-Soviet Marxists was structuralism, a scientific approach to the study of humankind whose proponents believed that all elements of culture, including literature, could be understood as parts of a system of signs. Using modern linguistics as a model, structuralists like Claude Lévi-Strauss broke down the myths of various cultures into "mythemes" in an attempt to show that there are structural correspondences, or homologies, between the mythical elements produced by various human communities across time.

Of the European structuralist Marxists, one of the most influential was Lucien Goldmann, a Rumanian critic living in Paris. Goldmann combined structuralist principles with Marx's base–superstructure model in order to show how economics determines the mental structures of social groups, which are reflected in literary texts. Goldmann rejected the idea of individual human genius, choosing to see works, instead, as the "collective" products of "trans-individual" mental structures. In early studies, such as *The Hidden God* (1955), he related seventeenth-century French texts (such as Racine's *Phèdre*) to the ideology of Jansenism. In later works, he applied Marx's base–superstructure model even more strictly, describing a relationship between economic conditions and texts unmediated by an intervening, collective consciousness.

In spite of his rigidity and perhaps because of his affinities with structuralism, Goldmann came to be seen in the 1960s as the proponent of a kind of watered-down, "humanist" Marxism. He was certainly viewed that way by the French Marxist Louis Althusser, a disciple not of Lévi-Strauss and structuralism but rather of the psychoanalytic theorist Jacques Lacan and of the Italian communist Antonio Gramsci, famous for his writings about ideology and "hegemony." (Gramsci used the latter word to refer to the pervasive, weblike system of assumptions and values that shapes the way things look, what they mean, and therefore what reality *is* for the majority of people within a culture.)

Like Gramsci, Althusser viewed literary works primarily in terms of their relationship to ideology, the function of which, he argued, is to (re)produce the existing relations of production in a given society. Dave Laing, in *The Marxist Theory of Art* (1978), has attempted to explain this particular insight of Althusser by saying that ideologies, through the "ensemble of habits, moralities, and opinions" that can be found in any literary text, "ensure that the work-force (and those responsible for re-producing them in the family, school, etc.) are maintained in their position of subordination to the dominant class" (91). This is not to say that Althusser thought of the masses as a brainless multitude following only the dictates of the prevailing ideology: Althusser followed Gramsci in suggesting that even working-class people have some freedom to struggle against ideology and to change history. Nor is it to say that Althusser saw ideology as being a coherent, consistent force. In fact, he saw it as being riven with contradictions that works of literature sometimes expose and even widen. Thus Althusser followed Marx and Gramsci in believing that although literature must be seen in *relation* to ideology, it — like all social forms — has some degree of autonomy.

Althusser's followers included Pierre Macherey, who in *A Theory of Literary Production* (1978) developed Althusser's concept of the relationship between literature and ideology. A realistic novelist, he argued, attempts to produce a unified, coherent text, but instead ends up producing a work containing lapses, omissions, gaps. This happens because within ideology there are subjects that cannot be covered, things that cannot be said, contradictory views that aren't recognized as contradictory. (The critic's challenge, in this case, is to supply what the text cannot say, thereby making sense of gaps and contradictions.)

But there is another reason why gaps open up and contradictions become evident in texts. Works don't just reflect ideology (which Goldmann had referred to as "myth" and which Macherey refers to as a system of "illusory social beliefs"); they are also "fictions," works of art, *products* of ideology that have what Goldmann would call a "world-view" to offer. What kind of product, Macherey implicitly asks, is identical to the thing that produced it? It is hardly surprising, then, that Balzac's fiction shows French peasants in two different lights, only one of which is critical and judgmental, only one of which is baldly ideological. Writing approvingly on Macherey and Macherey's mentor Althusser in *Marxism and Literary Criticism* (1976), Terry Eagleton says: "It is by giving ideology a determinate form, fixing it within certain fictional limits, that art is able to distance itself from [ideology], thus revealing . . . [its] limits" (19).

A follower of Althusser, Macherey is sometimes referred to as a "post-Althusserian Marxist." Eagleton, too, is often described that way, as is his American contemporary Fredric Jameson. Jameson and Eagleton, as well as being post-Althusserians, are also among the few Anglo-American critics who have closely followed and significantly developed Marxist thought.

Before them, Marxist interpretation in English was limited to the work of a handful of critics: Christopher Caudwell, Christopher Hill, Arnold Kettle, E. P. Thompson, and Raymond Williams. Of these, Williams was perhaps least Marxist in orientation: he felt that Marxist critics, ironically, tended too much to isolate economics from culture; that they overlooked the individualism of people, opting instead to see them as "masses"; and that even more ironically, they had become an elitist group. But if the least Marxist of the British Marxists, Williams was also by far the most influential. Preferring to talk about "culture" instead of ideology, Williams argued in works such as *Culture and Society 1780–1950* (1958) that culture is "lived experience" and, as such, an interconnected set of social properties, each and all grounded in and influencing history.

Terry Eagleton's *Criticism and Ideology* (1978) is in many ways a response to the work of Williams. Responding to Williams's statement in *Culture and Society* that "there are in fact no masses; there are only ways of seeing people as masses" (289), Eagleton writes:

> That men and women really are now unique individuals was Williams's (unexceptionable) insistence; but it was a proposition bought at the expense of perceiving the fact that they must mass and fight to achieve their full individual humanity. One has only to

adapt Williams's statement to "There are in fact no classes; there are only ways of seeing people as classes" to expose its theoretical paucity. (*Criticism* 29)

Eagleton goes on, in *Criticism and Ideology*, to propose an elaborate theory about how history — in the form of "general," "authorial," and "aesthetic" ideology — enters texts, which in turn may revivify, open up, or critique those same ideologies, thereby setting in motion a process that may alter history. He shows how texts by Jane Austen, Matthew Arnold, Charles Dickens, George Eliot, Joseph Conrad, and T. S. Eliot deal with and transmute conflicts at the heart of the general and authorial ideologies behind them: conflicts between morality and individualism, and between individualism and social organicism and utilitarianism.

As all this emphasis on ideology and conflict suggests, a modern British Marxist like Eagleton, even while acknowledging the work of a British Marxist predecessor like Williams, is more nearly developing the ideas of Continental Marxists like Althusser and Macherey. That holds, as well, for modern American Marxists like Fredric Jameson. For although he makes occasional, sympathetic references to the works of Williams, Thompson, and Hill, Jameson makes far more *use* of Lukács, Adorno, and Althusser as well as non-Marxist structuralist, psychoanalytic, and poststructuralist critics.

In the first of several influential works, *Marxism and Form* (1971), Jameson takes up the question of form and content, arguing that the former is "but the working out" of the latter "in the realm of superstructure" (329). (In making such a statement Jameson opposes not only the tenets of Russian formalists, for whom content had merely been the fleshing out of form, but also those of so-called vulgar Marxists, who tended to define form as mere ornamentation or window-dressing.) In his later work *The Political Unconscious* (1981), Jameson uses what in *Marxism and Form* he had called "dialectical criticism" to synthesize out of structuralism and poststructuralism, Freud and Lacan, Althusser and Adorno, a set of complex arguments that can only be summarized reductively.

The fractured state of societies and the isolated condition of individuals, he argues, may be seen as indications that there originally existed an unfallen state of something that may be called "primitive communism." History — which records the subsequent divisions and alienations — limits awareness of its own contradictions and of that

lost, Better State, via ideologies and their manifestation in texts whose
strategies essentially contain and repress desire, especially revolutionary
desire, into the collective unconscious. (In Conrad's *Lord Jim,* Jameson
shows, the knowledge that governing classes don't *deserve* their power
is contained and repressed by an ending that metaphysically blames
Nature for the tragedy and that melodramatically blames wicked Gentleman Brown.)

As demonstrated by Jameson in analyses like the one mentioned
above, textual strategies of containment and concealment may be discovered by the critic, but only by the critic practicing dialectical criticism, that is to say, a criticism aware, among other things, of its *own*
status as ideology. All thought, Jameson concludes, is ideological; only
through ideological thought that knows itself as such can ideologies be
seen through and eventually transcended.

In the essay that follows, David Simpson admits that his project —
to approach Coleridge's "Rime" from a Marxist perspective — is an
unusual one, for Marxist critics have generally been reluctant to engage
in "the historical-political interpretation of poetry" (149). The best-
known Marxist analyses of literature, Simpson explains, "have been
directed at the novel and the drama, which have been mythologized as
self-evidently within some or another public sphere, and as committed
to 'the people' in a way that poetry, with its mostly specialized and private readership, is not" (149). Simpson further notes that his decision
to offer "a Marxist account of *Romantic* poetry" must seem especially
unusual, given that poetry of the Romantic period is commonly viewed
as a "poetry of private vision and feeling" (150) that avoids, rather than
representing or responding to, social crises or even conditions.

Simpson insists, however, that no historical period or literary genre
is beyond the bounds of "good Marxist criticism," which he describes
as criticism that not only aims at "historical recovery" but also aspires
to offer "totalizing," or all-encompassing, historical "explanations."
Although Simpson recognizes that no act of recovery or explanation
can truly be complete, he nonetheless proposes that "the history of a
poem," no less than that of a novel or play, is "made up" of two kinds of
conditions — those that "continue to pertain to the modern condition
and of those that do not" (151). Those conditions are to be found even
in fanciful, Romantic works, and it is up to Marxist critics to find and
analyze them.

Having argued that all works are susceptible to an historical approach, Simpson proceeds by showing that Coleridge's "Rime" is sur-

prisingly responsive to such an approach. For starters, Simpson points out that the poem contains a framing narrative that tells the (hi)story of its own telling. The poem also offers an early instance of ecological concern, reflecting an emerging sense of "the similarities binding man and nature" and a "new need to define which animals deserved humane treatment and which might remain exempt from it" (158). The Ancient Mariner's ability to command the Wedding Guest's attention reflects another emerging, late-eighteenth-century interest: in "animal magnetism," now known as hypnotism (152). Suggesting that Coleridge's poem expresses "the desire for hypnotic power on the poet's part, and also the fear of such power on the part of the . . . hearer or reader," Simpson argues that the "Rime" indirectly raises, in a new light, Protestant issues regarding "free will, . . . choice, election, and damnation," as well as broader, philosophical questions regarding "epistemological consensus: (How) can one person's acts implicate another, (how) can one person know what another knows?" (152).

Because it raises these kinds of questions, Simpson argues that the "Rime" is both interested in and part of what he calls "the history of subjectivity" (152). He views the Romantic poets as writers who were "constantly concerned with whether or how one might tell the difference between what is 'in' the world and what is imagined or projected," and he suggests that this concern derived from wide-ranging contexts, including "the unstable relations between writers and readers in an increasingly free market for literary work" and the emergence of a "democratic-liberal social order in which the credibility of each person depended (as it often still does) on an ability to convince others" (153). (Note that the parenthetical phrase "as it often still does" indicates the presence, within Simpson's Marxist account of the "Rime," of a "historical condition" that "continue[s] to pertain to the modern condition" [151].)

Having argued that the "Rime" is both susceptible and responsive to a historical approach, Simpson fully admits that Coleridge's poem generally lacks historical specificity: nowhere does it mention the type of ship or kind of voyage involved nor even the ship's location when the events of the narrative befall it and its crew. But this lack of specificity, as Simpson shows, can itself be explained from the Marxist perspective. According to Simpson, "the poem registers . . . an acute version of what Marxists have called *alienation,* a separation of self from others, from the labor process, and from a comfortable relation to the world of things. The *work* of running a ship is completely effaced, and the Mariner's body is entirely a vehicle for metaphysical experience"

(153–54). Moreover, although most "voyage narratives" of the period featured physical descriptions and geographic discoveries, Coleridge's "Rime" is characterized by spirits and mysteries: "If the Enlightenment project was to know rationally all that could be known," Simpson writes, "then Coleridge's poem seems to stand in rebuke of an instrumental reason that would reduce all mysteries of rod and line" (157). Indeed, Simpson suggests that the "Rime," driven by an "agenda" of "remystifying the world" (158), undermines the reader's confidence in rationality and rationalist theories. It implicitly questions not only "the rationalist cartography that made [Captain] Cook's voyages possible" but also "any ambition we might have to devise a rationalist theory of the emotions, or of crime and punishment (of the sort that [Jeremy] Bentham was setting out to deduce)" (157).

Following this ambitious attempt to account historically for the poem's remystification "agenda," Simpson returns to what he calls "the basics," including the "literary marketplace" in which Coleridge's work was written (and consequently *re*written due to Wordsworth's dislike of the first edition and what Simpson calls "a shift in the class identity of the imagined reader" [162]). Even the degree to which the poem is open to interpretation, Simpson suggests, may be viewed as a market strategy; Coleridge may have realized, if only unconsciously, that "indeterminacy would keep his readers [most] satisfied" (163).

Simpson's essay involves classic Marxist paradigms (for instance, the view that aesthetic "superstructure" is determined by the economic "base") even as it employs two important contemporary Marxist paradigms. First, Simpson draws on the thinking of Adorno, Benjamin, Jameson, and Macherey in viewing literature as a medium that not only reflects social and cultural ideologies but that also "transcends or sees through the limitations of ideology." (For instance, the "Rime" both reflects and "rebukes" the Enlightenment fixation on reason.) Second, Simpson's essay attempts both to show the past as it "really was, even when seemingly irrelevant to the present," and to "make the past relevant to the present" (160).

Simpson achieves the latter end in arguing that "the continued popular reputation of 'The Ancient Mariner' and its availability for commonplace quotation (albatrosses, 'water water every where,' etcetera) bear witness to its success within a pedagogic tradition requiring that poems be at least loosely moralizing but at the same time obscure enough to be available for continual rereading and discussion" (163). With typical Marxist emphasis on commodities and consumption,

Simpson suggests that "the poem has itself become the very commodity whose transportation across the world is displaced from the voyage narrative. We do not know what the ship carried or what it sought — real slaves or real knowledge — but we happily consume the poem's memorable lines and images as the permanent gold standard of poetic excellence" (163).

Ross C Murfin

MARXIST CRITICISM: A SELECTED BIBLIOGRAPHY

Marx, Engels, Lenin, and Trotsky

Engels, Friedrich. *The Condition of the Working Class in England*. Ed. and trans. W. O. Henderson and W. H. Chaloner. Stanford: Stanford UP, 1968.

Lenin, V. I. *On Literature and Art*. Moscow: Progress, 1967.

Marx, Karl. *Selected Writings*. Ed. David McLellan. Oxford: Oxford UP, 1977.

Trotsky, Leon. *Literature and Revolution*. New York: Russell, 1967.

General Introductions to and Reflections on Marxist Criticism

Bennett, Tony. *Formalism and Marxism*. London: Methuen, 1979.

Demetz, Peter. *Marx, Engels, and the Poets*. Chicago: U of Chicago P, 1967.

Eagleton, Terry. *Literary Theory: An Introduction*. Minneapolis: U of Minnesota P, 1983.

———. *Marxism and Literary Criticism*. Berkeley: U of California P, 1976.

Elster, Jon. *An Introduction to Karl Marx*. Cambridge: Cambridge UP, 1985.

———. *Nuts and Bolts for the Social Sciences*. Cambridge: Cambridge UP, 1989.

Fokkema, D. W., and Elrud Kunne-Ibsch. *Theories of Literature in the Twentieth Century: Structuralism, Marxism, Aesthetics of Reception, Semiotics*. New York: St. Martin's, 1977. See ch. 4, "Marxist Theories of Literature."

Frow, John. *Marxism and Literary History*. Cambridge: Harvard UP, 1986.

Jefferson, Ann, and David Robey. *Modern Literary Theory: A Critical Introduction.* Totowa: Barnes, 1982. See the essay "Marxist Literary Theories," by David Forgacs.

Laing, Dave. *The Marxist Theory of Art.* Brighton: Harvester, 1978.

Selden, Raman. *A Readers' Guide to Contemporary Literary Theory.* Lexington: U of Kentucky P, 1985. See ch. 2, "Marxist Theories."

Slaughter, Cliff. *Marxism, Ideology, and Literature.* Atlantic Highlands: Humanities, 1980.

Some Classic Marxist Studies and Statements

Adorno, Théodor. *Prisms: Cultural Criticism and Society.* Trans. Samuel Weber and Sherry Weber. Cambridge: MIT P, 1982.

Althusser, Louis. *For Marx.* Trans. Ben Brewster. New York: Pantheon, 1969.

Althusser, Louis, and Étienne Balibar. *Reading Capital.* Trans. Ben Brewster. New York: Pantheon, 1971.

Bakhtin, Mikhail. *The Dialogic Imagination: Four Essays.* Ed. Michael Holquist. Trans. Caryl Emerson. Austin: U of Texas P, 1981.

———. *Rabelais and His World.* Trans. Hélène Iswolsky. Cambridge: MIT P, 1968.

Benjamin, Walter. *Illuminations.* Ed. with introd. by Hannah Arendt. Trans. H. Zohn. New York: Harcourt, 1968.

Caudwell, Christopher. *Illusion and Reality.* 1935. New York: Russell, 1955.

———. *Studies in a Dying Culture.* London: Lawrence, 1938.

Goldmann, Lucien. *The Hidden God.* New York: Humanities, 1964.

———. *Towards a Sociology of the Novel.* London: Tavistock, 1975.

Gramsci, Antonio. *Selections from the Prison Notebooks.* Ed. Quintin Hoare and Geoffrey Nowell Smith. New York: International UP, 1971.

Kettle, Arnold. *An Introduction to the English Novel.* New York: Harper, 1960.

Lukács, Georg. *The Historical Novel.* Trans. H. Mitchell and S. Mitchell. Boston: Beacon, 1963.

———. *Studies in European Realism.* New York: Grosset, 1964.

———. *The Theory of the Novel.* Cambridge: MIT P, 1971.

Marcuse, Herbert. *One-Dimensional Man.* Boston: Beacon, 1964.

Thompson, E. P. *The Making of the English Working Class.* New York: Pantheon, 1964.

————. *William Morris: Romantic to Revolutionary.* New York: Pantheon, 1977.

Williams, Raymond. *Culture and Society 1780–1950.* New York: Harper, 1958.

————. *The Long Revolution.* New York: Columbia UP, 1961.

————. *Marxism and Literature.* Oxford: Oxford UP, 1977.

Wilson, Edmund. *To the Finland Station.* Garden City: Doubleday, 1953.

Studies by and of Post-Althusserian Marxists

Dowling, William C. *Jameson, Althusser, Marx: An Introduction to "The Political Unconscious."* Ithaca: Cornell UP, 1984.

Eagleton, Terry. *Criticism and Ideology: A Study in Marxist Literary Theory.* London: Verso, 1978.

————. *Exiles and Émigrés.* New York: Schocken, 1970.

Goux, Jean-Joseph. *Symbolic Economies after Marx and Freud.* Trans. Jennifer Gage. Ithaca: Cornell UP, 1990.

Jameson, Fredric. *Marxism and Form: Twentieth-Century Dialectical Theories of Literature.* Princeton: Princeton UP, 1971.

————. *The Political Unconscious: Narrative as a Socially Symbolic Act.* Ithaca: Cornell UP, 1981.

Macherey, Pierre. *A Theory of Literary Production.* Trans. G. Wall. London: Routledge, 1978.

Other Marxist Approaches to the "Rime"

Keane, Patrick J. *Coleridge's Submerged Politics: The Ancient Mariner and Robinson Crusoe.* Columbia: U of Missouri P, 1994.

Kitson, Peter. "Coleridge, the French Revolution, and 'The Ancient Mariner': Collective Guilt and Individual Salvation." *Yearbook of English Studies* 19 (1989): 197–207.

Rubinstein, Chris. "A New Identity for the Mariner? A Further Exploration of 'The Rime of the Ancient Mariner.'" *The Coleridge Bulletin* 2 (1990): 16–29.

Watkins, Daniel P. "History as Demon in Coleridge's *The Rime of the Ancient Mariner.*" *Papers on Language and Literature* 24 (1988): 23–33.

DAVID SIMPSON

How Marxism Reads
"The Rime of the Ancient Mariner"

What might Karl Marx have made of Coleridge's most famous poem? Probably not much. Although he was uncommonly well read and obviously a lover of literature, Marx spent little time on literary criticism.[1] He makes reference to Shakespeare, Goethe, Aeschylus, and others when it suits his purpose, either for a telling illustration or a brief acknowledgment of literature's capacity for embodying social-historical energies. Thus "Timon of Athens" gives us insights into the nature of money, and *Robinson Crusoe* displays the personality of bourgeois-economic man (Marx 135–36, 318–19). Marx admired Heine and Shelley, saw some good in Byron, and advised Lassalle against making his characters mere "mouthpieces of the spirit of the age" (100). But the sphere of culture, and of literature in particular, was not a priority for Marx and Engels. According to Paul Lafargue, Marx intended to write at least an extended review of Balzac's novels (Marx 439). But he never did so. Only a creative adaptation of the major preoccupations of the writings of Marx and Engels has given us a Marxist literary criticism.

Furthermore, many have resisted the notion that a Marxist approach could make any sense at all of poetry, a genre habitually felt to consist of the most complex and refined language formed into the most intricate patterns and structures. To put Marxism and poetry together is to go against the grain of a long tradition positioning poetry as an alternative or antithesis to what Adorno called the "bustle and commotion" of sociological and historical analysis (1:37). Most readers unfamiliar with the complicated founding texts of the Marxist tradition, let alone with its even more complicated twentieth-century developments, tend to assume that Marxist literary criticism is all about sorting out politically acceptable books from politically unacceptable books, and disposing confident judgments about which works of literature present the workers in the proper light, or advance the cause of world revolution. This does reflect some of the polemical, illustrative literary references of Marx himself, but it is far from doing justice to the various efforts at fashioning a method or theory from the raw materials of Marxist analysis. Indeed, with the exception of some major studies by

---

[1]See S. S. Prawer, *Karl Marx and World Literature* (New York: Oxford UP, 1978).

Plekhanov, Bakhtin, and Trotsky, some fertile comments by Engels, and some important short essays by Lenin and Mao Tse Tung — many of these themselves far from tendentious — the most sustained and elaborate efforts at Marxist literary criticism have come with the movement called Western Marxism, that is, from within the capitalist world in the twentieth century and in response to a general if not absolute conviction that the impulse toward world revolution has slowed down if not stalled.[2]

Critics writing within the orbit of this Western Marxism, including such major figures as Lukács, Benjamin, Adorno, Della Volpe, Sartre, and Macherey, have not entirely given up on the idea that literature might stimulate or display the need for an incumbent socialism in political life; but the historical materialism governing their analysis has often been accompanied by a melancholy sense of the complicity of imaginative writing with the traditional vested interests of the world in which it has appeared. Marxist literary criticism has thus spent much of its effort on specifying the balance of revolutionary and reactionary elements in a given author or literary work, and its critical vocabulary is correspondingly complex. *Class, economy,* and *mode of production* indicate mechanisms of causality; *reification* and *alienation* signify consequences or effects; *ideology* and *mediation* refer to processes by which these results are brought about. Given the foundationally troubled or skeptical identity of the Western Marxist tradition, it is no surprise that there is to be found there very little of the tendentious and judgmental "Marxist" criticism that figures so prominently in the alarmed imaginations of Cold War liberals and conservatives. Such work can be found in the 1930s and (to a lesser degree) in the 1950s, but it is not typical of Marxist literary criticism at its best. And, at its worst, such criticism merely performs the same simplifications as does most other bad criticism.

Nonetheless, and despite this effusion of what I am claiming to be good Marxist literary criticism, there remains a visible recalcitrance about the historical-political interpretation of poetry. The most influential Marxist accounts of literature have been directed at the novel and the drama, which have been mythologized as self-evidently within some or other public sphere, and as committed to "the people" in a way that poetry, with its mostly specialized and private readership, is not. Bakhtin, one of the most influential Marxist critics in recent years,

[2]See Perry Anderson, *Considerations on Western Marxism* (London: New Left Books, 1976).

regarded the novel as the "leading hero in the drama of literary development in our time" because it "best of all reflects the tendencies of a new world still in the making" (7). Poetry has been felt to matter to Marxism when it is epic, oral or folk poetry, but not so much when it is offered for restricted circulation. Among the great critics, only Benjamin has set about the criticism of poetry in a major way, in his study of Baudelaire. But his work was unfinished, and was held by Adorno among others to be but dubious in its Marxist credentials as judged by its refusal or inability to produce grand narratives and theoretical totalities out of its local intuitions and conjunctions.[3]

How daunting it must seem, then, to project a Marxist account of *Romantic* poetry, already periodized in the popular literary consciousness as a poetry of private vision and feeling. Under the stern gaze of historical accountability that is the conventional mien of Marxist analysis, this poetry must all too often seem compensatory, self-deceiving and hopelessly alienated, not so much a response to social crisis as an avoidance of its implications. Recent leftist criticism has not dealt kindly with the humanitarian or activist claims of Wordsworth and Coleridge, even if Shelley and Blake have come off a bit more favorably.[4] We are going through a period in which most of the canonized writers of the past are being redefined as less worthy than they have seemed before, partly because of a shift in our own present concerns (feminism, multiculturalism, globalism), one that makes much of the past necessarily limited or blind, and partly because of an increased awareness of the failures of writing and teaching themselves as means to improve the social and political orders we inhabit. For these reasons among others we now tend to look critically upon the radical claims and aspirations of our literary forerunners (especially the males among them), and to find in literary history a long narrative of the cooperation of creative imagination with the reigning powers and interests.

What goals should Marxist criticism now set itself in the light of these constraints? Should it seek to become a comprehensive method, a protoscientific scheme aiming to explain everything, or should it remain a polemical, occasionalist rhetoric, meeting the needs of particular moments, as it so often was for Marx himself? The question is not a

---

[3]Adorno's comments and Benjamin's responses can be found in Ernst Bloch, George Lukács, Bertolt Brecht, Walter Benjamin, Theodor Adorno, *Aesthetics and Politics* (London: New Left Books, 1977).
    [4]The exemplary argument of recent years against a radical Romanticism is Jerome J. McGann, *The Romantic Ideology: A Critical Investigation* (Chicago: U of Chicago P, 1983).

trivial one, since the effort at comprehension must be understood as significantly conditioned by the demands of the academy and the traditions of Hegelian philosophy, while the embrace of contingency can also be validated by the more recent "postmodern" disapproval of grand theory in all its forms.[5] My argument is that good Marxist criticism will seek to achieve both historical and presentist goals, and will thereby propose that the history of a poem is made up both of conditions that continue to pertain to the modern condition and of those which do not. Neither is more valuable than the other, since the effort at historical understanding is itself of value for present orientation. Such criticism will make a commitment to historical recovery in the fullest and most exhaustive sense, because it is only to the degree that it is a historical discipline that Marxist criticism can be taken seriously in any address it might then go on to make to the world we now occupy. This historical recovery will of course be premised on an acceptance of incompletion, since total recall or reliving of the past is the promise made only by fiction itself or by necromancy. But the recognition of incompletion should be an incentive to more history rather than a closing off of inquiry, as it has so often been for the new historicism in its presentation of small (if vividly drawn) slices of vanished lives and in its reluctance to propose large historical explanations. Marxist criticism, conversely, must keep alive its ambition toward totalization and grand narrative — the very things most discredited in our postmodern ethos — even as it admits the difficulty and inadequacy of so many of its own findings. It must continue to aim toward a "big picture" analysis of the past — how things fitted together into patterns and even wholes — in the face of a contemporary culture that deems such ambitions either impossible or immoral. It looks to poetry as "a philosophical sundial telling the time of history" and the history for which it searches is that of an "entirety" (Adorno 46, 39). As such, Marxist criticism remains antagonistic to the way of our world, even when it is obliged to suspend any clear assurance of the desired social and political effects to be had from such antagonism.

What then does this mean for our reading of "The Ancient Mariner"? First, it is important to register the degree to which, like many Romantic poems, this is one that puts its address to "history" in a

---

[5]The exemplary rehearsal of these options is in the work of Fredric Jameson: see, especially, *The Political Unconscious: Narrative as a Socially Symbolic Act* (Ithaca: Cornell P, 1981); *Late Marxism: Adorno, or, the Persistence of the Dialectic* (New York: Verso, 1990); and *Postmodernism: or, the Cultural Logic of Late Capitalism* (Durham: Duke UP, 1991).

framing narrative foregrounding the act of telling the story itself. Part
of the history in the poem is the history of subjectivity. The old sailor
who "stoppeth one of three" (1.2) on the way to the wedding feast is a
proxy of the poet himself. As such, he expresses Coleridge's desire that
he too might have the power of commanding involuntary response —
for the Wedding Guest has no choice — at the same time representing
the obsessive late-eighteenth-century interest in hypnotism or, as it was
then called, animal magnetism.[6] This framing narrative of Mariner and
Wedding Guest is brilliantly oxymoronic. It expresses at once the desire
for hypnotic power on the poet's part, and also the fear of such power
on the part of the hearer or reader. To the degree that the Wedding
Guest takes on the Mariner's burden of thought, in a sort of compulsive
repetition that mirrors the Mariner's own irresistible urge to tell, he
has been captured by the spell of poetry, as we readers are in turn open
to capture. Coleridge wrote at a time when poets and writers were
especially anxious about questions of meaning and interpretation, and
about the writer's relation to his or her public. In "The Ancient
Mariner" he has fashioned a poem in which hypnotic authority commands attention and recreates for its hearer/reader exactly the dilemmas experienced by its protagonist. We take on the burden of trying to
fathom the morals and the meanings of the Mariner's adventure, but
also of its narration. Imaginatively we become both the teller and the
tale. Within the fiction that is the poem, we cannot know whether the
old man is telling a true story or experiencing some sort of hallucina-
tion. Coleridge described his purpose in the poem as the creation of
"characters supernatural, or at least romantic" that might stimulate the
"willing suspension of disbelief for the moment, which constitutes
poetic faith" (*Biographia* 2:6). The reader who chooses to read on
reads of the Wedding Guest's lack of free will. The foundational Protestant paradigms of choice, election, and damnation are written into the
framing narrative as well as the "story" of the poem. Coleridge has situated the urgent and for him "present" question about the writer's relation to his public in the (then) enduring contexts of theological and
epistemological consensus: (How) can one person's acts implicate
another, (how) can one person know what another knows? The Marxist
discussion of *alienation* has much to offer for an extended reading of
this component of Coleridge's poem.

[6]See Lane Cooper, "The Power of the Eye in Coleridge," *Late Harvest* (Ithaca: Cornell UP, 1962) 65–95.

The poem does not then offer itself as a conventional voyage narrative, but as a "supernatural" or "romantic" variation upon the genre of voyage narratives. The framing of the act of telling in such a dramatic and coercive way means that the details of the voyage, which would conventionally be thought of as the place where *history* comes into the poem, are presented by way of an already historical situation for subjectivity itself, conceived formally and abstractly. The Romantic poets were constantly concerned with whether or how one might tell the difference between what is "in" the world and what is imagined or projected. Coleridge presents the two together, and thus asks a radical question about how we are to receive the voyage narrative: did it happen this way? Was it a dream? Is the old man telling lies to hide some ghoulish crime, so that what he confesses to is but a screen for some other unspeakable deed? Is the old sailor simply mad? (How would you feel if someone popped out of the bushes and regaled you with this tale?) Romantic aesthetics loved to play with these questions, but not just for the fun of it. A Marxist account of this concern would include attention to the unstable relations between writers and readers in an increasingly free market for literary work, as well as to the long durational instability of subjectivity and personal identity in the philosophies of modernity at large, themselves evolving in an effort to describe a democratic-liberal social order in which the credibility of each person depended (as it often still does) upon an ability to convince others. Many of the social subgroups and convenient fictions employed to soften the force of these questions — the nation, the family, the profession, the religious community — were themselves in crisis as a result of the events surrounding and following the French Revolution. Commonplace as these explanations have become, it remains the task of Marxist criticism to make some detailed sense of these general conditions in relation to the specific thematic, formal, and semantic operations of literature. The Wedding Guest is plucked out of a ritual intended to celebrate the origins of a new family and the continuation of a traditional domestic order. He is compelled in imagination to roam the open seas in a world without women and without reliable social relations (for the crew is fickle) or clear moral guidance (for the Christian motifs in the poem intersect with all sorts of other supernatural energies). And having done so, he will never be the same again. The world has become more mysterious and more threatening, an environment that puts under pressure the homiletic or proverbial rules of operation ("He prayeth best, who loveth best" [l.618]) to which one turns for guidance. The poem registers, both in its framing narrative and in its narrated adventures, an acute version of what Marxists have called *alienation,* a separation of self from others, from the labor process, and from a comfortable relation to the world of things. The *work* of running a ship is completely effaced, and the Mariner's body is entirely a vehicle for metaphysical experience, itself confusing and unresolved.

The genre in which this kind of suspension of confident belief was being enacted in the late eighteenth century was, most commonly, the Gothic, which often functioned as an anti-Catholic rhetoric wherein the manipulation of and indulgence in superstition could be enjoyed exactly to the degree that it was positioned as the property of "them" and not "us." Often the invitation to experience the Gothic was held in check by a tendency to satire, and by a regular reminder of the literariness of it all, as if our English-language authors were not quite comfortable with the things by which they were also fascinated. Often, that is to say, the literary experience of the exotic, demonic, or perverted left one with a firm place to stand at the end of it all. Despite Coleridge's visible association with this Gothic pastiche — the Mariner is clearly a Catholic — the place to stand is what is finally refused in his poem. The domestic site has been unforgettably marked by the presence of the returned and traumatized sailor, and it will never be the same again. What happened far away has come home.

Let us then look to the voyage narrative itself to see what elements of "history" can be traced there. Fortunately, much if not most of the source-work for this poem has been excavated by John Livingston Lowes in his monumental *The Road to Xanadu,* first published in 1927. Lowes proved conclusively, I think, that the poem is a collage of hundreds of items and fragments in Coleridge's reading experiences — for at the time of composition he had never even been to sea — organized associationally into narrative. The poem, in other words, is not about a conventional "experience," and thus cannot be simply hooked into a straightforward realist exegesis whereby we can test out what we think really "happened" against what is described in the poem (as we can, for instance, with some of Wordsworth's poems, by reference to Dorothy Wordsworth's journals and other such records of events and encounters). The poem is fashioned from Coleridge's identity as a "library-cormorant" (*Collected Letters* 1:156), and is the product of his compulsive gathering up of interesting extracts. The history that Coleridge registers is a compendium of various voyage narratives: Purchas, Dampier, Shelvocke, Cook, Barents, and many others. It is just as eclectic in its literary borrowings and assimilations, for it draws, as Lowes has shown, on the whole ballad tradition from Chaucer to Bürger. What emerges is a coherent narrative, but the coherence is imaginative and derivative; it does not depend upon the raw material of a personal or personally witnessed experience. And it is not thematically exclusive enough to produce clear and conventional meaning.

This makes it difficult to assess the place of what we conventionally call "history" — real people in real places — in the poem. But the effort must be made, and indeed is worth making. Pierre Macherey has proposed that although the work of art is "precisely determined at every moment and at every level," the process of literary language is one that "distorts rather than imitates" (39, 61). Literature reflects history but also refigures it, to the point that much of what determines the work is not referenced at all, but only appears in the form of its silences, in what is not mentioned. Expression and repression occur together. No port of origin is specified in Coleridge's poem: we have just a church, a hill, and a lighthouse. It is clear that the ship sails around Cape Horn and up into the Pacific, even though the Mariner himself is not geographically literate enough to put things in these terms. Why does Coleridge (in the 1798 poem) make us work out where the ship is going by deduction from the Mariner's reports of where the sun rises and sets? Why does he blur the rather simple geography? Various answers are possible, and no one excludes the others. Clearly, it is part of the hypnotic effect that we be arrested at the point of immediate perception rather than guided comfortably through the experience by a detached, third-person narration (though this is one of the major shifts of emphasis produced by the marginal glosses added in 1817).

Coleridge also declines to specify what kind of a ship this is, and what kind of voyage it is on. Especially, we do not know if the voyage has a military, commercial, or scientific purpose — and all three were common at the time. The distinctions were not clear; naval ships were able to operate almost as privateers as well as taking on scientific tasks, and scientific expeditions had obvious military and commercial associations. Britain was explicitly or implicitly at war with France for most of the 1790s, and any British ship would have been deemed capable of military functions of one sort or another. One might suppose that Coleridge is somehow repressing the place of contemporary national events, or alluding implicitly to the matter of criminality and remorse as it had arisen around the execution of Louis XVI and the career of Robespierre (with which he and many others were fascinated), or seeking to put the question at a quite different level, in terms of ultimate guilt, innocence, and responsibility. One tradition, which began with

Southey's 1798 poem "The Sailor, who had served in the Slave Trade," interprets the historical emptiness of the voyage narrative as an allusion to or confession of complicity with the slave trade, a "fact" of which the Mariner cannot speak but that his voyage replicates.[7] Reference to the transportation of convicted persons to Australia may also be interpolated, and a silent allusion to the story of *The Bounty* is also plausible. Fletcher Christian was personally known to the Wordsworth-Coleridge circle, and the story of the mutiny was headline news in the early 1790s.[8] Another critic cogently associates the same emptiness of reference with Coleridge's massive disappointment at the utopian prospects generated and then destroyed by the violence of revolution (McKusick).

Most generally, it might be that the silence and emptiness of the southern seas traversed by the Mariner and his ship (a ship with no rank or hierarchy at a time when ships were *all* rank and hierarchy), serves as an eerie prefiguring of the mentality of international trade and global capital that governs us today, a poetic formalization of the attitude that sees only spaces for penetration rather than previously occupied territories. There are no people in the southern ocean as it is figured in the poem, and there is no reference to the countercultural utopias (sexual, political, economic) that various eighteenth-century voyagers had imaged in Tahiti and other such places. The Mariner is spared the ethical challenge of encounter with other human societies, who are replaced here by a bird and a ghost ship. It is as if the Mariner's story is the headline, and the surrounding world simply a backdrop. In this sense the poem may be proposed as a forerunner of a contemporary media culture in which "human drama" is enacted in exotic places with no worked out or implied relation to the dynamics of the anglophone subject.

All of these determinations may function as contributory explanations for Coleridge's decision to locate so much of the poem in the liminal spaces of the known world, and to make them even more mysterious by way of the sensationalist immediacy of the Mariner's narration. The mystery itself speaks for a "history." By about 1800 most of the known world had been explored and mapped: Cook's voyages around *Terra Australis Incognita* left it, too, finally open to settlement

---

[7]See Malcolm Ware, "Coleridge's 'Spectre-Bark': A Slave Ship?," *Philological Quarterly* 40 (1961): 589–93; William Empson, "The Ancient Mariner," *Critical Quarterly* 6 (1964): 298–319; J. R. Ebbatson, "Coleridge's Mariner and the Rights of Man," *Studies in Romanticism* 11 (1972): 171–206.

[8]See Charles S. Wilkinson, *The Wake of the Bounty* (London: Cassell, 1953); and Greg Dening, *Mr. Bligh's Bad Language: Passion, Power and Theatre on The Bounty* (Cambridge: Cambridge UP, 1992) 310 ff.

and development, and the first fleet set out for Australia in 1787. If the Enlightenment project was to know rationally all that could be known, then Coleridge's poem seems to stand in rebuke of an instrumental reason that would reduce all mysteries to rod and line. That ambition extended also to religion, so that it is not for nothing that Coleridge puts back into play not only a recognizable Christianity but also a whole litany of daemonic powers and principles excluded or suppressed by the Church of England, the embodiment of national religion. The archaic language of the 1798 poem, and the still anachronistic glosses of the 1817 poem (pitched somewhere in the diction and sources of the seventeenth century), enforce an impression of deliberate pastness behind and within an Enlightenment culture whose emphasis is upon a rational and progressive present and future. The poem, if you like, is an albatross around the neck of modernization, and one that cannot or should not, perhaps, be shaken off. The poem refutes the rationalist cartography that made Cook's voyages possible, as it also complicates any ambition we might have to devise a rationalist theory of the emotions, or of crime and punishment (of the sort that Bentham was setting out to deduce). The social isolation and abstract personality of the old Mariner seem to parody the Enlightenment ideal whereby we should become citizens of the world (an ideal resurrected by communism). He has indeed transcended local custom and narrow vision and come to embody some sort of general human nature, but that nature brings with it a loss of community instead of an integration into benign cosmopolitanism and brotherhood. Such compulsory internationalism is neither desired nor enjoyed.

If the Enlightenment project was one of demystification then Coleridge might be said to be in the business of remystification. This turning to the past was mocked by Peacock in *The Four Ages of Poetry* (1820) as "a modern-antique compound of frippery and barbarism" producing only a "heterogeneous congeries of unamalgamating manners" (476). This captures exactly the uneasiness and indecisiveness of tone and reference that marks "The Ancient Mariner." For Coleridge's Gothicism brings no comfort, and contributes to no project of national-Protestant consolidation. The Mariner's return to his "own countrée" is not an act of reintegration into an intact local community, but a further exacerbation of his isolation and his inability to live in his actual place and time. Coleridge tells us that dim sympathies should matter as much as clear accounts, that love matters more than reason, that cause and effect cannot be plotted accurately enough to guide us through life according to simple epistemological principles, but such homilies are cold comfort to his protagonist and to the reader haunted by him. In this sense the poem's refutation of Enlightenment rationalism is itself incomplete and hesitant: the traumatic state of storyteller and listener projects a need or desire for a world free from such mysteries (anticipating the trajectory of modern psychoanalysis) at the very moment that remystification seems to be the poem's primary agenda. "The Ancient Mariner" is not so much for or against Enlightenment as it is revelatory of the ambivalence that makes implausible any simple definition of this historical moment as one of pure enlightening. Neither the rationalist project nor its theological antagonist are here vindicated. We are presented with an indecisive to-ing and fro-ing (an existentially loaded version of the "free play" of the imagination) between the two.

The poem also addresses what we would now call an "ecological" question, one pertaining to the relation between humankind and other species. The Albatross is rarely seen by man, and had presumably never been seen before by the Ancient Mariner. Keith Thomas has written well on the cultural shift whereby, within fifty years of the poem's first appearance in 1798, Britain produced a spate of bills forbidding cruelty to various animals (149). The whimsical and unexplained cruelty typified by the Mariner's act was no longer deemed acceptable to the common mind, and gave way to a new interest in exploring the similarities binding man and nature, and to a new need to define which animals deserved humane treatment and which might remain exempt from it. The Mariner and the crew, in their incompatible and changing estimates of what the bird portends, function very much as representatives of an amoral and incoherent folk culture. The final commendation of an ethic of love replaces this sequence of folk superstitions by recognizing a higher and consistent order, true for all times and places. As Blake had put it: "every thing that lives is Holy" (45). In its rebuke of irrational violence and opportunistic justifications, the poem is engaging with nothing less than the theology of the fall of man, but it does so within a specific historical moment that inaugurates the familiar present-day connection between the ecological consciousness and the critique of the Enlightenment in its attributed relation to destructive technologies.

At this point it might seem that we have come a long way from the avowed priorities of Marxist criticism. But the kinds of historical coordinates I have been describing — and there are surely others — are of exactly the sort that must be gathered into a Marxist reading in its effort at totalization, exhaustive documentation, and inclusive theorization. There will be no final verdict, not least because the present situation within which all verdicts are returned is itself constantly changing. As Sartre puts it: "the supreme paradox of historical materialism is that it is, at one and the same time, the only truth of History and a total *indetermination* of the Truth" (19). Marxist critics have privileged various items in the Marxist roster as the primary determinants of literary expression. Most famously there is the economy, proposed as the "base" upon which the "superstructure" or art must be fashioned. But Marx's adumbration of this famous model, in the preface to his 1859 *Contribution to the Critique of Political Economy*, offers a very inclusive and flexible understanding of what "economy" means. Modes of production are at once social and material, each in and through the other, and they affect the entire development of life and culture, not just the sphere of art. Indeed, perhaps only by the most complex mediations do they determine the words on the page of a book of poetry. Thus the "economic" determination pertaining to "The Ancient Mariner" includes not only the authors' and publisher's calculations about the market for *Lyrical Ballads* (hypotheses or intuitions about consumption), but also the entire social and material field in which and through which such speculations took place.

One begins with the basics, the immediate conditions informing composition and publication. *Lyrical Ballads* was not just (if it was ever) a conscious and confident effort at redirecting the course of British poetry. It was a contribution to a literary marketplace in which ballads were almost surefire investments.[9] Percy, Burns, Macpherson, Chatterton, Bürger, and others had created and contributed to a market for archaic and folkloric verses, and Wordsworth and Coleridge were hoping to tap the same source. Coleridge imitates the traditional ballad stanza (quatrains of alternating three and four stress lines rhyming ABAB) but varies both stanza and rhyme scheme when it suits him, thus signaling both traditionalism and originality (another commodity in the literary marketplace). The eclectic diction, varying as it does between and among biblical, Scots (kirk, lavrock, cauld), and generally "medieval," signals both Coleridge's allegiance to the ballad tradition (wherein the Christian is often in tension with the pagan supernatural) and also his inability to reproduce it as other than pastiche. The historical identity of the poetic persona, and indeed its alienation from simple social affiliation, can be read in the form and matter

---

[9]See Robert Mayo, "The Contemporaneity of the *Lyrical Ballads*," *PMLA* 69 (1954): 486–522; and John E. Jordan, *Why the "Lyrical Ballads"?* (Berkeley: U of California P, 1976).

of the poem's local features. This identity is not simple, so that readers should be very cautious about employing the popular (Marxist and or not) term *ideology* in describing this poem. Coleridge does indeed have a view of the world that is the result of his particular connections with a variety of specific social groups: radical Christians, male scholars, anti-Gallicans, and so on. And none of these excludes a mediated relation to larger interests (a ruling class), even as none of them is on its own a simple facsimile or incarnation of such interests. The economic base, class, and ideology are interactive principles each requiring definition by way of the others. This is not to refute the strong economistic message of *Capital* so much as to insist on the recognition that what *Capital* described is not an ahistorical, autonomous mechanism true for all time but a particular moment in the evolution (and projected future of) the European (and especially British) factory economy. That this moment was not at all fully developed in 1798 makes the analysis of Coleridge a task for which we do not have the prospect of any simple application (as if there could ever be such) of Marx's major work.

But it does not make the analysis arbitrary. A Marxist reading, as I have said before, will want to make claims for its historical integrity as well as for a largeness-tending-toward-wholeness of the history that ensues. The wholeness is never complete, partly because we can never know everything about anything (the prospect indeed sits better with Borgesian fantasy than with the life of the literary critic) but also, as I have suggested, because the "we" who are conducting the inquiry are ourselves part of an ever-changing world, and are driven to notice and search for new things because of the demands of our own experience of the world. The same intuition might well have driven Coleridge to the extensive rewriting of his own poem. There are many insights into this process among Marxist theorists, and it has raised difficult questions for their attempts at telling things exactly "as they were." In his "Theses on the Philosophy of History" Walter Benjamin proposes that there would be no point in looking to the past if it were not for some motivating concern in the present. History is made by "the presence of the now" (261). It is not the disinterested accumulation of facts for their own sakes, but the result of an "experience" based on "a constructive principle" (262). Marxist criticism is often caught between an effort to make the past relevant to the present and a parallel effort at showing how it really was, even when seemingly irrelevant to the present. The first ambition responds to the forward-looking, socially activist component of Marxist thought, its belief in the possibility of a better world, and its hope of contributing to it. Pursuing this case we might, for example, speak of the traumas of alienated labor evident at all levels in "The Ancient Mariner," and its implicit recommendation of some kind of socialist economy and community: the crew of the Mariner's ship display neither common interests nor common affections. These syndromes are still with us and they are thus part of the poem's ongoing contemporaneity. The second ambition, that of describing the past in its own terms, emerges from the more traditional historical effort at showing the disposition of human relations in the past, both as they anticipate and differ from our own. Here the effort is to get it right, to produce a detailed description of Coleridge's world and the poem's message to it. The Marxist critic, unless he or she is a radical presentist willing to abandon all attention to the past in its own terms, will still hold a fairly conventional effort at historical understanding, at putting aside present preoccupations in hopes of coming back to them in a more informed state of mind.

This project is important not just because it gives Marxism a recognizable credibility in the traditional academy, or because it can ultimately sustain a more satisfying explanation of the present, but also because it is our best hope of resisting the blandishments of our own ideologies and our own complicities with the contemporary ruling class. Attention to the past produces recognitions that can be either merely projected or critically described. The play between the two is one of the things we learn from such attention. The pursuit of historical information is confusing, and it is in that confusion that we can find a means of *not* simply reading the past as a projection of the present. In this situation the seemingly irrelevant fact or item becomes valuable precisely because we cannot at once see what if anything it means. The most persuasive readings of history are always going to be those that put together a present preoccupation with a pattern in the past; but what is uninterpretable will, like a seed in the soil, provide the matter for meanings we cannot yet foresee.

Returning to Coleridge we can see that a sense of the shifting shape of the past is dramatically embodied in the textual evolution of "The Ancient Mariner." What began as a fairly straightforward poem in "olde" spelling became, by 1817, a modernized text with a historically distanced marginal gloss, a second narrative that sometimes clarifies, sometimes interprets, and arguably even confuses the Mariner's story.[10] Coleridge has thus written in the very model of interpretation of which

---

[10]Jack Stillinger, *Coleridge and Textual Instability: The Multiple Versions of the Major Poems* (New York: Oxford UP, 1994) 60–73, identifies no less than eighteen versions of the poem, though some are distinguished only by minor variations.

Benjamin speaks; he has distinguished the "experience" of 1817 from
that of 1798, reconstructing what has gone before according to present
motivations. The Latin epigraph and learned marginal references of the
1817 text seem to project a desire to appeal to a different sort of reader,
one less prone to be captured by the Gothic diction and paraphernalia
of the 1798 poem (which had, by the way, been one of the most frequent targets of the critics responding to *Lyrical Ballads*). This speaks
for a shift in the class identity of the imagined reader — and we must
stress the word *imagined*. Ballads were associated with (though not
limited to) the common or ordinary reader and with the spirit of the
folk, but this is hardly the tenor of the coauthored volume of 1798.
There is no suggestion of sung delivery (of the sort that Burns, for
example, encouraged), and if the poems are often *about* ordinary
people then they are less obviously *for* them. But there is nonetheless a
visible shift in the text of "The Ancient Mariner." The poem of 1817 is
unashamedly aimed at an educated mind.

Coleridge seems to have been consistently unsure of how to present
the poem, and unsure perhaps of what its appeal might be. In 1800 he
added the subtitle "A Poet's Reverie," which again attracted adverse
comment and was removed after 1805. The text was the object of both
constant tinkering and massive revision, making it a model of the past-
in-present conjunction specified by Benjamin as the process of writing
history. It is hard to be sure *which* poem Coleridge might have been
meaning when he made his famous remark to Mrs. Barbauld in 1830
about "the obtrusion of the moral sentiment so openly on the reader as
a principle or cause of action in a work of such pure imagination"
(*Table Talk* 2:100). At this time, thirty-two years after the first publication, he seems to have wanted the poem to be even more open to interpretation, or more subtle in its directives, than it had turned out to be.
Nor was the poem's fate simply the result of Coleridge's own choices
and preferences. Wordsworth was from the first at odds with the poem,
and moved it from the front of the 1798 volume to the middle of the
1800 volumes. Coleridge placed it fourth in his own volume of 1817,
Sibylline Leaves, as if to *almost* headline the poem after Wordsworth's
negative reshuffling. It seems as though "The Ancient Mariner" could
not appear twice in the same place or in the same way.

This textual instability mirrors the thematic openness of the poem,
which is of course the conventional attribute of good "literature" as we
have mostly defined it in the last three or four hundred years; it is what
traditionally distinguishes literature from philosophy or history. Literature is content to suggest where other disciplines seek to prove; that is

its approved task in the formation of modern cultural life and in the modern academy. Coleridge, then, is in a very basic way appealing to the market, as if he realized (though he probably did not) that indeterminacy would keep his readers satisfied when they were most hungry. Marx's famous but not very profound comment (in his *Introduction to the Critique of Political Economy*) on why we still enjoy Greek art and literature — because we feel nostalgia for the historical childhood of humanity — goes only part of the way toward explaining the appeal of the art of the past. Marx ignores the degree to which the aesthetic itself is premised on an indeterminate relation both to its own times and to the times inhabited by those who come after. The continued popular reputation of "The Ancient Mariner" and its availability for commonplace quotation (albatrosses, "water water, every where," etcetera) bear witness to its success within a pedagogic tradition requiring that poems be at least loosely moralizing but at the same time obscure enough to be available for continual rereading and discussion. It is as if the poem has itself become the very commodity whose transportation across the world is displaced from the voyage narrative. We do not know what the ship carried or what it sought — real slaves or real knowledge — but we happily consume the poem's memorable lines and images as the permanent gold standard of poetic excellence.

The critical-historical task is to understand this situation both then and now, and Coleridge seems to have understood it very well, if not with a conscious knowing. The indeterminacy he writes into the poem is not just a vulgar marketing ploy. Jerome McGann, following Elinor Shaffer's work, makes a very interesting case for the 1817 poem's participation in the Higher Criticism, a tradition of biblical exegesis wherein cumulative interpretation (of the sort that the glosses provide) is itself part of the truth to be revealed.[11] The various pre-Christian, Catholic, and Protestant motifs gathered into the poem thus become items for an "English national Scripture" (McGann 160), a totalizing accumulation through time that, ironically enough, instances Christianity's alternative version of the very same ambitions that Marxist doctrine would later embrace.

This might indeed be a description of what Coleridge had in mind by 1817. But it is not what he performed in 1798, nor does it completely describe the artifact of 1817. McGann convincingly interprets the major narrative but not the framing narrative, which seems to cast

---

[11]The place of the higher criticism in Romantic writing was first adumbrated in Elinor Shaffer, *"Kubla Khan" and the Fall of Jerusalem* (Cambridge: Cambridge UP, 1975).

into radical doubt the sufficiency of the higher critical analogue (or at least to make such doubt itself part of the its legacy). The large questions of right and wrong in relation to folk, Christian, and naturalist (or intuitive) ethics are floated in "The Ancient Mariner" but brought to a resolution that is only ever approximate, and thus haunting and compulsively repeated. That the Mariner and his hearer/reader are ultimately positioned as *alone* with the effort at moral intelligibility speaks for a loss of confidence in the consensual resolutions that churchgoing and orthodox faith (handed down by others) seem to offer, even if that is what the 1817 glosses were intended to provide. Engels famously remarked of Balzac that important messages came out "even in spite of the author's opinions" (Marx 91). Coleridge's efforts at making Christianity a viable address to the problems of modern life increased, if anything, with age. But the 1817 "Ancient Mariner" arguably comes no closer to satisfying this need than did Balzac, according to Engels, in his effort at producing a fictional legitimation of royalism and the conservative life in a historical climate that could not sustain such beliefs. One could say, for example, that the old sailor enacts a good-faith Christian conversion experience, or, alternatively, that his visibly Catholic affiliation marks him as out of step with the contemporary Protestant settlement; or that the clash between the two represents the settlement as less than settled (which was closer to the truth of things). If there is a God overseeing the narrative, then it is one who allows for apparently excessive punishments (the crew, the Pilot's boy) and for a range of supernatural agencies that seem to have little to do with a coherent theology.

To recreate, as Coleridge does, the dynamic of the early ballad's rehearsal of pagan-Christian alternatives is to propose the insufficiency of Christianity in coping with the great questions of human experience around 1800, as it is also to decompose Christianity itself into different and perhaps incommensurable primary elements. Coleridge's poem, in all its versions, reproduces more of alienation than of integration. But Coleridge does not produce this sensed alienation into a cult of "art for art's sake," despite his retrospective preference for the "pure imagination." In other words, even as the poem functions by a visible displacement of history conceived in social-realist terms, it does not give up on the quest for an urgent relation to history conceived in personal-interactive terms. One might say, furthermore, that the poem takes much of its energy from the effort at isolating the personal-interactive dimension *from* the social-real. This happens right at the start, when the likely readerly expectation that the old sailor is some sort of beggar (of the sort that populated the countryside at the time) is turned around by the way in which he commands rather than requests attention. And it continues right through the poem, where (as I have said already) the entire "social" and political fabric of the sea voyage is erased (or rather unimagined) in order to spotlight the Mariner's personal experience. There is no doubt that in some way the poem avoids its historical moment, one composed, for instance, of the recent (1797) mutinies in the naval bases at Spithead and the Nore, and by the daily cruelties of impressment on land and harsh discipline at sea, as well as of the geopolitical conditions I have previously sketched out. But in another way this avoidance is exactly the poem's "history"; instead of convicting Coleridge of some sort of moral failure in not being a good radical (whatever that was), we will find more out by historicizing his avoidance of certain kinds of historical reference.

Thus, in its silence about the contemporary realities of war, work, trade, and profit, the poem puts into suspension the regnant vocabulary of bourgeois optimism based on those very realities. Not for nothing does it begin with a disruption of the very social ritual, the wedding, that so often composes the end of literary narratives, where it signals the continuance of civic culture, sexual harmony, and economic growth. Coleridge's poem denies these consolations just as surely as do the adulteries and economic failures of nineteenth-century novels. The avoidance of expressed historical coordinates is not after all an avoidance of history. What should distinguish Marxist criticism from other sorts of historicism and historical research is, again, its commitment to an effort at totalization, at connecting up as many things (and meanings) as it can in an effort toward reconstructing a social-historical whole. The process must reckon with both short-durational history, in its references to naval events and national wars and displaced persons, and longer-durational history, of the sort that describes the general remystification of the world in reaction to a perceived excess of rationalism and modernization. This second, as I have suggested, is a process in which the institution of literature itself was (and remains) deeply involved. It must also include the sorts of cultural shifts such as that described by Keith Thomas as refiguring the relation between human and other species. What will keep emerging from this attention (for it is ongoing) is a complex interaction of personal, local, and general determinations within the poet's form and language, and with its literary history. Also ongoing is the question of why this matters to us, if it matters at all, and who is included within the "us." And for all the above reasons Marxist criticism must engage at all levels with what we call *theory,* as I have been doing throughout this essay, even as it admits that its reading practices can never complete themselves into immanent schemas. Such schemas are themselves nothing more than the commodified forms of intellectual inquiry, figments of an academy and a culture that would seek to separate out one school of thought, one "-ism," from another. Marxist criticism's openness, as I have described, is a refusal of this commodification; the risk it takes is that in this refusal it will become indistinguishable from criticism in general, which indeed it aspires to be. But it is in fact *more* open than many other criticisms in its refusal to conclude by invoking some or other transcendental standard, such as human nature or imagination or genius or experience. It recognizes all of these, and our current investment in them, as historical and variable, but without being simply arbitrary or relative. The study of literature in history and as past history produces describable and motivated variables, as does a consciousness of that same history and literature as in conjunction with "our" present. The findings of Marxist criticism are at once incomplete and definitive; that is to say, what is found must be retained and explained until it is superceded or proven wrong. In its determination to aim for the big picture without betraying the minute particulars, Marxist criticism is now as much as ever before, albeit in a more subdued voice, going against the grain, as Walter Benjamin insisted that it should.[12]

WORKS CITED

Adorno, Theodor W. "On Lyric Poetry and Society." *Notes to Literature*. Ed. Rolf Tiedemann. Trans. Shierry Weber Nicholsen. 2 vols. New York: Columbia UP, 1991–92.

Bakhtin, M. M. *The Dialogue Imagination: Four Essays*. Trans. Caryl Emerson and Michael Holquist. Austin: U of Texas P, 1981.

Benjamin, Walter. *Charles Baudelaire: A Lyric Poet in the Era of High Capitalism*. Trans. Harry Zohn. London: New Left, 1973.

———. "Theses on the Philosophy of History." *Illuminations*. Ed. Hannah Arendt. Trans. Harry Zohn. New York: Schocken, 1969. 253–64.

Blake, William. *The Complete Poetry and Prose of William Blake*. Ed. David V. Erdman. Berkeley: U of California P, 1982.

[12]This essay has been much improved by the responses and suggestions of audiences at the University of Colorado — Boulder, the University of California — Berkeley, and the University of Cambridge.

Bloch, Ernst, et al. *Aesthetics and Politics*. London: New Left, 1977.

Coleridge, Samuel Taylor. *Biographia Literaria*. Ed. James Engell and W. Jackson Bate. 2 vols. Princeton: Princeton UP, 1962.

———. *The Collected Letters of Samuel Taylor Coleridge*. Ed. Earl Leslie Griggs. Oxford: Clarendon, 1966.

———. *Table Talk*. Ed. Carl Woodring. 2 vols. Princeton: Princeton UP, 1990.

Dening, Greg. *Mr. Bligh's Bad Language: Passion, Power and Theatre on The Bounty*. Cambridge: Cambridge UP, 1992.

Lowes, John Livingston. *The Road to Xanadu: A Study in the Ways of the Imagination*. London: Constable, 1927.

Macherey, Pierre. *A Theory of Literary Production*. Trans. Geoffrey Wall. London: Routledge, 1978.

Marx, Karl, and Friedrich Engels. *Marx & Engels on Literature and Art*. Ed. Paul Lafargue. Moscow: Progress, 1976.

McGann, Jerome J. "The Ancient Mariner: The Meaning of the Meanings." *The Beauty of Inflections: Literary Investigations in Historical Method and Theory*. Oxford: Clarendon, 1988. 135–72.

McKusick, James C. " 'The Silent': Coleridge, Lee Boo, and the Exploration of the South Pacific." *The Wordsworth Circle* 24 (1993): 102–106.

Peacock, Thomas Love. "The Four Ages of Poetry." 1820. *The Norton Anthology of English Literature*. 6th ed. Ed. M. H. Abrams, et al. New York: Norton, 1993.

Sartre, Jean Paul. *Critique of Dialectical Reason. I: Theory of Practical Ensembles*. Ed. Jonathan Ree. Trans. Alan Sheridan-Smith. London: Verso, 1982.

Thomas, Keith. *Man in the Natural World: A History of the Modern Sensibility*. New York: Pantheon, 1983.

Wilkinson, Charles S. *The Wake of the Bounty*. London: Cassell, 1953.

The New Historicism and
"The Rime of the Ancient Mariner"

WHAT IS THE NEW HISTORICISM?

The title of Brook Thomas's *The New Historicism and Other Old-Fashioned Topics* (1991) is telling. Whenever an emergent theory, movement, method, approach, or group gets labeled with the adjective "new," trouble is bound to ensue, for what is new today is either established, old, or forgotten tomorrow. Few of you will have heard of the band called "The New Kids on the Block." New Age bookshops and jewelry may seem "old hat" by the time this introduction is published. The New Criticism, or formalism, is just about the oldest approach to literature and literary study currently being practiced. The new historicism, by contrast, is *not* as old-fashioned as formalism, but it is hardly new, either. The term "new" eventually and inevitably requires some explanation. In the case of the new historicism, the best explanation is historical.

Although a number of influential critics working between 1920 and 1950 wrote about literature from a psychoanalytic perspective, the majority took what might generally be referred to as the historical approach. With the advent of the New Criticism, however, historically oriented critics almost seemed to disappear from the face of the earth. The dominant New Critics, or formalists, tended to treat literary works as if they were self-contained, self-referential objects. Rather than basing their interpretations on parallels between the text and historical contexts (such as the author's life or stated intentions in writing the work), these critics concentrated on the relationships *within* the text that give it its form and meaning. During the heyday of the New Criticism, concern about the interplay between literature and history virtually disappeared from literary discourse. In its place was a concern about intratextual repetition, particularly of images or symbols but also of rhythms and sound effect.

About 1970 the New Criticism came under attack by reader-response critics (who believe that the meaning of a work is not inherent in its internal form but rather is cooperatively produced by the reader and the text) and poststructuralists (who, following the philosophy of Jacques Derrida, argue that texts are inevitably self-contradictory and that we can find form in them only by ignoring or suppressing conflicting details or elements). In retrospect it is clear that, their outspoken opposition to the New Criticism notwithstanding, the reader-response critics and poststructuralists of the 1970s were very much *like* their formalist predecessors in two important respects: for the most part, they ignored the world beyond the text and its reader, and, for the most part, they ignored the historical contexts within which literary works are written and read.

Jerome McGann first articulated this retrospective insight in 1985, writing that "a text-only approach has been so vigorously promoted during the last thirty-five years that most historical critics have been driven from the field, and have raised the flag of their surrender by yielding the title 'critic,' and accepting the title 'scholar' for themselves" (*Inflections* 17). Most, but not all. The American Marxist Fredric Jameson had begun his 1981 book *The Political Unconscious* with the following two-word challenge: "Always historicize!" (9). Beginning about 1980, a form of historical criticism practiced by Louis Montrose and Stephen Greenblatt had transformed the field of Renaissance studies and begun to influence the study of American and English Romantic literature as well. An by the mid-1980s, Brook Thomas was working on an essay in which he suggests that classroom discussions of Keats's "Ode on a Grecian Urn" might begin with questions such as the following: Where would Keats have seen such an urn? How did a Grecian urn end up in a museum in England? Some very important historical and political realities, Thomas suggests, lie behind and inform Keats's definitions of art, truth, beauty, the past, and timelessness.

When McGann lamented the surrender of "most historical critics," he no doubt realized what is now clear to everyone involved in the study of literature. Those who had *not* yet surrendered — had not yet "yield[ed] the title 'critic'" to the formalist, reader-response, and post-structuralist "victors" — were armed with powerful new arguments and intent on winning back long-lost ground. Indeed, at about the same time that McGann was deploring the near-complete dominance of critics advocating the text-only approach, Herbert Lindenberger was sounding a more hopeful note: "It comes as something of a surprise," he wrote in 1984, "to find that history is making a powerful comeback" ("New History" 16).

We now know that history was indeed making a powerful comeback in the 1980s, although the word is misleading if it causes us to imagine that the historical criticism being practiced in the 1980s by Greenblatt and Montrose, McGann and Thomas, was the same as the historical criticism that had been practiced in the 1930s and 1940s. Indeed, if the word "new" still serves any useful purpose in defining the historical criticism of today, it is in distinguishing it from the old historicism. The new historicism is informed by the poststructuralist and reader-response theory of the 1970s, plus the thinking of feminist, cultural, and Marxist critics whose work was also "new" in the 1980s. New historicist critics are less fact- and event-oriented than historical critics used to be, perhaps because they have come to wonder whether the truth about what really happened can ever be purely and objectively known. They are less likely to see history as linear and progressive, as something developing toward the present or the future ("teleological"), and they are also less likely to think of it in terms of specific eras, each with a definite, persistent, and consistent Zeitgeist ("spirit of the times"). Consequently, they are unlikely to suggest that a literary text has a single or easily identifiable historical context.

New historicist critics also tend to define the discipline of history more broadly than it was defined before the advent of formalism. They view history as a social science and the social sciences as being properly historical. In *Historical Studies and Literary Criticism* (1985), McGann speaks of the need to make "sociohistorical" subjects and methods central to literary studies; in *The Beauty of Inflections: Literary Investigations in Historical Method and Theory* (1985), he links sociology and the future of historical criticism. "A sociological poetics," he writes, "must be recognized not only as relevant to the analysis of poetry, but in fact as central to the analysis" (62). Lindenberger cites anthropology as particularly useful in the new historical analysis of literature, especially anthropology as practiced by Victor Turner and Clifford Geertz.

Geertz, who has related theatrical traditions in nineteenth-century Bali to forms of political organization that developed during the same period, has influenced some of the most important critics writing the new kind of historical criticism. Due in large part to Geertz's anthropological influence, new historicists such as Greenblatt have asserted that literature is not a sphere apart or distinct from the history that is relevant to it. That is what the old criticism tended to do: present the background information you needed to know before you could fully appreciate the separate world of art. The new historicists have used what Geertz would call "thick description" to blur distinctions, not only between history and the other social sciences but also between background and foreground, historical and literary materials, political and poetical events. They have erased the old boundary line dividing historical and literary materials, showing that the production of one of Shakespeare's historical plays was a political act and historical event, while at the same time showing that the coronation of Elizabeth I was carried out with the same care for staging and symbol lavished on works of dramatic art.

In addition to breaking down barriers that separate literature and history, history and the social sciences, new historicists have reminded us that it is treacherously difficult to reconstruct the past as it really was, rather than as we have been conditioned by our own place and time to believe that it was. And they know that the job is utterly impossible for those who are unaware of that difficulty and insensitive to the bent or bias of their own historical vantage point. Historical criticism must be "conscious of its status as interpretation," Greenblatt has written (*Renaissance* 4). McGann obviously concurs, writing that "historical criticism can no longer make any part of [its] sweeping picture unselfconsciously, or treat any of its details in an untheorized way" (*Studies* 11).

Unselfconsciously and *untheorized* are the key words in McGann's statement. When new historicist critics of literature describe a historical change, they are highly conscious of, and even likely to discuss, the *theory* of historical change that informs their account. They know that the changes they happen to see and describe are the ones that their theory of change allows or helps them to see and describe. And they know, too, that their theory of change is historically determined. They seek to minimize the distortion inherent in their perceptions and representations by admitting that they see through preconceived notions; in other words, they learn to reveal the color of the lenses in the glasses that they wear.

Nearly everyone who wrote on the new historicism during the 1980s cited the importance of the late Michel Foucault. A French philosophical historian who liked to think of himself as an archaeologist of human knowledge, Foucault brought together incidents and phenomena from areas of inquiry and orders of life that we normally regard as being unconnected. As much as anyone, he encouraged the new historicist critic of literature to redefine the boundaries of historical inquiry.

Foucault's views of history were influenced by the philosopher Friedrich Nietzsche's concept of a *wirkliche* ("real" or "true") history that is neither melioristic (that is, "getting better all the time") nor metaphysical. Like Nietzsche, Foucault didn't see history in terms of a continuous development toward the present. Neither did he view it as an abstraction, idea, or ideal, as something that began "In the beginning" and that will come to THE END, a moment of definite closure, a Day of Judgment. In his own words, Foucault "abandoned [the old history's] attempts to understand events in terms of . . . some great evolutionary process" (*Discipline and Punish* 129). He warned a new generation of historians to be aware of the fact that investigators are themselves "situated." It is difficult, he reminded them, to see present cultural practices critically from within them, and because of the same cultural practices, it is extremely difficult to enter bygone ages. In *Discipline and Punish: The Birth of the Prison* (1975), Foucault admitted that his own interest in the past was fueled by a passion to write the history of the present.

Like Marx, Foucault saw history in terms of power, but his view of power probably owed more to Nietzsche than to Marx. Foucault seldom viewed power as a repressive force. He certainly did not view it as a tool of conspiracy used by one specific individual or institution against another. Rather, power represents a whole web or complex of forces; it is that which produces what happens. Not even a tyrannical aristocrat simply wields power, for the aristocrat is himself formed and empowered by a network of discourses and practices that constitute power. Viewed by Foucault, power is "positive and productive," not "repressive" and "prohibitive" (Smart 63). Furthermore, no historical event, according to Foucault, has a single cause; rather, it is intricately connected with a vast web of economic, social, and political factors.

A brief sketch of one of Foucault's major works may help clarify some of his ideas. *Discipline and Punish* begins with a shocking but accurate description of the public drawing and quartering of a Frenchman who had botched his attempt to assassinate King Louis XV in 1757. Foucault proceeds by describing rules governing the daily life of modern Parisian felons. What happened to torture, to punishment as public spectacle? he asks. What complex network of forces made it disappear? In working toward a picture of this "power," Foucault turns up many interesting puzzle pieces, such as the fact that in the early years of the nineteenth century, crowds would sometimes identify with the prisoner and treat the executioner as if *he* were the guilty party. But Foucault sets forth a related reason for keeping prisoners alive, moving punishment indoors, and changing discipline from physical torture into mental rehabilitation: colonization. In this historical period, people were needed to establish colonies and trade, and prisoners could be used for that purpose. Also, because these were politically unsettled times, governments needed infiltrators and informers. Who better to fill those roles than prisoners pardoned or released early for showing a willingness to be rehabilitated? As for rehabilitation itself, Foucault compares it to the old form of punishment, which began with a torturer extracting a confession. In more modern, "reasonable" times, psychologists probe the minds of prisoners with a scientific rigor that Foucault sees as a different kind of torture, a kind that our modern perspective does not allow us to see as such.

Thus, a change took place, but perhaps not as great a change as we generally assume. It may have been for the better or for the worse; the point is that agents of power didn't make the change because mankind is evolving and, therefore, more prone to perform good-hearted deeds. Rather, different objectives arose, including those of a new class of doctors and scientists bent on studying aberrant examples of the human mind. And where do we stand vis-à-vis the history Foucault tells? We are implicated by it, for the evolution of discipline as punishment into the study of the human mind includes the evolution of the "disciplines" as we now understand that word, including the discipline of history, the discipline of literary study, and now a discipline that is neither and both, a form of historical criticism that from the vantage point of the 1980s looked "new."

Foucault's type of analysis has been practiced by a number of literary critics at the vanguard of the back-to-history movement. One of them is Greenblatt, who along with Montrose was to a great extent responsible for transforming Renaissance studies in the early 1980s and revitalizing historical criticism in the process. Greenblatt follows Foucault's lead in interpreting literary devices as if they were continuous with all other representational devices in a culture; he therefore turns to scholars in other fields in order to better understand the workings of literature. "We wall off literary symbolism from the symbolic structures operative elsewhere," he writes, "as if art alone were a human creation, as if humans themselves were not, in Clifford Geertz's phrase, cultural artifacts" (*Renaissance* 4).

Greenblatt's name, more than anyone else's, is synonymous with the new historicism; his essay entitled "Invisible Bullets" (1981) has been said by Patrick Brantlinger to be "perhaps the most frequently cited example of New Historicist work" ("Cultural Studies" 45). An English professor at the University of California, Berkeley — the early academic home of the new historicism — Greenblatt was a founding editor of *Representations,* a journal published by the University of California Press that is still considered today to be *the* mouthpiece of the new historicism.

In *Learning to Curse* (1990), Greenblatt cites as central to his own intellectual development his decision to interrupt his literary education at Yale University by accepting a Fulbright fellowship to study in England at Cambridge University. There he came under the influence of the great Marxist cultural critic Raymond Williams, who made Greenblatt realize how much — and what — was missing from his Yale education. "In Williams' lectures," Greenblatt writes, "all that had been carefully excluded from the literary criticism in which I had been trained — who controlled access to the printing press, who owned the land and the factories, whose voices were being repressed as well as represented in literary texts, what social strategies were being served by the aesthetic values we constructed — came pressing back in upon the act of interpretation" (2).

Greenblatt returned to the United States determined not to exclude such matters from his own literary investigations. Blending what he had learned from Williams with poststructuralist thought about the indeterminacy or "undecidability" of meaning, he eventually developed a critical method that he now calls "cultural poetics." More tentative and less overtly political than cultural criticism, it involves what Thomas calls "the technique of montage. Starting with the analysis of a particular historical event, it cuts to the analysis of a particular literary text. The point is not to show that the literary text reflects the historical event but to create a field of energy between the two so that we come to see the event as a social text and the literary text as a social event" ("New Literary Historicism" 490). Alluding to deconstructor Jacques Derrida's assertion that "there is nothing outside the text," Montrose explains that the goal of this new historicist criticism is to show the "historicity of texts and the textuality of history" (Veeser 20).

The relationship between the cultural poetics practiced by a number of new historicists and the cultural criticism associated with Marxism is important, not only because of the proximity of the two approaches but also because one must recognize the difference between the two to understand the new historicism. Still very much a part of the contemporary critical scene, cultural criticism (sometimes called "cultural studies" or "cultural critique") nonetheless involves several tendencies more compatible with the old historicism than with the thinking of new historicists such as Greenblatt. These include the tendency to believe that history is driven by economics; that it is determinable even as it determines the lives of individuals; and that it is progressive, its dialectic one that will bring about justice and equality.

Greenblatt does not privilege economics in his analyses and views individuals as agents possessing considerable productive power. (He says that "the work of art is the product of a negotiation between a creator or class of creators . . . and the institutions and practices of a society" [*Learning* 158]: he also acknowledges that artistic productions are "intensely marked by the private obsessions of individuals," however much they may result from "collective negotiation and exchange" [*Negotiations* vii].) His optimism about the individual, however, should not be confused with optimism about either history's direction or any historian's capacity to foretell it. Like a work of art, a work of history is the negotiated product of a private creator and the public practices of a given society.

This does not mean that Greenblatt does not discern historical change, or that he is uninterested in describing it. Indeed, in works from *Renaissance Self-Fashioning* (1980) to *Shakespearean Negotiations* (1988), he has written about Renaissance changes in the development of both literary characters and real people. But his view of change — like his view of the individual — is more Foucauldian than Marxist. That is to say, it is not melioristic or teleological. And, like Foucault, Greenblatt is careful to point out that any one change is connected with a host of others, no one of which may simply be identified as cause or effect, progressive or regressive, repressive or enabling.

Not all of the critics trying to lead students of literature back to history are as Foucauldian as Greenblatt. Some even owe more to Marx than to Foucault. Others, like Thomas, have clearly been more influenced by Walter Benjamin, best known for essays such as "Theses on the Philosophy of History" and "The Work of Art in the Age of Mechanical Reproduction." Still others — McGann, for example — have followed the lead of Soviet critic M. M. Bakhtin, who viewed literary works in terms of discourses and dialogues between the official, legitimate voices of a society and other, more challenging or critical voices echoing popular or traditional culture. In the "polyphonic" writings of Rabelais, for instance, Bakhtin found that the profane language of Carnival and other popular festivals offsets and parodies the "legitimate" discourses representing the outlook of the king, church, and socially powerful intellectuals of the day.

Moreover, there are other reasons not to consider Foucault the single or even central influence on the new historicism. First, he critiqued the old-style historicism to such an extent that he ended up being antihistorical, or at least ahistorical, in the view of a number of new historicists. Second, his commitment to a radical remapping of the relations of power and influence, cause and effect, may have led him to adopt too cavalier an attitude toward chronology and facts. Finally, the very act of identifying and labeling *any* primary influence goes against the grain of the new historicism. Its practitioners have sought to "decenter" the study of literature, not only by overlapping it with historical studies (broadly defined to include anthropology and sociology) but also by struggling to see history from a decentered perspective. That struggle has involved recognizing (1) that the historian's cultural and historical position may not afford the best purview of a given set of events and (2) that events seldom have any single or central cause. In keeping with these principles, it may be appropriate to acknowledge Foucault as just one of several powerful, interactive intellectual forces rather than to declare him the single, master influence.

Throughout the 1980s it seemed to many that the ongoing debates about the sources of the new historicist movement, the importance of Marx or Foucault, Walter Benjamin or Mikhail Bakhtin, and the exact locations of all the complex boundaries between the new historicism and other "isms" (Marxism and poststructuralism, to name only two) were historically contingent functions of the new historicism *newness.* In the initial stages of their development, new intellectual movements are difficult to outline clearly because, like partially developed photographic images, they are themselves fuzzy and lacking in definition. They respond to disparate influences and include thinkers who represent a wide range of backgrounds; like movements that are disintegrating, they inevitably include a broad spectrum of opinions and positions.

From the vantage point of the 1990s, however, it seems that the inchoate quality of the new historicism is characteristic rather than a function of newness. The boundaries around the new historicism remain fuzzy, not because it hasn't reached its full maturity but because, if it is to live up to its name, it must always be subject to revision and redefinition as historical circumstances change. The fact that so many critics we label new historicist are working right at the border of Marxist, poststructuralist, cultural, postcolonial, feminist, and now even a new form of reader-response (or at least reader-oriented) criticism is evidence of the new historicism's multiple interests and motivations, rather than of its embryonic state.

New historicists themselves advocate and even stress the need to perpetually redefine categories and boundaries — whether they be disciplinary, generic, national, or racial — not because definitions are unimportant but because they are historically constructed and thus subject to revision. If new historicists like Thomas and reader-oriented critics like Steven Mailloux and Peter Rabinowitz seem to spend most of their time talking over the low wall separating their respective fields, then maybe the wall is in the wrong place. As Catherine Gallagher has suggested, the boundary between new historicists and feminists studying "people and phenomena that once seemed insignificant, indeed outside of history: women, criminals, the insane" often turns out to be shifting or even nonexistent (Veeser 43).

If the fact that new historicists all seem to be working on the border of another school should not be viewed as a symptom of the new historicism's newness (or disintegration), neither should it be viewed as evidence that new historicists are intellectual loners or divisive outriders who enjoy talking over walls to people in other fields but who share no common views among themselves. Greenblatt, McGann, and Thomas all started with the assumption that works of literature are simultaneously influenced by and influencing reality, broadly defined. Whatever their disagreements, they share a belief in referentiality — a belief that literature refers to and is referred to by things outside itself — stronger than that found in the works of formalist, poststructuralist, and even reader-response critics. They believe with Greenblatt that the "central concerns" of criticism "should prevent it from permanently sealing off one type of discourse from another or decisively separating works of art from the minds and lives of their creators and their audiences" (*Renaissance* 5).

McGann, in his introduction to *Historical Studies and Literary Criticism,* turns referentiality into a rallying cry:

> What will not be found in these essays . . . is the assumption, so common in text-centered studies of every type, that literary works are self-enclosed verbal constructs, or looped intertextual fields of autonomous signifiers and signifieds. In these essays, the question of referentiality is once again brought to the fore. (3)

In "Keats and the Historical Method in Literary Criticism," he suggests a set of basic, scholarly procedures to be followed by those who have rallied to the cry. These procedures, which he claims are "practical derivatives of the Bakhtin school," assume that historicist critics will study a literary work's "point of origin" by studying biography and bibliography. The critic must then consider the expressed intentions of the author, because, if printed, these intentions have also modified the developing history of the work. Next, the new historicist must learn the history of the work's reception, as that body of opinion has become part of the platform on which we are situated when we study the work at our own particular "point of reception." Finally, McGann urges the new historicist critic to point toward the future, toward his or her *own* audience, defining for its members the aims and limits of the critical project and injecting the analysis with a degree of self-consciousness that alone can give it credibility (*Inflections* 62).

In his introduction to a collection of new historical writings on *The New Historicism* (1989), H. Aram Veeser stresses the unity among new historicists, not by focusing on common critical procedures but, rather, by outlining five "key assumptions" that "continually reappear and bind together the avowed practitioners and even some of their critics":

1. that every expressive act is embedded in a network of material practices;
2. that every act of unmasking, critique, and opposition uses the tools it condemns and risks falling prey to the practice it exposes;
3. that literary and non-literary texts circulate inseparably;
4. that no discourse, imaginative or archival, gives access to unchanging truths nor expresses inalterable human nature;
5. finally, . . . that a critical method and a language adequate to describe culture under capitalism participate in the economy they describe. (xi)

These same assumptions are shared by a group of historians practicing what is now commonly referred to as "the new cultural history." Influenced by *Annales*-school historians in France, post-Althusserian Marxists, and Foucault, these historians share with their new historicist counterparts not only many of the same influences and assumptions but also the following: an interest in anthropological and sociological subjects and methods; a creative way of weaving stories and anecdotes about the past into reveling thick descriptions; a tendency to focus on nontraditional, noncanonical subjects and relations (historian Thomas Laqueur is best known for *Making Sex: Body and Gender from the Greeks to Freud* [1990]); and some of the same journals and projects.

Thus, in addition to being significantly unified by their own interests, assumptions, and procedures, new historicist literary critics have participated in a broader, interdisciplinary movement toward unification virtually unprecedented within and across academic disciplines. Their tendency to work along disciplinary borderlines, far from being evidence of their factious or fractious tendencies, has been precisely what has allowed them to engage historians in a conversation certain to revolutionize the way in which we understand the past, present, and future.

Early in the essay that follows, Raimonda Modiano quotes Jerome McGann's assertion that Coleridge's "Rime" cries out for a new approach that will "historicize every aspect of the work" (187). Although Modiano accepts this assertion and challenge, she questions McGann's further assertion that, through the "Rime," Coleridge sought to defend and preserve the Bible's relevance by suggesting that all narratives grow "by accretion and interpolation" (188). Modiano suggests that her new historicist predecessor may have been trying too hard to do for Coleridge's "Rime" what Coleridge was supposedly trying to do for the Bible: namely, to prove its ongoing cultural predominance and relevance. She also indicts McGann for ignoring the many ways in which Coleridge's religious views changed between the period in which he wrote the poem's first draft and the time when he finished revising it, years later.

Having generally suggested that McGann incorrectly argued that the poem has "a Christian schema" demanding "a Christian framework of interpreting the Mariner's story," Modiano goes on to summarize the views of previous "historicist critics." Malcolm Ware was the first to suggest that the spectre-bark first viewed by the Mariner as an agent of salvation would, if real, have been a slave ship. (For Ware,

Coleridge's implicit reference to the slave trade supported the poem's overall theme regarding the consequences of violating principles of natural brotherhood.) J. B. Ebbatson subsequently suggested that if Coleridge's "Rimes" is, in fact, a "parable of guilt and redemption," it expresses guilt about slavery, specifically, the harm inflicted against "indigenous peoples."

Other historicist critics before McGann stressed the French Revolution rather than the slave trade as the defining historical context for Coleridge's "Rime." Peter Kitson argued that the terror and guilt expressed in the poem reflect the terror of the French Revolution — and the guilt felt by English Romantic poets who had supported it, believing idealistically that it would lead to human renewal and social betterment. Robert Maniquis subsequently hypothesized a connection between the French Revolution and the breakdown, in Coleridge's "Rime," of what Modiano calls "a sacrificial system that interprets violence in sacrificial terms" (198).

Patrick J. Keane, the last of the critics whose theses Modiano summarizes, "put the slave trade back on the map of historical criticism without losing sight of the French Revolution" by writing what Modiano judges to be "the first new historicist study of the poem" (198). (Keane relates the "Rime" to the French Revolution *and* the slave trade by seeing it in light of Coleridge's opposition, and later capitulation, to Prime Minister William Pitt, who waged war with revolutionary France, and whose opposition to slavery Coleridge found insincere.) Although Modiano finds fault with the logic of Keane's argument (which does not implicate Pitt in the shooting of the Albatross but does associate him with the water snakes the Mariner comes to bless), she credits Keane with producing what many new historicists, following Clifford Geertz, would call a "thick reading" of the poem's deeply interwoven contextual strands.

Modiano subsequently goes beyond Keane and older historicist critics by relating the "Rime" to known acts and even traditions of human sacrifice in the African land of Dahomey — acts and traditions that were used to justify the slave trade on the grounds that it removed people from a horrible place and from the possibility of a horrible fate. She even moves beyond McGann, who connected the "Rime" with the Bible, by specifically linking Coleridge's poem with the story of Cain and Abel. (That story recounts the first murder in human history, which occurred in the context of religious sacrifice.) Modiano argues that both in the "Rime" and in "The Wanderings of Cain," a poem coauthored with Wordsworth, Coleridge revised "biblical myth" by representing "Cain and Abel as doubles of each other" (205). As a result, "the Mariner carries a dual identity; he is at once the perpetrator and the victim of a transgression, both guilty and innocent, and in a sacrificial context, both sacrificer and sacrificed" (205–06). Modiano then reconnects the "Cain-Abel story" to the subject of the French Revolution; indeed, she maintains that the story became a popular means of thinking and talking about a revolution which, for all its emphasis on "fraternity," led to a fratricidal Reign of Terror in which "one radical group hunt[ed] down another, only to become the hunted victims of a next round of revolutionary wrath" (207).

Bringing her argument full circle, Modiano shows that "the Cain-Abel story also connects with the slave trade, thus functioning as a bridge between the two sites of violence identified in historicist readings of 'The Ancient Mariner'" (208). The association of the Mariner with Cain "does not prevent him from attaining the [Christlike] identity" accorded him by so many traditional critics; as Modiano points out, "it is not just Abel who is linked with Christ" by poets of the Romantic period "but also Cain, a development made possible by the transformation of the Cain-Abel pair into doubles of each other. In 'Adonais' Shelley makes an explicit connection between the mark of Cain and the crown of thorns worn by Christ, suggesting that both characters were subject to persecution" (210).

Modiano's essay exemplifies the new historicism in a number of ways. Rather than seeing a literary text as a discourse walled off from history, it views history as a complex web of discourses in which Shelley's poetry, the Old and New Testaments, English views of the French Revolution, and justifications for the slave trade all overlap and inform one another. Equally new historicist are Modiano's emphasis on the "Rime" as a text read and reread through time (each time within historical contexts that determine and/or provoke the next reading) and her assertion that Coleridge's poem at once reflects and challenges any number of ideologies or value systems (ranging from the Christian system in which sinners are ultimately redeemed no matter how much harm they have caused, to "radical political standpoints on the French Revolution or the slave trade" [215]). Moreover, Modiano sees political and religious standpoints as existing both inside and outside the text; they are seen not just as standpoints from which power may be critiqued but also as manifestations *of* power. Thus, though Modiano does not specifically allude to Michel Foucault (in the way she alludes to McGann), Foucault's concept of power is as deeply ingrained in her critical assumptions as Geertz's thick description and Greenblatt's montage technique are ingrained in her critical practices. Although Modiano may sometimes seem to range far from the "Rime," she ultimately draws us closer than previous critics have brought us to the forces that shaped the text and that, to no small extent, still shape us today.

Ross C Murfin

THE NEW HISTORICISM:
A SELECTED BIBLIOGRAPHY

The New Historicism: Further Reading

Brantlinger, Patrick. "Cultural Studies vs. the New Historicism." *English Studies/Cultural Studies: Institutionalizing Dissent.* Ed. Isaiah Smithson and Nancy Ruff. Urbana: U of Illinois P, 1994. 43–58.

Cox, Jeffrey N., and Larry J. Reynolds, eds. *New Historical Literary Study.* Princeton: Princeton UP, 1993.

Dimock, Wai-Chee. "Feminism, New Historicism, and the Reader." *American Literature* 63 (1991): 601–22.

Howard, Jean. "The New Historicism in Renaissance Studies." *English Literary Renaissance* 16 (1986): 13–43.

Lindenberger, Herbert. *The History in Literature: On Value, Genre, Institutions.* New York: Columbia UP, 1990.

———. "Toward a New History in Literary Study." *Profession: Selected Articles from the Bulletins of the Association of Departments of English and the Association of the Departments of Foreign Languages.* New York: MLA, 1984. 16–23.

Liu, Alan. "The Power of Formalism: The New Historicism." *English Literary History* 56 (1989): 721–71.

McGann, Jerome. *The Beauty of Inflections: Literary Investigations in Historical Method and Theory.* Oxford: Clarendon, 1985.

———. *Historical Studies and Literary Criticism.* Madison: U of Wisconsin P, 1985. See especially the introduction and the essays in the following sections: "Historical Methods and Literary Interpretations" and "Biographical Contexts and the Critical Object."

Montrose, Louis Adrian. "Renaissance Literary Studies and the Subject of History." *English Literary Renaissance* 16 (1986): 5–12.

Morris, Wesley. *Toward a New Historicism.* Princeton: Princeton UP, 1972.

New Literary History 21 (1990). "History and . . ." (special issue). See especially the essays by Carolyn Porter, Rena Fraden, Clifford Geertz, and Renato Rosaldo.

Representations. This quarterly journal, printed by the University of California Press, regularly publishes new historicist studies and cultural criticism.

Thomas, Brook. "The Historical Necessity for — and Difficulties with — New Historical Analysis in Introductory Courses." *College English* 49 (1987): 509–22.

———. *The New Historicism and Other Old-Fashioned Topics.* Princeton: Princeton UP, 1991.

———. "The New Literary Historicism." *A Companion to American Thought.* Ed. Richard Wightman Fox and James T. Klappenberg. New York: Blackwell, 1995.

———. "Walter Benn Michaels and the New Historicism: Where's the Difference?" *Boundary 2* 18 (1991): 118–59.

Veeser, H. Aram, ed. *The New Historicism.* New York: Routledge, 1989. See especially Veeser's introduction, Louis Montrose's "Professing the Renaissance," Catherine Gallagher's "Marxism and the New Historicism," and Frank Lentricchia's "Foucault's Legacy: A New Historicism?"

Wayne, Don E. "Power, Politics and the Shakespearean Text: Recent Criticism in England and the United States." *Shakespeare Reproduced: The Text in History and Ideology.* Ed. Jean Howard and Marion O'Connor. New York: Methuen, 1987. 47–67.

Winn, James A. "An Old Historian Looks at the New Historicism." *Comparative Studies in Society and History* 35 (1993): 859–70.

The New Historicism: Influential Examples

The new historicism has taken its present form less through the elaboration of basic theoretical postulates and more through certain influential examples. The works listed represent some of the most important contributions guiding research in this area.

Bercovitch, Sacvan. *The Rites of Assent: Transformations in the Symbolic Construction of America.* New York: Routledge, 1993.

Brown, Gillian. *Domestic Individualism: Imagining Self in Nineteenth-Century America.* Berkeley: U of California P, 1990.

Dollimore, Jonathan. *Radical Tragedy: Religion, Ideology and Power in the Drama of Shakespeare and His Contemporaries.* Brighton: Harvester, 1984.

Dollimore, Jonathan, and Alan Sinfield, eds. *Political Shakespeare: New Essays in Cultural Materialism*. Manchester: Manchester UP, 1985. This volume occupies the borderline between new historicist and cultural criticism. See especially the essays by Dollimore, Greenblatt, and Tennenhouse.

Gallagher, Catherine. *The Industrial Reformation of English Fiction*. Chicago: U of Chicago P, 1985.

Goldberg, Jonathan. *James I and the Politics of Literature*. Baltimore: Johns Hopkins UP, 1983.

Greenblatt, Stephen J. *Learning to Curse: Essays in Early Modern Culture*. New York: Routledge, 1990.

———. *Marvelous Possessions: The Wonder of the New World*. Chicago: U of Chicago P, 1991.

———. *Renaissance Self-Fashioning from More to Shakespeare*. Chicago: U of Chicago P, 1980. See chapter 1 and the chapter on *Othello* titled "The Improvisation of Power."

———. *Shakespearean Negotiations: The Circulation of Social Energy in Renaissance England*. Berkeley: U of California P, 1988. See especially "The Circulation of Social Energy" and "Invisible Bullets."

Liu, Alan. *Wordsworth, the Sense of History*. Stanford: Stanford UP, 1989.

Marcus, Leah. *Puzzling Shakespeare: Local Reading and Its Discontents*. Berkeley: U of California P, 1988.

McGann, Jerome. *The Romantic Ideology*. Chicago: U of Chicago P, 1983.

Michaels, Walter Benn. *The Gold Standard and the Logic of Naturalism: American Literature at the Turn of the Century*. Berkeley: U of California P, 1987.

Montrose, Louis Adrian. "'Shaping Fantasies': Figurations of Gender and Power in Elizabethan Culture." *Representations* 2 (1983): 61–94. One of the most influential early new historicist essays.

Mullaney, Steven. *The Place of the Stage: License, Play, and Power in Renaissance England*. Chicago: U of Chicago P, 1987.

Orgel, Stephen. *The Illusion of Power: Political Theater in the English Renaissance*. Berkeley: U of California P, 1975.

Sinfield, Alan. *Literature, Politics, and Culture in Postwar Britain*. Berkeley: U of California P, 1989.

Tennenhouse, Leonard. *Power on Display: The Politics of Shakespeare's Genres*. New York: Methuen, 1986.

Foucault and His Influence

As I point out in the introduction to the new historicism, some new historicists would question the "privileging" of Foucault implicit in this section heading ("Foucault and His Influence") and the following one ("Other Writers and Works"). They might cite the greater importance of one of those other writers or point out that to cite a central influence or a definitive cause runs against the very spirit of the movement.

Dreyfus, Hubert L., and Paul Rabinow. *Michel Foucault: Beyond Structuralism and Hermeneutics.* Chicago: U of Chicago P, 1983.

Foucault, Michel. *The Archaeology of Knowledge.* Trans. A. M. Sheridan Smith. New York: Harper, 1972.

———. *Discipline and Punish: The Birth of the Prison.* 1975. Trans. Alan Sheridan. New York: Pantheon, 1978.

———. *The History of Sexuality.* Trans. Robert Hurley. Vol. 1. New York: Pantheon, 1978.

———. *Language, Counter-Memory, Practice.* Ed. Donald F. Bouchard. Trans. Donald F. Bouchard and Sherry Simon. Ithaca: Cornell UP, 1977.

———. *The Order of Things: An Archaeology of the Human Sciences.* New York: Vintage, 1973.

———. *Politics, Philosophy, Culture.* Ed. Lawrence D. Kritzman. Trans. Alan Sheridan et al. New York: Routledge, 1988.

———. *Power/Knowledge.* Ed. Colin Gordon. Trans. Colin Gordon et al. New York: Pantheon, 1980.

———. *Technologies of the Self.* Ed. Luther H. Martin, Huck Gutman, and Patrick H. Hutton. Amherst: U of Massachusetts P, 1988.

Sheridan, Alan. *Michel Foucault: The Will to Truth.* New York: Tavistock, 1980.

Smart, Barry. *Michel Foucault.* New York: Tavistock, 1985.

Other Writers and Works of Interest
to New Historicist Critics

Bakhtin, M. M. *The Dialogic Imagination: Four Essays.* Ed. Michael Holquist. Trans. Caryl Emerson. Austin: U of Texas P, 1981. Bakhtin wrote many influential studies on subjects as varied as Dostoyevsky, Rabelais, and formalist criticism. But this book, in part due to Holquist's helpful introduction, is probably the best place to begin reading Bakhtin.

Benjamin, Walter. "The Work of Art in the Age of Mechanical

Reproduction." 1936. *Illuminations.* Ed. Hannah Arendt. Trans. Harry Zohn. New York: Harcourt, 1968.

Fried, Michael. *Absorption and Theatricality: Painting and Beholder in the Works of Diderot.* Berkeley: U of California P, 1980.

Geertz, Clifford. *The Interpretation of Cultures.* New York: Basic, 1973.

———. *Negara: The Theatre State in Nineteenth-Century Bali.* Princeton: Princeton UP, 1980.

Goffman, Erving. *Frame Analysis.* New York: Harper, 1974.

Jameson, Fredric. *The Political Unconscious.* Ithaca: Cornell UP, 1981.

Koselleck, Reinhart. *Futures Past.* Trans. Keith Tribe. Cambridge: MIT P, 1985.

Said, Edward. *Orientalism.* New York: Columbia UP, 1978.

Turner, Victor. *The Ritual Process: Structure and Anti-Structure.* Chicago: Aldine, 1969.

Young, Robert. *White Mythologies: Writing History and the West.* New York: Routledge, 1990.

Other New Historical Readings of the "Rime"

Keane, Patrick J. *Coleridge's Submerged Politics: The Ancient Mariner and Robinson Crusoe.* Columbia: U of Missouri P, 1994.

Kitson, Peter. "Coleridge, The French Revolution, and 'The Ancient Mariner': Collective Guilt and Individual Salvation." *Yearbook of English Studies* 19 (1989): 197–201.

McGann, Jerome J. "The Ancient Mariner: The Meaning of the Meanings." *The Beauty of Inflections: Literary Investigations in Historical Method and Theory.* Oxford: Clarendon, 1988. 135–72.

Modiano, Raimonda. "Coleridge and Wordsworth: The Ethics of Gift Exchange." *Wordsworth Circle* 20 (1989): 113–20.

Stevenson, Warren. "The Case of the Missing Captain: Power Politics in *The Rime of the Ancient Mariner.*" *Wordsworth Circle* 26 (1995): 112–18.

RAIMONDA MODIANO

Sameness or Difference? Historicist Readings of "The Rime of the Ancient Mariner"

We were the first that ever burst
Into that silent sea.

In his influential essay "The Meaning of *The Ancient Mariner*," Jerome McGann points out the pervasive "uniformity of approach" in nineteenth- and twentieth-century readings of this famous poem, arguing that critics have traditionally interpreted "The Ancient Mariner" according to the same Christian framework of interlocked images and ideas that had formed the basis of Coleridge's *own* "reading" of the world. McGann traces this tradition of reading literary texts in generally Christian terms back to an intellectual-historical movement — Higher Criticism — whose practitioners viewed scriptural and secular, biblical, and postbiblical works as contributing to a progressive process of divine revelation. He calls for a break with traditional criticism by means of a "critical method" which "must historicize every aspect of the work," and expose Coleridge's controlling interpretative model as representative of the predominant " 'concepts, schemes and values' of the Christian heritage" (65). In this essay I wish to examine the contention articulated most prominently by McGann but shared, among others, by critics such as Peter Kitson, Daniel Watkins, and Patrick J. Keane, that only a historical method will make a difference, and liberate readers from the "illusions" of a critical tradition "underwritten by Coleridge himself" (38).

Given McGann's claim that this difference will emerge only when we part ways with Coleridge's Christian hermeneutics, it is worth asking whether historicist readings of "The Ancient Mariner" have undermined or actually sustained Christian interpretations of the poem. In the following discussion I wish to demonstrate the frequent collusion between intended "radical" political readings and orthodox religious interpretations of "The Ancient Mariner" in historicist criticism. I will show that (1) McGann in particular (but not exclusively) gives us a more conservative religious perspective on "The Ancient Mariner" than critics with nonhistoricist leanings; (2) historicist critics both prior to and after McGann have privileged either the French Revolution or the slave trade as the relevant context in which the poem can be best understood, without looking for the connections between these two events;

and (3) an examination of the main sacrificial symbols in "The Ancient Mariner" and their sources in Old Testament (the Cain-Abel story), New Testament (Christ's crucifixion), and contemporary travel accounts and controversies about existing practices of human sacrifice (especially in the Kingdom of Dahomey in Western Africa) is crucial to an understanding of the poem's political as well as religious "signposts," and also provides a link between the French Revolution and the slave trade, both of which generated and were perceived at the time in terms of a sacrificial vocabulary.

McGann's essay has been often cited by critics with deserved respect and admiration, but few have given it more than cursory attention.[1] Briefly summarized, McGann's main arguments are as follows: Critics have often wondered what Coleridge's mysterious (and to his contemporaries often incomprehensible) poem might mean, without realizing that an answer to this question will be found by examining not the poem itself, but its critical tradition, that is, "the poem's historical relations with its readers and interpreters" (38). Coleridge himself, it turns out, composed a poem that specifically addressed the question of the cultural transmission and interpretation of texts, by constructing a narrative with several textual layers and temporal frames: the Mariner's original tale; the tale as passed on by a sixteenth-century balladeer and later edited by the seventeenth- or early-eighteenth-century scholar of the gloss, and finally, Coleridge's own nineteenth-century "point of view on his invented materials" (50). Coleridge's main goal in writing "The Ancient Mariner" was to illustrate "a special theory of the historical interpretation of texts" that made it possible to grasp the "significant continuity of meaning" between extremely diverse and seemingly irreconcilable "cultural phenomena" (50–51). Coleridge not only derived this method from the new interpretation of the bible introduced by Higher Criticism in Germany, but "he certainly intended his more perspicuous readers" to be familiar with this tradition and thus understand his attempt to show how a narrative grows "by accretion and interpolation," like the Scriptures, and incorporates material "from

---

[1]Watkins, for example, takes as his point of departure McGann's position that only a historical analysis can free readers from Coleridge's Christian hermeneutics, but he does not acknowledge the fact that his view of "The Ancient Mariner" as a story in which traditional Christian symbols are undermined by the "antagonistic forces of history," becoming "symbols of death and violence," (28) clashes with McGann's reading of the poem as a "salvation story" based on "Christian views about nature and human history" (McGann 54, 57). For a recent discussion of McGann's essay see Keane (188–90) and David Perkins (425–48).

the earliest and most primitive to the latest and most sophisticated" manifestations of religious experience (48–50).

McGann exhibits considerable enthusiasm for Coleridge's project because it is historicist in nature and appears to license his own method of historical analysis.[2] In fact McGann's own project is entirely parallel to Coleridge's: McGann treats "The Ancient Mariner" as Coleridge treats the Bible.[3] Just as in McGann's reading "The Ancient Mariner" is a story of "our salvation *of* Christ," (54) meaning, I assume, the salvation of the Christian heritage through a revisionist, historical reading, so McGann's own story here is that of the salvation of this "great literary ballad" (53) and of its author through a revisionist, historical methodology. It is this very coincidence between McGann's and Coleridge's project, as construed by McGann, that represents the most striking feature of this article.[4]

But this is not the impression that McGann wants to foster in his readers. On the contrary, McGann insists on differentiating himself from Coleridge lest one might think that he, like the generations of readers and academics before him, has fallen prey to the seduction of Coleridge's symbolist Christian hermeneutics. It appears then that McGann pursues two different projects in his article that often work at cross-purposes: one is to demonstrate that Coleridge was a historicist, which is a good thing; the other is to show that his ideas have dominated "Anglo-American culture during the past one hundred and fifty years" (53), which is a bad thing. The latter project is recognizably the one elaborated by McGann in *The Romantic Ideology,* where he represented "the scholarship and criticism of Romanticism" as "dominated by a Romantic ideology, by an uncritical absorption in Romanticism's own self-representations" (1). As this second project collides with the first, it introduces in McGann's essay a different set of terms and emphases. While an emphasis on continuity, coherence, congruence, and unity underlies McGann's construction of the historicist Coleridge in line with Higher Criticism, the second project brings in an emphasis on discontinuity and rupture and a new vocabulary strewn with terms such as "gulph," "alienation," "illusion," and "disbelief." While Coleridge's

---

[2]McGann himself admits that his "procedure" of historicizing "every aspect of the work" is one "which the poem's own method has initiated" (65).

[3]See, e.g., McGann's statement that "The Ancient Mariner" "is, as it were, an English national Scripture" (57).

[4]This point is emphasized by Perkins, who also questions McGann's construction of "a historicist Coleridge," arguing that "Coleridge's commitment to a historical point of view was limited by other premises" (446).

"hermeneutic" method enabled him to see "continuities with the past" (61), McGann's "critical" method does the opposite: it specifies "clearly the ideological gulph which separates" today's readers from Coleridge; it shows that even as this poem is not "as removed from the present" as the *Iliad* or *Oedipus*, "we must not allow its alienation to escape us"; and it offers an escape from our subjection to the "terms" and "illusions" of past ideological practices (54–55).

McGann first constructs two closed totalities (the absolute coherence of Coleridge's religious views[5] and the complete congruence between nineteenth- and twentieth-century interpretations of the poem), and then looks for an escape from such oppressive systems. But from the very beginning his analysis stands on shaky foundations. I have no room here even to begin to examine Coleridge's religious utterance, which is so varied and shifting that any paradigm such as McGann's looks like a straight road that conveniently bypasses the actual maze of Coleridge's thought. Let me just mention that even as Coleridge was a serious Christian in the 1790s or later on, he was also an immensely troubled one, often feeling faith slipping away from him, and unable to brush aside the assaults on orthodox Christianity that came from various philosophic, religious, and scientific quarters.[6] This is not to say that it is not possible to find points of continuity between Coleridge's early and later religious views, but simply that for a historicist critic to want to close the gap between the Coleridge of 1790s and the "Sage of Highgate" seems odd to me, given that the focus of a historical method should be precisely on the differences between time-bound and circumstance-bound points of view. One would also expect a historicist critic to demonstrate the differences, indeed the gulf, between nineteenth- and twentieth-century interpretations of "The Ancient Mariner" rather than their complete congruence. Otherwise, the break that McGann proposes between his "critical" view and previous "uncritical" ones becomes incomprehensible, for no historical explanation is provided to demonstrate how such a moment of illumination can occur in the 1980s that was completely unavailable to past interpreters.[7]

---

[5]We "must look again," McGann claims, "at the sorts of continuities which exist between the 'radical' Coleridge of the 1790s and the Sage of Highgate" (42).

[6]James Boulger's reading of "The Ancient Mariner" is much more attuned to Coleridge's religious anxieties and "the uneasy Christian skepticism that has been with us since Newton and Kant" than is McGann's.

[7]One wonders also whether McGann does not practice a version of Hegelian dialectics in this essay. Like Hegel, McGann stages a phase of negation, the encounter with "The Ancient Mariner" as an alien text, in order to propel critical consciousness to a higher level. McGann's reassurances to the reader that his critical analysis will increase the

My critique of McGann's reading of the "The Ancient Mariner" is admittedly one-sided and does not do justice to the subtlety and importance of his essay. I have no room here to highlight properly some of McGann's most valuable arguments, such as his deft demonstration of the significance of the gloss Coleridge added to the poem in 1817, which puts to rest William Empson's and David Pirie's uncomprehending rejection of it; his brilliant analysis of Rossetti's dealings with the Christian heritage compared with Coleridge's; and his persuasive point that as paradoxical as this may seem, it is only when works are perceived as truly historical products that they become transhistorical. My main disagreement with McGann's reading of "The Ancient Mariner" concerns the fact that the strict Christian schema he attaches to the poem does not allow him to contact even remotely the wrenching agony that we so often find in the poem, as in the following haunting lines:

Alone, alone, all, all alone,
Alone on a wide wide sea!
And never a saint took pity on
My soul in agony. (232–35)

Here is a voice that expresses unrelieved, naked, desperate suffering. It is the voice of a man with no place to go, no one to turn to, least of all providential aid. But McGann does not hear this voice because he assumes that "The Ancient Mariner" has a Christian and "ultimately redemptive meaning" (60), that it is about Christ's resurrection (in a symbolic sense), and that in it Coleridge "successfully sustained his theistic and Christian views about nature and human history" (57). At no point does McGann acknowledge the possibility that a Christian framework of interpreting the Mariner's story is in jeopardy at key moments in this poem, which has been pointed out by many critics from Edward Bostetter on. Instead, he readily embraces M. H. Abrams's reading of "the Mariner's experience as an instance of the Christian plot of moral error, the discipline of suffering, and a consequent change of heart," which he finds "right on the mark" (60–61). But in *The Romantic Ideology* McGann expressed considerable unhappiness with Abrams's way of reading Romanticism in terms of a Christian model that privileged

poem's significance shows how closely he works within the frame of Hegel's recuperative economy, in which ruptures and loss at one end of the system always spell out gain at the other. For McGann's critique of Hegel as generating an "explicitly Christian," erroneous, and reconciled theory of Romantic art that reproduces "the letter and not the spirit of its subject" see *The Romantic Ideology* (ch. 4).

hope, and "religious and spiritual success," making no room for the
despair that Keats or Byron articulated (25–26). And yet in his reading
of "The Ancient Mariner" McGann commits the same error as Abrams
by the same means: he reads the poem in terms of a conventional Christian plot that writes despair out of the picture. We do not need to turn
to Keats or Byron or Coleridge's later poetry to find despair.[8] It is
already here, at the very center of "The Ancient Mariner," all the more
haunting because of the Mariner's and other interpreters' attempts to
give his story a Christian significance.

In McGann's essay historicism sustains a Christian reading of the
poem that has been in place since the nineteenth century. We find similar collusions in other historicist interpretations of the poem, whether
of the "old" or "new" variety. But overall historicist critics have pursued
a different line of investigation from McGann's, turning their attention
to the contemporary events that have thrown their "gigantic shadow"
(in Kitson's nice metaphor [207]) across Coleridge's deceptively ahistorical work "of pure imagination." All have attempted to convey in
one form or another their sense that the poem, as David Erdman put
it in a succinct formulation, objectified "the dereliction and dismay of
the times in an imaginatively controlled nightmare" (268). For some
critics (William Empson, Malcolm Ware, J. B. Ebbatson, and Chris
Rubinstein), the primary source of "dereliction" for Coleridge was the
slave trade that implicated all of his countrymen in a most shameful
commerce; for other critics (Kitson and Robert Maniquis), it was the
violence of the French Revolution and England's "crimes against the
Revolution" (Kitson 203) that contributed to the "dismay of the times."

The first critic who emphasized the relevance of the slave trade to a
reading of "The Ancient Mariner" was Ware, who in a brief but suggestive article claimed that the terrifying spectre-bark mistakenly identified
at first by the Mariner as a ship of salvation was in fact a slave ship. Ware
points out relevant passages in Coleridge's political prose in which
images similar to those occurring in his poem or in Coleridge's marginal revisions are explicitly connected with the slave trade. He also
examines texts such as Rev. John Newton's *Authentic Narrative* or
Robert Southey's poem "The Sailor, Who Had Served in the Slave

---

[8]McGann claims that in Coleridge "the utter despair that might have been
Wordsworth's late or 'secondary' subject emerges" in "poems like 'Limbo,' 'Constancy
to an Ideal Object,' 'Nature,' and 'Love's Apparition and Evanishment,'" which "stand
in a secondary or critical relation to works like 'Kubla Khan' and 'The Rime of the
Ancient Mariner.' The despair of such later poetry is the sign of its ideological truthful-
ness." *The Romantic Ideology* (110).

Trade" that focus on the crimes and ensuing guilt of those involved in the slave trade. Ware ultimately marshals this evidence to justify the appropriateness of the poem's concluding moral against critics such as John Livingston Lowes who regarded it as no more than a superfluous expression of "valedictory piety" ("Coleridge's 'Spectre-Bark'" 592). In identifying the spectre-ship as a slave ship, Ware concludes, Coleridge "wished to demonstrate the consequences of violating the natural bonds of man to man, to justify thereby the moral stated, and to give his allegory a universality and scope quite consistent with the traditional Romantic concept of the oneness of nature and with Coleridge's own mature theory of the transcending unity of all creation" ("Coleridge's 'Spectre-Bark'" 593). For Ware, as this comment shows, the slave-trade issue does not conflict with a sacramental reading of "The Ancient Mariner." The fact that in a note written a year earlier Ware arrives at the same conclusion about the poem's moral without any reference to the slave trade, by pointing out the tight correspondence between the Mariner's experience and the five stages of prayer identified by Coleridge in an early notebook entry, indicates that Ware's Christian view of the poem does not permit him to understand the disturbing implications of his worthy effort to put the slave trade on the map of the poem's political landscape ("The Rime of the Ancient Mariner: A Discourse on Prayer").

Empson was the first critic to perceive a conflict between Coleridge's interest in the slave trade and a Christian interpretation of "The Ancient Mariner." In an essay published in 1964, Empson established what appeared to him to be two incontrovertible facts about the poem: (1) that it is not a "fanciful" apolitical "reverie" but "evokes a major historical event, the maritime expansion of the Western Europeans"; and (2) that it is definitely not "an allegory in favour of redemption by torment, the central tradition of Christianity," but if anything, a deliberate "parody of the traditional struggle for atonement" ("The Ancient Mariner" 298, 316). This enables him to reject a long line of criticism focusing on the severity of the Mariner's crime, viewed by some as "a ghastly violation of a great sanctity," symbolic of the murder of Christ (298). Empson argues that the Mariner is fundamentally innocent, even though he feels guilty, and that he shoots the Albatross for food, that is, for the benefit of a hungry crew, a common occurrence among navigators whose food supplies dwindled. In Empson's view, therefore, the Mariner has done no wrong; it is destiny that "has made him appear in the wrong; he has been framed by the supreme powers" (Introduction 40). As for the crew, they certainly did not deserve to be killed, being merely animated by "an appetite" for exploration and never abusing any natives or their symbolical substitutes. "Innocence could hardly be carried further" (31).

The problem with Empson's essays is that by declaring the Mariner innocent, he voids the historical context of its significance. The most Empson makes of the slave trade is to link it with the Mariner's encounter with the spectre-bark, which, like Ware before him, he identified as a slaver. The horror experienced by the Mariner at this moment in the poem, Empson argues, comes from his "premonition of a Slaver, with its planks rotted off by the insanitary exudation of the dying slaves," and his realization that slaving "was going to be the final result of his heroic colonial exploration" ("The Ancient Mariner: An Answer to Warren" 167). But Empson does not implicate the Mariner in the crimes associated with the slave trade, for the obvious reason that his innocence, which plays such a large part in Empson's reading, would then be in jeopardy. It is not surprising therefore to find that in his early 1964 essay, even as he introduces the important historical context of maritime expansion, Empson is quick to point out the error of interpreting the Albatross as a symbol of "the ill-treated natives" (305). It is indeed at the juncture of the killing of the Albatross (and not the later meeting with the spectre-bark) that a case for the Mariner's "real grounds for guilt" in his association with the slave trade can be made.[9] But in order to explain the Mariner's sense of guilt, Empson departs from the historical context altogether, showing this guilt to be the consequence of mistaken Christian scruples or a form of "neurotic guilt."[10] Hence Empson ultimately renders history marginal, having no meaningful way of connecting the slave trade with the Mariner's fate.

Subsequent critics have been more successful than Empson in showing the central role played by the slave trade in "The Ancient Mariner" because they involve the Mariner in slave-trading activities[11] and equate the Albatross with the victims of colonial exploitation, a leap Empson resisted. Whether this leap makes for a better or worse

[9]Perkins is right to point out that "If Empson could have said that the albatross symbolizes 'native peoples,' his interpretation would have been clearer and simpler in linking maritime expansion to colonialism and slavery. But he cannot say it, for it would make the remorse of the Mariner appropriate and his suffering a just punishment. In other words, it would reinstate the Christian interpretation of the poem . . ." (441).

[10]According to Empson, "The Ancient Mariner" is "the first and best study" of "neurotic guilt," which is essentially a state of feeling guilty without being able to "identify rationally any source of wrong doing." See *The Ancient Mariner* (306–14).

[11]Chris Rubinstein, for example, identifies the Mariner as "a sometime seafarer engaged in the slave trade, guilty of the most appalling atrocities, but now endeavouring to come to terms with his deep despair and mental torment . . ." (16). Cf. Keane (157).

reading of "The Ancient Mariner" remains to be seen. Ebbatson, for example, in his seminal 1972 essay "Coleridge's Mariner and the Rights of Man" advances the claim that "The Ancient Mariner" enacts the "gigantic historical process" of colonial conquest, and that the shoot-ing of the Albatross represents "a symbolic rehearsal of the crux of colonial expansion, the enslavement" and murder of "native peoples" (180, 198). Ebbatson conceives of his article as a modest expansion of Empson's "piercing insight" that "the theme of *The Ancient Mariner* is maritime expansion" (176), and he undoubtedly coincides with Empson on a number of points, not least of all an aversion to Christian readings of the poem, which in his view are "impervious to a weight" of contrary "evidence" (175). Like Empson, Ebbatson attempts to show how in interpretations of "The Ancient Mariner" an "inside" may be related to "an outside, " a "psychology" to a "history." But the psy-chology Ebbatson has in mind (which entails Coleridge's powerfully articulated sense of entrapment, due to his addiction to opium, which made him "feel a bond with the slave denied to a more robust soul like Wordsworth" [206]) is not equivalent to "neurotic guilt" as analyzed by Empson. The difference lies in the fact that for Empson it is precisely the innocence of the person who experiences guilt that leads to neuro-sis. Ebbatson, on the other hand, unambiguously legitimates the cause for guilt in the Mariner. In his view "The Ancient Mariner" is not a poem about a "motiveless" but a serious crime. The Mariner has after all "transgressed against the indigenous peoples of the globe, and his transgression is to be punished. The punishment, which might have been to die at the Negro slave's act of retribution (Death), is in fact a prolonged torment (Life-in-Death)" (205). In Ebbatson's reading there is no room for a plea of innocence on the Mariner's behalf, nor for a form of guilt that exceeds the "crime" from which it springs.

By connecting the Mariner's guilt with the slave trade and with Coleridge's full comprehension, based on his personal experiences, of the "inward humiliation and debasement" of a "Negro slave," Ebbat-son makes a more cogent case than Empson regarding the fit between the poem's "inside" and "outside." But this fit comes with a cost. Ebbatson's sense that "The Ancient Mariner" is a poem about just ret-ribution for a serious transgression makes his reading perfectly congru-ent with a Christian interpretation. If in "The Ancient Mariner" crime and punishment are in just proportion, a religious frame serves just as well as a historical frame to advance this point of view about the poem's meaning. It is therefore not surprising to observe that at one point in the essay Ebbatson admits the possibility of reading "The Ancient

Mariner" in religious terms, as "a parable of guilt and redemption" (198). Once again, as in McGann's essay, we arrive at a point of collusion between religious and historicist interpretations of the poem.

Ebbatson is the most notable critic prior to Keane to make a strong case concerning the importance of the slave trade to a reading of "The Ancient Mariner." He also alludes to the French Revolution as "the crucial contemporary fact" for both Coleridge and Wordsworth, claiming that "the Revolution itself was indissolubly linked with slave society in the French colonies" (187). But instead of showing how the connection between the French Revolution and the slave trade is represented in "The Ancient Mariner," Ebbatson uses it as a dispensation for dealing exclusively with the latter. While Ebbatson highlights the slave trade and marginalizes the French Revolution, Kitson does the opposite. For Kitson the French Revolution was unquestionably the event that had the most bearing on the composition of "The Ancient Mariner." "Without the experience of the French Revolution," he argues, " 'The Ancient Mariner' would not be the poem it is" (207). According to Kitson, the guilt so powerfully articulated in the poem stems from two sources connected with Coleridge's experience of the French Revolution: the collective guilt of the British nation whose actions against France generated the worst atrocities of the Revolution; and Coleridge's personal guilt for having believed that a political revolution could on its own bring about the regeneration of mankind. For Kitson therefore, the Mariner's guilt is appropriately large in congruence with the crimes that underwrite it, which are at once historically specific and "symbolical . . . of all sin." "It was a crime," Kitson claims, "for the Mariner to shoot the albatross just as it was a crime for Eve to eat the apple. It was also a crime for Coleridge to believe and encourage people to expect that mankind could improve itself by its own action unaided by grace" (205). As this statement indicates, for Kitson there appears to be no discrepancy between a religious reading of "The Ancient Mariner" in terms of original sin and a political reading in terms of the historically determined crimes of a given generation. Kitson disregards the evidence presented by Empson and Ebbatson concerning Coleridge's distaste for original sin in the 1790s due to his Unitarian affiliations, because in the end he needs this emphasis to advance a redemptive reading of the poem. The Mariner, Kitson writes, "commits a spiritual and symbolic sin when he shoots the benevolent albatross. He is punished for this by physical agony and by loneliness." For a time he becomes "totally alienated from nature" until he perceives the water snakes as beautiful and "his sympathy with them leads to love of God.

The curse is lifted. It is an act of grace that enables the mariner to begin the long process of restoration. . . . Following this the mariner is refreshed spiritually and physically by the fall of rain" (206–7). What is troublesome in this rendition of the poem is the extent to which the significance of the French Revolution as a devastating historical event becomes diminished. In Kitson's version of the poem, "the gigantic shadow" that the French Revolution supposedly cast across the poem begins to look more like a benign sun ray, dictating in Coleridge "a new faith in the restorative qualities of the imaginative perception of nature" (207). While Kitson's unwillingness to condemn Coleridge for this turn away from history to nature is refreshing in the current climate of stern disapprobation of such a move by new historicists, his happy version of "The Ancient Mariner" as a Christian story of sin, punishment, and ultimate salvation elides the disturbing terror that this poem conveys, a terror that could be, but is not meaningfully linked by Kitson with the French Revolution.

It was Maniquis who understood this link and who, although devoting only two paragraphs to "The Ancient Mariner," was able to capture much more accurately than Kitson the impact of the French Revolution on Coleridge's poem.[12] For Maniquis the French Revolution dealt a powerful blow to traditional ways of reading the universe in sacramental terms and rendered fragile all romantic attempts at "sacramentalizing" the "natural — and historical process" (389). The "savagery" unleashed by the French Revolution generated two conflicting perspectives on violence that account for the prevalent "expressions of sacramental failure" in romantic poetry. On the one hand, the Terror seemed like old violence and was linked with recurrent episodes of brutality throughout history, especially primitive rites of human sacrifice. On the other hand, the Terror appeared to have the characteristics of a new form of violence, for which the past offered no meaningful interpretative narratives. It was precisely this double consciousness of an event at once linked with the past and disconnected from it that generates the Romantic endeavour to invoke a sacramental order, and the disconcerting collapse of this order caused by the irruption of a violence "without any symbolic mediation" (385–86). Among the Romantics, Coleridge conveyed this dilemma more radically than either Blake or Wordsworth. In "The Ancient Mariner" he "pushed to the extreme . . . moments of void from which all meaning must then be reconstructed"

---

[12]For the view that history is a disruptive and demonic force in "The Ancient Mariner," undermining Christian values, see also Watkins.

(391). Indeed, no "other literary work in English literature so strikingly portrays violence stripped to such naked phenomenalism" (390), that is, a "pure act of violence before interpretation, not yet fitted into discourses of symbolic exchange." Maniquis is the only critic who points out the connection between the French revolution and the breakdown in "The Ancient Mariner" of a sacrificial system that interprets violence in sacramental terms. Although he does not provide an analysis of the various sacrificial layers in this poem, his view that the center of the poem is occupied by a symbol "devoid of all determinate sacrificial meaning" (391) — the Albatross hung around the Mariner's neck — sets up an illuminating path of inquiry, one that shall briefly pursue in the concluding part of this essay.

With Maniquis and Kitson the historical site most relevant to a reading of "The Ancient Mariner" shifts considerably from the slave trade to the French Revolution. It was Keane who put the slave trade back on the map of historical criticism without losing sight of the French Revolution. Keane's book offers by far the most informed and wide-ranging discussion of the sociopolitical context that influenced the composition of "The Ancient Mariner," and can be regarded as the first new historicist study of the poem, even as Keane practices a cautious as well as anxious brand of new historicism, constantly worrying about the danger of elevating the "historical resonance" of the poem at the expense of its "linguistic wonder" (184).[13] The first half of Keane's study offers an eminently painstaking, informed, and fair-minded assessment of Coleridge's views on race and the slave trade vis-à-vis Defoe's, neither overlooking Coleridge's occasional racist statements, nor simplifying his ambivalent reactions to the actual abolition of the slave trade. While Keane's documentation of Coleridge's career as an abolitionist and of the literature that directly influenced the poem's politically charged images is impressive, his actual interpretation of "The Ancient Mariner" does not move beyond the perspective articulated by previous critics who have dealt with the slave trade issue. Like Ebbatson, Keane declares the Mariner guilty of the crime of killing a slave and the crew complicit in it, and like Ware he brings the slave trade within the compass of a sacramental reading of the poem, arguing that the killing of the Albatross disturbs the "profound relationship unifying humanity, and in turn, humanity with the natural world" (144). Keane's more original as well as provocative contributions pertain not

[13]For the problems emerging in Keane's study from this uneasy relationship with New Historicism see my review in *JEGP* 95 (1996): 447–51.

to the slave trade or the French Revolution, but to a third historical site that is the actual focus of his study, namely domestic politics in the aftermath of the French Revolution and Coleridge's active opposition to Prime Minister William Pitt in the years prior to the poem's composition. Keane stresses the close connection between the "dungeon-grate" image and the blessing of the water snakes episode in the poem, arguing that both derive "from Coleridge's fears, in the Spring of 1798, that . . . without the political equivalent of the blessing of the water-snakes, the possibility of a dungeon-grate intruding between *Coleridge* and the sun was a real and present danger" (190). In a radical departure from other critical interpretations of the poem's main redemptive event, Keane claims that the water snakes embody the Pitt ministry, an association that often appears in Coleridge's political prose, and that their blessing reflects not love but "Coleridge's enforced prostration" before his political enemies out of fear of "being crushed" by them (336). In this context the Albatross no longer stands for a black slave but for the spirit of liberty that Coleridge betrays when he withdraws from political activities and that Pitt openly assaults through his continuing involvements. Likewise the Mariner's ship stands for the British ship of state under Pitt as represented in the period's cartoons, and its destruction "amid a submarine *rumbling*," is full of political implications, foretelling the coming of the revolution (268–69).

The problem with this reading is not simply that it is counterintuitive and incompatible with "the poem's manifest level or literal meaning," as Keane knows (174), but that it becomes contradictory in its own terms. Readers may find it odd that a sacramental reading of the poem is defended at the juncture where the Mariner kills the Albatross, but denied at the point he blesses the water snakes. As well may they wonder how the interpretation of the killing of the Albatross as symbolic of the sacrifice of slaves fits in with the view that the blessing of the water snakes reflects Coleridge's capitulation to Pitt. Given the strict parallelism and reverse implications of the two episodes, it would have made more sense to argue that the killing of the Albatross represents a symbolic assassination of Pitt for which Coleridge makes amends in the episode of the blessing; or that Pitt himself is implicated in the killing of slaves given Coleridge's distrust of the sincerity of Pitt's support of abolition bills.[14] Keane himself provides evidence for the former hypothesis

---

[14]See Coleridge's "Lecture on the Slave Trade," in which he accuses those who "think William Pitt sincere in his professions concerning the abolition of this diabolical Trade" of lack of "discernment." *Lectures 1795: On Politics and Religion*, 245.

when he suggests that the blessing does not stand just for Coleridge's prostration before the Pitt ministry out of fear, but also articulates his acceptance, even love of his enemies under the dispensation of a "benevolent Necessitarianism" that sees evil as part of the "benign Creator's grand scheme" (334). But if this is so, how does one account for the fact that later on in the poem Coleridge, as Keane points out, gives vent to his "revolutionary wrath," sinking "the *counter*revolutionary Ship of State steered by" the prime minister (269–70)? Even as one may accept an ambivalence in Coleridge's response toward Pitt that would take the form of both "revulsion and providential acceptance" (336), one would still expect a different sequence in the poem from wrath to love (in conjunction with the sequence from killing to blessing) and not vice versa.[15]

Despite such problems, Keane's study offers by far the most comprehensive picture of Coleridge's political voyaging in the years preceding the composition of the poem. On the subject of domestic politics Keane misses no piece of relevant historical data. But on the slave trade as a context for a political reading of "The Ancient Mariner," Keane, like all critics of the Romantic period, makes no mention of the crucial part played by Dahomey's scandalous rites of mass human sacrifices in the debates about the abolition of the slave trade in England.[16] In the

---

[15]There is also the further complication in which Keane acknowledges that it is the Mariner himself, who like "that divided patriot" Coleridge himself, is "aboard the doomed" and guilty ship (270). This implies, however, that Coleridge consciously or unconsciously erases all distinctions between himself and his political enemy, making both complicit in the assassination of liberty, which is highly improbable. Keane is also aware that the association of the Albatross with "freedom and the victims of slavery" undermines a "crudely" political definition of "this great symbolic bird" (358).

[16]It is peculiar that no mention is made of Dahomey in romantic studies, even in those specifically concerned with the slave trade. Dahomey was not an obscure but a notorious country, whose rise to power on the slave coast and rituals of human sacrifice had been observed by many Europeans and publicized in many captivating narratives, including William Snelgrave's *A New Account of Some Parts of Guinea and the Slave Trade* (1734); Robert Norris, *Memoirs of the Reign of Bossa Ahadee, King of Dahomey* (1789); Archibald Dalzel, *The History of Dahomey, An Inland Kingdom of Africa* (1793); and Richard Burton, *A Mission to Gelele, King of Dahomey* (1864). In the eighteenth and early part of the nineteenth century knowledge about Dahomey in England was disseminated through reviews of narratives in major periodicals. John Astley's ever-popular *A New General Collection of Voyages and Travels*, 4 vols. (1745–47); Joseph Ritson's *An Essay on Abstinence from Animal Food, as a Moral Duty* (1802); and most significantly, the parliamentary debates about the abolition of the slave trade. So well known was Dahomey in these debates that Reverend James Ramsey in *Objections to the Abolition of the Slave Trade with Answers* (1788) assigns it a case number, "nr. 65," which reads: *"The king of Dahomey murders his people for his amusement, therefore we may traffick in slaves."* (This statement captures the typical way in which slave traders made use of the sacrificial rites of Dahomey to justify their occupation.) In the latter part of the nineteenth century,

last two decades of the eighteenth century Dahomey became a test case in these debates, as witnesses called to testify before both houses of the Parliament were routinely asked to comment on the practice of human sacrifice in Dahomey and other parts of Africa.[17] For slave traders Dahomey was a lucky find, enabling them to offer a "humanitarian" argument in defense of their occupation, as is evident in the following slogan of antiabolitionist literature: "Suppress the Slave Trade and it is evident human sacrifices would be endless."[18] On the other hand, abolitionists consistently avoided any mention of Dahomey's rites of sacrifice, even when like Coleridge, or Thomas Clarkson, they specifically refer to this kingdom in their work.[19] I have no room to present this history here but I want to suggest that the intense focus on Dahomey's rites in parliamentary debates about the slave trade represents the

---

news about Dahomey's rituals appeared with regularity in the London *Times,* as many British officials, including Richard Burton, were sent to this country in a futile attempt to stop the slave trade and human sacrifices. See my article "Unremembered Sights of Violence: The Scandal of Dahormey's Rites of Human Sacrifice in the Debates about the Abolition of the Slave Trade in England."

[17]See, e.g., *Abridgement of the Minutes of the Evidence 1789–91.*

[18]This statement appears in *The True State of the Question.* Here the anonymous author regrets having ignorantly signed a petition at Derby in favor of the abolition of the slave trade, and, to justify his conversion to the cause of the antiabolitionists, lists a string of citations regarding the practice of human sacrifice in Africa from the testimony of various witnesses interviewed by the Parliament.

[19]Coleridge mentions Dahomey several times in his work, without any reference to this kingdom's rites of sacrifice. See *On the Constitution of Church and State* (16); his marginal note to Richard Payne Knight's *An Analytical Inquiry into the Principles of Taste* (I: 11–12 n5); and his *Essay on Taste* in *Shorter Works and Fragments* (I: 363–64). Thomas Clarkson was well-acquainted with Dahomey, being involved in a controversy with Robert Norris, the author of the well-reviewed *Memoirs of Bossa Ahadee, King of Dahomey,* which Clarkson read while it was still in manuscript form. This controversy was taken up by the Parliament who interviewed both witnesses regarding an original conversation they had in 1787 during which Clarkson formed the mistaken opinion that Norris supported the abolition of the slave trade. See *Abridgement of the Minutes of the Evidence* (III: 15–34). Although Clarkson, in the second edition of his prize-winning *An Essay on the Slavery and Commerce of the Human Species* (1786; 1788), added a brief section on Dahomey based on Norris's narrative, he leaves out any reference to the practice of human sacrifice in this country (39). The first time that Clarkson mentions this practice is in his retrospective account of the slave trade in *The History of the Rise, Progress, and Accomplishment of the Abolition of the African Slave Trade by the British Parliament* (1808), where he shows how devastating for the abolitionist cause were Norris's and other slavetraders' testimonies regarding human sacrifice in Africa (478–86). But even here Clarkson downplays the significance of these sacrifices, claiming that they were confined to only "one or two countries in Africa," that their frequency had been exaggerated, and that they were superstitious rites no different from those that took place "at Otaheite, or in Britain in the time of the Druids" (485). For Coleridge's review of Clarkson's *History* and his familiarity with the Clarkson-Norris controversy see *Shorter Works and Fragments* (I: 216–243) and "Unremembered Sights of Violence" (12–14).

covert referent in the predominant sacrificial rhetoric of abolitionist tracts, and might also have a bearing on the prevalence of sacrificial themes in Romantic literature. It was not just the French Revolution, but also the slave trade that put into circulation and gave new life to the paradigm of sacrifice, fueling the Romantics' keen sense that rituals of human sacrifice were not a thing of the past, but a most distressing contemporary practice. Hence one way of connecting the French Revolution with the slave trade in historicist readings of "The Ancient Mariner" is through an exploration of the poem's sacrificial symbols, a subject insufficiently dealt with by critics thus far. In what follows I want to examine the poem's handling of sacrifice within three contextual frameworks: the Old Testament murder/sacrifice of Abel, the New Testament sacrifice of Christ, and pagan or Christian sacrifices from the travel literature that Coleridge read.

Perhaps no biblical story connects more deeply with the breakdown of a sacrificial economy in "The Ancient Mariner," as pointed out by Maniquis, than the Old Testament recounting of the murder of Abel. From its very inception the story has been, as Ricardo J. Quinones eloquently puts it, about "a breach in existence, a fracture at the heart of things" (3), highlighting the *"tragedy of differentiation"* brought about by divine *"arbitrariness of preference"* (9), and, in its nineteenth-century transformations, the necessary "flight from an undifferentiated communion" for the sake of individuation (19). Thus the Cain-Abel story either refers nostalgically to an ideal of unity at the very moment of its dissolution, or may present this very ideal as illusory, and its violation as a necessary condition of subjectivity, an ambiguity that is at the heart of Coleridge's poem. Furthermore, this story radically destabilizes the significance of sacrificial rites, identifying this very practice as the source of the first murder in human history. No other biblical narrative makes more explicit the dangerous proximity of "legitimate" and "criminal" violence that is already embedded in the structure of sacrifice, allowing for their "reciprocal substitution."[20] Its central event, the killing of Abel, inhabits a liminal space between profane and sacred violence, appearing in turn as an unauthorized murder caused by Cain's corrupt nature, or as an actual sacrifice, yielding in the long run a beneficial return. As commentators have shown, from Augustine on, the Cain-Abel story has been often read as a foundation sacrifice, similar to the Romulus-Remus myth with which it shares the connection between

---

[20]This is a central component of René Girard's theory of sacrifice in *Violence and the Sacred*.

fratricide and the building of a city.[21] Moreover, the slaying of Abel has been also interpreted as a prefiguration of the sacrifice of Christ, although in the nineteenth century this was a highly disputed subject, tied to the controversial issue as to whether Old Testament sacrifices were a purely human institution or ordained by God.[22]

Coleridge shared with other Romantics a keen interest in the character of Cain, which he developed at an early stage of his poetic career. As is well known, Coleridge had planned to write a poem on Cain in 1796, which eventually led to his abortive collaboration with Wordsworth on "The Wanderings of Cain," and subsequently on "The Ancient Mariner." For his poem on Cain Coleridge turned to two main sources, Flavius Josephus's *Antiquities of the Jews* and Pierre Bayle's *Historical and Critical Dictionary*.[23] The two authors represent Cain in such strikingly divergent ways that any attempt at reconciliation would have been fruitless, and Coleridge drew his inspiration mainly from Bayle's typically irreverent rendition of biblical material, even as Josephus's pinpointing of Cain's avaricious nature as the origin of his crime would have interested Coleridge, given his views on private property in the 1790s.[24] In Josephus Cain appears as an unredeemably wicked

[21]See Quinones, Introduction (10–11, ch. 1).

[22]The view that sacrifice was a human institution rather than divinely ordained has had various proponents throughout history, including Maimonides, Tertullian, and Cyril of Alexandria. See William Magee, *Discourses on the Scriptural Doctrines of Atonement and Sacrifice* (1801) 283–86 (i.e. note 2 to p. 47). In the late seventeenth and eighteenth centuries, this view was vindicated, among others, by John Spencer in *De Legibus Hebraearum ritualibus, et earum rationibus, libri tres* (1685), and by William Warburton in *The Divine Legation of Moses* (IX: ch. 2). *Works* (1788) III: 660–62. In the nineteenth century William Magee in *Discourses* launched a powerful attack against this position, arguing that the sacrifices of the law, such as Abel's animal offering, were a divine institution, and intimately connected with the sacrifice of Christ, being in effect "but preparations for this one great sacrifice . . . ordained by God . . . in which all others were to have their consummation" (53). See esp. *Discourses* (Sermon II: 45–71, 282–374nn). Later in the century John Davidson refuted Magee's arguments, reasserting the view that Old Testament sacrifices, unlike the sacrifice of Christ, were of purely human origin, stirring further controversies. See John Davison, *An Inquiry into the Origin and Intent of Primitive Sacrifice, and the Scripture Evidence Respecting It* (1825), and John Edward Nassau Molesworth, *An Answer to Davison's Inquiry into the Origin and Intent of Primitive Sacrifice* (1826). Coleridge refers to Magee's often reprinted *Discourses* in a notebook entry tentatively dated by Kathleen Coburn as 1812. See *Notebooks* III: #4140n and cf. IV: #5215, 5384. He engages the issue as to whether Old Testament sacrifices "were types and shadows of Christ's Death" in two late notebook entries of summer or fall of 1831 (British Museum Add. ms. 47545 ff. 28ᵛ–29 and 29ᵛ–30). I am grateful to Anthony Harding for bringing these entries to my attention.

[23]For the history of the "Wanderings of Cain" and its sources in Josephus, Bayle, as well as Salomon Gessner's *The Death of Abel* (1760), see John Livingston Lowes, *The Road to Xanadu*. (236–38, 255–60).

[24]See Kathleen Coburn's note to entry 277 of vol. I of *Notebooks*.

character, already bent on violence prior to the killing of Abel due to his acquisitive predisposition, and continuing to amass "much wealth, by rapine and violence" (I.2:42) after he settled in the city of Nod. Josephus contends that Cain's offering to God was "the invention of a covetous man," obtained "by forcing the ground," in contrast to Abel's offering of "what grew naturally of its own accord" (I.2:42). Bayle, on the other hand, ridicules such fanciful interpretations of Cain's offering as defective or unnatural, reminding Josephus that the Law of Moses ordains the offering of the first ears of corn to God. He also challenges Josephus's reading of Cain's invention of weights and measures, arguing that this did not change "the world into cunning craftiness," but on the contrary was designed to prevent cheating among Cain's descendants who had become a "wicked" and "dissolute" people.[25]

"When once a Man," Bayle writes, "is grown scandalous for his ill Actions, the very Good he does shall be condemned: of this *Cain* is an Example" (248). This statement would have struck a sympathetic chord in Coleridge at a time when domestic terror rendered everyone liable to persecution, and connects with the Mariner's irreversible damnation, even though, unlike Josephus's Cain, he engages in no further acts of violence after the initial killing, clinging to a new ethos of love of "All things both great and small." But of greater relevance to a reading of "The Ancient Mariner" are Bayle's entries on the Canites' views on tutelary genii "principally called *Demons*" (249), which might have contributed to the presence of supernatural spirits in the poem. According to Bayle, the Canites believed that the God of the Old Testament "had sown Discord in the World"; that the tutelary genius who "produced *Abel* was of an Order much inferior" (that is, weaker) to "that which produced *Cain*"; and that the attachment of a particular genius to a person is a matter of pure accident, for as "the Souls that were sent into this World were drawn by Lot, so was likewise the Tutelar Genius of Every Person" (249). It is therefore possible to see how "Evil may exist as well as Good" just as "there may be mischievous *Genii* as well as beneficent ones" (251).

Several strands from Bayle's entries on Cain leave visible traces on "The Ancient Mariner," as well as "The Wanderings of Cain." The motiveless and sudden killing of the Albatross as if the Mariner yields to the "innate promptings of an evil 'Imp of the Perverse,' as Poe called it";[26] the dice game played by the spectral Death and Life-in-Death;

[25]See the entry on Cain and Cainites in Pierre Bayle, *The Dictionary Historical and Critical,* II: 246–51.
[26]Cited by Keane, 201.

and Coleridge's notorious statement to Mrs. Barbauld that the poem "ought to have had no more moral than the *Arabian Nights'* tale" of the unlucky merchant whose date shell accidentally puts out the eye of a geni's son[27] — all have obvious connections with Bayle's *Dictionary* entries that suggest that evil actions may be the consequence of the sport of some whimsical supernatural agency. Furthermore, these entries call into question a single center of divine authority, introducing a proliferation of spirits who use human hosts for their actions and who may be more powerful than the Jehovah of the Old Testament. For the two protagonists of Coleridge's works the very uncertainty concerning the ruling deity in a world in which spirits rise everywhere represents the greatest source of their existential perplexity and suffering. In "The Wanderings of Cain" this perplexity becomes especially acute, given the presence of two rival deities, the God of the Living and the God of the Dead, each requiring different, though unknowable kinds of sacrifices. Abel's warning to Cain that "Wretched shall they be all the days of their mortal life . . . who sacrifice worthy and acceptable sacrifices to the God of the Dead" (291) highlights the collapse of a predictable sacrificial order which is already at the center of the biblical myth, and further hints at the possibility that one might unwittingly offer the right sacrifice to the wrong deity. But who is the *right* deity in "The Wanderings of Cain"? Since Abel presumably offered the proper sacrifice to the proper deity, why is it, as Cain rightly asks, that the Creator forsook Abel and left him in a state of distress and lamentation no different from that of Cain (291–92)?

Cain's anxious questions point to what is undoubtedly Coleridge's most significant revision of the biblical myth, namely the representation of Cain and Abel as doubles of each other. In "The Wanderings of Cain" not only do the two characters share the same pallid appearance "like the white sands beneath their feet" (291), but their fate appears to be identical: both are stricken by misery and lament their existence, and both are bereft of divine favor. Cain's sole experience of God is one of such intense persecution that he wishes himself as inert as a lifeless rock. Conversely, Abel feels persecuted by the God of the Dead with no hope of help from the God of the Living. "The Rime of the Ancient Mariner" takes this resemblance between the two characters a step further, merging them into a single figure. The Mariner, as Susan Eilenberg notes, is a "composite of Cain" and "of the brother he murdered" (46). This means that the Mariner carries a dual identity; he is at once

[27]See *Table Talk,* I: 149, 272–73. Cf. Keane, 129n8.

the perpetrator and the victim of a transgression, both guilty and innocent, and in a sacrificial context, both sacrificer and sacrificed. Furthermore, like the protagonists of "The Wanderings of Cain," and in
keeping with Bayle's representation of Cain, the Mariner is not justly
punished, as he has been represented in both historicist and Christian
readings, but remains a persecuted figure, thrown into an irrational
world of "warring and delusive spirits" that exceeds the "terribleness of
a dream," and suspends all certainty as to "whether the cosmos is a cosmos, united under a single, benevolent God" (Eilenberg 46).

Such ambiguities are intimately connected with the difficulty of
interpreting the Mariner's crime in terms of either profane or sacred
violence which, as seen before, is at the root of the Cain-Abel myth and
its critical tradition. Critics who have read "The Ancient Mariner" as a
story of ultimate salvation have implicitly invoked the recuperative
economy of sacrifice in which violence serves a redemptive purpose.
Hence the killing of the Albatross functions as a foundation sacrifice,
setting up the necessary precondition for the blessing of the water
snakes and the new covenant between God, man, bird, and beast, as
stated in the poem's concluding moral. In this reading the Mariner's
world is sacramental through and through, and the Albatross is from
the very beginning a sacred bird. But this is a highly questionable
hypothesis, because in the poem the identity of either the world or of
the bird is largely undetermined, and yields conflicting perspectives.
The Albatross appears in turn as an ordinary bird upon whom a superstitious crew confers supernatural powers, as Empson contended, or as
totemic bird, which the Mariner, ignorant of its high status unwittingly
kills. Conversely, while several of the poem's main events suggest the
existence of some primitive pre-Christian sacred order ruled by spirits,
at the beginning of the poem there are certainly no signs whatsoever of
a sacramental unity of deity, man, and beast. On the contrary, the universe in which the Mariner finds himself is alien, inhospitable, and lifeless ("Nor shapes of men nor beast we ken — / The ice was all
between" [ll.57–8]. The killing of the Albatross reflects at some level
the Mariner's need to ascertain the sacred boundaries of this unknown
environment and it does in fact release spiritual forces, just as the rav-
aging of the bower in Wordsworth's "Nutting" establishes the presence
of a "spirit in the wood. " In this sense both acts bear a certain resemblance to sacrificial practices, in that it is precisely through violence that
the sacred is instantiated. Yet neither character reaps the benefits of a
sacrificial economy, in part because they act without the consent of a
community, and expose themselves to the threat of vengeance, which is

already an indication of a failed sacrifice, as the Cain-Abel story amply attests. Furthermore, the documented parallels between the killing of the Albatross and the hunting of a stag in Bürger's "Der Wilde Jaeger" or the shooting of a bird in Philip Quarll's *The England Hermit*[28] seriously jeopardize the interpretation of the Mariner's act in terms of sacrifice by introducing the competing paradigm of hunting. Although, as Walter Burkhert has shown, sacrifice might have originated from hunting rituals, writers throughout the ages from Aeschylus on have used hunting as the most powerful tool of exposing the profane nature of crimes performed under a false sacrificial dispensation. This is also why the theme of the hunt is so often linked with that of a curse; while in sacrifice violence yields the blessing of a divinity, the hunt is sacrilegious, attracting a curse.[29] In both *The Oresteia* and "Der Wilde Jaeger" the curse takes a particular form of immediate relevance to the fate of the Mariner: "the hunter becomes the hunted" (Parsons 114).

The prominence of the theme of hunting in "The Ancient Mariner" and other romantic poems has a historical referent in the violence of the French Revolution and the daily experience during the Reign of Terror of one radical group hunting down another, only to become the hunted victims of a next round of revolutionary wrath. This also explains the popularity of the Cain-Abel story at this time, as evinced by one of the most widely circulating slogans during the French Revolution, *fraternité ou la mort* (fraternity or death) (Quinones 1–6), which captured the violent conjunction between two absolute and contradictory principles, brotherhood and death, the sacrality of the social bond and its profane violation, a fact painfully demonstrated by the course of the Revolution. It is surprising that historicist critics have not exploited more the Cain-Abel story in relation to "The Ancient Mariner," for it is this story that provides the mediating link desired by Maniquis between the "massive violence of the French Revolution and the killing of a seabird" (391). The very fact that the Mariner kills the Albatross shortly after he perceives it as a possibly kindred spirit, "a Christian soul," shows how dangerously close the ideal of brotherhood has come to its complete negation. This is one of the painful lessons of history that Coleridge and other contemporaries of the French revolution

[28]Coleman O. Parsons, "The Mariner and the Albatross," 112–17, cf. Lowes, 16, 458–60, 478, 484, 486, 497.
   [29]Walter Burkhert, *Homo Necans. The Anthropology of Ancient Greek Sacrificial Ritual and Myth*. The theme of the hunt and of sacrifice is prevalent in Wordsworth's poetry. See my article "Blood Sacrifice, Gift Economy and the Edenic World: Wordsworth's 'Home at Grasmere.'"

experienced again and again: generalized violence, like an infernal God, arbitrarily picks its victims and turns people into unwitting instruments of violence; that at such times the distinguishing boundaries between friends and foes, brothers and murderers disappears.

The Cain-Abel story also connects with the slave trade, thus functioning as a bridge between the two sites of violence identified in historicist readings of "The Ancient Mariner." The theme of violated brotherhood is paramount in antislavery documents and resonates fully in "The Rime of the Ancient Mariner." Its presence is also apparent in "The Wanderings of Cain," which makes a direct reference to the slave trade. Here Cain encounters the voice of Abel as "thin and querulous, like that of a feeble slave in misery, who despairs altogether, yet can not refrain himself from weeping and lamentation" (290). By killing Abel, Cain in effect has reduced him to the condition of slavery — a state of grief and lamentation when one is neither fully alive nor dead, leading a ghostlike existence, which, as shown before, becomes precisely Cain's own predicament. What Coleridge suggests in both fragment and poem is the equivalence between murder, slavery and self-enslavement. By killing the Albatross the Mariner has in effect become trapped in an existential state equivalent to that of a slave. In this context it is useful to note Ebbatson's valuable comment that "the act of hanging the albatross round the Mariner's neck" might "be an image of the slave laden with ball and chain" (201n76; cf. Rubinstein 21). But Ebbatson seems unaware that this comment undermines his equation of the Mariner with a violent colonialist and of the Albatross with a gentle native or innocent slave, for it demonstrates that it is the Mariner rather than the Albatross that carries on the yoke of the agonizing existence of a slave. It is also difficult to identify the Albatross with a slave, because it roams freely, or with a happy and generous-minded free native, because it is solitary, disconnected from a community, and possibly "disconsolate," as it is described in Shelvocke's narrative.[30] The Albatross in fact embodies an alienated existence akin to that of the Mariner, but eagerly attaches itself to a new community by partaking of its food, play, and religious ceremonies. It is possible to suggest that for the Mariner, who neither plays with nor feeds the Albatross like his shipmates,[31] this rep-

---

[30]The relevant passage from Shelvocke's *A Voyage round the World by the Way of the Great South Sea* . . . (London, 1726) is cited in Lowes 226.

[31]This point is emphasized by O. Brian Fulmer, who notes that "Although the Mariner joined the crew in welcoming the bird when it first appeared, he seems to stand in sharp contrast to the seamen even before his cruel act. The bird returns each day 'to the mariners' hollo!' not to his . . ." (807).

resents a false attempt to resolve alienation through a naive faith in the goodness and hospitality of human beings. In killing the Albatross the Mariner instinctively destroys this very assumption of brotherly love and unity for which he finds no immediate corroboration in the ice-bound and distinctly hostile environment around him, nor for that matter did Coleridge find much evidence of it in his world, where the daily traffic in slaves and slaughter of human beings not only in France and other European countries, but also in African countries by Africans themselves, offered a demoralizing picture of "humanity cannibalizing itself" (Maniquis 377).

While the Old Testament Cain-Abel story connects with "The Ancient Mariner" on many levels, the New Testament story of Christ's crucifixion has a more limited range of applicability, even though it has dominated the critical interpretation of the poem. Critics who have invoked this biblical context have generally emphasized the severity of the Mariner's crime, either to reveal the wonder of redemptive mercy, or to explain why his crime is "unforgivable." For example, O. Bryan Fulmer, like W. H. Auden, equates the Albatross with the Holy Ghost and Christ, but he perceives the Mariner's predicament in terms of eternal damnation rather than Auden's paradigm of the fortunate fall. Fulmer argues that the Mariner is conflated with the legendary figure of the Wandering Jew who refused hospitality to Christ, and that in effect he "crucifies Christ again by killing the albatross, just as according to the Jew in the *Reliques* ballad, blasphemers re-crucify their Saviour" (807–8).[32] Yet oddly enough, Fulmer provides the best arguments against the full equation of the Albatross with Christ, noting that the ritual whereby the shipmates hang the Albatross around the Mariner's neck represents "an ironic reversal of the crucifixion. The cross-like brand of sin, which is also a promissory indication of retribution to be made, is in direct contrast with the symbol of the innocent Christ" (807). The lines "Instead of the cross, the Albatross / About my neck was hung" (ll.141–2) highlight the dissociation between the Albatross and Christ, undoing their tenuous connection as constructed by the crew earlier: "As if it had been a Christian soul, / We hailed it in God's name" (ll.65–6). In fact it is possible to suggest, along with Fulmer, that the Mariner "rejects the associations which the albatross has with Christ and Christian rituals" (807), not because he is intent on destroy-ing "sanctity itself," as the critic contends, but because he perceives a

[32]On the connection between "The Ancient Mariner" and the legend of the Wan-dering Jew see Lowes (ch. xiv).

disjunction between this constructed symbol of a Christian order and the alien and terrifying world he inhabits. The Christian myth is further subverted by an even more glaring "reversal of the crucifixion," when the Albatross, instead of rising back to life, like Christ, sinks "Like lead into the sea" (1.295). The Albatross has become dead matter, a leftover from a symbolic system that can no longer reclaim it.

At the same time it is impossible to void the Albatross entirely of Christian significance, for the simple reason that it is represented in the poem as a substitute for the cross and, in any substitutive process the exchanged objects maintain a link with each other. By being connected with "him who died on the cross," the Albatross is represented as a sacrificial figure, an identity it passes on to the Mariner, when it is hung around his neck. Fulmer interprets the hung Albatross as related to "the burning cross Lewis's Wandering Jew bore as a mark of sin, a mark ultimately derived from Cain," in contrast to the cross, which represents "the symbol on innocent Christ" (807). But the critic misses the important clue that through the Albatross the Mariner assumes a Christlike identity. The association of the Mariner with Cain does not prevent his attaining this identity, for by the nineteenth century it is not just Abel who is linked with Christ but also Cain, a development made possible by the transformation of the Cain-Abel pair into doubles of each other. In "Adonais" Shelley makes an explicit connection between the mark of Cain and the crown of thorns worn by Christ, suggesting that both characters were subject to persecution (34: 306). It is indeed the emphasis on persecution in Coleridge's poem, as distinct from punishment for the purpose of moral regeneration, that turns the Mariner into a Christlike figure, with the difference that there is no ultimate salvation for the Mariner, nor does his suffering offer the sacrificial benefit of a united community.

The religious context I have examined shows the extent to which "The Ancient Mariner" both carries a significant number of sacrificial markers and subverts a sacrificial economy. But as Lowes contends, "Cain and the Wandering Jew are venerable figures, but they have no inherent associations with the sea," whereas "The Ancient Mariner" is "a sea-tale *par excellence*" (261). Ebbatson also argues that the literature of maritime expansion rather than biblical mythology is the "right starting-point for an interpretation of *The Ancient Mariner*" (175), and he identifies some sources from this vast material that are crucial to a sacrificial reading of the poem. In the concluding section of this essay I want to investigate this third sacrificial context by reviewing Ebbatson's examples, and pointing out the mistaken inferences this critic derives from them.

Ebbatson rightly directs our attention to "the murderous instinct for survival in an alien world" (177) so often described in the literature of colonial discovery, and he cites two particularly evocative examples from Vasco da Gama's and Columbus's journals. In the former we witness the violent encounter between Diaz and natives who "pelted him with stones from a hill," to which he retaliated by killing "one of them with a crossbow" (177). In the latter, a crew finds itself "in great peril" due to a squall "which tore all the sails," and consequently a victim is selected by the drawing of lots (the admiral) to be "sent to Santa Maria de la Cinta in Hueva" (177–78). These examples provide a revealing perspective on the killing of the Albatross or the crew's action of turning the Mariner into a sacrificial scapegoat, but Ebbatson either aligns them with the wrong stanzas in "The Ancient Mariner" or ignores important differences between text and source. It certainly makes sense, given the identity of the used weapons, to correlate the stanza about the killing of the Albatross with Diaz's action, but Ebbatson fails to note that while Diaz kills because he is being attacked first, the Albatross initiates no violent action. Ebbatson's linking of Diaz's with the Mariner's action would have been more plausible if the critic was willing to entertain the idea that the Albatross could be construed (or misconstrued) as dangerous, like the natives encountered by Diaz. But Ebbatson maintains that the Albatross is a benign creature representing a symbol of the kind of natives Columbus met in Hispaniola in 1492, who "are so guileless and so generous with all they possess that no one would believe it who has not seen it" (177); or those natives met by Captain Cook in Tahiti or Australia who "enjoy liberty in its fullest extent" and "live in a tranquility that is not disturbed by the inequality of condition" (179). But here again, regarding Columbus's journal, Ebbatson misses the point that the Albatross is not a host who gives everything away but is the receiver of acts of benefaction from the crew; and, regarding Captain Cook, the critic makes no mention of the explorer's discovery of rituals of human sacrifice at Otaheite, which are given a central place in the narrative of his voyage to the South Pacific.[33] Inadvertently, Ebbatson has actually located one of the most salient

---

[33]In *A Voyage to the Pacific Ocean,* Captain Cook often notes "barbarous" customs "still prevailing amongst this benevolent, humane people." For his description of the human sacrifices at Otaheite see vol. II, bk. III, ch. 2. On human sacrifice see also vol. I: 350–51; vol. II, ch. 10: 200–5; vol. III, ch. 8: 132, 161.

features of the literature of colonial expansion with which "The Ancient Mariner" might be connected. This concerns the explorers' pervasive uncertainties as to what sort of natives they would encounter in the unknown parts of the world, and their fears that violence was around the corner even where natives seemed most friendly and welcoming.

It is then possible to speculate that when the Mariner crosses the boundary of the known world ("We were the first that ever burst / Into that silent sea" [1817 105–06]), he would be apprehensive of possible threats to his life, apprehensions that are immediately confirmed by the inhospitable ice-bound environment whose sounds ominously resemble those of a hungry pack of wolves. For this reason the arrival of the Albatross superimposed on the growling sounds of cracking ice can only be confusing. In this context it is useful to recall the passage in Shelvocke's *Voyage round the World* that served as the immediate source of the killing of the Albatross. Here too a crew of mariners is exposed to "continual squals of sleet, snow and rain" in an environment where no "thing living" can be imagined to "subsist," and where they "had not had sight of one fish of any kind . . . nor sea-bird" with the exception of a single "disconsolate black *Albitross*" that followed them for several days "as if he had lost himself" (cited in Lowes 226). What triggers Hatley's killing of this albatross is precisely his inability to determine why this particular bird appears in a world where nothing else lives and his suspicion that it might be a supernatural bird of bad omen. Like Hatley, the Mariner himself is confronted with the incongruity between a live bird and a world with no other evidence of living creatures ("Nor shapes of men nor beasts we ken — / The ice was all between" [ll.57–8]), which, coupled with the extreme weather conditions, is sufficient to alert him to the dangerous potential of this uninvited guest. What is this playful bird that exacts hospitality from the crew doing in an alien place where hospitality is nowhere in sight? Is the Albatross a mere bird that seeks food, a tutelary spirit of this new world, or a deceptive symbol of Christian values liable to expose his crew to danger? While the motive for the killing of the Albatross can never be fully determined, surely the literature of discovery in which explorers so often articulate fears of survival and uncertainty about the disposition of indigenous beings, human or animal, provides a better ground of interpretation than original sin.

The second example cited by Ebbatson from Columbus's journal, which features a crew's arbitrary selection of a sacrificial victim to intervene with a deity on their behalf, raises a different set of questions that are not addressed by the critic. By a logic that is incomprehensible to me, Ebbatson connects this episode with the stanza in "The Ancient Mariner" describing the Hermit who lives in the wood and "loves to talk with marineres" (178). But this passage has more direct links with the crew's action of hanging the Albatross around the Mariner's neck, since it demonstrates how under extreme conditions of survival a community is liable to fall back on sacrificial practices. The shipmates certainly act like a sacrificial community in this instance, choosing one of their members to incur the punishment for an act that any of them could have easily committed, as their unanimous approval of the murder when their lot seems to improve indicates.[34] Ebbatson is aware that the shipmates are complicit in the Mariner's crime and that the Mariner expiates the collective "guilt of the European powers in their treatment of newly discovered people" (176), but he does not see how the Mariner's function as a scapegoat of European racial guilt changes his identity. In this light the Mariner appears as a victim, not just a victimizer, and his new condition is appropriately marked by the slain Albatross around his neck. As I have already argued, the Mariner and the Albatross become one, just as Cain and Abel become conflated into a single figure in Coleridge's reworking of the biblical myth. Such a merging of identities and erasure of distinctions is bound to lead to what René Girard calls a "sacrificial crisis," in which violence can no longer be contained. Indeed, what we witness in the poem is a cycle of violence that cannot be halted. The Albatross is merely the first victim; followed by the Mariner, who becomes the victim of the crew; followed by the crew, who become victims of the violent forces of Life and Death-in-Life; followed by the Pilot and the Pilot's boy, who are permanently damaged by their encounter with the ghostly figure of the Mariner; followed by the Wedding Guest, and by countless future Wedding Guests who will be "stunned, / And [of] sense forlorn" (ll.622–23) after hearing the Mariner's agonizing tale, and rendered unfit to return to the world of festive communal celebrations.

Violence, as it were, spills over the edges of the poem's narrative, pointing to the past as well as the future, to "agonies that had been, and were, and were still to continue to be" ("The Wanderings of Cain" 289). The poem conveys a strong sense that violence does not begin with the slaying of the Albatross but antecedes it. The. past may be as distant as biblical history or as recent as the war that branded the sailor

---

[34]See Empson, Introduction (35, 37) where the critic points out that the Mariner functions as a scapegoat for a community whose members might have committed the same murderous act.

in Wordsworth's "Adventures on Salisbury Plain."[35] Or the past may be the Mariner's previous experience on a slave ship, as Rubinstein contends (see n12). If there is any credence to the notion that the Mariner had been aboard a slave ship earlier, then his crime and the sailor's crime in Wordsworth's "Adventures on Salisbury Plain" may have similar sources. Both characters have witnessed violence and injustice of such proportion that they need to master, express, and fully inhabit it, in order to make visible the "dereliction and dismay of the times." In this sense they become the living symbols and spokesmen of the crimes committed by their contemporaries. It is important to note the degree to which neither character resists the punishment inflicted on them in the name of retributive justice. The sailor commits himself to the law and the Mariner accepts the hanging of the Albatross around his neck without protest. A sacrificial society has thus found its perfect victims, those who accept their doom without the least struggle. But by this very token the characters attain a Christlike identity, taking, as it were, the sins of the world upon themselves, without, however, any prospect of redeeming the sins of the world.

Historical readings of "The Ancient Mariner" have to contend with a major stumbling block, namely the fact that its main character appears in a dual light, as both Cain and Abel, Cain and Christ, sacrificer and sacrificed, criminal and persecuted victim. As we have observed earlier, within a political and religious framework, the Mariner's crime has been judged severely, his punishment appearing proportional to his offense. But consistently the Mariner slips to the victim side of a polarized identity. A violation is inflicted not just *by* him upon an innocent victim, but also *to* him, as if by an external force. Like the Wedding Guest, who is "stunned" by the Mariner's tale, the Mariner is stunned by his own act of violence, which is disconnected from his self, and ultimately incomprehensible. It is therefore fallacious to pin the guilt of a colonialist squarely onto the Mariner, because it is the Mariner who embodies the condition of slavery (whose identifying marks are entrapment, loss of a homeland, loss of freedom, and physical and spiritual suffering of nightmarish proportion), and because, as Empson intuited, he remains at some level innocent even as he is implicated in guilt, an Abel "framed by the supreme powers" (Introduction 40) who inadvertently turns into a Cain.[36]

---

[35]On Wordsworth's "Salisbury Plain" poems as a source for "The Ancient Mariner" see Eilenberg (47–49); Keane (160, 220–21); and Magnuson (84–95).

[36]For the significance of the Mariner's identification with Cain and of his voyage as "an objectification of the isolation and aloneness of all men" see Charles E. May, 47.

"The Ancient Mariner" is then not a story about "salvation" either "in Christ" or "of Christ," in McGann's terms (54), but about a "fracture at the heart of things" (Quinones 3), as the enduring Cain-Abel story commemorates. This fracture is caused by history itself,[37] which in Coleridge's time provided terrifying spectacles of what "man can do to man" in every corner of the world,[38] posing a formidable challenge to Christian values as well as radical political standpoints on the French Revolution or the slave trade, a fact that some historicist critics have not fully taken into account, hanging on to sacramental readings of the poem. The presence in the poem of Christian symbols and of a code of brotherly love opposed to violence is unmistakable, but it only heightens the pathos of an ideal that is irretrievably lost, as the substitution of the cross with the Albatross powerfully conveys. There is no need to undo the Mariner's blessing of the water snakes by reading sinister political implications into it, as does Keane, nor dismiss the poem's concluding moral, for both project a healing ethos whose absolute desirability, coupled with its irreparable violation, compound the Mariner's tragic predicament. Ironically, the Mariner, who begins his journey distrusting the compatibility between Christian symbols and a world where "God himself / Scarce seemed there to be," (1817 l.603–04) ends up constructing a narrative that circumscribes terror within the framework of conventional Christian beliefs.[39] By this very process, however, the Mariner "cannibalizes" himself, just as he sucks his own blood at the sight of the spectre-bark, becoming the sacrificial victim of his own tale, which forever must begin anew, "from that zero point of initial, violent fracture" (Maniquis 391):

"God save thee, ancient Mariner!
From the fiends, that plague thee thus! —
Why look'st thou so?" — With my cross-bow
I shot the ALBATROSS! (79–82)

[37]As Quinones notes, the Cain-Abel myth represents at its very core "an encounter with history — oppressive, inevitable history, or history transcended and transformed, but never ignored" (20).

[38]In a review of Norris's book on Dahomey in the *Gentleman's Magazine* 59 (1789), the author notes that this narrative "makes our blood run cold at the recital of what man can do to man, in a state of nature . . ." (433). This review might have been the source of Wordsworth's lines in his poem "Lines Written in Early Spring": "And much it grieved my heart to think / What man has made of man." I am grateful to Charles Rzepka for pointing out to me this intriguing connection.

[39]See my essay "Words and 'Languageless' Meanings: Limits of Expression in *The Rime of the Ancient Mariner*" and Watkins.

WORKS CITED

Abridgment of the Minutes of the Evidence Taken before a Committee of the Whole House, to Whom It Was Referred to Consider of the Slave-Trade 1789–1791. 4 vols. London, 1789 (1791).

Astley, John. *A New General Collection of Voyages and Travels.* 4 vols. London, 1745–47

Auden, W. H. *The Enchafèd Flood.* New York: Vintage, 1967.

Bayle, Peter. *The Dictionary Historical and Critical of Mr. Peter Bayle.* 1734–38. 5 vols. New York: Garland, 1984.

Burkhert, Walter. Homo Necans. *The Anthropology of Ancient Greek Sacrificial Ritual and Myth.* Berkeley: U of California P, 1983.

Boulger, James. "Christian Skepticism in *The Rime of the Ancient Mariner.*" *From Sensibility to Romanticism.* Ed. Frederick W. Hilles and Harold Bloom. New York: Oxford UP, 1965. 439–52.

Burton, Richard. *A Mission to Gelele, King of Dahomey.* London, 1864.

Clarkson, Thomas. *An Essay on the Slavery and Commerce of the Human Species.* 2nd ed. London, 1788.

———. *The History of the Rise, Progress, and Accomplishment of the Abolition of the African Slave Trade by the British Parliament.* 2 vols. London, 1808.

Coleridge, Samuel Taylor. *The Complete Poetical Works of Samuel Taylor Coleridge.* Ed. E. H. Hartley. 2 vols. Oxford: Oxford UP, 1912.

———. *The Friend.* Ed. Barbara Rooke. No. 4. 2 vols. Bollingen Ser. 75. *The Collected Works of Samuel Taylor Coleridge.* London: Routledge, 1969.

———. *Lectures 1795: On Politics and Religion.* Ed. Lewis Patton and Peter Mann. No. 1. Bollingen Ser. 75. *The Collected Works of Samuel Taylor Coleridge.* London: Routledge, 1971.

———. *The Notebooks of Samuel Taylor Coleridge.* Bollingen Ser. 50. Vols. I and II. New York: Pantheon, 1957, 1961. Vols. III and IV. Princeton: Princeton UP, 1973, 1990.

———. *On the Constitution of Church and State.* Ed. John Colmer. No. 10. Bollingen Ser. 75. *The Collected Works of Samuel Taylor Coleridge.* London: Routledge, 1976.

———. *Shorter Works and Fragments.* Ed. H. J. Jackson and J. R. de J. Jackson. No. 11. 2 vols. Bollingen Ser. 75. *The Collected Works of Samuel Taylor Coleridge.* London: Routledge, 1994.

———. *Table Talk.* Ed. Carl Woodring. No. 14. 2 vols. Bollingen Ser.

75. *The Collected Works of Samuel Taylor Coleridge*. London: Routledge, 1990.

Cook, Capt. James and Capt. James King. *A Voyage to the Pacific Ocean*. 3 vols. London, 1784.

Dalzel, Archibald. *The History of Dahomey, An Inland Kingdom of Africa*. London, 1793.

Davison, John. *An Inquiry into the Origin and Intent of Primitive Sacrifice, and the Scripture Evidence Respecting It*. London, 1825.

Ebbatson, J. B. "Coleridge's Mariner and the Rights of Man." *Studies in Romanticism* 11 (1972): 171–206.

Eilenberg, Susan. *Strange Power of Speech: Wordsworth, Coleridge, and Literary Possession*. New York: Oxford UP, 1992.

Empson, William. *"The Ancient Mariner." Critical Quarterly* 6 (1964): 298–319.

———. " 'The Ancient Mariner': An Answer to Warren." *The Kenyon Review* 15 (1993): 155–77.

Empson, William, and David Pirie, eds. Introduction. *Coleridge's Verse: A Selection*. London: Faber, 1972. 13–100.

Erdman, David. *Blake: Prophet Against Empire*. 3rd ed. Princeton: Princeton UP, 1977.

Fulmer, O. Brian. "The Ancient Mariner and the Wandering Jew." *Studies in Philology* 66 (1969): 797–815.

Girard, René. *Violence and the Sacred*. Baltimore: Johns Hopkins UP, 1972.

Josephus, Flavius. *Antiquities of the Jews*. Trans. William Whiston. Hartford: Scranton, 1910.

Keane, Patrick J. *Coleridge's Submerged Politics: The Ancient Mariner and Robinson Crusoe*. Columbia: U of Missouri P, 1994.

Kitson, Peter. "Coleridge, the French Revolution, and 'The Ancient Mariner': Collective Guilt and Individual Salvation." *Yearbook of English Studies* 19 (1989): 197–207.

Lowes, John Livingston. *The Road to Xanadu: A Study in the Ways of the Imagination*. Boston: Houghton, 1930.

Magee, William. *Discourses on the Scriptural Doctrines of Atonement and Sacrifice*. London, 1801.

Magnuson, Paul. *Coleridge and Wordsworth: The Lyrical Dialogue*. Princeton: Princeton UP, 1988.

Maniquis, Robert M. "Holy Savagery and Wild Justice: English Romanticism and the Terror." *Studies in Romanticism* 28 (1989): 365–95.

May, Charles E. "Objectifying the Nightmare: Cain and the Mariner." *Ball State University Forum* 14 (1973): 45–8.

McGann, Jerome. "The Meaning of 'The Ancient Mariner.'" *Critical Inquiry* 8 (1981): 35–67.

———. *The Romantic Ideology: A Critical Investigation.* Chicago: U of Chicago P, 1983.

Modiano, Raimonda. "Blood Sacrifice, Gift Economy and the Edenic World: Wordsworth's 'Home at Grasmere'." *Studies in Romanticism* 32 (1993): 481–521.

———. Rev. of *The Ancient Mariner and Robinson Crusoe,* by Patrick Keane. *JEGP* 95 (1996): 447–51.

———. "Unremembered Sights of Violence: The Scandal of Dahomey's Rites of Human Sacrifice in the Debates about the Abolition of the Slave Trade in England." *The Poetics of Memory.* Ed. Thomas Wägenbaur. Tübingen: Stauffenburg, 1988. 173–89.

———. "Words and 'Languageless' Meanings: Limits of Expression in *The Rime of the Ancient Mariner.*" *Modern Language Quarterly* 38 (1977): 40–61.

Molesworth, John Edward Nassau. *An Answer to Davidson's Inquiry into the Origin and Intent of Primitive Sacrifice.* London, 1826.

Norris, Robert. *Memoirs of the Reign of Bossa Ahadee, King of Dahomey.* London, 1789.

Parsons, Coleman O. "The Mariner and the Albatross." *Virginia Quarterly Review* 26 (1950): 102–23.

Perkins, David. "'The Ancient Mariner' and Its Interpreters: Some Versions of 'Coleridge.'" *Modern Language Quarterly* 57 (1996): 425–48.

Quinones, Ricardo J. *The Changes of Cain: Violence and the Lost Brother in Cain and Abel Literature.* Princeton: Princeton UP, 1991.

Ramsey, James. *Objections to the Abolution of the Slave Trade with Answers.* London, 1788.

Ritson, Joseph. *An Essay on Abstinence from Animal Food, as a Moral Duty.* London, 1802.

Rubinstein, Chris. "A New Identity for the Mariner? A Further Exploration of 'The Rime of the Ancient Mariner.'" *The Coleridge Bulletin* 2 (1990): 16–29.

Shelley, Percy Bysshe. "Adonais." *Shelley's Poetry and Prose.* Ed. Donald H. Reiman and Sharon B. Powers. New York: Norton, 1977.

Shelvocke, Captain George. *A Voyage round the World by the Way of the Great South Sea.* London, 1726.

Snelgrave, William. *A New Account of Some Parts of Guinea and the Slave Trade*. London, 1734.

Spencer, John. *De Legibus Hebraearum ritualibus, et earum rationibus, libri tres*. Cantabrigiae, 1685.

The True State of the Question, Addressed to the Petitioners for the Abolition of the Slave Trade. London, 1792.

Warburton, William. *The Divine Legation of Moses. The Works of the Right Reverend William Warburton, Lord Bishop of Gloucester*. 7 vols. London, 1788.

Ware, Malcolm. "Coleridge's 'Spectre-Bark': A Slave Ship?" *Philological Quarterly* 40 (1961): 589–93.

———. "*The Rime of the Ancient Mariner*: A Discourse on Prayer." *Review of English Studies* 11 (1960): 303–04.

Watkins, Daniel. "History as Demon in Coleridge's *The Rime of the Ancient Mariner*." *Papers on Language and Literature* 24 (1988): 23–33.

Psychoanalytic Criticism and "The Rime of the Ancient Mariner"

WHAT IS PSYCHOANALYTIC CRITICISM?

It seems natural to think about literature in terms of dreams. Like dreams, literary works are fictions, inventions of the mind that, although based on reality, are by definition not literally true. Like a literary work, a dream may have some truth to tell, but, like a literary work, it may need to be interpreted before that truth can be grasped. We can live vicariously through romantic fictions, much as we can through daydreams. Terrifying novels and nightmares affect us in much the same way, plunging us into an atmosphere that continues to cling, even after the last chapter has been read — or the alarm clock has sounded.

The notion that dreams allow such psychic explorations, of course, like the analogy between literary works and dreams, owes a great deal to the thinking of Sigmund Freud, the famous Austrian psychoanalyst who in 1900 published a seminal text, *The Interpretation of Dreams*. But is the reader who feels that Emily Brontë's *Wuthering Heights* is dreamlike — who feels that Mary Shelley's *Frankenstein* is nightmarish — necessarily a Freudian literary critic? To some extent the answer has to be yes. We are all Freudians, really, whether or not we have read a single work by Freud. At one time or another, most of us have referred to ego, libido, complexes, unconscious desires, and sexual repression. The premises of Freud's thought have changed the way the Western world thinks about itself. Psychoanalytic criticism has influenced the teachers our teachers studied with, the works of scholarship and criticism they read, and the critical and creative writers *we* read as well.

What Freud did was develop a language that described, a model that explained, a theory that encompassed human psychology. Many of the elements of psychology he sought to describe and explain are present in the literary works of various ages and cultures, from Sophocles' *Oedipus Rex* to Shakespeare's *Hamlet* to works being written in our own day. When the great novel of the twenty-first century is written, many of these same elements of psychology will probably inform its discourse as well. If, by understanding human psychology according to Freud, we can appreciate literature on a new level, then we should acquaint ourselves with his insights.

Freud's theories are either directly or indirectly concerned with the nature of the unconscious mind. Freud didn't invent the notion of the unconscious; others before him had suggested that even the supposedly "sane" human mind was conscious and rational only at times, and even then at possibly only one level. But Freud went further, suggesting that the powers motivating men and women are *mainly* and *normally* unconscious.

Freud, then, powerfully developed an old idea: that the human mind is essentially dual in nature. He called the predominantly passional, irrational, unknown, and unconscious part of the psyche the *id*, or "it." The *ego*, or "I," was his term for the predominantly rational, logical, orderly, conscious part. Another aspect of the psyche, which he called the *superego*, is really a projection of the ego. The superego almost seems to be outside of the self, making moral judgments, telling us to make sacrifices for good causes even though self-sacrifice may not be quite logical or rational. And, in a sense, the superego *is* "outside," since much of what it tells us to do or think we have learned from our parents, our schools, or our religious institutions.

What the ego and superego tell us *not* to do or think is repressed, forced into the unconscious mind. One of Freud's most important contributions to the study of the psyche, the theory of repression, goes something like this: much of what lies in the unconscious mind has been put there by consciousness, which acts as a censor, driving underground unconscious or conscious thoughts or instincts that it deems unacceptable. Censored materials often involve infantile sexual desires, Freud postulated. Repressed to an unconscious state, they emerge only in disguised forms: in dreams, in language (so-called Freudian slips), in creative activity that may produce art (including literature), and in neurotic behavior.

According to Freud, all of us have repressed wishes and fears; we all have dreams in which repressed feelings and memories emerge disguised, and thus we are all potential candidates for dream analysis. One of the unconscious desires most commonly repressed is the childhood wish to displace the parent of our own sex and take his or her place in the affections of the parent of the opposite sex. This desire really involves a number of different but related wishes and fears. (A boy — and it should be remarked in passing that Freud here concerns himself mainly with the male — may fear that his father will castrate him, and he may wish that his mother would return to nursing him.) Freud referred to the whole complex of feelings by the word *oedipal,* naming the complex after the Greek tragic hero Oedipus, who unwittingly killed his father and married his mother.

Why are oedipal wishes and fears repressed by the conscious side of the mind? And what happens to them after they have been censored? As Roy P. Basler puts it in *Sex, Symbolism, and Psychology in Literature* (1975), "from the beginning of recorded history such wishes have been restrained by the most powerful religious and social taboos, and as a result have come to be regarded as 'unnatural,'" even though "Freud found that such wishes are more or less characteristic of normal human development":

> In dreams, particularly, Freud found ample evidence that such wishes persisted. . . . Hence he conceived that natural urges, when identified as "wrong," may be repressed but not obliterated. . . . In the unconscious, these urges take on symbolic garb, regarded as nonsense by the waking mind that does not recognize their significance. (14)

Freud's belief in the significance of dreams, of course, was no more original than his belief that there is an unconscious side to the psyche. Again, it was the extent to which he developed a theory of how dreams work — and the extent to which that theory helped him, by analogy, to understand far more than just dreams — that made him unusual, important, and influential beyond the perimeters of medical schools and psychiatrists' offices.

The psychoanalytic approach to literature not only rests on the theories of Freud; it may even be said to have *begun* with Freud, who was interested in writers, especially those who relied heavily on symbols. Such writers regularly cloak or mystify ideas in figures that make sense only when interpreted, much as the unconscious mind of a neurotic disguises secret thoughts in dream stories or bizarre actions that need to be interpreted by an analyst. Freud's interest in literary artists led him to make some unfortunate generalizations about creativity; for example, in the twenty-third lecture in *Introductory Lectures on Psycho-Analysis* (1922), he defined the artist as "one urged on by instinctive needs that are too clamorous" (314). But it also led him to write creative literary criticism of his own, including an influential essay on "The Relation of a Poet to Daydreaming" (1908) and "The Uncanny" (1919), a provocative psychoanalytic reading of E. T. A. Hoffmann's supernatural tale "The Sandman."

Freud's application of psychoanalytic theory to literature quickly caught on. In 1909, only a year after Freud had published "The Relation of a Poet to Daydreaming," the psychoanalyst Otto Rank published *The Myth of the Birth of the Hero*. In that work, Rank subscribes to the notion that the artist turns a powerful, secret wish into a literary fantasy, and he uses Freud's notion about the "oedipal" complex to explain why the popular stories of so many heroes in literature are so similar. A year after Rank had published his psychoanalytic account of heroic texts, Ernest Jones, Freud's student and eventual biographer, turned his attention to a tragic text: Shakespeare's *Hamlet*. In an essay first published in the *American Journal of Psychology*, Jones, like Rank, makes use of the oedipal concept: he suggests that Hamlet is a victim of strong feelings toward his mother, the queen.

Between 1909 and 1949, numerous other critics decided that psychological and psychoanalytic theory could assist in the understanding of literature. I. A. Richards, Kenneth Burke, and Edmund Wilson were among the most influential to become interested in the new approach. Not all of the early critics were committed to the approach; neither were all of them Freudians. Some followed Alfred Adler, who believed that writers wrote out of inferiority complexes, and others applied the ideas of Carl Gustav Jung, who had broken with Freud over Freud's emphasis on sex and who had developed a theory of the *collective* unconscious. According to Jungian theory, a great work of literature is not a disguised expression of its author's personal, repressed wishes; rather, it is a manifestation of desires once held by the whole human race but now repressed because of the advent of civilization.

It is important to point out that among those who relied on Freud's models were a number of critics who were poets and novelists as well. Conrad Aiken wrote a Freudian study of American literature, and poets such as Robert Graves and W. H. Auden applied Freudian insights when writing critical prose. William Faulkner, Henry James, James Joyce, D. H. Lawrence, Marcel Proust, and Toni Morrison are only a few of the novelists who have either written criticism influenced by Freud or who have written novels that conceive of character, conflict, and creative writing itself in Freudian terms. The poet H. D. (Hilda Doolittle) was actually a patient of Freud's and provided an account of her analysis in her book *Tribute to Freud*. By giving Freudian theory credibility among students of literature that only they could bestow, such writers helped to endow earlier psychoanalytic criticism with a largely Freudian orientation that has begun to be challenged only in the last two decades.

The willingness, even eagerness, or writers to use Freudian models in producing literature and criticism of their own consummated a relationship that, to Freud and other pioneering psychoanalytic theorists, had seemed fated from the beginning; after all, therapy involves the close analysis of language. René Wellek and Austin Warren included "psychological" criticism as one of the five "extrinsic" approaches to literature described in their influential book *Theory of Literature* (1942). Psychological criticism, they suggest, typically attempts to do at least one of the following: provide a psychological study of an individual writer; explore the nature of the creative process; generalize about "types and laws present within works of literature"; or theorize about the psychological "effects of literature upon its readers" (81). Entire books on psychoanalytic criticism began to appear, such as Frederick J. Hoffman's *Freudianism and the Literary Mind* (1945).

Probably because of Freud's characterization of the creative mind as "clamorous" if not ill, psychoanalytic criticism written before 1950 tended to psychoanalyze the individual author. Poems were read as fantasies that allowed authors to indulge repressed wishes, to protect themselves from deep-seated anxieties, or both. A perfect example of author analysis would be Marie Bonaparte's 1933 study of Edgar Allan Poe. Bonaparte found Poe to be so fixated on his mother that his repressed longing emerges in his stories in images such as the white spot on a black cat's breast, said to represent mother's milk.

A later generation of psychoanalytic critics often paused to analyze the characters in novels and plays before proceeding to their authors. But not for long, since characters, both evil and good, tended to be seen by these critics as the author's potential selves or projections of various repressed aspects of his or her psyche. For instance, in *A Psychoanalytic Study of the Double in Literature* (1970), Robert Rogers begins with the view that human beings are double or multiple in nature. Using this assumption, along with the psychoanalytic concept of "dissociation" (best known by its result, the dual or multiple personality), Rogers concludes that writers reveal instinctual or repressed selves in their books, often without realizing that they have done so.

In the view of critics attempting to arrive at more psychological insights into an author than biographical materials can provide, a work of literature is a fantasy or a dream — or at least so analogous to daydream or dream that Freudian analysis can help explain the nature of the mind that produced it. The author's purpose in writing is to gratify secretly some forbidden wish, in particular an infantile wish or desire that has been repressed into the unconscious mind. To discover what the wish is, the psychoanalytic critic employs many of the terms and procedures developed by Freud to analyze dreams.

The literal surface of a work is sometimes spoken of as its "manifest content" and treated as a "manifest dream" or "dream story" would be treated by a Freudian analyst. Just as the analyst tries to figure out the "dream thought" behind the dream story — that is, the latent or hidden content of the manifest dream — so the psychoanalytic literary critic tries to expose the latent, underlying content of a work. Freud used the words *condensation* and *displacement* to explain two of the mental processes whereby the mind disguises its wishes and fears in dream stories. In condensation, several thoughts or persons may be condensed into a single manifestation or image in a dream story; in displacement, an anxiety, a wish, or a person may be displaced onto the image of another, with which or whom it is loosely connected through a string of associations that only an analyst can untangle. Psychoanalytic critics treat metaphors as if they were dream condensations; they treat metonyms — figures of speech based on extremely loose, arbitrary associations — as if they were dream displacements. Thus figurative literary language in general is treated as something that evolves as the writer's conscious mind resists what the unconscious tells it to picture

or describe. A symbol is, in Daniel Weiss's words, "a meaningful concealment of truth as the truth promises to emerge as some frightening
or forbidden idea" (20).

In a 1970 article entitled "The 'Unconscious' of Literature," Norman Holland, a literary critic trained in psychoanalysis, succinctly sums
up the attitudes held by critics who would psychoanalyze authors, but
without quite saying that it is the *author* that is being analyzed by the
psychoanalytic critic. "When one looks at a poem psychoanalytically,"
he writes, "one considers it as though it were a dream or as though
some ideal patient [were speaking] from the couch in iambic pentame-
ter." One "looks for the general level or levels of fantasy associated with
the language. By level I mean the familiar stages of childhood development — oral [when desires for nourishment and infantile sexual desires
overlap], anal [when infants receive their primary pleasure from defeca-
tion], urethral [when urinary functions are the locus of sexual plea-
sure], phallic [when the penis or, in girls, some penis substitute is of
primary interest], oedipal." Holland continues by analyzing not Robert
Frost but Frost's poem "Mending Wall" as a specifically oral fantasy
that is not unique to its author. "Mending Wall" is "about breaking
down the wall which marks the separated or individuated self so as to
return to a state of closeness to some Other" — including and perhaps
essentially the nursing mother ("'Unconscious'" 136, 139).

While not denying the idea that the unconscious plays a role in creativity, psychoanalytic critics such as Holland began to focus more on
the ways in which authors create works that appeal to *our* repressed
wishes and fantasies. Consequently, they shifted their focus away from
the psyche of the author and toward the psychology of the reader and
the text. Holland's theories, which have concerned themselves more
with the reader than with the text, have helped to establish another
school of critical theory: reader-response criticism. Elizabeth Wright
explains Holland's brand of modern psychoanalytic criticism in this
way: "What draws us as readers to a text is the secret expression of what
we desire to hear, much as we protest we do not. The disguise must
be good enough to fool the censor into thinking that the text is respectable, but bad enough to allow the unconscious to glimpse the
unrespectable" (117).

Holland is one of dozens of critics who have revised Freud significantly in the process of revitalizing psychoanalytic criticism. Another
such critic is R. D. Laing, whose controversial and often poetical writings about personality, repression, masks, and the double or "schizoid"

self have (re)blurred the boundary between creative writing and psychoanalytic discourse. Yet another is D. W. Winnicott, an "object relations" theorist who has had a significant impact on literary criticism. Critics influenced by Winnicott and his school have questioned the tendency to see reader/text as an either/or construct; instead, they have seen reader and text (or audience and play) in terms of a *relationship* taking place in what Winnicott calls a "transitional" or "potential" space — space in which binary terms such as *real* and *illusory, objective* and *subjective,* have little or no meaning.

Psychoanalytic theorists influenced by Winnicott see the transitional or potential reader/text (or audience/play) space as being *like* the space entered into by psychoanalyst and patient. More important, they also see it as being similar to the space between mother and infant: a space characterized by trust in which categorizing terms such as *knowing* and *feeling* mix and merge and have little meaning apart from one another.

Whereas Freud saw the mother-son relationship in terms of the son and his repressed oedipal complex (and saw the analyst-patient relationship in terms of the patient and the repressed "truth" that the analyst could scientifically extract), object-relations analysts see both relationships as *dyadic* — that is, as being dynamic in both directions. Consequently, they don't depersonalize analysis or their analyses. It is hardly surprising, therefore, that contemporary literary critics who apply object-relations theory to the texts they discuss don't depersonalize critics or categorize their interpretations as "truthful," at least not in any objective or scientific sense. In the view of such critics, interpretations are made of language — itself a transitional object — and are themselves the mediating terms or transitional objects of a relationship.

Like critics of the Winnicottian school, the French structuralist theorist Jacques Lacan focused on language and language-related issues. He treated the unconscious *as* a language and, consequently, viewed the dream not as Freud did (that is, as a form and symptom of repression) but rather as a form of discourse. Thus we may study dreams psychoanalytically to learn about literature, even as we may study literature to learn more about the unconscious. In Lacan's seminar on Poe's "The Purloined Letter," a pattern of repetition like that used by psychoanalysts in their analyses is used to arrive at a reading of the story. According to Wright, "the new psychoanalytic structural approach to literature" employs "analogies from psychoanalysis . . . to explain the workings of the text as distinct from the workings of a particular author's, character's, or even reader's mind" (125).

Lacan, however, did far more than extend Freud's theory of dreams, literature, and the interpretation of both. More significantly, he took Freud's whole theory of psyche and gender and added to it a crucial third term — that of language. In the process, he both used and significantly developed Freud's ideas about the oedipal stage and complex.

Lacan pointed out that the pre-oedipal stage, in which the child at first does not even recognize its independence from its mother, is also a pre*verbal* stage, one in which the child communicates without the medium of language, or — if we insist on calling the child's communications a language — in a language that can only be called *literal*. ("Coos," certainly, cannot be said to be figurative or symbolic.) Then, while still in the pre-oedipal stage, the child enters the *mirror* stage.

During the mirror period, the child comes to view itself and its mother, later other people as well, *as* independent selves. This is the stage in which the child is first able to fear the aggressions of another, to desire what is recognizably beyond the self (initially the mother), and, finally, to want to compete with another for the same desired object. This is also the stage at which the child first becomes able to feel sympathy with another being who is being hurt by a third, to cry when another cries. All of these developments, of course, involve projecting beyond the self and, by extension, constructing one's own self (or "ego" or "I") as others view one — that is, as *another*. Such constructions, according to Lacan, are just that: constructs, products, artifacts — fictions of coherence that in fact hide what Lacan called the "absence" or "lack" of being.

The mirror stage, which Lacan also referred to as the *imaginary* stage, is fairly quickly succeeded by the oedipal stage. As in Freud, this stage begins when the child, having come to view itself as self and the father and mother as separate selves, perceives gender and gender differences between its parents and between itself and one of its parents. For boys, gender awareness involves another, more powerful recognition, for the recognition of the father's phallus as the mark of his difference from the mother involves, at the same time, the recognition that his older and more powerful father is also his rival. That, in turn, leads to the understanding that what once seemed wholly his and even indistinguishable from himself is in fact someone else's: something properly desired only at a distance and in the form of socially acceptable *substitutes*.

The fact that the oedipal stage roughly coincides with the entry of the child into language is extremely important for Lacan. For the linguistic order is essentially a figurative or "Symbolic" order; words are not the things they stand for but are, rather, stand-ins or substitutes for those things. Hence boys, who in the most critical period of their development have had to submit to what Lacan called the "Law of the Father" — a law that prohibits direct desire for and communicative intimacy with what has been the boy's whole world — enter more easily into the realm of language and the Symbolic order than do girls, who have never really had to renounce that which once seemed continuous with the self: the mother. The gap that has been opened up for boys, which includes the gap between signs and what they substitute — the gap marked by the phallus and encoded with the boy's sense of his maleness — has not opened up for girls, or has not opened up in the same way, to the same degree.

For Lacan, the father need not be present to trigger the oedipal stage; nor does his phallus have to be seen to catalyze the boy's (easier) transition into the Symbolic order. Rather, Lacan argued, a child's recognition of its gender is intricately tied up with a growing recognition of the system of names and naming, part of the larger system of substitutions we call language. A child has little doubt about who its mother is, but who is its father, and how would one know? The father's claim rests on the mother's *word* that he is in fact the father; the father's relationship to the child is thus established through language and a system of marriage and kinship — names — that in turn is basic to rules of everything from property to law. The name of the father (*nom du père*, which in French sounds like *non du père*) involves, in a sense, nothing of the father — nothing, that is, except his word or name.

Lacan's development of Freud has had several important results. First, his sexist-seeming association of maleness with the Symbolic order, together with his claim that women cannot therefore enter easily into the order, has prompted feminists not to reject his theory out of hand but, rather, to look more closely at the relation between language and gender, language and women's inequality. Some feminists have gone so far as to suggest that the social and political relationships between male and female will not be fundamentally altered until language itself has been radically changed. (That change might begin dialectically, with the development of some kind of "feminine language" grounded in the presymbolic, literal-to-imaginary communication between mother and child.)

Second, Lacan's theory has proved of interest to deconstructors and other poststructuralists, in part because it holds that the ego (which in Freud's view is as necessary as it is natural) is a product or construct. The ego-artifact, produced during the mirror stage, *seems* at once unified, consistent, and organized around a determinate center. But the unified self, or ego, is a fiction, according to Lacan. The yoking together of fragments and destructively dissimilar elements takes its psychic toll, and it is the job of the Lacanian psychoanalyst to "deconstruct," as it were, the ego, to show its continuities to be contradictions as well.

In the essay that follows, Anne Williams regularly cites the work of Julia Kristeva, a psychoanalytic theorist commonly associated with feminist advocates of feminine language but who eschews the feminist label. Kristeva accepts Freud's concepts of the pre-oedipal stage, in which the child initially feels undifferentiated from its mother, and the oedipal stage, during which the emergent ego, subject, or self views itself as fully independent from the mother. She also accepts Lacan's theory that there is a mirror stage that comes toward the end of the pre-oedipal stage. (During the mirror stage, the child begins to imagine itself as a unified being distinct from all others.) Following Lacan, Kristeva suggests that the subsequent, oedipal stage roughly coincides with the child's entry into language, which she generally views as patriarchal and symbolic in the Lacanian sense of being abstract, definitive, and systematic.

What distinguishes Kristeva's work from that of other psychoanalytic critics is her belief that there is another kind or mode of language that is *semiotic* (loosely associational) rather than *symbolic* (more rigidly representational) — and that semiotic language is derived from the pre-oedipal stage and is associated with the feminine and the maternal. Indeed, Kristeva suggests that the language we think of as being "poetic" is language interrupted and disrupted by semiotic, rhythmic urgings emanating from the psychically repressed realm of the maternal. Feminist critics have suggested that "feminine language" or "feminine writing" should be based on semiotic language, which seems chaotic from the vantage point of symbolic language, masculinist culture.

Williams begins her psychoanalytic analysis of the "Rime" by stating that Coleridge' s poem "enacts the process by which the speaking subject — the user of language — is constituted," adding that the "creation of the I" and "the subject's entry into language" involve a "flight" from the world of the maternal and from the associated, material world of the "eye," that is, the world simply seen but not imaginatively or symbolically "envisioned" (239). Arguing that Freudian analysis has inadequately elucidated the "Rime" due to Freud's failure fully to perceive the (repressed) power of the mother, Williams grounds her post-Freudian analysis in Kristeva's alternative account of the "abjection" of the maternal by the developing self (the "not yet self"). Williams maintains that the "horror" at the heart of Coleridge's poem is a "symptom of the not yet self's 'abjection' (casting off) of the maternal" (240) and semiotic in favor of the paternal and symbolic. Yet the poem also exemplifies poetic language as Kristeva defines it; indeed, "Coleridge's narrative (including frame and gloss) may be read as a representation of semiotic intrusion into the symbolic universe" (240). Although the Mariner may seem, and at one level may be, the archetypal "wise old man," Coleridge's poem "also repeatedly links him with the conventionally female in Western culture: the sea, irrationality, motherhood, and nature — 'spontaneous energies' that challenge and disrupt the symbolic order" (241).

This "fusion of female with male," this confusion of maternal and paternal, contradicts what Lacan called "the law of the father," or, as Williams explains it, "the symbolic law of identity (which dictates that a mariner is only a mariner and a mother is only a mother)" (242). Similarly confused — and confusing — is the Mariner's tale, which contradicts the laws (conventions) that govern most such shipboard adventure tales. First, the Mariner's tale is told in poetic (as opposed to ordinary) language. Second, his tale is "dreamlike," at times even "nonsensical," for it involves a ship (which Williams views as "a basic metaphor for the body") subject to "random motions punctuated with periods of stasis and stagnation" (243).

Williams argues that certain natural entities depicted in the "Rime" are associated primarily with the masculine or the feminine (for instance, the sun with fatherhood, the moon with motherhood) but that *all* such entities — including the albatross itself — are "linked . . . with both pleasant and unpleasant sensations" (244). The Albatross thus "connotes mother *and* father in both good and bad aspects," and its shooting represents "the attainment of selfhood and subjectivity" gained in the "separation from matter and from *mater* [mother]. This experience," Williams argues, "inaugurates what Kristeva calls the thetic stage — the crucial, inexorable emergence of a sense of self and not self — beginning with the mirror stage" (245).

In Williams' view, the second part of Coleridge's "Rime" chronicles the sense of absence, physical revulsion, and ultimately horror that "the fragile and not yet self exhibits when *about* to separate from the mother" (246) (emphasis added). This part also chronicles the transformation of the (dead) Albatross into a sign, if not a symbol, thereby inviting traditional, Christian interpretations of the text. In the third part, the horrifying figures seen aboard the "spectre bark" propel the Mariner into a new psychic stage, the stage in which the "not yet self" *actually* separates from or sublimates the maternal. In the "Night-mare Life-in-Death," he confronts a woman who is "Eros and Thanatos (Love [Sex] and Death) in the same boat," a woman who gambles with the masculine figure Death in a scene whose nightmarish quality, Williams suggests, "appears to confirm Madelon Sprengnether's argument in *The Spectral Mother* that maternal desire is the one thing that patriarchy cannot accommodate" (249).

The third part subsequently chronicles the rapid development of the "I"; the Mariner develops "the guilty sense that he is looked at (the gaze, according to Lacan, effects alienation)" and subsequently "denies the family of nature and humankind" by symbolizing and spiritualizing the maternal and material world (251). As Williams puts it, the Mariner "sublimat[es] the abject by leaping into a 'true' and satisfying spiritual membership in the family of God the Father, and by crossing the threshold of the symbolic" (251). The Mariner makes this leap, achieves this break, when he transforms dark sea creatures that Williams says "epitomize the horrors of materiality" by naming them ("O happy living things!") and blessing them, thereby symbolically including them in the single, unified whole envisioned by Western culture and traditions.

Later parts of Coleridge's poem, according to Williams, chronicle the development of the "I," or what Freud called the "ego," into what Freud called "superego," as when the Mariner faints and hears voices that "attribute a spiritual cause to the albatross's death: 'a spirit . . . loved the bird that loved the man / Who shot him with his bow.'" With the development of the ego and the superego, Williams suggests, the imagination comes into being. Viewing the "Rime" as a work that "traces the means by which meaning is constructed out of separation, need, fear, guilt, and a need to repair the primal break," Williams says that "The fragile I, to mend the break its birth necessitates, imagines a higher realm where no such gap exists. Entry into the symbolic is a creative act, for the self is thereby constituted" (256). Thus, in Williams's view, "Imagination is defensive," for its construction of a world unified by language and symbol is, in fact, a reaction against the horrifying loss of a boundariless, pre-oedipal world in which the infant, mother, and natural world are one.

In her essay on Coleridge's "Rime," Williams both uses and breaks with Freud, appropriating Freudian concepts like that of the superego while castigating Freud for his failure to understand the repressed power of the mother and the maternal over the self and, especially, over poetic language. She shows her indebtedness to Lacan not only in her use of his concepts of the "law of the father" and the related law of "symbolic identity" but also in her use of his concept of "the gaze" — the sense of being looked at that creates both a sense of alienation and of individuality (self). And, although Kristeva is the post-Lacanian theorist to whom Williams owes the greatest debt, she also alludes to the work of Melanie Klein, who, in Williams's words, argues that "since infantile connections with the mother cannot be literally reestablished once they are severed, the adult re-creates them in symbolic modes" (254–55).

Ross C Murfin

PSYCHOANALYTIC CRITICISM: A SELECTED BIBLIOGRAPHY

Some Short Introductions to Psychological and Psychoanalytic Criticism

Holland, Norman. "The 'Unconscious' of Literature: The Psychoanalytic Approach." *Contemporary Criticism.* Ed. Malcolm Bradbury and David Palmer. Stratford-upon-Avon Studies 12. New York: St. Martin's, 1971. 131–53.

Natoli, Joseph, and Frederik L. Rusch, comps. *Psychocriticism: An Annotated Bibliography.* Westport: Greenwood, 1984.

Scott, Wilbur. *Five Approaches to Literary Criticism.* London: Collier-Macmillan, 1962. See the essays by Burke and Gorer as well as Scott's introduction to the section "The Psychological Approach: Literature in the Light of Psychological Theory."

Wellek, René, and Austin Warren. *Theory of Literature.* New York: Harcourt, 1942. See the chapter "Literature and Psychology" in pt. 3, "The Extrinsic Approach to the Study of Literature."

Wright, Elizabeth. "Modern Psychoanalytic Criticism." *Modern Literary Theory: A Comparative Introduction.* Ed. Ann Jefferson and David Robey. Totowa: Barnes, 1982. 113–33.

Freud, Lacan, and Their Influence

Basler, Roy P. *Sex, Symbolism, and Psychology in Literature.* New York: Octagon, 1975. See especially 13–19.

Bowie, Malcolm. *Lacan*. Cambridge: Harvard UP, 1991.

Clément, Catherine. *The Lives and Legends of Jacques Lacan*. Trans. Arthur Goldhammer. New York: Columbia UP, 1983.

Freud, Sigmund. *Introductory Lectures on Psycho-Analysis*. Trans. Joan Riviere. London: Allen, 1922.

Gallop, Jane. *Reading Lacan*. Ithaca: Cornell UP, 1985.

Hoffman, Frederick J. *Freudianism and the Literary Mind*. Baton Rouge: Louisiana State UP, 1945.

Hogan, Patrick Colm, and Lalita Pandit, eds. *Lacan and Criticism: Essays and Dialogue on Language, Structure, and the Unconscious*. Athens: U of Georgia P, 1990.

Kazin, Alfred. "Freud and His Consequences." *Contemporaries*. Boston: Little, 1962. 351–93.

Lacan, Jacques. *Écrits: A Selection*. Trans. Alan Sheridan. New York: Norton, 1977.

———. *Feminine Sexuality: Lacan and the École Freudienne*. Ed. Juliet Mitchell and Jacqueline Rose. Trans. Rose. New York: Norton, 1985.

———. *The Four Fundamental Concepts of Psychoanalysis*. Trans. Alan Sheridan. London: Penguin, 1980.

Macey, David. *Lacan in Contexts*. New York: Verso, 1988.

Meisel, Perry, ed. *Freud: A Collection of Critical Essays*. Englewood Cliffs: Prentice, 1981.

Muller, John P., and William J. Richardson. *Lacan and Language: A Reader's Guide to "Écrits."* New York: International UP, 1982.

Porter, Laurence M. *"The Interpretation of Dreams": Freud's Theories Revisited*. Twayne's Masterwork Studies Ser. Boston: Hall, 1986.

Reppen, Joseph, and Maurice Charney. *The Psychoanalytic Study of Literature*. Hillsdale: Analytic, 1985.

Schneiderman, Stuart. *Jacques Lacan: The Death of an Intellectual Hero*. Cambridge: Harvard UP, 1983.

———. *Returning to Freud: Clinical Psychoanalysis in the School of Lacan*. New Haven: Yale UP, 1980.

Selden, Raman. *A Reader's Guide to Contemporary Literary Theory*. 2nd ed. Lexington: U of Kentucky P, 1989. See "Jacques Lacan: Language and the Unconscious."

Sullivan, Ellie Ragland. *Jacques Lacan and the Philosophy of Psychoanalysis*. Champaign: U of Illinois P, 1986.

Sullivan, Ellie Ragland, and Mark Bracher, eds. *Lacan and the Subject of Language*. New York: Routledge, 1991.

Trilling, Lionel. "Art and Neurosis." *The Liberal Imagination*. New York: Scribner's, 1950. 160–80.

Wilden, Anthony. "Lacan and the Discourse of the Other." In Lacan, *Speech and Language in Psychoanalysis*. Trans. Wilden. Baltimore: Johns Hopkins UP, 1981. (Published as *The Language of the Self* in 1968.) 159–311.

Žižek, Slavoj. *Looking Awry: An Introduction to Jacques Lacan through Popular Culture*. Cambridge: MIT P, 1991.

Psychoanalysis, Feminism, and Literature

Chodorow, Nancy. *The Reproduction of Mothering: Psychoanalysis and the Sociology of Gender*. Berkeley: U of California P, 1978.

Gallop, Jane. *The Daughter's Seduction: Feminism and Psychoanalysis*. Ithaca: Cornell UP, 1982.

Garner, Shirley Nelson, Claire Kahane, and Madelon Sprengnether. *The (M)other Tongue: Essays in Feminist Psychoanalytic Interpretation*. Ithaca: Cornell UP, 1985.

Grosz, Elizabeth. *Jacques Lacan: A Feminist Introduction*. New York: Routledge, 1990.

Irigaray, Luce. *The Speculum of the Other Woman*. Trans. Gillian C. Gill. Ithaca: Cornell UP, 1985.

———. *This Sex Which Is Not One*. Trans. Catherine Porter. Ithaca: Cornell UP, 1985.

Jacobus, Mary. "Is There a Woman in This Text?" *New Literary History* 14 (1982): 117–41.

Kristeva, Julia. *The Kristeva Reader*. Ed. Toril Moi. New York: Columbia UP, 1986. See especially the selection from *Revolution in Poetic Language*, 89–136.

Mitchell, Juliet. *Psychoanalysis and Feminism*. New York: Random, 1974.

Mitchell, Juliet, and Jacqueline Rose. "Introduction I" and "Introduction II." Lacan, *Feminine Sexuality: Jacques Lacan and the École Freudienne*. New York: Norton, 1985. 1–26, 27–57.

Sprengnether, Madelon. *The Spectral Mother: Freud, Feminism, and Psychoanalysis*. Ithaca: Cornell UP, 1990.

Psychological and Psychoanalytic Studies of Literature

Bettelheim, Bruno. *The Uses of Enchantment: The Meaning and Importance of Fairy Tales*. New York: Knopf, 1976. Although this book is about fairy tales instead of literary works written for publication, it offers model Freudian readings of well-known stories.

Crews, Frederick C. *Out of My System: Psychoanalysis, Ideology, and Critical Method*. New York: Oxford UP, 1975.

——. *Relations of Literary Study*. New York: MLA, 1967. See the chapter "Literature and Psychology."

Diehl, Joanne Feit. "Re-Reading *The Letter:* Hawthorne, the Fetish, and the (Family) Romance." *Nathaniel Hawthorne, The Scarlet Letter*. Ed. Ross C Murfin. Case Studies in Contemporary Criticism Ser. Ed. Ross C Murfin. Boston: Bedford, 1991. 235–51.

Hallman, Ralph. *Psychology of Literature: A Study of Alienation and Tragedy*. New York: Philosophical Library, 1961.

Hartman, Geoffrey, ed. *Psychoanalysis and the Question of the Text*. Baltimore: Johns Hopkins UP, 1978. See especially the essays by Hartman, Johnson, Nelson, and Schwartz.

Hertz, Neil. *The End of the Line: Essays on Psychoanalysis and the Sublime*. New York: Columbia UP, 1985.

Holland, Norman N. *Dynamics of Literary Response*. New York: Oxford UP, 1968.

——. *Poems in Persons: An Introduction to the Psychoanalysis of Literature*. New York: Norton, 1973.

Kris, Ernest. *Psychoanalytic Explorations in Art*. New York: International, 1952.

Lucas, F. L. *Literature and Psychology*. London: Cassell, 1951.

Natoli, Joseph, ed. *Psychological Perspectives on Literature: Freudian Dissidents and Non-Freudians: A Casebook*. Hamden: Archon, 1984.

Phillips, William, ed. *Art and Psychoanalysis*. New York: Columbia UP, 1977.

Rogers, Robert. *A Psychoanalytic Study of the Double in Literature*. Detroit: Wayne State UP, 1970.

Skura, Meredith. *The Literary Use of the Psychoanalytic Process*. New Haven: Yale UP, 1981.

Strelka, Joseph P. *Literary Criticism and Psychology*. University Park: Pennsylvania State UP, 1976. See especially the essays by Lerner and Peckham.

Weiss, Daniel. *The Critic Agonistes: Psychology, Myth, and the Art of Fiction*. Ed. Eric Solomon and Stephen Arkin. Seattle: U of Washington P, 1985.

Lacanian Psychoanalytic Studies of Literature

Collings, David. "The Monster and the Imaginary Mother: A Lacanian Reading of *Frankenstein*." *Mary Shelley, Frankenstein*. Ed. Johanna M. Smith. Case Studies in Contemporary Criticism. Ser. Ed. Ross C Murfin. Boston: Bedford, 1992. 245–58.

Davis, Robert Con, ed. *The Fictional Father: Lacanian Readings of the Text*. Amherst: U of Massachusetts P, 1981.

———. "Lacan and Narration." *Modern Language Notes* 5 (1983): 848–59.

Felman, Shoshana, ed. *Jacques Lacan and the Adventure of Insight: Psychoanalysis in Contemporary Culture*. Cambridge: Harvard UP, 1987.

———. *Literature and Psychoanalysis: The Question of Reading: Otherwise*. Baltimore: Johns Hopkins UP, 1982.

Froula, Christine. "When Eve Reads Milton: Undoing the Canonical Economy." *Canons*. Ed. Robert von Hallberg. Chicago: U of Chicago P, 1984. 149–75.

Homans, Margaret. *Bearing the Word: Language and Female Experience in Nineteenth-Century Women's Writing*. Chicago: U of Chicago P, 1986.

Mellard, James. *Using Lacan, Reading Fiction*. Urbana: U of Illinois P, 1991.

Muller, John P., and William J. Richardson, eds. *The Purloined Poe: Lacan, Derrida, and Psychoanalytic Reading*. Baltimore: Johns Hopkins UP, 1988. Includes Lacan's seminar on Poe's "The Purloined Letter."

Other Psychoanalytic Approaches to the "Rime"

Beres, David. "A Dream, a Vision, and a Poem: A Psycho-Analytic Study of the Origins of the Rime of the Ancient Mariner." *International Journal of Psycho-Analysis* 32 (1951): 97–116.

Bodkin, Maud. "A Study of 'The Ancient Mariner' and of the Rebirth Archetype." *Archetypal Patterns in Poetry: Psychological Studies of Imagination*. 1934. New York: Vintage, 1958. 25–85.

Harding, Davis W. "The Theme of 'The Ancient Mariner.'" *Scrutiny* 9 (1941): 334–42.

Knight, G. Wilson. *The Starlit Dome: Studies in the Poetry of Vision*. 1941. London: Oxford, 1971.

Sitterson, Joseph. "'The Rime of the Ancient Mariner' and Freudian Dream Theory." *Papers on Language and Literature* 18 (1982): 17–35.

Whalley, George. "The Mariner and the Albatross." *University of Toronto Quarterly* 16 (1946): 381–98.

ANNE WILLIAMS

An I for an Eye: "Spectral Persecution" in "The Rime of the Ancient Mariner"

Here . . . consciousness has not assumed its rights and transformed into signifiers those fluid demarcations of yet unstable
territories where an "I" that is taking shape is ceaselessly
straying.
–JULIA KRISTEVA Powers of Horror: An Essay on Abjection (11)

Coleridge's definition of "Imagination," though notoriously
obscure, is clear in affirming that this "esemplastic power" "struggles to
idealize and to unify" (*Biographia* 1: 295, 304). It follows (according
to chapter 14 of his *Biographia Literaria*) that the true poem is "a
graceful and intelligent *whole*" (2: 18; my emphasis). With these statements and the declaration that "The Rime of the Ancient Mariner" is
"a poem of pure imagination" (*Table Talk* 273), Coleridge inspired a
critical search for this work's inherent unity.

This quest impelled Robert Penn Warren to view the "Rime," in his
canonical reading, as a narrative of the "one life" and of the "sacramental unity" of the creative imagination (222, 214). Jerome McGann's
essay "*The Rime of the Ancient Mariner:* The Meaning of the Meanings" has been hailed as a definitive escape from Warren. A refreshing
demystifier of musty critical metaphysics, McGann argues that Coleridge's faith in symbolism is itself "epochal," founded on a "Romantic
ideology"; hence the poet's "much-discussed symbolic method is nothing more (or less) than rhetorical machinery for producing . . . interpretive results" (152). In recognizing the poem's ideology, he
concludes, one may reclaim the text as a "human — a social and historical — resource" (172). Even McGann, however, presupposes a
Coleridgean ideology: the "meanings" have one "meaning."

Yet the "Rime" seems extravagantly *dis*unified, composed of inter-
ruptions, disruptions, and irruptions. Split between gloss and ballad,

prose and verse, the two-column poem partitions commentary and narrative, philosophical and emotive languages. A disjointed, seven-part
story, the ballad concerns an interrupted wedding and describes abrupt
appearances and vanishings, intense, unmotivated passions. Even the
divisions between gloss, frame, and tale are interrupted: the wedding
guest twice stops the Mariner, and in the pivotal gloss about the "journeying Moon" (263–71), poetry intrudes into the prose. The work's
generic affinities represent another kind of boundary violation — Coleridge's appropriation of popular Gothic conventions to "serious"
poetic purpose.

Thus the Mariner's cognitive conclusion — "He prayeth best, who
loveth best" (614) — concludes nothing. He is doomed to repeat forever the struggle "to idealize and to unify." (As many readers have
noted, the Mariner suffers from "repetition compulsion.") Moreover, it
seems that the Mariner has jumped to his conclusion, for his spiritual
moral curiously elides the material horrors of his experience. The
"Rime" is like a figure-ground paradox — the rabbit-duck drawing, for
instance. In describing his "spectral persecution," as Wordsworth called
it, and then asserting its lesson of Fatherly love, the Mariner delineates a
rabbit and then declares it a duck. Yet the poem's coherence resides in
the interdependence of meaning and of experience. I propose, therefore, that the "Rime" enacts the process by which the speaking
subject — the user of language, the teller of tales — is constituted. The
poem concerns not the creative Imagination so much as the creation of
Imagination. There may be less frightful roads to language, but for
Coleridge's Mariner, the creation of the I in the perception of the eye is
a spectral flight from unspeakable horrors.

THE MARINER'S (M)OTHER

Gothic conventions are thus suited to this tale, a fact that might —
in another argument altogether — suggest a new theory of the Gothic.
But Coleridge's material debt to this mode has been denied, ignored,
and repressed by professional Romanticists. James D. Boulger's remark that "Coleridge was not a fool writing a pot-boiler for an audience of 'Gothic' sensibility" (14) candidly expresses the mainstream
assumption that the mode merely panders to readers of slight intellect
and low taste. (Indeed, Coleridge's ambivalent review of *The Monk*
contains some similar pronouncements about "the horrible and the

preternatural" ["*Monk*" 370].[1]) This repression of the Gothic is congruent with the philosophical and theological critics' confidence that the "Night-mare Life-in-Death" (193) reveals the law of the father, for the Gothic expresses dark, distant otherness — the culturally female at its most extravagant and threatening. And though the Mariner's bizarre, dreamlike story might seem to invite a Freudian hermeneutic, classical psychoanalysis has also failed the "Rime." As Freud's feminist critics have pointed out, the father of psychoanalysis did not admit, or even perceive, the power of the mother.

Julia Kristeva's theories concerning the emergence of the subject offer a powerful alternative framework for understanding the "Rime." According to Kristeva, the speaking subject is split, inhering in the dynamic interdependence of the symbolic and the semiotic, figuring the law of the father against the unrepresentable ground of the repressed mother. The formation of the subject is a process: "Discrete quantities of energy move through the body of the subject who is not yet constituted as such and, in the course of his development they are arranged according to the various constraints imposed upon this body . . . by family and social structures" (*Black Sun* 264).[2] Horror is the symptom of the not yet self's "abjection" (casting off) of the maternal and material. Once constituted, the speaking subject is not fixed but is always *en procès* (both in process and on trial). Poetic language, in its sounds, rhythms, and disruptions of the symbolic's semantic and syntactic laws, evokes the pulsions and drives of the semiotic maternal *chora*, "this rhythmic space, which has no thesis and no position, the process by which significance is constituted" (Kristeva, *Revolution* 26). Of course, any poem, no matter how poetic, in Kristeva's sense, always remains within the symbolic, because poetry is composed of language; a text may, nevertheless, manifest the semiotic's disruptive, even revolutionary, energies.

Coleridge's narrative (including frame and gloss) may be read as a representation of semiotic intrusion into the symbolic universe.[3] The

---

[1]Coleridge may owe something to Lewis's plot, however. Lewis's Wandering Jew (who cannot remain in one place more than fourteen days) interrupts Raymond de las Cisternas's "wedding" to the Bleeding Nun, who is literally a nightmare life-in-death. (Ann B. Tracy's index of Gothic motifs lists the interrupted wedding as the most frequent device in Gothics published between 1790 and 1830.)

[2]The semiotic's "vocal and gestural organization is subject to an objective *ordering* (*ordonnancement*), which is dictated by nature or socio-historical constraints such as the biological difference between the sexes or family structure" (Kristeva, *Revolution* 26–27).

[3]Coleridge's addition of the glosses in 1817 itself implies an effort to assimilate the semiotic to the symbolic. Like Kristeva's essay *"Stabat Mater,"* the annotated poem juxtaposes two modes and hence exemplifies their incompatibility.

Mariner appears as if from nowhere (the nonworld of the unspeakable), and when he leaves, the guest is "like one that hath been stunned, . . . sadder and . . . wiser" (622, 624), realizing new, though unspeakable and unspoken, dimensions of reality. Not only does the Mariner express the hitherto unimaginable; he also, peculiarly, represents the mother. He is an archetype (i.e., a culture-wide symbol), the wise old man, whose hypnotic "glittering eye" (3) implies the Lacanian phallic gaze of simultaneous identity and alienation. But the text also repeatedly links him with the conventionally female in Western culture: the sea, irrationality, motherhood, and nature — "spontaneous" energies that challenge and disrupt symbolic order. The guest calls him a "grey-beard loon" (11); when the Mariner moved his lips, the pilot shrieked and "fell down in a fit," while the pilot's boy "doth crazy go" (560–61, 565). The Mariner's purpose in life is to instruct the young, a role traditionally relegated to mothers: the wedding guest is like a "three years' child" (15) compelled to listen to a nightmare nanny's terrible bedtime story.[4]

The Mariner chooses his listeners with "feminine" intuitiveness, and he describes the repeated reproduction of his tale in terms suggesting the onset of birth:

> [T]his frame of mine was wrenched
> With a woful agony,
> Which forced me to begin my tale;
> And then it left me free.
>
> Since then, at an uncertain hour,
> That agony returns. . . . (578–83)

This unwilling bearer of the word is associated with Mother Nature's cyclic rhythms: he is "long, and lank, and brown, / As is the ribbed sea-sand" (226–27); he says, "I pass, like night, from land to land" (586). His ship reminds the hermit of nature's brutality, of the season when "the owlet whoops to the wolf below, / That eats the she-wolf's young" (536–37). His "strange power of speech" (587), though more intelligible than that of Keats's Belle Dame, brings the sort of message from the beyond that Romantic poets usually hear in a female voice.

This fusion of female with male both represents poetic discourse and may exemplify how I believe the text "means." This mariner-mother

---

[4]See Cixous and Clément on madness and hysteria as signifiers of the repressed other.

ignores the symbolic law of identity (which dictates that a mariner is only a mariner and a mother only a mother); yet the figure is still readable if other symbolic connections are attended to. As a whole, the Mariner's tale ignores the symbolic law of cause and effect, but his vivid images link with other powerful but usually tacit ways of making sense. These alternatives include assumptions about what is male and what female — fundamental and virtually unconscious ordering principles — and the perceptual and cognitive "maps" that George Lakoff and Mark Turner call "basic metaphors," whose use is "conventional, unconscious, automatic, and typically unnoticed" (80): "life is a journey," for instance, or "freedom is up" (221–22).

As a speaking subject, the Mariner exists within the symbolic; but he disrupts its present order in and through his tale, which so disturbs the wedding guest. And in affirming the love of an absent, distant, ideal father, his words, like his person, imply that the other of which he speaks remains incommensurate, unassimilated, and powerful. Thus it is appropriate that in conclusion the Mariner describes the model community, family members who in praying to their invisible "great Father" are related by spirit, not blood. He insists that life's greatest sweetness is "To walk together to the kirk, / And all together pray": "Old men, and babes, and loving friends / And youths and maidens gay!" (601–09). And yet no married women and mothers appear in his congregation (not surprising for one who keeps young men from weddings). In compulsively speaking of love as ideal, universal, asexual, and fatherly, he ignores its concrete, erotic, and social dimensions culturally linked with the mother: agape represses eros. Though he has left the ocean for the land, he must wander eternally from one surrogate "child" to another, telling and retelling his story. In his strangeness, his marginality, he is the exception that proves the rule (or the neurosis that discloses the unconscious structure). He is a speaking subject whose subject is his own subjectivity; he exists only as a subject manifestly and eternally *en procès*.

"VOYAGING THROUGH STRANGE SEAS OF THOUGHT"

A wedding is an appropriate occasion for this revolutionary disruption of the law of the father, for the ceremony is patriarchy's central ritual for regulating the female — the bride takes her husband's name and her place in the culture. The Mariner's dreamlike tale, though told and heard, is virtually nonsensical, almost failing to mesh with the structures that impart meaning to experience. But only such a tale could represent the semiotic — a series of disjointed, emotionally charged images evoking the eye's oceanic voyage toward the I-land of self-consciousness. After the Mariner emerges from the water, his first act is a speech act, a response to the hermit's question "What manner of man art thou?" (577).

Coleridge's seven parts imply what the story relates: that this process is no smooth, overtly purposeful voyage but a series of violent, often apparently random motions punctuated with periods of stasis and stagnation. The tale begins with an unquestionable first premise: "There was a ship" (10). The vessel setting out on its journey constitutes a basic metaphor for the body beginning life. The ship's movements follow the pulsions and rhythms of fluid, preoedipal drives, of the semiotic *chora*. As Wordsworth observed, the Mariner is extraordinarily passive (361). In part I this passivity appears not only in the narrator's grammar, characterized by passive voice and intransitive verbs: "The ship was cheered . . ."; "Merrily did we drop . . ." (21, 22). Coleridge's language here also tends to decenter the subject position; the narrator uses the first-person plural, barely distinguishes chronological sequence, and lacks both a precise perspective on the action and a firm sense of cause and effect.

At first the mariners perceive only a rhythm of natural variation — the rising and the setting of the sun. They already associate this elemental cyclicality, however, with a rudimentary sense of spatiality, of right and left. The rhythm is disturbed by the "Storm-blast," which drives the vessel into the frozen Antarctic. These early stanzas contain no speculation, as opposed to observation, no sense of sequence or cause — only recognition of events: "And now the STORM-BLAST came . . ."; "And now there came both mist and snow . . ." (41, 51). These experiences, pleasant and unpleasant, evoke intense though general sensations, of violent motion, loud noise, bright color (the ice is as "green as emerald" [54]).

Most important, these natural phenomena are always already gendered. The sun and the storm are "he," while the moon is "she." Warren rightly emphasizes the contrasting and complementary functions of sun and moon in the "Rime." But his contention that these figures represent "reason" and "imagination" is, as many have noted, debatable. I propose that their function is simpler, more concrete: in the mariners' evolving sense of reality, the sun, like the wind, is associated with father and the male, and the moon, like the water, is related to mother and the female.[5]

The masculine and feminine are each linked, however, with both pleasant and unpleasant sensations. The father sun first implies comforting regularity, something to wonder at (26) and to depend on — at least until hidden by storm clouds. But the storm blast, also male, is experienced as an abusive father who "Was tyrannous and strong: / He struck with his o'ertaking wings, / And chased us south along" (42–44). The epic simile describing the ship's response evokes a cowering child who can only flee:

> As who pursued with yell and blow
> Still treads the shadow of his foe,
> And forward bends his head,
> The ship drove fast, loud roared the blast,
> And southward aye we fled. (46–50)

This "paternal" violence drives the vessel into the cold. A familiar metaphor for rejection, ice is an apt figure for the transformation of good mother into bad: the tropically warm, liquid medium hitherto supporting the ship turns hard and frigid, frustrating (e)motion.

When the albatross appears, both of these external and gendered forces have already caused suffering: the warm father sun has disappeared, and the father wind has rained down hostile blows; the mother ocean has turned to ice. The albatross, however, connotes mother *and* father in both good and bad aspects. A creature of sea and air, it is associated both with "mist and snow" and with the beneficent moonshine. Winged like the masculine storm blast, it also seems to bring "the good south wind." The bird, however, is consistently called "it." In making the albatross a pet (it shares the childish activities of "food or play"), the sailors establish a quasi-familial relationship with this external object that is almost, though not quite, a person (greeted "As *if* it had been a Christian soul" [my emphasis]). The bird also evokes the mariners' first purposeful articulation. ("Hail" and "hollo" are emotive rather than denotative but are more focused than the poem's previous noises, the

---

[5] I do not imply that anything is essentially masculine or feminine. Instead, these figures already express a metonymic association derived from the earliest infantile sensations. In a patriarchal family, the infant associates the maternal and feminine with a nurturing proximity, a materiality, that the father can simply never match. The father and the masculine principle therefore connote the nonmaterial, abstract, ideal.

"loud roar" of the blast, the "crack," "growl," "roar," and "howl" of the ice.) The whole episode is indeterminate, however, shrouded in "mist," "cloud," "fog-smoke," and "Moonshine" (41–78).

As the closest thing to a personal object yet encountered, the albatross appears to draw the hostility aroused in the Mariner by the forces harrying the vessel; the creature affords him the first opportunity for self-expression (and hence for selfhood), a virtually automatic imitation of blows experienced, implying a physics in which every psychic action is answered by an equal and opposite reaction. Shooting the albatross, the Mariner destroys the mistily pleasurable community of sailors and bird — a relation of not yet self and not quite other.

From the symbolic retrospect of language, the shooting represents an experience inevitable in the attainment of selfhood and subjectivity: separation from matter and from *mater*. This experience inaugurates what Kristeva calls the thetic stage — the crucial, inexorable emergence of a sense of self and not self — beginning with the mirror stage and ending with the discovery of castration (*Revolution* 46). From this perspective, the most familiar, bewildering question about the poem — why the Mariner shoots the albatross — appears utterly irrelevant. Notions of cause and effect (or of psychological motivation) are created by the symbolic order: not effects but affects are relevant to the preoedipal. The Mariner's tale is disturbing and original because it shows preoedipal affects coalescing and transforming into symbolic faith in effects. The painful intensity of this first self-recognition, the Mariner's mirror stage, is represented by the violence of the act. A striking detail of grammar confirms that the shooting is significant precisely as a first deed, a self-creating act: here the Mariner uses the pronoun "I" for the first time — "I shot the ALBATROSS" (82).

Part 2 chronicles the mariners' resulting recognition of absence. The familiar natural rhythms continue, but the missing bird excites the sailors' first speculation (of a double kind: they scrutinize their surroundings and construct a hypothesis). In this early attempt at "reading," they try out the possibility that contingency and causation are the same. Since the good breeze followed the bird's arrival, they expect that the breeze will vanish after the killing. Initially inclined to think that the deed is "hellish" (the vanished bird is called "sweet"), they subsequently see the rising of the "glorious Sun" as affirmation that the killing is "right" (87–102).[6]

---

[6]The sun previously came up on the "right" (83). The association of sun, light, and right may illustrate a metonymy by which patriarchy justifies itself. If the sun is linked with the paternal (a connection established by masculine characterizations of energy and

Increasingly specific perceptions accompany these tentative gestures. Other modes of absence intrude on the senses of the mariners, who notice silence and in the lack of wind feel the lack of motion. Matter seems to shrink away, like the boards of the ship. And though it may have been right to slay the albatross, the emptiness is painful. The Mariner reports that the sailors "speak only to break" the silence (109), though his narrative contains as yet no direct discourse. But horror — physical revulsion — is their most salient response:

> The very deep did rot: O Christ!
> That ever this should be!
> Yea, slimy things did crawl with legs
> Upon the slimy sea. (123–26)

Such a response is predicted by Kristeva's theory of abjection, in which horror is the symptom the fragile not yet self exhibits when about to separate from the mother: "the abject confronts us . . . with our earliest attempts to release the hold of *maternal* entity even before ex-isting outside of her, thanks to the autonomy of language. It is a violent, clumsy breaking away. . . ." In abjection, the subject inescapably responds to corporeality, recognizes its own dependence on materiality. As Kristeva notes, "Food loathing is perhaps the most elementary and archaic form of abjection" (*Powers* 15, 2). The mariners experience the waters of the sea, of the "mother" of life, as undrinkable; hence its "slimy" surface teems with "rot," or the opposite of nourishment.

The intensifying stress of part 2 ends with the poem's second explicit action. Having begun with the mariners' attempt to see meaning in the albatross's death, the section concludes with a quasi-symbolic gesture: "Instead of the cross, the Albatross / About my neck was hung" (141–42). The gloss declares, "The shipmates, in their sore distress, would fain throw the whole guilt on the ancient Mariner: in sign whereof they hang the dead sea-bird round his neck." But in the poem, the passive voice again masks the subject; the Mariner merely records that the bird was put there, as a clumsy replacement intended to alleviate the symptoms of losing the living albatross. In *Powers of Horror* Kristeva argues that as waste is a source of abjection, the corpse mani-

---

light and, in this passage in the "Rime," by the Mariner's likening the newly risen sun to "God's own head" [97]), then when the dawn banishes the mist, the paternal pushes the traditionally feminine and maternal toward otherness. The incontestable benefits of solar warmth and light give this result the stamp of rightness.

fests the condition most potently (18). The carcass of the albatross represents the abject becoming the object. The difference here between gloss and Mariner's narrative is significant in showing that separation and the attempt to mark or mask the gap created with a substitute are coeval with guilt. In establishing a link between "cause" and affect, the dead bird is not yet a symbol, however. The mariners grope toward the symbolic, the conventional substitution of one thing for an absent other, but the abject corpse of the albatross represents the bird's own death. The sign of the albatross's death is the dead albatross. The concept of substitution has appeared, but the signifier virtually *is* the signified.

Nevertheless, this event marks the second stage of the Mariner's voyage. The Warren tradition reads the curious phrase "Instead of the cross" as support for a Christian interpretation of the text. What is fundamental, crucial, in both the Warren reading and mine is the role of substitution in the constitution of the symbolic. Christian atonement is effected when innocent Christ replaces guilty humanity. The mariners' action thus discloses a link among the structure of the symbolic, the theological concept of redemptive sacrifice, and an idea of the sacred. In the "Rime" the death of the "harmless Albatross" (401) gives rise to the notion of guilt as both having offended and having merely acted,[7] a notion that motivates the idea of symbolic substitution. The Mariner's existence as a speaking subject, his "salvation," coincides with his escape from oceanic isolation, his capacity to tell his tale. Only then, when the albatross's death is mediated through speech, a system itself dependent on substitution, does it become possible to interpret the killing as redemptive. Indeed, only at this point is the death a sacrifice; only then does this creature, which impels the transition from nonself to I, become sacred. (For until there is a speaking subject, there is no meaning, sacred or otherwise; and, conversely, as Kristeva comments, "[s]acrifice reminds us that the symbolic emerges out of material continuity, through a violent and unmotivated leap" [*Revolution* 77].) The uncanny resonance of the albatross's death, I suspect, thus springs from the bird's symbolic dissonance within the ballad. The death fails to conform to the symbolic rules of sacrifice even while exposing their

---

[7]According to the *Oxford English Dictionary*, one of the earliest senses of *guilt* (current from the twelfth century to 1671) was "[r]esponsibility for an action or event." The placement of the albatross marks the agency of the Mariner; he is singled out. (The glossist uses "guilt" in the more familiar sense of "[t]he fact of having committed . . . some specified or implied offense," an extension of the earlier one, and assumes subjectivity in mariners and Mariner alike, since the notion of offense presupposes responsibility.)

fundamental principle — the notion of substitution as a reparation for loss, lack, absence.

THE MARINER'S FAMILY ROMANCE

In part 3 the horror of the persons on board the "spectre-bark" shocks the Mariner into a new stage of development. After appearing at the climax of part 1, the pronoun "I" alternates with "we" in part 2. In part 3, though "we" still appears occasionally, the narrative voice increasingly shares the Mariner's perspective, as if his vision were becoming more focused, giving another signal of emerging selfhood. He describes the approaching ship with increasing specificity, seeing first a "something" and then "a little speck," "a mist," a "shape," and finally "a sail!" (148–61). At this recognition he utters the first direct discourse of his narrative — words spoken out of a need so terrible that he sucks his own blood to pronounce them. (This blood is the first hint that the Mariner has an interior dimension; the "autovampirism" may suggest the presence of a kind of literal inner resource, as well as connoting the sublimation of the abject.) He expresses a devout, enthusiastic faith that "she" comes "[h]ither to work us weal" (168). Yet the first spoken words — "A sail! a sail!" — name and summon not the nourishing mother but the specter bark: his first denotative use of language is ambiguous. The Mariner's developing negative experience of the maternal as ice and as rot is now realized in the person of the "Nightmare Life-in-Death."

The vessel's passengers offer considerable insight into the Mariner's avoidance of weddings. He asks a series of questions that lead toward certainty:

And is that Woman all her crew?
Is that a DEATH? and are there two?
Is DEATH that woman's mate?

Her lips were red, *her* looks were free,
Her locks were yellow as gold:
Her skin was white as leprosy,
The Night-mare LIFE-IN-DEATH was she,
Who thicks man's blood with cold. (187–94)

Here are Eros and Thanatos in the same boat, as it were, and one remarkably like the Mariner's own, as the Hermit's later description reveals (529–37).

Classical Freudian theory would interpret this grouping as an oedipal triangle, but the configuration is bizarrely skewed in a decidedly unclassical way. The woman has the gold hair, red lips, white skin of many a ballad heroine, but her erotic beauty implies danger and disease — no temptations to incest here. The climax of the passage occurs when the Mariner names her by her function, to "thick man's blood with cold" — the sign that represents her is still virtually metonymic, contingent. The father figure here is Death himself, instrument of the last and greatest "castration." This mother comes hither not to "work us weal" but to gamble with Death. Indeed, this Nightmare appears to confirm Madelon Sprengnether's argument in *The Spectral Mother* that maternal desire is the one thing that patriarchy cannot accommodate: what is most horrible here is the implication that the figure is powerful, free, and indifferent to the nascent subject. The Mariner, like the protagonists in all Gothic romance, holds a family secret in his heart of darkness. These apparitions are his "parents," their legacy the knowledge that he belongs — randomly and temporarily — to mother, the fatal woman, the slimy sea, rotting *mater,* darkness.

As Life-in-Death claims victory, the sun sets, darkness falls, and the specter bark vanishes. The mariners now experience motionlessness as suspense while, for a terrible moment, they wait: "We listened and looked sideways up! / Fear at *my* heart, as at a cup, / *My* life-blood seemed to sip!" (203–05; my emphases). The Mariner and his shipmates outwardly behave alike, though the blood the Mariner drank in summoning the bark is now echoed figuratively by his simile, as if feeding the private fear that sets him apart and marking his progress toward the symbolic. In responding to the absence of the bark, displaying anxiety about the nonmaterial, about the future, he implies an incipient capacity for imagination.

The suspense resolves itself by the rising of "The hornéd Moon, with one bright star / Within the nether tip" (210–11). The vessel that had materialized out of the sun vanishes like the sun over the horizon, seemingly beneath the ocean's surface. In a movement emblematic of primal repression, the Madonna-like moon appears in place of the bark. Intolerably erotic, personified horror disappears, and its opposite — distant rather than near, moving gently and predictably, summoning rather than being summoned — rises from the depths of the ocean. The moon reappears with "*one* bright star / Within the nether tip"; won by Life-in-Death, the Mariner is one indeed. Hence the shipmates die as the moon rises, a development that realizes his condition. The identity or agency hitherto diffused among the group now entirely coalesces into an agonizing self-consciousness: the mariners become the Mariner.

Now he must relive, and more intensely, the miseries following the death of the albatross. Part 4 recounts the pains of "I-solation," of one man as an island in the "wide wide sea" (237). This section repeats the pronoun "I" fifteen times, and the long *i* is almost obsessively echoed in rhyme and patterns of assonance. The very sounds of the words point to the source of the Mariner's anxiety. He is an I — one and alone — and yet he shares "I-ness," life, with everything around him. He experiences life as horrible because it suggests the indeterminacy, the fragility, of his own I. Painfully aware of himself, he also perceives the horrible materiality of the other *i*'s in the world: "And a thousand thousand slimy things / Lived on; and so did I" (238–39).

Furthermore, the Mariner recognizes the others' deaths as an unambiguously personal reproach, for the stronger his identity as an agent, the stronger his capacity for guilt:

> An orphan's curse would drag to hell
> A spirit from on high;
> But oh! more horrible than that
> Is the curse in a dead man's eye! (261–264)

The Mariner's I is confirmed by his guilty sense that he is looked at — the gaze, according to Lacan, effects alienation. Of course, the Mariner *is* responsible, the agent of the others' deaths, for it was the consequence of his emerging I. And like the albatross, the corpses remain as signs of the abject, of the cast off, horrible reminders of the self's painful, violent birth through separation and isolation.

At this point, the Mariner is an orphan — his father and mother have vanished — and his brother sailors are dead. His feeling of lack (which is partly a relief, given the horror of the parental figures) explains his eventual allegiance to the family of God the Father. As Freud writes in "Family Romances," imagining a father who is a nobleman or king enables the neurotic to deal with intolerable familial circumstances. This, I suggest, is the situation of the Mariner just before he blesses the water snakes: he is a child terrified and abandoned, afloat on the loathsome, slimy bosom of terrible Mother Nature.[8] Dawning

---

[8]Camille Paglia argues that the Mariner is a "male heroine" who is appalled by the horrors of female nature (323–27). According to Kristeva's theory of abjection, however, horror springs from the fact of separation instead of inhering in nature, in the female, as Paglia seems to assume.

self-consciousness is coeval with guilt. Where can he go but up? He denies the family of nature and humankind by sublimating the abject — by leaping into a "true" and satisfying spiritual membership in the family of God the Father, by crossing the threshold of the symbolic.

SEEING EYE TO AYE

Through part 4 the Mariner's account of his experiences portrays the world through the eyes of an I in formation. As materiality forces itself on the mariners' notice and a sense of spatiality begins to emerge, the world becomes increasingly complex. To this point, this vessel has been voyaging on the surface of the ocean, and what is underneath belongs to a beyond of which he has no concept. The Mariner apparently never sleeps, though he says that others dream (131–32). The mariners' psychic stirrings, their primitive attempts to find meaning in events, have been focused on the horizontal plane and have been fundamentally metonymic — meaning arises from contiguity (as when the sailors use the albatross as a sign of its own death).

When the moon displaces the specter bark in part 3, the Mariner's world begins to reorganize itself along the vertical plane: displacement, a metonymic primary process hitherto dominant, is replaced by the metaphoric function of condensation. The disappearance of the bark and the reappearance of the moon not only "cause" the death of the other mariners; the events also imply that the ocean's depths effect some transforming magic. In Freudian depth psychology, this substitution is called a "compromise formation": the specter bark with its horrible figures becomes tolerable when contemplated as the moon, a maternal presence now distant in the fatherly mode. But such a compromise does not entirely allay anxiety. The moon becomes desirable when it creates the possibility of desire by becoming unreachable.

The same moon, now risen much higher, presides over the Mariner's blessing of the water snakes. The detail of a "star or two beside" gives the moon a maternal quality (266), reinforced by the reference to an "orphan's curse." The relationship between orphan child and mother moon is still metonymic but barely so, since the chief effect of the conjunction is to contrast a low realm (of orphans, curses, guilt, vile ocean, repellent life, stasis), occupied by the Mariner, with a high one (of mother and child, softness, movement). Thus the moon, though unreachable, at least displays to the Mariner an alternative to his miserable state. The power of the affect that the moon provokes is demonstrated by the glossist, who waxes poetic for the first and only time. The annotative simile of celestial homecoming parallels and affirms the Mariner's displacement upward. What happens can be expressed only by using home as a metaphor for the lost bliss of pure nonselfhood.

Then the Mariner looks again at the snakes, those ambiguously phallic creatures of the mother that epitomize the horrors of materiality. When he sees the snakes in the light of the moon, his eye effects an affirmative transformation, a comic re-vision of nature, a repression of the abject: "Her beams bemocked the sultry main, / Like April hoar-frost spread," he says (267–68). "Beams," referring to irradiation, conotes smiles, while "bemocked" means "laughed at," and the simile "Like April hoar-frost spread" is comically incongruous, a natural joke, for frost in April is transient and delusive. The moonlight on the "sultry" waves makes them appear the opposite of what they seemed before — they appear cool rather than hot, light rather an dark, attractive rather than repellent.

The Mariner's response to this transformation expresses his first recognition:

O happy living things! no tongue
Their beauty might declare:
A spring of love gushed from my heart,
And I blessed them unaware:
Sure my kind saint took pity on me,
And I blessed them unaware. (282–87)

In naming the sea creatures, he escapes into the symbolic, where love, life, and beauty are aspects of a single, unified whole. This re-vision is the Mariner's first, empowering experience of the eye-I's capacity to dominate and organize perception, a discovery that frees him from *mater* and matter. Most telling, this liberating love (and its adequate expression) presupposes the unknowable and the unspeakable, in the repression of the maternal and the material. "Spring," "love," and "gushed" all figuratively represent the fluid, feminine other that now belongs to the unconscious (personified as "my kind saint").[9] The other functions both as a sign of this new organization of the eye-I and

---

[9]Numerous critics have assumed that the Mariner unambiguously states that the blessing comes from his "kind saint." But he says, "*Sure* my kind saint took pity on me"— in other words, he is speculating, guessing.

as a necessary source of vital energy from beyond.[10] At last the Mariner's words rise up to heaven. Prayer is surely language at its most symbolic, communication directed "upward" toward an unseen and invisible other. The albatross falls "[l]ike lead into the sea" (291). The ocean, now functioning as the unconscious, mercifully hides the body, abject reminder of self-creating guilt.

SPECTRAL PERSECUTION

The Mariner's journey homeward is undoubtedly less compelling than his outward voyage. Between his blessing and his confession to the hermit — the Mariner's first experience as a speaking subject[11] — the tale confirms the symbolically ordered structure of the I. Yet the supernatural machinery in this segment lacks the uncanny materiality of the earlier specters, as well as their vivid hues.[12] In blessing the snakes, the Mariner enacts and at the same time participates in the system founded on a recognized distinction between self and other, matter and spirit, speakable and unspeakable, conscious and unconscious. His subsequent experiences confirm these boundaries and divisions. Having known

[10]The Mariner's experience here appears to confirm Kristeva's assertion, in contrast to Melanie Klein's and D. W. Winnicott's emphasis on the centrality of the preoedipal mother, that "the father of personal pre-history" affects the child's capacity for agape, or love as metaphoric identification, as "movement toward the discernible, a journey toward the visible" ("Freud" 247). The infant responds to a triangular configuration that includes itself, the mother, and the "phallus of the father," the last item designating the mother's desire for something other than the child. The Mariner's "salvation" involves such a triangle — his I-eye, the phallic-feminine water snakes, and the moon — that also incorporates qualities associated with the masculine (motion and distance). Explicit — though metaphoric — recognition of the moon's "desire" (and the emergence of desire in the Mariner) is displaced into the famously poetic gloss: "In his loneliness and fixedness he yearneth towards the journeying Moon . . ." (263–71). He reads in the heavenly bodies a story about the homecoming of "lords."

[11]Though the Mariner must have spoken with his fellow sailors before they died, the poem records no speech among them — indeed a rather odd omission. Even the "vespers" of part 1 (76) are sung prayers (and so more semiotic than symbolic). Thus this argument demonstrates the power of the symbolic to create expectations about experience in narrative.

[12]The major exception is the "crimson shadows" rising from the moonlit bay (482–85). The gloss identifies them with the seraphs' "forms of light." These apparitions may be linked with the "still and awful red" of the ship's shadow (271), just before the blessing of the water snakes. The reappearance of crimson shadows from the depths brings to mind the animating life force of the lost mother repressed into the unconscious. Coleridge associates red with the female: the bride is as "[r]ed as a rose" (34), as are Life-in-Death's vampiric lips (190).

consciousness for the first time, he finally sleeps. His dreams reiterate the new primacy of spirit: "I dreamt that [the buckets] were filled with dew; / And when I awoke, it rained." His mind feels separate from his body — he feels liberated from matter altogether — as if he were "a blesséd ghost" (299–300, 308).

The wind returns in a sublime mode reminiscent of the Pentecostal wind, and the rainstorm comes on. (Perhaps in the phrase "upper air" [313] Coleridge unconsciously echoes the "upper room" where the apostles received the gift of tongues.) But now natural forces are neither male nor female. Lunar movement and windstorm are magnificent but utterly remote celestial events. The reanimation of the dead sailors further affirms the power of spirit. As cast-off (abject) parts of the Mariner himself, their bodies neither "rot nor reek" (254), but the revival of the sailors through spiritual intervention suggests that they continue to inhabit the Mariner's unconscious. Their language is now the sweet music of birdsong, the echolalia of the semiotic.[13]

Parts 5 and 6 describe the appearance of the superego, unconscious parental voice of right and wrong. After fainting from a sudden rush of blood to his head, the Mariner hears two voices that attribute a spiritual cause to the albatross's death: a "spirit . . . loved the bird that loved the man / Who shot him with his bow." Experienced within the structure of the patriarchal symbolic, the voices belong to spiritual beings assimilated to the masculine, yet the one identified as "he" and who calls the other "brother" has a voice as "soft as honey-dew." They speak authoritatively about moral and physical cause and effect (though their explanation of the ship's motion is dubious). The Mariner, while unconscious, overhears their talk of expiation: "The man hath penance done, / And penance more will do" (402–20).

Warren assumes that the moral law the Mariner overhears is the Christian paradigm of "crime and punishment and reconciliation" (233), finding in this reading affirmation of Coleridge's "sacramental unity." But in fact the law seems closer to the "love, guilt, and reparation" that Melanie Klein argues is the main theme of preoedipal experience. Since infantile connections with the mother cannot be literally reestablished once they are severed, the adult re-creates them in sym-

---

[13]This music is connected with that "sweet bird" the albatross. Tracing the word "sweet" through the poem appropriately reveals that a quality beginning in sensuous experience emerges as a concept: "no sweet bird did follow . . ." (88); "Sweet sounds rose slowly through their mouths . . ." (352); "Around, around, flew each sweet sound . . ." (354); "With their sweet jargoning" (362); "How loudly his sweet voice [the hermit] rears!" (516); "O sweeter than the marriage-feast, / 'Tis sweeter far to me, / To walk together to the kirk . . ." (601–03).

bolic modes. Ideas of "penance" or expiation discover a principle of cause and effect in the ideal or psychological realm as well as in the physical one. Indeed, Freud's observation of his grandson's *fort-da* game is also relevant. The child invented the ritual of throwing away and retrieving a spool to relieve his anger over his mother's departure: "At the outset he was in a *passive* situation — he was overpowered by the experience; but, by repeating it, unpleasurable though it was, as a game, he took on an *active* part . . ." (*Pleasure Principle* 15–16). Freud tells this anecdote in the course of trying to account for repetition compulsion, the Mariner's permanent neurosis. The principle of moral reparation, established in the Mariner's unconscious, offers a panacea for guilt — the curse is finally snapped, and he can move forward once again.

Even after the Mariner reaches land, his identity as speaking subject is fragile, for the *procès* of his creation returns intermittently to consciousness. Even as the curse is broken, his words declare that it is only tentatively repressed. He says:

> [O]nce more
> I viewed the ocean green,
> And looked far forth, yet little saw
> Of what had else been seen. . . . (442–45)

This passage curiously unites active and passive voices; the I dimly intuits the presymbolic experience but can barely express it, doing so in the passive construction of his earlier, semiotic phase.

Though the Mariner now barely notices the horrors before him, he retains a sense of spectral persecution: he is

> Like one, that on a lonesome road
> Doth walk in fear and dread,
> And having once turned round walks on,
> And turns no more his head;
> Because he knows a frightful fiend
> Doth close behind him tread. (446–51)

Like the earlier simile describing the ship's flight before the storm, this image concerns pursuit. But in contrast to the ship's frantic forward motion, the movement here is deliberate. Alone, the subject refuses to look back at what he knows is behind him — at what he has already seen. What is seen is connected to what is ghostly through *spectral,* for the word's meanings have included "[c]apable of seeing spectres," "[h]aving the character of a spectre or phantom," "ghostly, unsubstantial, unreal," and even "[p]roduced merely by the action of light on the eye or on a sensitive medium" (*OED*). The spectral is now both past (repressed) and eternally present. Turned spectral himself (as the pilot's boy confirms), the Mariner leaves the ocean forever, for his ship follows the albatross into the depths. Once the infant (the root *infans* means "incapable of speech") becomes a compulsive talker, it will never forget speech. The specters of the Mariner's past continue to pursue him and always will, for they are intrinsic to his being. His I, consisting of what his eye has seen, has defined itself in trying to escape.

AN I FOR AN EYE

If the "Rime" expresses, within the resources of the symbolic, the semiotic prehistory of a speaking subject, it follows that the narrative also provides a genealogy of the Coleridgean Imagination. As I read the poem, it traces the means by which meaning is constructed out of separation, need, fear, guilt, and a need to repair the primal break. The fragile I, to mend the break its birth necessitates, imagines a higher realm where no such gap exists. Entry into the symbolic is a creative act, for the self is thereby constituted. Though Coleridge was Romantic in taking this process as his subject, he dis-covers an ideology not merely Romantic, as McGann claims it was, but also patriarchal in its horrified repression of the female. In this context, Coleridge's famous definition of Imagination and his comments on the symbol appear somewhat less enigmatic. In regard to Imagination, he writes:

> The IMAGINATION then I consider either as primary, or secondary. The primary IMAGINATION I hold to be the living Power and prime Agent of all human Perception, and a repetition in the finite mind of the eternal act of creation in the infinite I AM. The secondary I consider as an echo of the former. . . . [I]t struggles to *idealize* and to *unify* [my emphases]. It is essentially *vital,* even as all objects (*as* objects) are essentially fixed and dead. (*Biographia* 1: 304)

Imagination is an active power, an agent whose perception gives it knowledge of its own identity — of its experience of "I am," in contrast to the otherness of the fixed and dead. Cut off by definition from the material world, the "shaping spirit of Imagination" idealizes and unifies, re-creating the world in its own image (Coleridge, "Dejection"

86). The Mariner's most horrible experience is his isolation, his oneness. Perhaps Imaginative unity is most important to the Mariner in
serving his desire to make everything one with him, to reestablish the
preoedipal world, where there were no boundaries, where everything
shared one life — which was of course his own.

Thus Imagination is defensive; the Mariner's leap into the symbolic
is a reaction against the horrifying vacancy inherent in separation from
the maternal and material. Coleridge's obsessive use of abstractions
repeats this leap — indeed, could his fondness for philosophy and theology be a similar flight? Such a reaction also informs his definition of
the symbol and underlies his privileging of the symbolic. Coleridge
writes in *The Statesman's Manual* that the symbol is "the translucence
of the Eternal through and in the Temporal. It always partakes of the
reality it renders intelligible" (30). This definition takes on new and
ironic resonance in the light of the "Rime," as does the meditation
Coleridge recorded in 1804:

> In looking at objects of Nature while I am thinking, as at yonder
> moon dim-glimmering thro' the dewy window-pane, I seem
> rather to be seeking, as it were *asking*, a symbolical language for
> something within me that already and forever exists, than observ-
> ing anything new. (*Collected Notebooks* 2546)

The intuition that the symbol is somehow always already constituted within the subject is congruent with Kristeva's notion of the
semiotic within the symbolic. Coleridgean Imagination seems to be
fatally weakened: it exists only insofar as it is separated from what in fact
is its life. This "shaping spirit" sustains itself through its self-conscious
experience of its difference from the "natural," spontaneous, "feminine"
force in the beyond. To the extent that Imagination is self-confident
and self-absorbed, it may vanish altogether, according to its own rules.
It is thus strongest at its borders (as in the Mariner's moment of beatific
vision) or in writing elegies for itself (like "Dejection: An Ode").

The "Rime"'s great power — and readers' urge to interpret the
text — lies in the poem's discovery of intense, primitive anxieties fundamental to the self. Coleridge's reply to Anna Barbauld, who complained
that the "Rime" "lacked a moral," reveals his unconscious sense of this
strength: the work's

> only, or chief fault . . . was the obtrusion of the moral sentiment
> so openly on the reader as a principle or cause of action in a work

of pure imagination. . . . It ought to have had no more moral than
the *Arabian Nights'* tale of the merchant's sitting down to eat
dates by the side of a well and throwing the shells aside, and lo! a
genie starts up and says he *must* kill the aforesaid merchant *because*
one of the date shells had, it seems, put out the eye of the genie's
son. (272–73)

These comments affirm that both the *Arabian Nights* anecdote and
the "Rime" are concerned with the making of morals — with how
the concept of crime and punishment rushes in as a way of ensuring
order in the universe. The merchant has simply been going about his
business — eating dates (i.e., passing the time?) — when the avenging
father appears (out of a body of water) and announces a law that out-
does the Old Testament equity of an eye for an eye by requiring an I
for an eye — the genie demands the merchant's existence in repay-
ment. Humphry House points out that in the story as it appears in the
Arabian Nights, the date shell kills the genie's son (90–92). Norman
Fruman suggests that Coleridge's change may indicate a wish to "establish the *irrationality* of the *Arabian Nights* story" (545). In the context
of my reading, however, the change signals the "Rime"'s link between
vision and death, the specters of speculation. Perhaps most horrible to
Coleridge is the unconscious implication of this parable: that morality is
a response to meaningless change and loss. Imagination defends against
this knowledge. Small wonder, then, that Coleridge could not produce the discursive analysis an extended definition of Imagination demands; the Gothic horror of the "Rime" was as close as he could come
to imagining the unspeakable.

WORKS CITED

Beres, David. "A Dream, a Vision, and a Poem: A Psychoanalytic
    Study of the Origins of *The Rime of the Ancient Mariner.*"
    International Journal of Psychoanalysis 32 (1951): 97–116.
Boulger, James D. Introduction. *Twentieth-Century Interpretations of*
    The Rime of the Ancient Mariner. Ed. Boulger. Englewood Cliffs:
    Prentice, 1968. 1–20.
Cixous, Hélène, and Catherine Clément. *The Newly Born Woman.*
    Trans. Betsy Wing. Minneapolis: U of Minnesota P, 1985.
Coleridge, Samuel Taylor. *Biographia Literaria; or, Biographical
    Sketches of My Literary Life and Opinions.* Ed. James Engell and

W. Jackson Bate. Princeton: Princeton UP, 1983. 2 vols. No. 7 of *The Collected Works of Samuel Taylor Coleridge*.

———. *Coleridge: Poetical Works*. Ed. E. H. Coleridge. Oxford Standard Authors. London: Oxford UP, 1912.

———. *Collected Notebooks of Samuel Taylor Coleridge*. Ed. Kathleen Coburn. Pt. 2. Vol. 1. New York: Pantheon, 1957.

———. "Dejection: An Ode." Coleridge, *Coleridge* 362–68.

———. *The Statesman's Manual. Lay Sermons*. Ed. R. J. White. Princeton: Princeton UP, 1972. 3–114. No. 6 of *The Collected Works of Samuel Taylor Coleridge*.

———. *The Rime of the Ancient Mariner*. Coleridge, *Coleridge* 186–209.

———. *Table Talk*. Ed. Carl Woodring. Vol. 1. Princeton: Princeton UP, 1990. No. 14 of *The Collected Works of Samuel Taylor Coleridge*.

———. "*The Monk*, a Romance." *Coleridge's Miscellaneous Criticism*. Ed. T. M. Raysor. Cambridge: Harvard UP, 1936. 370–78.

Freud, Sigmund. *Beyond the Pleasure Principle*. Trans. and ed. James Strachey. Introd. Peter Gay. New York: Norton, 1989.

———. "Family Romances." *The Freud Reader*. Ed. Peter Gay. New York: Norton, 1989. 297–300.

Fruman, Norman. *Coleridge: The Damaged Archangel*. New York: Braziller, 1971.

House, Humphry. *Coleridge: The Clark Lectures, 1951–1952*. London: Hart, 1953.

Klein, Melanie. "Love, Guilt, and Reparation." *Writings of Melanie Klein, 1921–1945*. Ed. R. E. Money-Kyrle. New York: Dell, 1977. 306–43.

Kristeva, Julia. *Black Sun: Depression and Melancholia*. Trans. Leon S. Roudiez. New York: Columbia UP, 1989.

———. "Freud and Love: Treatment and Its Discontents." *Moi* 240–71.

———. *Powers of Horror: An Essay on Abjection*. Trans. Leon S. Roudiez. New York: Columbia UP, 1982.

———. *Revolution in Poetic Language*. Trans. Margaret Waller. New York: Columbia UP, 1984.

———. "Stabat Mater." *Moi* 160–86.

Lakoff, George, and Mark Turner. *More Than Cool Reason: A Field Guide to Poetic Metaphor*. Chicago: U of Chicago P, 1989.

McGann, Jerome. "*The Rime of the Ancient Mariner*: The Meaning of the Meanings." *The Beauty of Inflections: Literary Investigations in Historical Method and Theory.* Oxford: Clarendon, 1985. 135–72.

Modiano, Raimonda. "Words and 'Languageless' Meanings: Limits of Expression in *The Rime of the Ancient Mariner.*" *Modern Language Quarterly* 38 (1977): 40–61.

Moi, Toril, ed. *The Kristeva Reader.* New York: Columbia UP, 1986.

Paglia, Camille. *Sexual Personae: Art and Decadence from Nefertiti to Emily Dickinson.* New Haven: Yale UP, 1990.

Schulz, Max F. "Samuel Taylor Coleridge." *The English Romantic Poets: A Review of Research and Criticism.* Ed. Frank Jordan. 4th ed. New York: MLA, 1985. 341–463.

Sprengnether, Madelon. *The Spectral Mother: Freud, Feminism, Psychoanalysis.* Ithaca: Cornell UP, 1990.

Tracy, Ann B. *The Gothic Novel, 1790–1830: Plot Summaries and Index to Motifs.* Lexington: UP of Kentucky, 1981.

Warren, Robert Penn. 1946. "*The Rime of the Ancient Mariner:* A Poem of Pure Imagination." *Selected Essays of Robert Penn Warren.* New York: Vintage, 1956. 198–305.

Wordsworth, William. *The Poetical Works of William Wordsworth.* 1st ed. Ed. Ernest de Selincourt and Helen Darbishire. Vol. 1. Oxford: Oxford UP, 1940.

Deconstruction and
"The Rime of the Ancient Mariner"

WHAT IS DECONSTRUCTION?

Deconstruction has a reputation for being the most complex and forbidding of contemporary critical approaches to literature, but in fact almost all of us have, at one time, either deconstructed a text or badly wanted to deconstruct one. Sometimes when we hear a lecturer effectively marshal evidence to show that a book means primarily one thing, we long to interrupt and ask what he or she would make of other, conveniently overlooked passages that seem to contradict the lecturer's thesis. Sometimes, after reading a provocative critical article that *almost* convinces us that a familiar work means the opposite of what we assumed it meant, we may wish to make an equally convincing case for our former reading of the text. We may not think that the poem or novel in question better supports our interpretation, but we may recognize that the text can be used to support *both* readings. And sometimes we simply want to make that point: texts can be used to support seemingly irreconcilable positions.

To reach this conclusion is to feel the deconstructive itch. J. Hillis Miller, the preeminent American deconstructor, puts it this way: "Deconstruction is not a dismantling of the structure of a text, but a demonstration that it has already dismantled itself. Its apparently solid ground is no rock but thin air" ("Stevens' Rock" 341). To deconstruct a text isn't to show that all the high old themes aren't there to be found in it. Rather, it is to show that a text — not unlike DNA with its double helix — can have intertwined, opposite "discourses" — strands of narrative, threads of meaning.

Ultimately, of course, deconstruction refers to a larger and more complex enterprise than the practice of demonstrating that a text can have contradictory meanings. The term refers to a way of reading texts practiced by critics who have been influenced by the writings of the French philosopher Jacques Derrida. It is important to gain some understanding of Derrida's project and of the historical backgrounds of his work before reading the deconstruction that follows, let alone attempting to deconstruct a text.

Derrida, a philosopher of language who coined the term *deconstruction,* argues that we tend to think and express our thoughts in terms of opposites. Something is black but not white, masculine and therefore not feminine, a cause rather than an effect, and so forth. These mutually exclusive pairs or dichotomies are too numerous to list but would include beginning / end, conscious / unconscious, presence / absence, and speech / writing. If we think hard about these dichotomies, Derrida suggests, we will realize that they are not simply oppositions; they are also hierarchies in miniature. In other words, they contain one term that our culture views as being superior and one term viewed as negative or inferior. Sometimes the superior term seems only subtly superior (*speech, cause*), but at other times we know immediately which term is culturally preferable (*presence, beginning,* and *consciousness* are easy choices). But the hierarchy always exists.

Of particular interest to Derrida, perhaps because it involves the language in which all the other dichotomies are expressed, is the hierarchical opposition "speech/writing." Derrida argues that the "privileging" of speech, that is, the tendency to regard speech in positive terms and writing in negative terms, cannot be disentangled from the privileging of presence. (Postcards are written by absent friends; we read Plato because he cannot speak from beyond the grave.) Furthermore, according to Derrida, the tendency to privilege both speech and presence is part of the Western tradition of *logocentrism,* the belief that in some ideal beginning were creative *spoken* words, such as "Let there be light," spoken by an ideal, *present* God.[1] According to logocentric tra-

---

[1]Derrida sometimes uses the word *phallogocentrism* to indicate that there is "a certain indissociability" between logocentrism and the "phallocentrism" (Derrida, *Acts* 57) of a culture whose God created light, the world, and man before creating woman — from

dition, these words can now be represented only in unoriginal speech or writing (such as the written phrase in quotation marks above). Derrida doesn't seek to reverse the hierarchized opposition between speech and writing, or presence and absence, or early and late, for to do so would be to fall into a trap of perpetuating the same forms of thought and expression that he seeks to deconstruct. Rather, his goal is to erase the boundary between oppositions such as speech and writing, and to do so in such a way as to throw the order and values implied by the opposition into question.

Returning to the theories of Ferdinand de Saussure, who invented the modern science of linguistics, Derrida reminds us that the association of speech with present, obvious, and ideal meaning — and writing with absent, merely pictured, and therefore less reliable meaning — is suspect, to say the least. As Saussure demonstrated, words are *not* the things they name and, indeed, they are only arbitrarily associated with those things. A word, like any sign, is what Derrida has called a "deferred presence"; that is to say, "the signified concept is never present in itself," and "every concept is necessarily . . . inscribed in a chain or system, within which it refers to another and to other concepts" ("Différance" 138, 140). Neither spoken nor written words have present, positive, identifiable attributes themselves. They have meaning only by virtue of their difference from other words (*red, read, reed*) and, at the same time, their contextual relationship to those words. Take *read* as an example. To know whether it is the present or past tense of the verb — whether it rhymes with *red* or *reed* — we need to see it in relation to some other words (for example, *yesterday*).

Because the meanings of words lie in the differences between them and in the differences between them and the things they name, Derrida suggests that all language is constituted by *différance*, a word he has coined that puns on two French words meaning "to differ" and "to defer": words are the deferred presences of the things they "mean," and their meaning is grounded in difference. Derrida, by the way, changes the *e* in the French word *différence* to an *a* in his neologism *différance;* the change, which can be seen in writing but cannot be heard in spoken French, is itself a playful, witty challenge to the notion that writing is inferior or "fallen" speech.

In *Dissemination* (1972) and *De la grammatologie* [*Of Grammatology*] (1967), Derrida begins to redefine writing by deconstructing some

Adam's rib. "Phallocentrism" is another name for patriarchy. The role that deconstruction has played in feminist analysis will be discussed later.

old definitions. In *Dissemination*, he traces logocentrism back to Plato, who in the *Phaedrus* has Socrates condemn writing and who, in all the great dialogues, powerfully postulates that metaphysical longing for origins and ideals that permeates Western thought. "What Derrida does in his reading of Plato," Barbara Johnson points out in her translator's introduction to *Dissemination*, "is to unfold dimensions of Plato's *text* that work against the grain of (Plato's own) Platonism" (xxiv). Remember: that is what deconstruction does, according to Miller; it shows a text dismantling itself.

In *Of Gramatology*, Derrida turns to the *Confessions* of Jean-Jacques Rousseau and exposes a grain running against the grain. Rousseau — who has often been seen as another great Western idealist and believer in innocent, noble origins — on one hand condemned writing as mere representation, a corruption of the more natural, childlike, direct, and therefore undevious speech. On the other hand, Rousseau acknowledged his own tendency to lose self-presence and blurt out exactly the wrong thing in public. He confesses that, by writing at a distance from his audience, he often expressed himself better: "If I were present, one would never know what I was worth," Rousseau admitted (Derrida, *Of Grammatology* 142). Thus, Derrida shows that one strand of Rousseau's discourse made writing seem a secondary, even treacherous supplement, while another made it seem necessary to communication.

Have Derrida's deconstructions of *Confessions* and the *Phaedrus* explained these texts, interpreted them, opened them up and shown us what they mean? Not in any traditional sense. Derrida would say that anyone attempting to find a single, homogeneous or universal meaning in a text is simply imprisoned by the structure of thought that would oppose two readings and declare one to be right and not wrong, correct rather than incorrect. In fact, any work of literature that we interpret defies the laws of Western logic, the laws of opposition and noncontradiction. From deconstruction's point of view, texts don't say "A and not B." They say "A and not-A." "Instead of a simple 'either/or' structure," Johnson explains, "deconstruction attempts to elaborate a discourse that says *neither* 'either/or' *nor* 'both/and' nor even 'neither/nor,' while at the same time not totally abandoning these logics either. The word deconstruction is meant to undermine the either/or logic of the opposition 'construction/destruction.' Deconstruction is both, it is neither, and it reveals the way in which both construction and destruction are themselves not what they appear to be" (Johnson, *World* 12–13).

Although its ultimate aim may be to criticize Western idealism and logic, deconstruction began as a response to structuralism and to formalism, another structure-oriented theory of reading. Using Saussure's theory as Derrida was to do later, European structuralists attempted to create a *semiology*, or science of signs, that would give humankind at once a scientific and a holistic way of studying the world and its human inhabitants. Roland Barthes, a structuralist who later shifted toward poststructuralism, hoped to recover literary language from the isolation in which it had been studied and to show that the laws that govern it govern all signs, from road signs to articles of clothing. Claude Lévi-Strauss, a structural anthropologist who studied everything from village structure to the structure of myths, found in myths what he called *mythemes*, or building blocks, such as basic plot elements. Recognizing that the same mythemes occur in similar myths from different cultures, he suggested that all myths may be elements of one great myth being written by the collective human mind.

Derrida did not believe that structuralists had the concepts that would someday explain the laws governing human signification and thus provide the key to understanding the form and meaning of everything from an African village to Greek myth to Rousseau's *Confessions*. In his view, the scientific search by structural anthropologists for what unifies humankind amounts to a new version of the old search for the lost ideal, whether that ideal be Plato's bright realm of the Idea or the Paradise of Genesis or Rousseau's unspoiled Nature. As for the structuralist belief that texts have "centers" of meaning, in Derrida's view that derives from the logocentric belief that there is a reading of the text that accords with "the book as seen by God." Jonathan Culler, who thus translates a difficult phrase from Derrida's *L'Écriture et la différence* [*Writing and Difference*] (1967) in his book *Structuralist Poetics* (1975), goes on to explain what Derrida objects to in structuralist literary criticism:

> [When] one speaks of the structure of a literary work, one does so from a certain vantage point: one starts with notions of the meaning or effects of a poem and tries to identify the structures responsible for those effects. Possible configurations or patterns that make no contribution are rejected as irrelevant. That is to say, an intuitive understanding of the poem functions as the "centre". . . . : it is both a starting point and a limiting principle. (244)

Deconstruction calls into question assumptions made about literature by formalist, as well as by structuralist, critics. Formalism, or the

New Criticism as it was once commonly called, assumes a work of literature to be a freestanding, self-contained object, its meanings found in the complex network of relations that constitute its parts (images, sounds, rhythms, allusions, and so on). To be sure, deconstruction is somewhat like formalism in several ways. Both formalism and deconstruction are text-oriented approaches whose practitioners pay a great deal of attention to rhetorical *tropes* (forms of figurative language including allegory, symbol, metaphor, and metonymy). And formalists, long before deconstructors, discovered counterpatterns of meaning in the same text. Formalists find ambiguity: deconstructors find undecidability. On close inspection, however, the formalist understanding of rhetorical tropes or figures is quite different from that of deconstruction, and undecidability turns out to be different from the ambiguity formalists find in texts.

Formalists, who associated literary with figurative language, made qualitative distinctions between types of figures of speech; for instance, they valued symbols and metaphors over metonyms. (A metonym is a term standing for something with which it is commonly associated or contiguous; we use metonymy when we say we had "the cold plate" for lunch.) From the formalist perspective, metaphors and symbols are less arbitrary figures than metonyms and thus rank more highly in the hierarchy of tropes: a metaphor ("I'm feeling blue") supposedly involves a special, intrinsic, nonarbitrary relationship between its two terms (the feeling of melancholy and the color blue); a symbol ("the river of life") allegedly involves a unique fusion of image and idea.

From the perspective of deconstruction, however, these distinctions are suspect. In "The Rhetoric of Temporality," Paul de Man deconstructs the distinction between symbol and allegory; elsewhere, he, Derrida, and Miller have similarly questioned the metaphor/metonymy distinction, arguing that all figuration is a process of linguistic substitution. In the case of a metaphor (or symbol), they claim, we have forgotten what juxtaposition or contiguity gave rise to the association that now seems mysteriously special. Derrida, in "White Mythology," and de Man, in "Metaphor (*Second Discourse*)," have also challenged the priority of literal over figurative language, and Miller has gone so far as to deny the validity of the literal/figurative distinction, arguing that all words are figures because all language involves *catachresis*, "the violent, forced, or abusive importation of a term from another realm to name something which has no proper name" (Miller, *Ariadne* 21).

The difference between the formalist concept of literary ambiguity and the deconstructive concept of undecidability is as significant as the gap between formalist and deconstructive understandings of figurative language. Undecidability, as de Man came to define it, is a complex notion easily misunderstood. There is a tendency to assume that it refers to readers who, when forced to decide between two or more equally plausible and conflicting readings, throw up their hands and decide that the choice can't be made. But undecidability in fact debunks this whole notion of reading as a decision-making process carried out on texts by readers. To say we are forced to choose or decide, or that we are unable to do so, is to locate the problem of undecidability falsely within ourselves, rather than recognizing that it is an intrinsic feature of the text.

Undecidability is thus different from ambiguity, as understood by formalists. Formalists believed that a complete understanding of a literary work is possible, an understanding in which ambiguities will be resolved objectively by the reader, even if only in the sense that they will be shown to have definite, meaningful functions. Deconstructors do not share that belief. They do not accept the formalist view that a work of literary art is demonstrably unified from beginning to end, in one certain way, or that it is organized around a single center that ultimately can be identified and defined. Neither do they accept the concept of irony as simply saying one thing and meaning another thing that will be understood with certainty by the reader. As a result, deconstructors tend to see texts as more radically heterogeneous than do formalists. The formalist critic ultimately makes sense of ambiguity; undecidability, by contrast, is never reduced, let alone mastered by deconstructive reading, although the incompatible possibilities between which it is impossible to decide can be identified with certainty.

For critics practicing deconstruction, a literary text is neither a sphere with a center nor an unbroken line with a definite beginning and end. In fact, many assumptions about the nature of texts have been put in question by deconstruction, which in Derrida's words "dislocates the borders, the framing of texts, everything which should preserve their immanence and make possible an internal reading or merely reading in the classical sense of the term" ("Some Statements" 86). A text consists of words inscribed in and inextricable from the myriad discourses that inform it; from the point of view of deconstruction, the boundaries between any given text and that larger text we call language are always shifting.

It was that larger text that Derrida was referring to when he made his famous statement *"there is nothing outside the text"* (*Grammatology*

158). To understand what Derrida meant by that statement, consider the following: we know the world through language, and the acts and practices that constitute that "real world" (the Oklahoma City bombing, the decision to marry) are inseparable from the discourses out of which they arise and as open to interpretation as any work of literature. Derrida is not alone in deconstructing the world/text opposition. De Man viewed language as something that has great power in individual, social, and political life. Geoffrey Hartman, who was closely associated with deconstruction during the 1970s, wrote that "nothing can lift us out of language" (xii).

Once we understand deconstruction's view of the literary text — as words that are part of and that resonate with an immense linguistic structure in which we live and move and have our being — we are in a better position to understand why deconstructors reach points in their readings at which they reveal, but cannot decide between, incompatible interpretive possibilities. A text is not a unique, hermetically sealed space. Perpetually open to being seen in the light of new contexts, any given text has the potential to be different each time it is read. Furthermore, as Miller has shown in *Ariadne's Thread: Story Lines* (1992), the various "terms" and "famil[ies] of terms" we use in performing our readings invariably affect the results. Whether we choose to focus on a novel's characters or its realism, for instance, leads us to different views of the same text. "No one thread," Miller asserts, "can be followed to a central point where it provides a means of overseeing, controlling, and understanding the whole" (21).

Complicating matters still further is the fact that the individual words making up narratives — the words out of which we make our mental picture of a character or place — usually have several (and often have conflicting) meanings due to the complex histories of their usage. (If your professor tells the class that you have written a "fulsome report" and you look up the word *fulsome* in a contemporary dictionary, you will learn that it can mean either "elaborate" or "offensive"; if, for some reason, you don't know what *offensive* means, you will find out that it can equally well describe your favorite quarterback and a racist joke.) "Each word," as Miller puts it, "inheres in a labyrinth of branching interverbal relationships"; often there are "forks in the etymological line leading to bifurcated or trifurcated roots." Deconstructors often turn to etymology, not to help them decide whether a statement means this or that, but rather as a way of revealing the coincidence of several meanings in the same text. "The effect of etymological retracing," Miller writes, "is not to ground the work solidly but to render it unstable, equivocal, wavering, groundless" (*Ariadne* 19).

Deconstruction is not really interpretation, the act of choosing between or among possible meanings. Derrida has glossed de Man's statement that "there is no need to deconstruct Rousseau" by saying that "this was another way of saying: there is always already deconstruction, at work *in* works, especially *literary* works. It cannot be applied, after the fact and from outside, as a technical instrument. Texts deconstruct *themselves* by themselves" (Derrida, *Memoires* 123). If deconstruction is not interpretation, then what is it? Deconstruction may be defined as reading, as long as reading is defined as de Man defined it — as a process involving moments of what he called *aporia* or terminal uncertainty, and as an act performed with full knowledge of the fact that all texts are ultimately unreadable (if reading means reducing a text to a single, homogeneous meaning). Miller explains unreadability by saying that although there are moments of great lucidity in reading, each "lucidity will in principle contain its own blind spot requiring a further elucidation and exposure of error, and so on, ad infinitum. . . . One should not underestimate, however, the productive illumination produced as one moves through these various stages of reading" (*Ethics* 42, 44).

Miller's point is important because, in a sense, it deconstructs or erases the boundary between the readings of deconstructors and the interpretations of more traditional critics. It suggests that all kinds of critics have had their moments of lucidity; it also suggests that critics practicing deconstruction know that their *own* insights — even their insights into what is or isn't contradictory, undecidable, or unreadable in a text — are hardly the last word. As Art Berman writes, "In *Blindness and Insight* de Man demonstrates that the apparently well-reasoned arguments of literary critics contain contradiction at their core; yet there is no alternative path to insight. . . . The readers of criticism recognize the blindness of their predecessors, reorganize it, and thereby gain both the insight of the critics and a knowledge of the contradiction that brings forth insight. Each reader, of course, has his own blindness; and the criticism of criticism is not a matter of rectifying someone else's mistakes" (Berman 239–40).

When de Man spoke of the resistance to theory he referred generally to the antitheoretical bias in literary studies. But he might as well have been speaking specifically of the resistance to deconstruction, as expressed not only in academic books and journals but also in popular magazines such as *Newsweek*. Attacks on deconstruction became more common and more personal some four years after de Man's death in 1983. That was the year that a Belgian scholar working on a doctoral thesis discovered ninety-two articles that de Man had written during World War II for the Brussels newspaper *Le Soir*, a widely read French-language daily that had fallen under Nazi control during the German occupation of Belgium. Ultimately, one hundred and seventy articles by de Man were found in *Le Soir;* another ten were discovered in *Het Vlaamsche Land*, a collaborationist newspaper published in Flemish. These writings, which date from 1941 (when de Man was twenty-one years old), ceased to appear before 1943, by which time it had become clear to most Belgians that Jews were being shipped to death camps such as Auschwitz.

De Man's wartime journalism consists mainly, but not entirely, of inoffensive literary pieces. In one article de Man takes Germany's triumph in World War II as a given, places the German people at the center of Western civilization, and foresees a mystical era involving suffering but also faith, exaltation, and rapture. In another article, entitled *"Les Juifs dans la littérature actuelle"* ["Jews in Present-day Literature"], de Man scoffs at the notion that Jewish writers have significantly influenced the literature of his day and, worse, considers the merits of creating a separate Jewish colony that would be isolated from Europe.

No one who had known de Man since his immigration to the United States in 1948 had found him to be illiberal or anti-Semitic. Furthermore, de Man had spent his career in the United States demystifying or, as he would have said, "debunking" the kind of ideological assumptions (about the relationship between aesthetics and national cultures) that lie behind his most offensive Belgian newspaper writings. The critic who in *The Resistance to Theory* (1986) argued that literature must not become "a substitute for theology, ethics, etc." (de Man 24) had either changed radically since writing of the magical integrity and wholeness of the German nation and its culture or had not deeply believed what he had written as a young journalist.

These points have been made in various ways by de Man's former friends and colleagues. Geoffrey Hartman has said that de Man's later work, the work we associate with deconstruction, "looks like a belated, but still powerful, act of conscience" (26–31). Derrida, who like Hartman is a Jew, has read carefully de Man's wartime discourse, showing it to be "split, disjointed, engaged in incessant conflicts" (Hamacher, Hertz, and Keenan 135). "On the one hand," Derrida finds *"unpardonable"* de Man's suggestion that a separate Jewish colony be set up; "on the other hand," he notes that of the four writers de Man praises in the same article (André Gide, Franz Kafka, D. H. Lawrence, and Ernest Hemingway), not one was German, one (Kafka) *was* Jewish, and all four "represent everything that Nazism . . . would have liked to extirpate from history and the great tradition" (Hamacher, Hertz, and Keenan 145).

While friends asserted that some of de Man's statements were unpardonable, deconstruction's severest critics tried to use a young man's sometimes deplorable statements as evidence that a whole critical movement was somehow morally as well as intellectually flawed. As Andrej Warminski summed it up, "the 'discovery' of the 1941–42 writings is being used to perpetuate the old myths about so-called 'deconstruction'" (Hamacher, Hertz, and Keenan 389). Knowing what some of those myths are — and why, in fact, they *are* myths — aids our understanding in an indirect, contrapuntal way that is in keeping with the spirit of deconstruction.

In his book *The Ethics of Reading* (1987), Miller refutes two notions commonly repeated by deconstruction's detractors. One is the idea that deconstructors believe a text means nothing in the sense that it means whatever the playful reader *wants* it to mean. The other is the idea that deconstruction is "immoral" insofar as it refuses to view literature in the way it has traditionally been viewed, namely, "as the foundation and embodiment, the means of preserving and transmitting, the basic humanistic values of our culture" (9). Responding to the first notion, Miller points out that neither Derrida nor de Man "has ever asserted the freedom of the reader to make the text mean anything he or she wants it to mean. Each has in fact asserted the reverse" (10). As for the second notion — that deconstructors are guilty of shirking an ethical responsibility because their purpose is not to (re)discover and (re)assert the transcendent and timeless values contained in great books — Miller argues that "this line of thought" rests "on a basic misunderstanding of the way the ethical moment enters into the act of reading" (9). That "ethical moment," Miller goes on to argue, "is not a matter of response to a thematic content asserting this or that idea about morality. It is a much more fundamental 'I must' responding to the language of literature in itself. . . . Deconstruction is nothing more or less than good reading as such" (9–10). Reading itself, in other words, is an act that leads to further ethical acts, decisions, and behaviors in a real world involving relations to other people and to society at large. For these, the reader must take responsibility, as for any other ethical act.

A third commonly voiced objection to deconstruction is to its playfulness, to the evident pleasure its practitioners take in teasing out all the contradictory interpretive possibilities generated by the words in a text, their complex etymologies and contexts, and their potential to be read figuratively or even ironically. Certainly, playfulness and pleasure are aspects of deconstruction. In his book *The Post Card* (1987), Derrida specifically associates deconstruction with pleasure; in an interview published in a collection of his essays entitled *Acts of Literature* (1992), he speculates that "it is perhaps this *jouissance* which most irritates the all-out adversaries of deconstruction" (56). But such adversaries misread deconstruction's "jouissance," its pleasurable playfulness. Whereas they see it as evidence that deconstructors view texts as tightly enclosed fields on which they can play delightfully useless little word games, Derrida has said that the "subtle and intense pleasure" of deconstruction arises from the "dismantl[ing]" of repressive assumptions, representations, and ideas — in short, from the "lifting of repression" (*Acts* 56–57). As Gregory S. Jay explains in his book *America the Scrivener: Deconstruction and the Subject of Literary History* (1990), "Deconstruction has been not only a matter of reversing binary oppositions but also a matter of disabling the hierarchy of values they enable and of speculating on alternative modes of knowing and of acting" (xii).

Far from viewing literature as a word-playground, Derrida, in Derek Attridge's words, "emphasizes . . . literature as an institution," one "not given in nature or the brain but brought into being by processes that are social, legal, and political, and that can be mapped historically and geographically" (*Acts* 23). By thus characterizing Derrida's emphasis, Attridge counters the commonest of the charges that have been leveled at deconstructors, namely, that they divorce literary texts from historical, political, and legal institutions.

In *Memoires for Paul de Man* (1986), Derrida argues that, where history is concerned, "deconstructive discourses" have pointedly and effectively questioned "the classical assurances of history, the genealogical narrative, and periodizations of all sorts" (15) — in other words, the tendency of historians to view the past as the source of (lost) truth and value, to look for explanations in origins, and to view as unified epochs (for example, the Victorian period, 1837–1901) what are in fact complex and heterogeneous times in history. As for politics, Derrida points out that de Man invariably "says something about institutional structures and the political stakes of hermeneutic conflicts," which is to say that de Man's commentaries acknowledge that conflicting interpretations reflect and are reflected in the politics of institutions (such as the North American university).

In addition to history and politics, the law has been a subject on which deconstruction has had much to say of late. In an essay on Franz Kafka's story "Before the Law," Derrida has shown that for Kafka the law as such exists but can never be confronted by those who would do so and fulfill its commands. Miller has pointed out that the law "may only be confronted in its delegates or representatives or by its effects on us or others" (*Ethics* 20). What or where, then, is the law itself? The law's presence, Miller suggests, is continually deferred by narrative, that is, writing about or on the law which constantly reinterprets the law in the attempt to reveal what it really is and means. This very act of (re)interpretation, however, serves to "defer" or distance the law even further from the case at hand, since the (re)interpretation takes precedence (and assumes prominence) over the law itself. (As Miller defines it, narrative would include everything from a Victorian novel that promises to reveal moral law to the opinion of a Supreme Court justice regarding the constitutionality of a given action, however different these two documents are in the conventions they follow and the uses to which they are put.) Miller likens the law to a promise, "the validity of [which] does not lie in itself but in its future fulfillment," and to a story "divided against itself" that in the end "leaves its readers . . . still in expectation" (*Ethics* 33).

Because the facts about deconstruction are very different from the myth of its playful irreverence and irrelevance, a number of contemporary thinkers have found it useful to adapt and apply deconstruction in their work. For instance, a deconstructive theology has been developed. Architects have designed and built buildings grounded, as it were, in deconstructive architectural theory. In the area of law, the Critical Legal Studies movement has, in Christopher Norris's words, effectively used "deconstructive thinking" of the kind de Man used in analyzing Rousseau's *Social Contract* "to point up the blind spots, conflicts, and antinomies that plague the discourse of received legal wisdom." Critical legal theorists have debunked "the formalist view of law," that is, the "view which holds law to be a system of neutral precepts and principles," showing instead how the law "gives rise to various disabling contradictions," such as "the problematic distinction between 'private' and 'public' domains." They have turned deconstruction into "a sophisticated means of making the point that all legal discourse is performative in character, i.e., designed to secure assent through its rhetorical power to convince or persuade" (Norris, *Deconstruction and the Interests* 17). Courtroom persuasion, Gerald Lopez has argued in a 1989 article in the *Michigan Law Review*, consists of storytelling as much as argument (Clayton 13).

In the field of literary studies, the influence of deconstruction may be seen in the work of critics ostensibly taking some other, more political approach. Barbara Johnson has put deconstruction to work for the feminist cause. She and Shoshana Felman have argued that chief among those binary oppositions "based on repression of differences with entities" is the opposition man/woman (Johnson, *Critical* x). In a reading of the "undecidability" of "femininity" in Balzac's story "The Girl with the Golden Eyes," Felman puts it this way: "the rhetorical hierarchization of the . . . opposition between the sexes is . . . such that woman's *difference* is suppressed, being totally subsumed by the reference of the feminine to masculine identity" ("Rereading" 25).

Elsewhere, Johnson, Felman, and Gayatri Spivak have combined Derrida's theories with the psychoanalytic theory of Jacques Lacan to analyze the way in which gender and sexuality are ultimately textual, grounded in language and rhetoric. In an essay on Edmund Wilson's reading of Henry James's story *The Turn of the Screw*, Felman has treated sexuality as a form of rhetoric that can be deconstructed, shown to contain contradictions and ambiguities that more traditional readings of sexuality have masked. Gay and lesbian critics have seen the positive implications of this kind of analysis, hence Eve Kosofsky Sedgwick's admission in the early pages of her book *Epistemology of the Closet* (1990): "One main strand of argument in this book is deconstructive, in a fairly specific sense. The analytic move it makes is to demonstrate that categories presented in a culture as symmetrical binary oppositions . . . actually subsist in a more unsettled and dynamic tacit relation" (9–10).

In telling "The Story of Deconstruction" in his book on contemporary American literature and theory, Jay Clayton assesses the current status of this unique approach. Although he notes how frequently deconstructive critics have been cited for their lack of political engagement, he concludes that deconstruction, "a movement accused of formalism and arid intellectualism, participates in the political turn of contemporary culture" (34). He suggests that what began as theory in the late 1960s and 1970s has, over time, developed into a method employed by critics taking a wide range of approaches to literature —

ethnic, feminist, new historicist, Marxist — in addition to critics outside of literary studies per se who are involved in such areas as Critical Legal Studies and Critical Race Theory, which seeks to "sustain a complementary relationship between the deconstructive energies of Critical Legal Studies and the constructive energies of civil rights activism" (58).

Clayton cites the work of Edward Said as a case in point. Through 1975, the year that his *Beginnings: Intention and Method* was published, Said was employing a form of deconstructive criticism that, in Clayton's words, emphasized the "power" of texts "to initiate projects in the real world" (45–46). Said became identified with cultural and postcolonial criticism, however, beginning in 1978 with the publication of his book *Orientalism,* in which he deconstructs the East/West, Orient/Occident opposition. Said argues that Eastern and Middle Eastern peoples have for centuries been stereotyped by the Western discourses of "orientalism," a textuality that in no way reflects the diversity and differences that exist among the peoples it claims to represent. According to Said, that stereotyping not only facilitated the colonization of vast areas of the globe by the so-called West but also still governs, to a great extent, relations with the Arab and the so-called Eastern world. The expansion of Said's field of vision to include not just literary texts but international relations is powerfully indicative of the expanding role that deconstruction currently plays in developing contemporary understandings of politics and culture, as well as in active attempts to intervene in these fields.

In the essay that follows, Susan Eilenberg views Coleridge's "Rime" in terms of its linguistic strangeness, as a "series of dislocations — translations, displacements, metonymies" — that "dares its audience to make sense of it" (283). Readers and critics typically "respond" to the challenge "by talking about madness or the supernatural," thereby rescuing the poem from what Eilenberg calls "the failure of signification" by tracing this failure to determinable causes, that is the Mariner's insanity and/or the "spirits and demons" that "cause the effects we cannot otherwise explain" (283). For Eilenberg, however, the "supernatural" of "The Rime of the Ancient Mariner," rather than explaining the poem's strangeness, in fact reside *in* its strangeness. This is a poem that "pulls not rabbits out of hats but voices out of voices," a tale that posits as its origin or source a Mariner who "has no name because he has no identity," the "dummy" of an "absent ventriloquist" (282).

Quoting Arden Reed's remark that the Mariner is "more the effect

of the 'Rime' than its cause," the "by-product of a text that wills its
own repetition," Eilenberg argues that the tale ultimately "dissociates
itself from both teller and theme and takes its place *en abyme,* generating its own linguistic origins and constituting itself as the object of its
own signification" (285). Explaining her assertion that the tale "gen-
erat[es] its own linguistic origins," Eilenberg points out that the
Mariner does not wish to tell the tale; rather, he is "forc'd" to "begin"
(and repeatedly rebegin) it by a "strange power of speech." (The
Mariner is thus, in a sense, "the perpetual, helplessly uncomprehending
audience to the tale that speaks itself through him" [286].) As for her
assertion that the tale is the "object of its own signification," Eilenberg
makes two points. First, the tale is its own subject, that is, it is about
its own (re)telling. Second, the tale is, in a sense, the crime that it
recounts, for, as Homer Brown has argued, the story "identifies the
self-assertion of the crime with the self-assertion of the telling — the
killing of the albatross with the usurpation of the wedding guest"
(286).

Eilenberg maintain that the tale is not really the Mariner's (insofar
as he is its victimized vehicle) — and therefore that "the Mariner's
speech . . . must be regarded as enclosed in invisible quotation marks"
(286). She goes on to suggest that "the Mariner is not the only victim"
of "the anonymous voice of this self-propagating tale" (289). She
grounds her argument in an analysis of quotation marks (and their
often strange absence) within the tale. In a poem "founded upon the
power of quotation," Eilenberg writes, "quotation marks are strangely
unreliable indices of the borders of speech" (287). Punctuational lapses
and inconsistencies allow the reader to hear one voice as two in some
places, two voices as one in others. Thus we, too, are victims of the
absent ventriloquist's voice. It may be that we define our feeling of disease as a maddening "linguistic problem," whereas "the tale's characters register [it] as a demonological one," coming to view the Mariner
as "a dead man possessed." But readers, Eilenberg suggests, are not
entirely immune to a sense of supernatural agency. "By giving the
Mariner the air of a zombie," she maintains, "the poem forces the
reader to confront a radical split between speaker and speech, both
of which seem haunted" (290). In suggesting that "speech" seems
haunted, Eilenberg refers to the fact that the Mariner "is not the tale's
only teller; his story is enclosed and repeated by others over whom the
Mariner (as opposed to the tale) has no influence" (290). Thus, unless
we assume that everyone who tells or retells the tale is identically pos-

sessed or insane, we cannot ascribe the haunting quality of "speech" entirely to the "speaker."

In the later stages of her argument, Eilenberg draws a connection between the Mariner's endless retelling of the tale with the poet's "more limited compulsion to repeat himself" via his two major revisions of the "Rime," the second of which contains a prose gloss that, in a sense, repeats or "doubles" the poem. In discussing the poem's different versions, she also discusses its archaic language (a feature that "involves" still more "echoes and ventriloquies" and that contributes significantly to the poem's strangeness) and the fact that the "Rime" began as a collaborative effort between Coleridge and Wordsworth. Eilenberg deftly suggests a subtle relationship between several factors: the poem's doomed collaborative beginnings; its status as a "conversation turned monologue"; its theme of the double (each person who hears the story becomes, like the Mariner, the teller of that story); its often confusing use of several voices (prose commentary on poetic narrative, for instance); and its relationship to various poetic sources (including the ballad tradition, the poetry of Edward Spenser, and Coleridge's own poem "The Wanderings of Cain"). Viewing "the contest of voices within the 'Rime'" as a result of Coleridge's "uneasiness" or "anxiety" regarding his debt to various and varied sources, Eilenberg concludes by arguing that the sources themselves reflect the same kind of authorial uneasiness or anxiety, for they also included voices within voices responding to other voices. However much they appeared to be works by a single author narrating, in a determinable way, an account of a single, determinate, unique event, no event understood in language (which is, after all, what makes understanding possible) is single or determinate, unique or original. The shooting of the Albatross has meaning within a deep context of tales, narratives, and other histories that are sometimes self-contradictory, in addition to being in conflict with one another.

Eilenberg makes any number of moves associated with deconstruction. Focusing on dislocations and metonymies rather than consistencies and metaphors, she draws our attention to all the ways in which the text seems arbitrary and contradictory rather than determinate and determinable, an invitation to interpretive play rather than a mandate for fixed and stable reading. Equally typical of the deconstructive approach to literature is Eilenberg's idea that the text is self-propagating, that is, its own origin rather than the identifiably belated outgrowth of some text that has been true since the beginning. The idea that the text is self-propagating might seem to conflict with Eilenberg's interest in poets and poems that influenced Coleridge and the "Rime," but does not in the sense that Eilenberg embeds the poem within numerous sources, implying that her list is limited. Furthermore, she makes clear that all of the sources she identifies are fed by multiple sources, few of which would be shared by a single reader of the "Rime" — and all of which are: (1) self-conflicted; and (2) themselves fed by numerous, self-conflicted sources.

Ross C Murfin

DECONSTRUCTION:
A SELECTED BIBLIOGRAPHY

Writings on Deconstruction

Arac, Jonathan, Wlad Godzich, and Wallace Martin, eds. *The Yale Critics: Deconstruction in America.* Minneapolis: U of Minnesota P, 1983. See especially the essays by Bové, Godzich, Pease, and Corngold.

Berman, Art. *From the New Criticism to Deconstruction: The Reception of Structuralism and Post-Structuralism.* Urbana: U of Illinois P, 1988.

Butler, Christopher. *Interpretation, Deconstruction, and Ideology: An Introduction to Some Current Issues in Literary Theory.* Oxford: Oxford UP, 1984.

Clayton, Jay. *The Pleasure of Babel: Contemporary American Literature and Theory.* New York: Oxford UP, 1993.

Culler, Jonathan. *On Deconstruction: Theory and Criticism After Structuralism.* Ithaca: Cornell UP, 1982.

———. *Structuralist Poetics: Structuralism, Linguistics, and the Study of Literature.* Ithaca: Cornell UP, 1975. See especially ch. 10.

Esch, Deborah. "Deconstruction." *Redrawing the Boundaries: The Transformation of English and American Literary Studies.* Ed. Stephen Greenblatt and Giles Gunn. New York: MLA, 1992. 374–91.

Feminist Studies 14 (1988). Special issue on deconstruction and feminism.

Hamacher, Werner, Neil Hertz, and Thomas Keenan. *Responses: On Paul de Man's Wartime Journalism.* Lincoln: U of Nebraska P, 1989.

Hartman, Geoffrey. "Blindness and Insight." *The New Republic*, 7 Mar. 1988.

Jay, Gregory S. *America the Scrivener: Deconstruction and the Subject of Literary History*. Ithaca: Cornell UP, 1990.

Leitch, Vincent B. *American Literary Criticism from the Thirties to the Eighties*. New York: Columbia UP, 1988. See especially ch. 10, "Deconstructive Criticism."

——. *Cultural Criticism, Literary Theory, Poststructuralism*. New York: Columbia UP, 1992.

Loesberg, Jonathan. *Aestheticism and Deconstruction: Pater, Derrida, and de Man*. Princeton: Princeton UP, 1991.

Melville, Stephen W. *Philosophy Beside Itself: On Deconstruction and Modernism*. Theory and History of Lit. 27. Minneapolis: U of Minnesota P, 1986.

Norris, Christopher. *Deconstruction and the Interests of Theory*. Oklahoma Project for Discourse and Theory 4. Norman: U of Oklahoma P, 1989.

——. *Deconstruction: Theory and Practice*. London: Methuen, 1982. Rev. ed. London: Routledge, 1991.

——. *Paul de Man, Deconstruction and the Critique of Aesthetic Ideology*. New York: Routledge, 1988.

Weber, Samuel. *Institution and Interpretation*. Minneapolis: U of Minnesota P, 1987.

Works by de Man, Derrida, and Miller

de Man, Paul. *Allegories of Reading*. New Haven: Yale UP, 1979. See especially ch. 1, "Semiology and Rhetoric," and ch. 7, "Metaphor *(Second Discourse)*."

——. *Blindness and Insight*. New York: Oxford UP, 1971. Minneapolis: U of Minnesota P, 1983. The 1983 edition contains important essays not included in the original edition. See especially "Rhetoric of Temporality."

——. "Phenomenality and Materiality in Kant." *Hermeneutics: Questions and Prospects*. Ed. Gary Shapiro and Alan Sica. Amherst: U of Massachusetts P, 1984. 121–44.

——. *The Resistance to Theory*. Minneapolis: U of Minnesota P, 1986.

——. *Romanticism and Contemporary Culture*. Ed. E. S. Burt, Kevin Newmarkj, and Andrzej Warminski. Baltimore: Johns Hopkins UP, 1993.

———. *Wartime Journalism, 1939–1943*. Lincoln: U of Nebraska P, 1989.

Derrida, Jacques. *Acts of Literature*. Ed. Derek Attridge. New York: Routledge, 1992.

———. "Différance." *Speech and Phenomena*. Trans. David B. Alison. Evanston: Northwestern UP, 1973.

———. *Dissemination*. 1972. Trans. Barbara Johnson. Chicago: U of Chicago P, 1981. See especially the concise, incisive "Translator's Introduction," which provides a useful point of entry into this work and others by Derrida.

———. "Force of Law: The 'Mystical Foundation of Authority.' " Trans. Mary Quaintance. *Deconstruction and the Possibility of Justice*. Ed. Drucilla Cornell, Michel Rosenfeld, and David Gray Carlson. New York: Routledge, 1992. 3–67.

———. *Given Time. 1, Counterfeit Money*. Trans. Peggy Kamuf. Chicago: U of Chicago P, 1992.

———. *Margins of Philosophy*. Trans. Alan Bass. Chicago: U of Chicago P, 1982. Contains the essay "White Mythology: Metaphor in the Text of Philosophy."

———. *Memoires for Paul de Man*. Wellek Library Lectures. Trans. Cecile Lindsay, Jonathan Culler, and Eduardo Cadava. New York: Columbia UP, 1986.

———. *Of Grammatology*. Trans. Gayatri C. Spivak. Baltimore: Johns Hopkins UP, 1976. Trans. of *De la grammatologie*. 1967.

———. "Passions." *Derrida: A Critical Reader*. Ed. David Wood. Cambridge: Blackwell, 1992.

———. *The Post Card: From Socrates to Freud and Beyond*. Trans. with intro. Alan Bass. Chicago: U of Chicago P, 1987.

———. "Some Statements and Truisms about Neo-logisms, Newisms, Postisms, and Other Small Seisisms." *The States of "Theory."* New York: Columbia UP, 1990. 63–94.

———. *Specters of Marx*. Trans. Peggy Kamuf. New York: Routledge, 1994.

———. *Writing and Difference*. 1967. Trans. Alan Bass. Chicago: U of Chicago P, 1978.

Miller, J. Hillis. *Ariadne's Thread: Story Lines*. New Haven: Yale UP, 1992.

———. *The Ethics of Reading: Kant, de Man, Eliot, Trollope, James, and Benjamin*. New York: Columbia UP, 1987.

———. *Fiction and Repetition: Seven English Novels*. Cambridge: Harvard UP, 1982.

————. *Hawthorne and History: Defacing It.* Cambridge: Basil Blackwell, 1991. Contains a bibliography of Miller's work from 1955 to 1990.

————. *Illustrations.* Cambridge: Harvard UP, 1992.

————. "Stevens' Rock and Criticism as Cure." *Georgia Review* 30 (1976): 3–31, 330–48.

————. *Typographies.* Stanford: Stanford UP, 1994.

————. *Versions of Pygmalion.* Cambridge: Harvard UP, 1990.

Essays on Deconstruction and Poststructuralism

Barthes, Roland. *S/Z.* Trans. Richard Miller. New York: Hill, 1974. In this influential work, Barthes turns from a structuralist to a post-structuralist approach.

Benstock, Shari. *Textualizing the Feminine: On the Limits of Genre.* Norman: U of Oklahoma P, 1991.

Bloom, Harold, et al., eds. *Deconstruction and Criticism.* New York: Seabury, 1979. Includes essays by Bloom, de Man, Derrida, Miller, and Hartman.

Chase, Cynthia. *Decomposing Figures.* Baltimore: Johns Hopkins UP, 1986.

Cohen, Tom. *Anti-Mimesis: From Plato to Hitchcock.* Cambridge: Cambridge UP, 1994.

Elam, Diane. *Feminism and Deconstruction: Ms. en Abyme.* New York: Routledge, 1994.

Felman, Shoshana. "Rereading Femininity." Special Issue on "Feminist Readings: French Texts/American Contexts," *Yale French Studies* 62 (1981): 19–44.

————. "Turning the Screw of Interpretation." *Literature and Psychoanalysis: The Question of Reading: Otherwise.* Special issue, *Yale French Studies* 55–56 (1978): 3–508. Baltimore: Johns Hopkins UP, 1982.

Harari, Josué, ed. *Textual Strategies: Perspectives in Post-Structuralist Criticism.* Ithaca: Cornell UP, 1979.

Johnson, Barbara. *The Critical Difference: Essays in the Contemporary Rhetoric of Reading.* Baltimore: Johns Hopkins UP, 1980.

————. *A World of Difference.* Baltimore: Johns Hopkins UP, 1987.

Krupnick, Mark, ed. *Displacement: Derrida and After.* Bloomington: Indiana UP, 1987.

Meese, Elizabeth, and Alice Parker, eds. *The Difference Within: Feminism and Critical Theory.* Philadelphia: Benjamins, 1989.

Sedgwick, Eve Kosofsky. *Epistemology of the Closet.* Berkeley: U of California P, 1990.

Ulmer, Gregory L. *Applied Grammatology.* Baltimore: Johns Hopkins UP, 1985.

————. *Teletheory: Grammatology in the Age of Video.* New York: Routledge, 1989.

Other Poststructuralist/Deconstructive Approaches to the "Rime"

Galperin, William. "Coleridge and Critical Intervention." *Wordsworth Circle* 22 (1991): 56–64.

Kramer, Lawrence. "The Other Will: The Daemonic in Coleridge and Wordsworth." *Philological Quarterly* 58 (1979): 298–320.

Reed, Arden. "The Riming Mariner and the Mariner Rimed." *Romantic Weather: The Climates of Coleridge and Baudelaire.* Hanover: UP of New England, 1983. 147–81.

SUSAN EILENBERG

Voice and Ventriloquy in "The Rime of the Ancient Mariner"

The ordinary tale of the supernatural is like the magician's trick of pulling a rabbit out of a hat. It depends upon a false bottom, an illusion of sourcelessness. Bad metaphysics, it exploits our confusion about the relationship between cause and effect, appearance and reality, body and soul. The supernatural of "The Rime of the Ancient Mariner" pulls not rabbits out of hats but voices out of voices. It makes its home in the space between speaker and spoken, motivation and action, intention and meaning. Instead of pretending there is no source, it pretends there is one, that behind the Mariner-as-dummy there is a ventriloquist, a figure or language or system of meanings in the context of which the tale that comes out of the Mariner's mouth makes sense.

The "Rime" evades the question any reader asks upon opening to this first poem in the originally anonymous *Lyrical Ballads:* "Whose voice is this?" The "Rime," one of the most deeply and elaborately anonymous poems ever written, comes to speech through the medium of an alien voice — archaic, inhuman, uncanny — in response to an impossible demand. "What manner man art thou?" the Hermit cries out in horror at the speaking corpse. It is a question derived anagrammatically from the answer the corpse is unable to give: man < manner < Mariner. The question contains the fragments of the word that, fleeing into anonymity, the Mariner leaves behind. "I am an Ancient Mariner" becomes "There was a ship." It is the first in a series of dislocations — translations, displacements, metonymies — that spring from the Mariner's refusal of his own name. It is a revelation of the anonymity whose power calls into being both the "Rime" and the collaborative project — the *Lyrical Ballads* — that the "Rime" inaugurates.

The impropriety of the "Rime"'s language, suited neither to the expression of anything we would regard as sound character nor to the evocation of any familiar system of reference, dares its audience to make sense of it.[1] We respond by talking about madness and the supernatural, notions that convert the failure of signification into evidence of significance and allow us to defer the unwelcome recognition of our interpretive helplessness. We sacrifice our belief in the Mariner's sanity on the altar of "character" or admit the possibility that spirits and demons cause the effects we cannot otherwise explain. Thus we attempt to rescue a purely ideal propriety.

Why can the Mariner not name himself? Perhaps because, as Wordsworth, obtusely accurate, seems to have been the first to notice, he is a man without "distinct character, either in his profession of Mariner, or as a human being."[2] He has no name because he has no identity. Ignorant of who he is, unable to recognize his fears and desires as his own or distinguish himself from his surroundings, and practically devoid of conscious intention and affect, the Mariner apprehends the contents of his own psyche as alien and inexplicable, perceptible only in the forms of an unnatural nature, frightened and hostile men, and spirits. Everywhere he looks he sees with no recognition versions of himself, the

---

[1]"The difficulty of the poem," writes Frances Ferguson, "is that the possibility of learning from the Mariner's experience depends upon sorting that experience into a more linear and complete pattern than the poem ever agrees to do." See "Coleridge and the Deluded Reader: 'The Rime of the Ancient Mariner,'" pages 113–30 in this book.

[2]Wordsworth's remarks can be found in *Lyrical Ballads: The text of the 1798 edition with the additional 1800 poems and the Prefaces,* edited by R. L. Brett and A. R. Jones (London: Methuen, 1963), p. 277.

human and natural worlds he moves in functioning as agents of his psy-che,[3] their energies and actions displacements of his own.[4]

The Mariner's empty world is crowded with what he cannot own, cannot distinguish, and therefore cannot name; anonymity is the com-mon linguistic condition of people and things in his tale. There are strangely few proper names here; the Mariner identifies almost no one, and names even of simple abstractions elude him. Despite the excesses of his later speech, his relation to language is, like that of so many of Wordsworth's early protagonists, that almost of an aphasic. With the single exception of his painful exclamation at the sight of the spec-tre ship, "A sail! a sail!", the Mariner seems to say nothing during the length of his voyage. When he does speak, he speaks like a man suffer-ing from what Roman Jakobson describes as a similarity disorder.[5] How appropriate that the Mariner's cry should trope Coleridge's own stan-dard example of synecdoche:[6] "A sail" for "a ship" whose sails have rot-ted away.[7]

The Mariner's difficulties with language and his reluctance to abstract judgments from the mass of discrete observations he presents may signal intellectual deficiency, but they could also indicate the impossibility of such identifications and judgments as we are accus-tomed to expect. We cannot discount the possibility that what look like distortions of language and logic in the Mariner's rendition reflect truly the incoherence of the world he has passed through.

[3]In the best reading of this kind, Lawrence Kramer discusses the poem in terms of demonic imagination, which reveals itself "as a kind of anti-self" or "hostile other," "the personification of an unconscious will to represent whatever aspects of the self that the self chooses to forget — the side of the self we can still call repressed, if we use the term loosely." See "That Other Will: The Daemonic in Coleridge and Wordsworth," *Philolog-ical Quarterly* 58 (1979), 298–320.

[4]The Wedding Guest may be regarded as what Paul Magnuson has called "a psycho-logical double of the mariner." Magnuson, *Coleridge's Nightmare Poetry* [Charlottesville: University Press of Virginia, 1974], p. 84. See also Ward Pafford, "Coleridge's Wedding Guest," *Studies in Philology* 60 [1963], 618–26, and Arnold E. Davidson, "The Conclud-ing Moral in Coleridge's *The Rime of the Ancient Mariner*" *Philological Quarterly* 60 [1981], 90).

[5]See "Two Aspects of Language and Two Types of Aphasic Disturbances," in Roman Jakobson and Morris Halle, *Fundamentals of Language,* 4th ed. (1956; New York: Mouton, 1980).

[6]*Miscellaneous Criticism,* edited by Thomas Middleton Raysor (London: Constable & Co., 1936), p. 99.

[7]His exclamation identifies the unnameable "something in the Sky" that, when it "took at last / A certain shape," proves to be not only an image of what the Mariner's ship will become but an emblem of the story they are living through: the very vehicle of contagion, metonymy turned literal.

The Sun came up upon the left,
Out of the Sea came he:
And he shone bright, and on the right
Went down into the Sea.

Higher and higher every day
Till over the mast at noon —[8]

Unlike the Wedding Guest, who beats his breast in an agony of impatience, we may recognize in the Mariner's somewhat pedantic attention to days and directions an attempt to defend against cosmic derangement. But readerly dependence upon the Mariner — an obviously unreliable narrator — limits our ability to distinguish with any degree of certainty between psychological or linguistic and physical or metaphysical effects; we have a hard time deciding how much the tale's oddity has to do with the oddity of its teller and how much it has to do with the oddity of its material. Ultimately, however, the tale dissociates itself from both teller and theme and takes its place *en abyme,* generating its own linguistic origins and constituting itself as the object of its own signification.

As Arden Reed remarks, the Mariner is "more the effect of the 'Rime' than its cause," "the by-product of a text that wills its own repetition."[9] The Mariner's relation to his tale is tautological, at once totally arbitrary and totally determined. The Mariner tells his tale to explain that he is the man who tells the tale in order to explain what manner man he is. It is only after the end of his marine adventures, when the Hermit questions him, that the Mariner becomes aware of the unnaturalness of his relation to the story he tells:

Forthwith this frame of mine was wrench'd
With a woeful agony,
Which forc'd me to begin my tale
And then it left me free.

Since then at an uncertain hour,
Now ofttimes and now fewer,
That anguish comes and makes me tell
My ghastly aventure. (611–18)

---

[8]Lines 29–34. Unless otherwise noted, all citations will be from the 1798 edition of the poem printed in *Lyrical Ballads 1798,* edited by W. J. B. Owen, 2nd ed. (Oxford: Oxford University Press, 1969).

[9]Arden Reed, *Romantic Weather: The Climates of Coleridge and Baudelaire* (Hanover, NH: University Press of New England, 1983), p. 177.

A "strange power of speech" forces him out of silence. His aphasia vio-
lently reverses itself as language steps into the role of persecutor left
vacant by the avenging *genii loci,* vestigial guardians of the proprieties
the Mariner has violated.[10] An alien spirit thus comes to inhabit the
body of the Mariner's speech, which, endlessly iterated and claiming no
source in the Mariner's will, must be regarded as enclosed in invisible
quotation marks. The tale that comes out of his mouth is not his.
Prophet rather than source, the Mariner is only the perpetual, helplessly
uncomprehending audience to the tale that speaks itself through him.[11]
    Clearly, the Mariner's recital is no mere history. He does not choose
his words; he suffers them, reliving what he tells. Who can tell whether
he does not relive even his impulse to kill?

> "God save thee, ancyent Marinere!
> "From the fiends that plague thee thus —
> "Why lookst thou so?" — with my cross bow
> I shot the Albatross. (77–80)

The fiends that plague him may be simultaneously those of bitter remorse and those that tormented him at the time of his original violence:
the penitential representation comes very close to repeating the crime
the Mariner is trying to expiate. No wonder the penance must be repeated so often. As Homer Brown puts it, "The tale that repeats the
crime 'repeats' it in a double sense: it tells the story which identifies the
self-assertion of the crime with the self-assertion of the telling — the killing of the albatross with the usurpation of the Wedding Guest."[12]
In the words of Jonathan Arac, "Repetition solicits repetition."[13] The

---

[10]Geoffrey H. Hartman, *Beyond Formalism: Literary Essays, 1958–1970* (New
Haven: Yale University Press, 1970), p. 334.

[11]Not until the end of the poem does the Mariner attempt to direct the course of
his narration, and the resulting moral stanzas strike many readers as the most incredible
part of the poem. For various theories regarding these stanzas see Smith's argument
"A Reappraisal of the Moral Stanzas in *The Rime of the Ancient Mariner,*" *Studies in
Romanticism* 3 (1963), 42–52. For Wallen's argument see "Return and Representation:
The Revisions of 'The Ancient Mariner,'" *Wordsworth Circle* 17 (1986), 148–56. For
Koestenbaum's remarks, see *Double Talk: The Erotics of Male Literary Collaboration* (New
York: Routledge, 1989), p. 76.

[12]Homer Obed Brown, "The Art of Theology and the Theology of Art: Robert
Penn Warren's Reading of Coleridge's *The Rime of the Ancient Mariner,*" in William V.
Spanos, Paul A. Bové, and Daniel O'Hara, eds., *The Question of Textuality: Strategies of
Reading in Contemporary American Criticism* (Bloomington: Indiana University Press,
1982), p. 254.

[13]Jonathan Arac, "Repetition and Exclusion: Coleridge and New Criticism Reconsidered," in Spanos et al., eds., *The Question of Textuality,* p. 269

effect is to implicate the ancient Mariner so deeply in the circumstances of his younger self as to discredit the authority of his final moral summing up: its lesson is either irrelevant or impermanent; it cannot save the Mariner from an endless repetition of his agony, from being possessed by the voice of the past.

But the Mariner is not the only victim of his voice. In this poem founded upon the power of quotation, quotation marks are strangely unreliable indices of the borders of speech. The Minstrel indicates when the Mariner is speaking with "quoth he" and "thus spake on that ancient man," and he consistently punctuates the openings of speeches by the Wedding Guest, the spirits, the Hermit, the Pilot, and the Boy. But he is not always careful to mark the end of a speech. To a reader careless of the convention — not observed in every poem in this volume[14] — that places a quotation mark in front of every line in a quoted speech and one last mark at the end of the final line, one voice may seem suddenly to become two.

> He holds him with his skinny hand,
> Quoth he, there was a Ship —
> "Now get thee hence, thou grey-beard Loon!
> "Or my Staff shall make thee skip.
>
> He holds him with his glittering eye —
> The wedding guest stood still
> And listens like a three year's child;
> The Marinere hath his will. (13–20)

A punctuational lapse, the absence of a closing quotation mark, allows the reader also to hear the two voices as one and so to perceive the dialogue as monologue.[15] The story dissolves the distinction between the

---

[14]In this same volume, two of Wordsworth's poems, "Anecdote for Fathers" and "The Mad Mother," contain examples of similar carelessness with regard to closing quotation marks, suggesting that no reader would be greatly surprised by Coleridge's handling of punctuation in the "Rime." Coleridge himself was habitually careless about closing quotation marks in his informal writing. In his early letters, especially, he is willing to indicate where a quotation begins but liable not to reclaim authority from those he is quoting, so that other men's voices blend into his own.

[15]For a more detailed examination of this effect and a fuller reading of its implications, see Wallen, pp. 151–56. Arden Reed observes of the first of the two following stanzas that although "it is not difficult to sort out the pronouns' references . . . as one reads straight through the stanza, the diction tends to confuse the interlocutor's [sic] separate identities in one's mind, an effect redoubled thematically over the course of the poem" (*Romantic Weather*, p. 158).

roles of speaker and audience: both here are equally in thrall to the tale,
the Wedding Guest no more capable of closing his ears against the tale
than the Mariner is of closing his mouth against it.

It hardly seems to matter who speaks the words the tale requires;
for the purposes of vocalization, one character is as good as another.
Characters confuse their own identities and voices with those of others,
and so, in matters of revision, does Coleridge. In 1798, for example,
the Mariner and the reanimated body of his nephew are pulling together at one rope when the Mariner's horror of zombies suddenly
becomes a horror of himself:

> The body and I pull'd at one rope,
> But he said nought to me —
> And I quakd to think of my own voice
> How frightful it would be!
>
> The day-light dawn'd — they dropp'd their arms,
> And cluster'd round the mast:
> Sweet sounds rose slowly thro' their mouths
> And from their bodies pass'd. (335–42)

In 1800 the nephew remains silent. But instead of the Mariner's fears,
we get the Wedding Guest's:

> "I fear thee, ancient Mariner!"
> Be calm thou Wedding-Guest!
> 'Twas not those souls who fled in pain
> Which to their corses came again,
> But a troop of spirits blest: (345–49)

Fearing at that uncanny moment the sound of his own voice, lest it *not*
be his, the Mariner hears instead the Wedding Guest's, whose ventriloquy gives voice and fulfillment to the Mariner's fears. Taken by itself,
the 1800 text provides reassurance for the reader who, with the Wedding Guest, fears that the Mariner might be a ghoul; the Mariner's
reply to the Wedding Guest[16] allays his suspicions. But the relationship

---

[16]It is a curiously shrewd reply, reinterpreting the Wedding Guest's exclamation at
the possibility that he might be possessed as a question about the nature of the spirits
inhabiting the bodies of others. His reassurance that the spirits are not the original inhabitants of the bodies is not really reassuring, however.

between the revised and the original text lends support to the possibility that the words of 1800 deny. As the spirits bless'd work through the
bodies of the crew, so the spirit of the Mariner speaks through the Wedding Guest. Both men become functions of the tale whose telling they
must endure and to whose impersonal power they must bear witness.

Having begun by crossing the boundaries of speech and character
ordinarily marked by punctuation, the anonymous voice of this self-
propagating tale develops into full-scale ventriloquism. What we register as a linguistic problem, however, the tale's characters register as a
demonological one; they see the Mariner himself, and not the tale that
he tells and that they enter, as the problem. Instrument rather than
author of the tale he tells, the Mariner appears to them a dead man possessed by a demon of loquacity.

To the Hermit. the Pilot, and the Pilot's boy, who assume that
the body they draw from the sea at the sinking of the ship is that of
a corpse, the sight — or sound — of the Mariner's attempt to speak is
uncanny:

> Stunn'd by that loud and dreadful sound,
> Which sky and ocean smote:
> Like one that hath been seven days drown'd
> My body lay afloat:
> But, swift as dreams, myself I found
> Within the Pilot's boat.
>
> .   .   .   .
>
> I mov'd my lips: the Pilot shriek'd
> And fell down in a fit.
> The holy Hermit rais'd his eyes
> And pray'd where he did sit. (583–88, 593–96)

They do not recover from their horror when he takes the oars. They do
not react with relief that one they mistook for dead should prove still to
be alive. Nothing the Mariner does convinces them that he is a living
man. And although the Wedding Guest, not having seen him rise from
the waters, is not as immediately or as forcibly affected as they are, he
also soon becomes uneasy. Something, presumably, in the Mariner's
manner — his mesmeric power the unnatural concentration of vitality
in his glittering eye and his unstoppable mouth, perhaps — causes the
Wedding Guest to wonder what sort of creature he has before him. Nor
can he believe that the tale the Mariner tells can be told by a living man.

Hence his fear that he may be talking to a zombie.[17] Hence too the
question that calls forth the tale.

By giving the Mariner the air of a zombie, the poem forces the
reader to confront a radical split between speaker and speech, both of
which seem haunted. The connection between possession and ventriloquy is made explicit late in the poem, when the spirits that have been
inhabiting the dead bodies of the crew take the form of embodied imitative voice:

> The day-light dawn'd — they dropp'd their arms,
> And cluster'd round the mast:
> Sweet sounds rose slowly thro' their mouths
> And from their bodies pass'd.
>
> Around, around, flew each sweet sound,
> Then darted to the sun:
> Slowly the sounds came back again
> Now mix'd, now one by one. (339–46)

It would be a display of exquisitely acrobatic voice-throwing if the
voices had an origin to be thrown from, but the circumstances forbid us
to locate the source of voice in its apparent speakers; these voices no
more belong to the crew out of whose mouths they pass than the tale
belongs to the Mariner.

Were it not for the fact that the Mariner is but the first victim of the
tale's compulsive repetitions, we might attribute his behavior to hysteria. But he is not the tale's only teller; his story is enclosed and repeated
by others over whom the Mariner (as opposed to the tale) has no influence. That the later narrators are even more deeply anonymous than
the Mariner himself (whose appearance, social demeanor, and history
we know) is, of course, a problem; their retellings can neither authorize
the truth of the original tale nor enable us to sort out its errors. But
unless we decide that everyone who tells or retells the tale is mad in precisely the same way, we cannot read the tale's peculiarities as symptoms

---

[17]I cannot entirely agree with Arden Reed, who believes that the Wedding Guest
finds the Mariner ghostly (*Romantic Weather*, p. 153). Although given the Mariner's
insistence that he is a living man I cannot convincingly argue that the Mariner is really and
literally a zombie, I find him more zombie-like than ghostly: the Wedding Guest is horri-
fyingly aware of the details of his quite physical appearance. It is telling, however, that he
arouses the fears of the Wedding Guest and the men who row out to save him not so
much by his appearance as by his speech: he speaks as if it were not himself speaking. And
in the world this poem describes, speech seems to be more important than action. It is,
after all, for their irresponsible speech that the crew are punished with death.

of pathology either psychological or ethical. Indeed, the framing of the tale calls into question the very notion of character upon which considerations of psychology and ethics — and hence, of course, propriety — depend.

The reduction of the poem's characters to reflections and echoes of the tale-ridden Mariner could, one imagines, be the work of the minstrel who narrates the tale that the antiquarian would gloss. But the tale's curse is not so easily explained; it exercises its power on figures whom one would like to assume stand beyond its reach, outside its fictional space — on those figures precisely who determine the boundaries of the tale. Both minstrel and antiquarian are absorbed into the mechanism of the tale's telling. With no punctuation distinguishing the minstrel's voice from the Mariner's, both voices seem to emanate from the same source, and the poor minstrel, his independence thus undermined, transmits to the antiquarian (not yet, in 1798, brought into being) the compulsion to repeat.

The poem's strange power to bring itself to voice against the knowledge or will of its sometimes arbitrary subject is something other than a simple fiction: it affects Coleridge too.[18] As the Mariner is subject to a "strange power of speech" that forces him to repeat his tale endlessly, so the poet himself lay under a similar though more limited compulsion to repeat himself, revising the poem in 1800 and again in 1817, when he doubled it with a prose gloss in the style of a learned seventeenth-century antiquarian. "Each revision," writes Homer Brown, "is an apparent attempt to define and control the wandering meaning — in a sense the reading — of the poem. . . . And each version of this tale is allegorical in relationship to the one prior to it."[19] The gloss attempts to prop up the original narrative, making explicit what the Mariner either left implicit or, perhaps, missed. The brief "Argument," though tracing little more than the ship's movements and holding out the bare lure of "strange things that befell," does in little what the gloss does in full. Both repeat to rationalize or explain — to reclaim sense from

---

[18]The Mariner is something of a self-portrait of the poet, who was at the time of the poem's composition only slightly less odd than his creation. Coleridge was still a young man when he wrote the poem and, though a great talker, not yet the notorious glittery-eyed monologuist of the Highgate years. He did have a weakness for recycling his words; when the demands of correspondence became too great, he would repeat not only the same bits of news but the same wording, sometimes pages at a time, letter after letter. His penchant for reusing poetry and prose was still probably a matter of efficiency, not pathology. It was only later that Coleridge began drawing parallels between his experience and the Mariner's.

[19]Brown, "The Art of Theology," p. 249.

apparent nonsense. But an uncanny motive behind the retellings gives itself away; rationalization reveals itself as an attempt to conceal the nature of the Mariner's story.

For the reader who accepts the authority of the gloss and the connections the gloss makes, the commentary is the completion of an otherwise incomplete structure. Walter Jackson Bate speaks for these readers when he asserts that Coleridge added "the beautiful gloss in order to flesh out the otherwise skeletal bones of the supernatural machinery and also to help smooth the flow of the narrative."[20] If we can take Bate's words more seriously than he meant them, the gloss humanizes the supernatural, animates the dead — worthy aims both, from the Wordsworthian perspective. But Bate's image suggests an unwitting interpretive necromancy, for the literary critical raising of bones merely repeats one of the "Ancient Mariner" 's objectionable wonders. The gloss does to the poem what the spirits do to the bodies of the crew, and what the spirits do to the crew the tale does to its explicators. A structure of nested quotations, the poem behaves in linguistic terms like its own ventriloquist, appropriated by and taking possession of one voice after another: the Mariner's, the minstrel's, the antiquarian's, the critic's. Acknowledging no author, the tale dominates its speakers. To encounter it is to be infected.

The "Rime" 's ventriloquisms are both fictions and realities. When the Wedding Guest, preternaturally sensitive to the presence of linguistic demons, realizes that the voice that has been telling him about the strange death of the crew could not belong to the terrifying body whose glittering eye and rigid hand have immobilized him, we should listen carefully:

"I fear thee, ancyent Marinere!
"I fear thy skinny hand;
"And thou art long and lank and brown
"As is the ribb'd Sea-sand.

"I fear thee and thy glittering eye
"And thy skinny hand, so brown —
Fear not, fear not, thou wedding guest!
This body dropt not down. (216–23)

[20]Walter Jackson Bate, *Coleridge* (1968; rpt. Cambridge: Harvard University Press, 1987), pp. 56–57. What Frances Ferguson says of the gloss is true of any possible remark on the poem: "In assuming that things must be significant and interpretable, [the gloss] finds significance and interpretability, but only by reading ahead of — of beyond — the main text" ("Coleridge and the Deluded Reader," 119).

It is the body, and particularly the hand, that terrifies the Wedding Guest, and it is about the body, though not the hand, that the Mariner tries to reassure him. But he says nothing about the voice. In fact there is an alien voice, and even an alien hand, in the vicinity; it belongs, as Coleridge points out in a note appended in 1817, to Wordsworth, who contributed the lines about the Mariner's ghoulish appearance. Coleridge's uneasiness about the Wordsworthian lines he uses finds expression in the Wedding Guest's cry of apprehension; the Wedding Guest — or is it Wordsworth? — serves as ventriloquist to voice Coleridge's fears of ventriloquy. But if Wordsworth is the ventriloquist here, he is only the nearest to hand; there are others behind him. The voice that repeats the "Rime" is strange not only because it is mysteriously motivated, and not only because it fails to explain anything more than its frame or the reason it is being told, but also because it is archaic, as indeed is the language of the entire poem. The style of the "Rime" seems strange because its familiarity goes too far back for us to recognize it. "A Dutch attempt at German sublimity," Southey called it,[21] his desire to poke fun accidentally leading him in the direction of a truth. An earlier English style[22] has returned sounding almost foreign.

So carefully did Coleridge set about archaizing the vocabularies of the poem and establishing plausibility of the historical details that scholars can guess with fair assurance when the voyage was supposed to have been undertaken,[23] when the minstrel was supposed to have made the "Rime,"[24] and when the commentator was supposed to have written

[21] *Critical Review,* October, 1798; in John O. Hayden, ed., *Romantic Bards and British Reviewers: A Selected Edition of the Contemporary Reviews of the Works of Wordsworth, Coleridge, Byron, Keats and Shelley* (Lincoln: University of Nebraska Press, 1971), p. 4. In a letter written a decade later, Coleridge gets Southey's witticism interestingly wrong: "'over-polished in the diction with *Dutch* industry'" (Letter #762, to Thomas Longman, 27 April 1809, *STCL,* III, p. 203).

[22] Richard Payne has demonstrated that "Coleridge was attempting, in the idiom of the 'Ancient Mariner,' to recapture the lost natural idiom" of the "elder poets" and that he succeeded in producing "a quite authentic rendition of the idioms of a broad section of the British literary tradition" of the sixteenth and seventeenth centuries" ("'The Style and Spirit of the Elder Poets': The *Ancient Mariner* and English Literary Tradition," *Modern Philology* 75 [1978], 368–84).

[23] "There is . . . enough historical evidence to date the imaginary voyage, very broadly, around 1500, a natural date for a late-medieval ballad, and consistent with the elaborately Catholic and medieval detail," writes George Watson (*Coleridge the Poet* [London: Routledge and Kegan Paul, 1966], p. 90). See also Huntington Brown, "The Gloss to *The Rime of the Ancient Mariner,*" *Modern Language Quarterly* 6 (1945), 319.

[24] The purity and simplicity of the minstrel's language mark him as a medieval minstrel, as opposed to one of "the broadside journalists of Shakespeare's London," observes Huntington Brown, p. 319. Coleridge copied this particular ballad form keeping an eye on Percy's *Reliques,* particularly "Sir Cauline" (*STCL* I, p. 379 n.). John Livingston

the gloss.[25] But Coleridge's scholarly success worked against him. His contemporaries, responding not to the authenticity of the details but to the fact of their unfamiliarity and their suggestion of stylistic ventriloquism, reacted to the poet the way the Hermit reacted to the Mariner: with deep suspicion about the source of so obviously unnatural an utterance. Speaking anonymously for the *Critical Review*, Southey objected to what he regarded as the inauthenticity of the poem:

> We are tolerably conversant with the early English poets; and can discover no resemblance whatever, except in antiquated spelling and a few obsolete words. This piece appears to us perfectly original in style as well as in story.[26]

Others took exception to the diction while appreciating the overall style. An anonymous critic for *The British Critic* wrote,

> The author . . . is not correctly versed in the old language, which he undertakes to employ. "Noises of a *swound*,". . . and "broad as a *weft*,". . . are both nonsensical; but the ancient style is so well imitated, while the antiquated words are so very few, that the latter might with advantage be entirely removed without any detriment to the effect of the Poem.[27]

When he revised the poem in 1800, Coleridge did change the phrases to which critics had raised particular objections.[28]

Perhaps one reason for the critics' displeasure at the language of the "Ancient Mariner" as it appeared in 1798 is that others before Coleridge had drawn so heavily upon archaic and pseudo-archaic English as to have given the public a disgust for the style. During the 1780s and 1790s sophisticated writers of "ballads of simplicity" had their productions "encrusted with a patina spuriously induced by consonants doubled at random and superfluous *e*'s" in order to make them seem older

---

Lowes traces another large portion of the 'Ancient Mariner's vocabulary to Chaucer, Spenser, William Taylor's translations of Burger's "Lenore," Chatterton, Hakluyt, Purchas, Martens, and Harris (*The Road to Xanadu: A Study in the Ways of the Imagination* [Boston: Houghton Mifflin Company, 1927], pp. 296–308).

[25]The writer of the gloss was an inhabitant of the seventeenth century. See Huntington Brown, pp. 322, 320.

[26]Quoted in Hayden, p. 4.

[27]Hayden, p. 6.

[28]B. R. McElderry, Jr., "Coleridge's Revision of 'The Ancient Mariner,'" *Studies in Philology* 29 (1932), 71.

than they really were.[29] The fraud was not always so transparent. Lowes remarks that

> nine out of ten of the archaisms which went into the earliest version of "The Ancient Mariner" had already imparted a would-be romantic flavour to the pages of Chatterton, and Shenstone, and Thomson, and of such smaller fry as Mickle, and Wilkie, and William Thompson, and Moses Mendez, and Gilbert West.[30]

Some readers were tired of antiquity. Others had never had a taste for it. Charles Burney, speaking for the eighteenth century generally, expressed uneasiness about poetic regression:

> Would it not be degrading poetry, as well as the English language, to go back to the barbarous and uncouth numbers of Chaucer? Suppose, instead of modernizing the old bard, that the sweet and polished measures, on lofty subjects, of Dryden, Pope, and Gray, were to be transmuted into the dialect and versification of the XIVth century? Should we be gainers by the retrogradation? *Rust* is a necessary quality to a counterfeit old medal: but, to give artificial rust to modern poetry, in order to render it similar to that of three or four hundred years ago, can have no better title to merit and admiration than may be claimed by any ingenious forgery.[31]

Yet the style of the "Ancient Mariner" would fool no reader into thinking the poem ancient. Even the 1798 version, its archaic words and spellings not yet removed, would have looked odd to a sixteenth-century reader, for, despite its curiosities of diction, the basis of the poem is the English of 1798.[32] To use Coleridge's own distinction,[33]

[29]Albert Friedman, *The Ballad Revival: Studies in the Influence of Popular on Sophisticated Poetry* (Chicago: University of Chicago Press, 1961), p. 269.

[30]*The Road to Xanadu*, p. 307.

[31]Quoted in J. R. de J. Jackson, ed., *Coleridge: The Critical Heritage* (London: Routledge & Kegan Paul, 1970), p. 55.

[32]Despite the similarity of their sources, Coleridge was no Chatterton. Henry A. Beers writes, "It might be hard to prove that the Rowley poems had very much to do with giving shape to Coleridge's own poetic output. Doubtless, without them, 'Christabel,' and 'The Ancient Mariner,' and 'The Dark Ladye' would still have been; and yet it is possible that they might not have been just what they are" (*A History of English Romanticism in the Eighteenth Century* [New York: Henry Holt and Company, 1899], p. 369). Chatterton conscientiously mined Chaucer, Speght's Chaucer glossary, Kersey's dictionary, Spenser, Drayton, Marlowe, Shakespeare, Percy's *Reliques*, as well as Elizabeth Cooper's *Muses' Library*, Ossian, Dryden, and Pope. See Donald S. Taylor, ed., *The Complete Works of Thomas Chatterton* (Oxford: Oxford University Press, 1971), p. xliv, and Bertrand H. Bronson, "Thomas Chatterton," in Frederick W. Hilles, ed., *The Age of*

his poem was meant to imitate and not copy ancient poetic language. It seems to have been this mixture of the strange and the familiar, more than the strangeness itself, that disturbed contemporary readers.

Coleridge himself may have been uneasy about the unnaturalness of his imitation-antique language. He disparaged badly managed archaisms in others' poems, expressing particular dislike for "their inverted sentences, their quaint phrases, and incongruous mixture of obsolete and spenserian words."[34] Praising the ballad in Monk Lewis's *Castle Spectre,* a work he otherwise disparaged as "a mere patchwork of plagiarisms," he wrote,

> The simplicity & naturalness is his own, & not imitated, for it is made to subsist in contiguity with a language perfectly modern — the language of his own times, in the same way that the language of the writer of "Sir Cauline" was the language of *his* times. This, I think, a rare merit: at least, *I* cannot attain this innocent nakedness, except by *assumption* — I resemble the Dutchess [sic] of Kingston, who masqueraded in the character of "Eve before the Fall" in flesh-coloured Silk.[35]

If to copy "innocent nakedness" is lascivious, to copy primitive language is sophisticated. In both cases the imitation offends because it pretends to imitate what is valued precisely for its freedom — as object and as subject — from the taint of imitation. It offends because it acts out of awareness of that which must be unconscious.

But the objects of the "Rime"'s mimetic intentions are hardly innocent victims. Deeply and consciously involved in echoes and ventriloquies, the "Rime" derives from, or echoes, sources that are themselves perplexed. It is not simply the echoic structure that denaturalizes the language; the earlier voices are no more natural than those they haunt. There was never a first time the Mariner recited his "Rime." From the outset the tale was a repetition — of the experience itself, which the Mariner relives as he retells it, of the words in which he retells it, and of other words, with which Coleridge and Wordsworth had been telling or

---

Johnson: Essays Presented to Chauncey Brewster Tinker (1949; rpt. New York: AMS Press, 1978), pp. 244, 245.

[33]"The composition of a poem is among the *imitative* arts; and . . . imitation," as opposed to copying, consists either in the interfusion of the SAME throughout the radically DIFFERENT, or of the different throughout a base radically the same" (*BL,* II, p. 72).

[34]*CPW,* II, p. 1139.

[35]Letter #225, to William Wordsworth, 23 January 1798, in *STCL,* I, p. 379.

trying to tell other tales during the last half-dozen years. The poem's obvious and exotic anachronisms cover more recent and more local influences, particularly "The Wanderings of Cain" and "Salisbury Plain."

The "Rime" was the result of two separate collaborative failures. It was meant to be a joint project, like the *Lyrical Ballads* to which it gave rise. As Wordsworth told Isabella Fenwick the story of the poem's inception and early development, he, Dorothy, and Coleridge were on a walk when they decided to write a poem in order to finance a tour. Parts of the idea for it came from the dream of a Mr. Cruikshank; other parts, such as the shooting of the albatross, the navigation of the ship by the dead men, and the spirits' revenge, were suggested by Wordsworth, who also contributed a few lines. But "as we endeavoured to proceed conjointly (I speak of the same evening) our respective manners proved so widely different that it would have been presumptuous in me to do anything but separate from an undertaking upon which I could only have been a clog."[36] Thus even before the poem took definite shape it was already a conversation turned monologue; years before the gloss was written there were voices other than the narrator's telling versions of parts of the same tale. The final form recapitulates what would otherwise seem to be irrelevant facts about its production.

The plan Wordsworth tells about was already a repetition of, or substitution for, an earlier plan. In his "Prefatory Note" to the fragmentary "Wanderings of Cain," Coleridge writes:

The work was to have been written in concert with another [Wordsworth], whose name is too venerable within the precincts of genius to be unnecessarily brought into connection with such a trifle, and who was then residing at a small distance from Nether Stowey. The title and subject were suggested by myself, who likewise drew out the scheme and contents for each of the three books or cantos, of which the work was to consist, and which, the reader is to be informed, was to have been finished in one night! My partner undertook the first canto: I the second: and whichever had *done first,* was to set about the third. Almost thirty years have passed by; yet at this moment I cannot without something more than a smile moot the question which of the two things was the more impracticable, for a mind so eminently original to compose another man's thoughts and fancies, or for a taste so austerely pure and simple to imitate the Death of Abel? Methinks I see his grand and noble countenance as at the moment when having despatched my own portion of the task at full finger-speed, I

[36] *WPW,* I, p. 361.

hastened to him with my manuscript — that look of humourous despondency fixed on his almost blank sheet of paper, and then its silent mock piteous admission of failure struggling with the sense of the exceeding ridiculousness of the whole scheme — which broke up in a laugh: and the Ancient Mariner was written instead.[37]

Coleridge's account of the poem's "birth, parentage, and premature decease" (as he calls it) inadvertently suggests a parallel between the writing and the story being written. In stressing the absurdity of one man attempting to offer what is not his to offer, Coleridge's account cannot help but remind us that Abel the shepherd was killed because his offering of sheep was accepted while Cain the farmer's offering of grain — he had no sheep to sacrifice — was not. The brother poets proved unable to cooperate on a story centering around the fratricidal consequences of that unequally regarded sacrifice. It is no coincidence that so many of the poems on which Wordsworth and Coleridge tried to collaborate concern violence and envy.

As so often is the case, Coleridge's remarks on textual history provide a key to reading the text as an allegory of its own production. His remarks raise questions about the authenticity of expression that "The Wanderings of Cain" and its successor will dramatize. Though it may be ridiculous for one man "to compose another man's thoughts," Coleridge found the possibility of such an impersonation sufficiently intriguing to make it one of "Cain"'s major themes. Ventriloquism may be no proper source of poetry, but the "Rime," "Cain"'s stepchild, depends on it, internalizing the relationship that Coleridge now writes off.

"The Wanderings of Cain" matters to a reading of the "Rime" because of the relationships among its history, its subject, and its formal structure — if one can call a text so confused, so nonsensical, either formal or structured. In "The Wanderings of Cain" as in the "Rime," different voices and different versions of the same story compete with one another. The relationship among the introductory verse stanza Coleridge claimed to have reconstructed from memory ("Encinctured with a twine of leaves," etc.), the prose version of canto II, and the "rough draft of a continuation or alternative version . . . found among Coleridge's papers"[38] is not clear. It is hard to say whether we are dealing with different versions of the same events or with different, although

---

[37] *CPW*, I, pp. 285–87.
[38] *Ibid.*, p. 285.

perhaps similar, events — a problem the reader of the "Rime" and its gloss should recognize.

Though the plot of "The Wanderings of Cain" is too baffling to recount, it is — happily — not as a narrative but as a collection of themes, images, and questions about representation that "The Wanderings of Cain" finds its way into the "Rime." "The Wanderings of Cain" contains the raw materials for the "Rime": killing, punishment by solitude, spirits, trances, the sacrifice of blood from an arm, and wandering. It contains passages that translate almost immediately into the words of the later poem. One such passage follows:

> And Cain lifted up his voice and cried bitterly, and said, "The Mighty One that persecuteth me is on this side and on that; he pursueth my soul like the wind, like the sand-blast he passeth through me; he is around me even as the air! O that I might be utterly no more! I desire to die — yes, the things that never had life, neither move they upon the earth — behold! they seem precious to mine eyes. O that a man might live without the breath of his nostrils. So I might abide in darkness, and blackness, and an empty space! . . . For the torrent that roareth far off hath a voice: and the clouds in heaven look terribly on me; the Mighty One who is against me speaketh in the wind of the cedar grove; and in silence am I dried up."

Cain's complaints resemble the Mariner's: he is persecuted by storm and by freakish winds; he wishes he could die; he learns to love the slimy things that crawl with legs upon the slimy sea; the bodies of the dead crew move with no breath in their nostrils; he is alone, alone, on a wide, wide sea; he can hear the winds roaring far off; drought silences him. Both Cain and the shape of Abel resemble the Mariner: Cain whose eye "glared . . . fierce and sullen" and whose "countenance told in a strange and terrible language of agonies that had been, and were, and were still to continue to be"; and the shape of Abel, who cries, "Woe is me! woe is me! I must never die again, and yet I am perishing with thirst and hunger." The Mariner is in part a composite of Cain and the delusive representation of the brother he murdered, uncertain what god or what spirits may have dominion over him now.

In neither poem is it apparent whether the cosmos *is* a cosmos, united under a single, benevolent God, or a place of warring and delusive spirits. We see the spirits and hear their reports, but are they reliable? The Mariner asserts the unity of God and the universality of His

laws of love, but the evidence suggests that the shape of Abel may have
spoken the truth when he talked of another God ruling over the nightmare world of sin and death. "The Wanderings of Cain" articulates the
heresy that the "Rime" rehearses to deny.

A work of Wordsworth's variously entitled "A Night on Salisbury
Plain," "Adventures on Salisbury Plain,",, and "Guilt and Sorrow"
looks like another possible source for the "Rime." Coleridge saw a draft
of this larger work, which was begun probably in 1793, about a year
before he began the "Rime." Like "The Wanderings of Cain" and like
"The Ancient Mariner," "Adventures on Salisbury Plain" lacks a single
authoritative narrator or narrative, repeating the same story in different
voices and with different sets of characters, trapped in representations
of the past. Like the "Rime," it is deeply concerned with traumatic
repetition.

The protagonist, long the victim of official injustice, becomes an
agent of private injustice himself, robbing and killing a man on his way
home after years away at sea. This crime, which he commits near his
own doorstep, drives him back into exile, now self-imposed: dreading
to show himself to his family as a murderer, he wanders anxiously,
wearily, over Salisbury Plain as over a stage on which his past is being
continually reenacted and his future — or lack of it — continually fore-
shadowed. Making his way through a storm to "the dead house of the
Plain," he encounters a Female Vagrant, who, after briefly mistaking
the guilty sailor for an unburied corpse, tells him the story of her own
wanderings. Her life, which Wordsworth excerpted to print as "The
Female Vagrant" in the 1798 *Lyrical Ballads,* only a few pages further
on from the "Rime," is guiltless but apparently cursed in much the
same way as the Mariner's; she remembers her anguish and her calm at
sea in words almost identical to those in which the Ancient Mariner
remembers his. At dawn the two leave the dead house and come upon a
beaten child lying as if dead on the ground. For an instant the sailor sees
in the child a reflection of the man he himself has killed: the murder
seems to have repeated itself before his eyes and accused him of his
crime. The child's father frightens them off. Walking on, they meet an
ailing woman who proves to be the sailor's wife, driven from her home
by her neighbors' suspicions of her husband's involvement in the murder. Recognizing her long-lost husband, she is overcome with emotion
and dies of joy. A couple of innkeepers realize at that instant who the
sailor must be and urge him to surrender to the law. He does so and is
hanged.

The killing of the traveler, like the killing of the albatross, is a form of what the gloss to the "Rime" calls inhospitality. Both murderers are hosts,[39] and both are punished with homelessness for their offenses against hospitality. Yet neither crime is a narrative turning point. Although their punishment is wandering, both are already wanderers. Their crimes change things less than one might expect; indeed, it is that changelessness of things that is their true punishment. Both men are doomed to inhabit a time that cannot progress normally and a space that turns in every direction to the scene of the crime. Instead of returning to his family, the sailor enters a world in which everyone and everything is related to him; he becomes the traveler he kills and the hanged man he sees; he looks at his victim bleeding again in the guise of a child and hears himself as a brutal father threaten himself with the gallows. The vagrant's story of a family lost through war is a counterpart to his own.[40] His reunion with his wife kills her, and the hospitality of the innkeepers kills him. Although the sailor himself never tells his tale except (out of our hearing) to the judges, the stories everyone else tells echo the story he could have told.

Despite its contemporary social relevance, "The Female Vagrant" was almost as much an anachronism in that volume as the "Rime." Wordsworth's poem participates in Spenserian patterns of behavior, confronting men with aspects of their own motives and destinies. Its stanzas, aspects of its style,[41] and its symbolic space[42] are Spenserian, too. But, unlike "The Ancient Mariner" and unlike *The Faerie Queene* or *The Shepheardes Calendar,* "Salisbury Plain" does not flaunt its archaism. Samuel Schulman observes that "Wordsworth's use of the Spenserian mode in a poem like this — contemporary, socially advanced, anti-war — is a repudiation of the antiquarian sensibility that

[39]The sailor is at the point of stepping inside his own door when he comes upon his victim; the Mariner has, presumably, with the rest of the crew, been feeding the albatross crumbs.

[40]J. R. Watson recognizes the similarity but stresses differences between the two poems in his book *Wordsworth's Vital Soul: The Sacred and Profane in Wordsworth's Poetry* [London: Macmillan, 1982], p. 68). It is possible to make too much of the contrast. The differences between the poems are real, of course, but what is telling is how alike the structures of two such apparently unlike poems turn out to be. Lines 392–96, 427–35, and 546–49 are strikingly similar to passages in the "Rime."

[41]Hartman points out the poem's Spenserian consonance, caesurae, inversion, and "multiplication of monosyllables," in *Wordsworth's Poetry, 1787–1814* (1964; rpt. New Haven: Yale University Press, 1977), p. 119.

[42]Samuel Schulman compares Salisbury Plain with the topography of *The Faerie Queene* in "Wordsworth's Spenserian Voice," Ph.D. diss., Yale University 1978, p. 30.

had, up to now, cherished and promoted the appreciation of Spenser."[43]
By the time Wordsworth came to write "Salisbury Plain" its Spenserian
stanzas no longer brought Spenser to the mind of the average reader,
who was more familiar with the neoclassical derivative than with the
bewildering original. No anonymous seventeenth scholar glosses its
antique meaning; no E. K. remarks upon its "straungenesse." "Salisbury Plain" establishes no distance between barbarous past and barbarous present. It reminds us how history uncannily persists, bringing
itself to voice through the voices of strangers, reenacting itself in fragments, defying the silence of its protagonist.[44]

"The Wanderings of Cain" and "Salisbury Plain" provided Coleridge with a store of material to use in the "Rime." Some of this material was available elsewhere (in *The Borderers*, in "The Destiny of
Nations"); much of it was simply in the air between the two poets. The
poems also provided examples of a puzzling aspect of the relationship
between representation and repetition: the multiplication of signs and
the splitting of their referents. But perhaps the particular content or the
particular source matters less than what it all represented for Coleridge:
material that arrived between quotation marks, fuel for a literary
machine that could transform problems of intertextuality into problems
of intratextuality.

The Ancient Mariner's uneasiness at the sound of his voice
expresses Coleridge's own uneasiness. Both know the tale they tell is of
alien origin, and for both of them, though for different reasons, this
fact comes laden with anxiety. The "Rime"'s archaism, like its thematic
ventriloquism. expresses the poet's consciousness of what he owes to
his sources — one of whom was himself. But the anxiety he feels is not
the kind that can be soothed by acknowledgment; his sources suffer
from the same embarrassments he does. If the contest of voices within
the "Rime" acts out that poem's relation to its sources, what is one to
say about similar contests in the sources themselves? It is not the bor-
rowing of material that generates the "Rime"'s anxiety, for the anxiety
was there in the original; it is part of what Coleridge borrows. So is the
penitential repetition. Cain and the sailor both sinned before Coleridge

---

[43]Schulman, p. 17.

[44]In the course of a full and meticulous analysis of the "Rime"'s debt to "Salisbury
Plain," Paul Magnuson argues that "'The Ancient Mariner' alters the Salisbury Plain
poems, not only in giving a voice to suffering, but also in characterizing the voice as dis-
sociated from the mariner." Persuasive as Magnuson's reading is, I am not convinced that
what Coleridge has done in the "Rime" amounts to "giving a voice" to its protagonist.
See *Coleridge and Wordsworth: A Lyrical Dialogue* (Princeton: Princeton University
Press, 1988), pp. 68–84.

sat down to his "Rime." No matter how much he tries, the Mariner cannot expiate a sin committed before he was created.

A summary of the "Rime," a transcription of a recital of a repeatedly ventriloquized tale, might go, " " " 'I' can't stop talking." ' " The Mariner's compulsive self-quotation, which calls into question the self he quotes, expresses on the level of individual character a compulsion to repeat that constitutes not just the poem's psychology and genealogy but also its morphology. Stanzas, lines, phrases, and even individual words reveal the same penchant for repetition and self-quotation as do the poem's ancestors, inhabitants, and redactors.

Echoes and patterns of imagistic repetition ordinarily invite comparisons: we take them as indices — straight or ironic — of continuity, coherence, or analogy. Some of the "Rime"'s echoes — verbal, imagistic, and structural — behave as we expect them to; others do not. As Arden Reed points out,

> The process of doubling in the "Ancient Mariner" operates in two directions. One is the creation of resemblance or identity out of difference, when the poem demonstrates how two things that seem unrelated or even opposite can come to mirror each other. . . . But . . . the poem is also engaged in splitting identity (the presence of the word to itself, for instance) into differences, in turning the singular "rime" into two meanings that are not necessarily commensurate. This second process may be related to a more general fragmentation that marks the entire poem. Both of these operations, the making and unmaking of congruence, take place throughout the text and are woven together; but they do not form any regular, much less any dialectical pattern.[45]

Through much of the poem, the tendency to repeat disguises itself as balladic repetition:

> Water, water, every where,
> And all the boards did shrink;
> Water, water, every where,
> Nor any drop to drink. (115–18)

Traditional balladic repetitions depend for their effect either upon their rhythmic value alone or upon their ability to unfold an irony or a

[45]Reed, *Romantic Weather,* p. 150.

revelation. The "Rime"'s repetitions sometimes seem to function the same way, as forms of punctuation laden at once with musical and with thematic value. One of the more accessible of such clusters involves interruption. The "loud bassoon" that announces the entrance of the bride into the hall interrupts the Mariner's tale just when the ship has reached the equator, where twice later its voyage will be interrupted. The voyage is interrupted first by a deadly calm that brings the specter ship bearing Life-in-Death, whose appearance parodies the bride's. It is interrupted again by the changing of the spirit-guard that makes the ship pause and rock and lunge. The "roaring wind" that approaches the becalmed ship makes "the upper air burst into life" and sets "fire-flags sheen" and stars dancing in a fashion that anticipates the conclusion of the wedding, when "what loud uproar bursts from that door!" at the singing of the bride and her maids. These echoes hint at a relationship of inverse analogy between the Mariner's journey and the wedding that his tale prevents the Wedding Guest from celebrating.

Clusters such as this one, much favored by those who insist upon the organic unity and Christian implications of the poem, lend them-selves to analysis into categories of life and death, vitality and stasis, love and hate, good and evil. Taken by themselves, these patternings seem to set human life and love into the context of universal life and love, giving cosmic overtones to the wedding and affirming the universality of the human moral and epistemological codes. They suggest that what happens in the middle of the ocean remains comparable to what hap-pens in ordinary English villages and remains interpretable by terrestrial rules. But of course the analogy can work the other way around as well, suggesting that what happens in the villages is properly interpretable only in terms of what happens to unlucky mariners at sea. It is a disturb-ing thought, but when — as here — the alternative is total unreadabil-ity, even a sinister interpretation may be better than none at all.

Most of the "Rime"'s repetitions are neither unmeaning "hey nonny noes" nor clues whose meaning will have become clear by the end of the poem but passages in which the mere mechanism or materi-ality of language seems almost — but not quite — to deny the possibil-ity of sense. "Alone, alone, all all alone, / Alone on a wide wide Sea," laments the Mariner. The cry approaches the condition of a wordless moan. At the same time, it dramatizes a solitude that seems to imply its absoluteness by verbal necessity. The line resembles both a stutter, mere sound haunted by its own terrifyingly arbitrary and disparate possibili-ties, and an oxymoron, "all" being an unfinished "alone," "alone" being a portmanteau of "all" and "lone" or "one." The barely articulate wail contains its own comfort and the germ of one of Coleridge's favorite intellectual convictions, that the "all" and the "one" could be reconciled. But little other than wistful thinking holds the line's paradoxical echoes together; and even so it is unclear whether the wistful thinking is the critic's or the Mariner's.

Many of the "Rime"'s apparent echoes and symmetries resemble accidents rather than analogies. These repetitions, instances of what one might call the *instance de la lettre,* suggest primarily the power of images to recur and the powerlessness of the Mariner or the narrator to dispose of them. They seem not merely the objects of obsession but agents of contagion, infecting those who behold them. Their metonymy exercises a metaphoric, even metamorphic, effect. For this reason both looking and speaking can be dangerous activities.

In the "Rime" you become what you meet. This principle dictates the poem's structure and plot. The hypnotic power the Mariner exercises over the Wedding Guest he has absorbed, painfully, from the dead crew, who, having met Death and Life-in-Death, experience the meaning of the first and enact the meaning of the second:

All stood together on the deck,
For a charnel-dungeon fitter:
All fix'd on me their stony eyes
That in the moon did glitter.

The pang, the curse, with which they died,
Had never pass'd away:
I could not draw my een from theirs
Ne turn them up to pray. (439–46)

The Mariner's ship displays a similar vulnerability during its transformation into an image of the two things it encounters at sea, the albatross and the specter ship. By the time it returns to port, the Mariner's ship is inhabited by Death in the several persons of the crew and Life-in-Death in the person of the Ancient Mariner, an apparent corpse still capable of both speech and movement. The ship itself, says the Hermit, "hath a fiendish look": "The planks looked warped! and see those sails, / How thin they are and sere!" It has become a skeleton ship. Though it does not plunge and tack and veer, it does, like the specter ship, move "without a breeze, without a tide," powered by

supernatural forces.[46] The wind that blows as it comes to land has no
navigational use:

> But soon there breath'd a wind on me,
> Ne sound ne motion made:
> Its path was not upon the sea
> In ripple or in shade.
> .   .   .   .
> Swiftly, swiftly flew the ship,
> Yet she sail'd softly too:
> Sweetly, sweetly blew the breeze —
> On me alone it blew. (457–60, 465–68)

The ship shares too the fate of the albatross, whose behavior fore-
shadows elements of the coming catastrophe. "It ate the food it ne'er
had eat," as the Mariner will shortly after, although perhaps a diet of
blood is not strictly comparable to one of biscuit worms. The ship,
doomed to go "down like lead" when the Hermit approaches it in his
boat singing "godly hymns," suffers a fate not unlike that of the albatross, which falls into the sea at an "unaware" blessing from the
Mariner. The ship sinks to the sound of underwater thunder that "split
the bay." Its sinking creates a whirlpool in which the Hermit's boat
"spun round and round." Both ships together thus reenact in a sinister
fashion the scenes in which the playful albatross first comes to the
frozen ship: "round and round it flew: / The Ice did split with a Thunder fit; / The Helmsman steer'd us thro'" (66–68).[47]

It is not necessary, however, actually to encounter a physical object in order to feel its metamorphosing influence. Sometimes a merely
verbal encounter is enough. Passing through the neighborhood of a
simile or even a submerged metaphor puts you (even, perhaps, you the
reader) at risk; the words are capable of realizing themselves at your
expense. So the ship's very setting off is a sinking, as it "drop[s] /
Below the Kirk, below the Hill, / Below the Light-house top"; its final

---

[46]Presumably now that the crew have absorbed the wind into themselves in the form
of singing spirits they no longer need an external wind to sail the ship. The Mariner suggests that a spirit moves the ship from below.

[47]From all this a reader bent on finding a certain kind of poetic unity might deduce a
kind of poetic justice: as the albatross responds to the ship, so the ship responds to the
spirits who administer its doom. The Mariner's perception that the death of the crew was
linked to the death of the albatross might support such a reading. But it does not take us
far, partly because we see so little into the spirits' motivations, partly because the behavior
of a living albatross does not shed much light on the behavior of a skeleton ship.

moments realize in literal terms the implications of its first ones. The cracking and growling and roaring and howling of the ice at the south pole, "like noises of a swound," anticipate the trance in which the Mariner later hears two spirits discussing his past and his future. And the first hint that the Mariner is in trouble comes before the commission of the crime, when the Mariner compares the force of the storm that drives the ship south to the violence of persecution. In 1798 a fairly impersonal tempest "play'd us freaks." In 1817 the tempest became a hostile spirit:

> And now the STORM-BLAST came, and he
> Was tyrannous and strong;
> He struck us with o'ertaking wings,
> And chased us south along.

> With sloping masts and dipping prow,
> As who pursued with yell and blow
> Still treads the shadow of his foe
> And forwards bends his head,
> The ship drove fast, loud roared the blast,
> And southward aye we fled.[48]

When the albatross appears, as Paul Magnuson points out, "the mariner unconsciously associates the albatross with the storm while he and the crew outwardly receive the bird as a member of their Christian community."[49] The shooting of the Albatross, which most readers regard as the single event that produces the more dramatic misfortune that follows,[50] may have been a consequence of that unconscious association; alternatively, it may have been an attempt to produce belatedly a reason for what would otherwise lack explanation. A figure of the effect produces the reality of its own cause.

But to speak of before and after, anticipation and fulfillment, may be inappropriate here, where chronology is a blur, events are metalepses, and what drives the plot is the conversion of figures into literal realities and sometimes back into figures again. Chronology does not really apply to the events of this poem: its temporality is rhetorical. The

[48]Lines 41–50. I am quoting here from the 1817 version printed in *CPW*, I.
[49]Magnuson, *Coleridge's Nightmare Poetry*, p. 58.
[50]But see Lawrence Kramer, who argues that the appearance of the albatross means a respite from the nightmare of the ice and that "by killing the albatross, therefore, the Mariner does not initiate his nightmare; he returns to it, and allows it to perpetuate itself" ("That Other Will," 307).

same scenes — or at least the same figures — are always before our
eyes, even if we cannot see them or understand what they represent.
Things we never saw before are greeted like sudden recognitions, as if
successful interpretation had called them into being. Thus the odd
sense of familiarity at the appearance of the specter ship:

> Alas! (thought I, and my heart beat loud)
> How fast she neres and neres!
> Are those *her* Sails that glance in the Sun
> Like restless gossameres? (173–76)

This itself echoes the gesture of recognition that opens the poem. "It is
an ancient Mariner," says the narrator, as if we had already seen "it" and
wanted to know what it was.[51] The lack of antecedent is no obstacle to
recurrence in a poem like this, in which a figure may generate its own
etymon and interpretation precedes its own object.

While the "Rime" deprives its declared and undeclared origins of
originality, it also produces the image of a linguistic genesis of sorts. At
the heart of the poem (if it can be said to have such a thing) one finds a
passage in which the poem's principal obsessions and paradoxes con-
verge. The appearance of the specter ship, an emblem of what he is
about to become, inspires the Mariner to invent a rash method of what
the gloss calls "free[ing] his speech from the bonds of thirst":

> I bit my arm and suck'd the blood
> And cry'd, A sail! a sail! (152–53)

The lines intimate a close relation among naming, violence, and death.
Bloodshed, after all, is bloodshed: with the killing of the albatross so
recently past, the Mariner's desperate attempt to quench his thirst cannot help but suggest murder.[52] Even worse, the bloodsucking conjures
up superstitions about how the dead prey upon the living. But although
the poem elsewhere provides what may be evidence for such a reading,
one need not think solely in terms of vampires and ghouls. Odysseus
offered bloody oblations to the most respectable shades in Hades in

---

[51]See Lawrence Lipking's remarks on the opening "phantom reference" in "The
Marginal Gloss," *Critical Inquiry* 3 (1977), 615.
   It is curious to note that the first of the two spirits whose voices the Mariner hears in
his trance begins in a similar manner. " 'Is it he?' quoth one, 'Is this the man?' "
[52]Shipwrecked men were known to commit cannibalism in order to survive, however, and maritime law made allowance for the fact.

order to release them from speechlessness.[53] When he drinks his own blood, the Mariner puts himself in the position of one already dead, and this despite the fact that Death and Life-in-Death are only at that moment coming over the horizon. Whereas in Homer the dead drink blood so that they can address the living, the Mariner drinks blood in order to hail the dead.

The act is a parody of the archaic rite, itself a Hadean inversion of divine inspiration: drinking blood in the underworld is a necessary prelude to true speech, just as inhaling divine breath is — or was — the necessary prelude to true song. In either rite, one takes into oneself the essence of another's life or spirit.[54] If the drinking of his own blood can be considered the Mariner's version of inspiration and not merely a novel way to clear his throat, then the source of his inspiration is not a higher being but himself. Paradoxically, the traditional gesture of poetic dependence has become an assertion of vocal and imaginative autonomy. It is the physiological equivalent of self-quotation and the literary equivalent of suicide.[55]

This is not the first time the Mariner has been inspired by the blood he sheds. It was the killing of the albatross that first enabled him to identify himself, at least retrospectively, as an "I"; it may have been what provided him with a self to refer to.[56] This second shedding of blood functions like the first, enabling the Mariner to identify an inchoate "something" as a ship. It provides him too with the words that will prove to be the germ of his tale, the vocabulary (a literalization of an earlier vehicle) with which he will later try to answer the Hermit's question about his own identity. "A sail! a sail!" becomes the first line of the Mariner's autobiography: "There was a Ship."

The moment that brings into view that incarnation of the principle of uncanniness, Life-in-Death, brings also the mind's recognition of its own originary power. What answers to the Mariner's cry is an engine of

---

[53] *The Odyssey* offers at different points somewhat different explanations for the ceremony: that it enables the ghosts to speak, that it forces them to speak truly, and that it rouses them from oblivion. It could well be that the offering of blood derives from the archaic belief in the chthonic divinity of the dead and the necessity to offer sacrifice to them.

[54] The very next passage, in which the crew "all at once their breath drew in / As they were drinking all" (ll. 157–58), contributes to the confusion, or identification, of drinking and inhaling, liquid and air.

[55] It is linked as well to familial violence, a connection the Hermit makes for us when the sight of the ghastly returning ship leads him to free-associate to "the wolf below / That eats the she-wolf's young" (ll. 569–70).

[56] See Richard Haven, *Patterns of Consciousness*, pp. 29–30, and Paul Magnuson, *Coleridge's Nightmare Poetry*, p. 62.

autonomy and the first violation of the laws of nature. The specter ship moves without wind, without indeed any apparent motive power at all — as fits the instrument of retribution for a motiveless crime. When the Mariner's ship becomes spectral itself, it moves the same way, powered by the absence of wind, which in this case is something other than mere stillness.

> And soon I heard a roaring wind:
> It did not come anear;
> But with its sound it shook the sails,
> That were so thin and sere.
>
> . . . .
>
> The loud wind never reached the ship,
> Yet now the ship moved on!
> Beneath the lightning and the Moon
> The dead men gave a groan.
>
> They groaned, they stirred, they all uprose,
> Nor spake, nor moved their eyes:
> It had been strange, even in a dream,
> To have seen those dead men rise.
> The helmsman steered, the ship moved on;
> Yet never a breeze up-blew. . . . (309–12, 327–36, 1817 ed.)[57]

Natural wind exists as a constant moving away from itself; its condition, like that of language, is differential. This wind, curiously independent of the movement of air, affects things not by presence, not by absence, but — so to speak — by the absence of that natural absence in which normal wind consists: only the sound or voice of its roaring ever reaches the ship. It behaves like a metonymy of its own metonymic potential, a deconstructive metalepsis that leaves nature, causality, and identity behind. Its appearance amounts to a confession of allegory, voice that lives in despair of its object.

The association between wind and language is, of course, ancient and universal.[58] Traditionally, poetic wind, bearing the voice and breath

---

[57] In 1798 the wind "reach'd the ship . . . And dropp'd down, like a stone!"

[58] In Sanskrit, Hebrew, Greek, Latin, Japanese, and other languages, the word for "wind" doubles as the word for "spirit." M. H. Abrams discusses the ubiquity of the association and Coleridge's relationship to it in "The Correspondent Breeze: A Romantic Metaphor," in *The Correspondent Breeze: Essays on English Romanticism* (New York: W. W. Norton, 1984), pp. 37–54.

Many critics have seen in the wind of the *Rime* a symbol of the mind or the creative of the muse into the very body of the human singer, guaranteed the truth of song: it testified to a metaphysics of presence. And so Coleridge was content to regard it until as late at least as 1795, when he imagined it sweeping, "Plastic and vast, one intellectual breeze, / At once the Soul of each, and God of all," over a world of Eolian harps.[59] A similar ideal, albeit expressed in the mode of despair, would lie behind the "Dejection" ode, whose wind the poet imagines no longer as an ecstatic, impersonal power but now as the magical counterpart to his own blocked voice, capable not only of expressing all he cannot but also of reviving that lost state in which nature and consciousness were one. He wants, in Frost's words, not "copy speech" but "original response," neither inspiration nor an interpreter but an echo that reestablishes his dialogue with what now he only gazes at " — and with how blank an eye!" Though he argues that "from the soul itself must there be sent / A sweet and potent voice, of its own birth," the priority of the internally generated voice is uncertain; the poet still yearns for the "wonted impulse" of a storm that "Might startle this dull pain, and make it move and live!" By the time the storm has risen and Coleridge has realized that he has recovered his voice, the wind has become his double, and it is impossible to locate the origin of the voice it represents.

The "Rime"'s uncanny wind, like those of the "Eolian Harp" and the "Dejection" ode, is allied with language and with spirit, but in uncomfortable ways. It is not life-giving, truthful, or cathartic, and the way it raises spirits is not cheering. Though it takes the form of spirits, it is not spiritual: insisting upon its independence, it usurps upon the souls and bodies of those it occupies, substituting voice for intentionality and turning those it inspires into zombies. It is a demonic version of the force the two conversation poems invoke, an allegory of influence, enacting the horrors against which those more traditional representations are meant to defend.

The "Rime," like the Mariner, is obsessed with its need to talk about itself and its relation to speech but never quite manages to name

impulse. See, for example, Maud Bodkin, *Archetypal Patterns in Poetry: Psychological Studies of Imagination* (London: Oxford University Press, 1934), pp. 30, 34–35; Richard Harter Fogle, "The Genre of The Ancient Mariner," *Tulane Studies in English* 7 (1957), 123–24; and Robert Penn Warren, "A Poem of Pure Imagination: An Experiment in Reading," in *Selected Essays* (1941; rpt. New York: Random House, 1958), pp. 237–38.

[59]Eight years later Coleridge was still playing with the image. Ideas, he wrote, do not recall ideas "any more than Leaves in a forest create each other's motion — The Breeze it is that runs thro' them / it is the Soul, the state of Feeling — ." See letter #510, to Robert Southey, 7 August 1803, in *STCL*, II, p. 961.

its subject. The poem is filled with emblems and allegories of its history and constitution: the Mariner possessed by his "strange power of speech" and the dead crew whose bodies house the spirits that sometimes sing and sometimes sail are working through aspects of inspiration, influence, and intertextuality. Just how terrifying these issues could seem to Coleridge we may see in a passage that appeared in the 1798 edition before being suppressed. The Mariner has just encountered the specter ship. Life-in-Death whistles, and a wind responds by whistling back at her through Death:

> A gust of wind sterte up behind
> And whistled thro' his bones;
> Thro' the holes of his eyes and the hole of his mouth
> Half-whistles and half-groans. (195–98)

It plays upon him as upon some ghastly Aeolian harp — a strange power of speech indeed. These lines, along with some other details of grossly Gothic character, were purged from the poem by 1800 in an attempt to placate the critics,[60] whose voices, like so many others, found lodging in Coleridge's text. But the mysterious behavior of the wind, something hostile critics pounced upon as "absurd, or unintelligible"[61] and even friendly readers found disturbing,[62] remained in place.

Like the wind, the "Rime" denies its origins: no original language, no language of spirits, no motivation, no proper causes. It gives us imitations, repetitions, representations — but no originals. It constitutes its own motivation; its telling demands the explanation its retelling, like the reenactment of Freudian transference, fails to provide. Yet the surprising thing is not, finally, that the "Rime" feels and fears the influence of outer or earlier voices, that its originality is open to question, but that the poem works so hard to put itself in second place, to confess and exhibit its secondariness. It shudders at alien voices, but it shudders at its own voice — thoroughly haunted, possessed, dispossessed,

---

[60]B. R. McElderry, Jr., shows that Coleridge took his critics' criticisms seriously enough to follow whatever particular changes in diction they recommended and to work on passages that aroused special ire ("Coleridge's Revision of 'The Ancient Mariner,'" p. 71).

[61]Robert Southey, quoted in Hayden, p. 4.

[62]For example, Lamb, in a letter to Southey intended as a defense of the poem, deplored a passage about the supernatural behavior of the wind as "fertile in unmeaning miracles." See Jackson, p. 60.

and characterless, and thereby most deeply and characteristically Coleridgean — most of all.

Divided from himself as from other men, inhabiting a world of baffling disjunction, and speaking a language neither whose motive force nor whose meaning is apparent, the Mariner is in no position to tell who he is. In a world where identity fails to coincide with character, where motivations are external and apparently autonomous, the difficulty of naming himself would be enormous. Perhaps the "Rime" really is the shortest answer to the Hermit's question, demonstrating the difficulty of saying "I am" in one's own voice.

WORKS CITED

Arac, Jonathan. "Repetition and Exclusion: Coleridge and New Criticism Reconsidered," *The Question of Textuality: Strategies of Reading in Contemporary American Criticism.* Ed. William V. Spanos, Paul A. Bové, and Daniel O'Hara. Bloomington: Indiana UP, 1982.

Bate, Walter Jackson. *Coleridge.* 1968. Cambridge: Harvard UP, 1987.

Brown, Homer Obed. "The Art of Theology and the Theology of Art: Robert Penn Warren's Reading of Coleridge's *The Rime of the Ancient Mariner.*" *The Question of Textuality: Strategies of Reading in Contemporary American Criticism.* Ed. William V. Spanos, Paul A. Bové, and Daniel O'Hara. Bloomington: Indiana UP, 1982.

Coleridge, Samuel Taylor. *Collected Letters of Samuel Taylor Coleridge.* Ed. Earl Leslie Griggs. 6 vols. Oxford: Clarendon, 1956–1971.

———. *Miscellaneous Criticism.* Ed. Thomas Middleton Raysor. London: Constable, 1936.

———. *The Poetical Works of Samuel Taylor Coleridge.* 1912. Ed. Ernest Hartley Coleridge. 2 vols. Oxford: Clarendon, 1979.

Friedman, Albert. *The Ballad Revival: Studies in the Influence of Popular on Sophisticated Poetry.* Chicago: U of Chicago, 1961.

Hartman, Geoffrey H. *Beyond Formalism: Literary Essays, 1958–1970.* New Haven: Yale UP, 1970.

Jackson, J.R. de J., ed. *Coleridge: The Critical Heritage.* London: Routledge, 1970.

Jakobson, Roman and Morris Halle. "Two Aspects of Two Types of Aphasic Disturbances." *Fundamentals of Language.* 4th ed. New York: Mouton, 1980.

Lowes, John Livingston. *The Road to Xanandu: A Study in the Ways of the Imagination.* Boston: Houghton, 1927.

———. *Coleridge's Nightmare Poetry.* Charlottesville: U of Virginia, 1974.

Reed, Arden. *Romantic Weather: The Climates of Coleridge and Baudelaire.* Hanover, NH: U of New England, 1983.

Schulman, Samuel. "Wordsworth's Spenserian Voice." Diss. Yale U, 1978.

Southey, Robert. *Critical Review.* October, 1798. *Romantic Bards and British Reviewers: A Selected Edition of the Contemporary Reviews of the Works of Wordsworth, Coleridge, Byron, Keats and Shelley.* Ed. John O. Hayden. Lincoln: U of Nebraska P, 1971.

Wordsworth, William. *Lyrical Ballads: The texts of the 1798 edition with the additional 1800 poems and the Prefaces.* Ed. R. L. Brett and A. R. Jones. London: Methuen, 1963.

———. *Lyrical Ballads 1798.* 2nd ed. Ed. W. J. B. Owen. Oxford UP, 1969.

———. *The Prose Works of William Wordsworth.* Ed. W. J. B. Owen and Jane Worthington Smyser. 3 vols. Oxford: Clarendon, 1974.

Combining Perspectives
on the "Rime"

Each of the previous essays exemplifies, as much as possible, a "pure" reading from a single contemporary critical perspective. As much as possible, each of the previous essays: (1) reflects the relatively consistent assumptions held by those who practice one well-established approach to literature; and (2) demonstrates the rhetorical moves of those who have written in that particular tradition of criticism.

But much hangs on the phrase "as much as possible." Criticism emerges from the interplay of the traditional (what has been thought and expressed before) and the individual (the critical intellect that any single reader brings to the text). Arguably, only Freud could have written a "pure" example of psychoanalytic criticism, only Marx a "pure" example of the Marxist approach, only Derrida a "pure" deconstruction. And even those thinkers were hardly pure originals; each would see himself as working in a tradition of analysis — though swerving usefully, perhaps uniquely, from what had gone before.

So far, then, this volume's emphasis has been on mapping out and demonstrating the broad outlines of particular, influential modern critical traditions. In examining this final essay, by Paul H. Fry, the emphasis is reversed, for "Wordsworth in the 'Rime'" demonstrates the permeability of those traditions, implicitly suggesting how supposedly disparate assumptions can be held simultaneously and how supposedly diverse rhetorical conventions can mix, merge, and metamorphose. To

put it more plainly, Fry's essay allows us to see how a critic can draw on
the insights of *several* critical traditions (in effect, combining perspectives) to present a view of a work unavailable from any one window, any
single critical perspective.

Admittedly, Fry begins his analysis by promising to "perform an
exercise in reader-response criticism" insofar as that "to study a human
relationship is always to perform an exercise in reader-response criticism" and insofar as his essay, though focused on Coleridge's "Rime,"
is fundamentally "about the relationship between Wordsworth and
Coleridge" (320). Immediately thereafter, however, he signals his
intention to push the envelope of the reader-response approach, admitting that he has exercised a "bold choice among the 'reader-response'
options" by focusing not on the reader-'Rime' relationship but, rather,
on the Wordsworth-Coleridge relationship as one involving *readers*
reading and responding to one another in their writings. Arguing that
this influence, or *inter*fluence, began as the two poets read and
responded to one another's drafts even before the first edition of *Lyrical Ballads* had been published, Fry writes: "I shall make the riskier
decision to refer to a tissue of allusions to the "Rime" in Wordsworth's
1798 poems . . . as though Wordsworth in these poems were saying,
'This is what Coleridge evidently thinks I would say, and to some extent
he is right, but he misunderstands why I would say it, and I am now
going to set him straight'" (321).

Before Fry reads Wordsworth's readings of Coleridge, however, he
approaches Coleridge as a "reader" of Wordsworth — and the "Rime"
as a reading of Wordsworth's earliest poetry. Maintaining that Coleridge "read" Wordsworth as a "'Semi-atheist,'" Fry goes on to suggest
that the "Rime" may be "considered a commentary on Wordsworth's
alleged version of natural religion" (323) (a religion perhaps best
summed up in Wordsworth's "Tintern Abbey," in which Wordsworth
calls himself a "worshipper of nature"). Coleridge's depiction of the
Wedding Guest listening to the Mariner as would a "three-years' child"
is said by Fry to be "pure Wordsworth," but the nature depicted for the
Wedding Guest by the Mariner is less than pure (and remains so
throughout the "Rime"'s various editions). For Coleridge, "there is
only one state of nature, benign but amoral and lacking in freedom, and
curative only to a relative degree of the wounds for which it is responsible" (329).

In the "Rime" and in Wordsworth's poem "The Idiot Boy," both
of which were published in the first edition of *Lyrical Ballads,* calm is
portrayed through a state — Fry calls it one of "indifference" — in

which the unification of disparate things is symbolized by a sun confused with a moon. (In "The Idiot Boy," a nighttime sun "did shine so cold"; in Coleridge's "Rime," "the bloody sun" appears "No bigger than the moon.") But Wordsworthian calm, in Coleridge's poetry, is a "terrifying," *non*beatific, state; indeed, according to Fry, "the state of Wordsworthian indiscrimination is a horrific nightmare" (330) for Coleridge. Treating this difference of opinion as one between writers who are reading one another and readers who are (re)writing one another, Fry identifies the Hermit in the "Rime" as Wordsworth (who puts a reconfigured version of the questions Coleridge's Hermit asks the Mariner to the Leech Gatherer in his later poem "Resolution and Independence" [1807]).

In the last analysis, Fry sides with Wordsworth against Coleridge, suggesting that Wordsworth "saw farther into the penetralium of the mystery" than did his coauthor and collaborator (336). After viewing the "Rime" as Coleridge's argument with poems Wordsworth had written and was likely to write, Fry reads "The Thorn," "The Idiot Boy," and other poems by Wordsworth as more successful arguments by Wordsworth — as arguments *against* Coleridge's anti-Wordsworthian devaluation of the (hermitlike) life in nature, and as arguments *for* his own, anti-Coleridgean views that nature is harmonious and instructive, and that dwelling in place, in nature, is as valuable as voyaging afar in search of truth because nature is mind as well as world.

By revealing his own personal, critical preferences, Fry exhibits a tendency emerging among practitioners of several contemporary critical approaches: the tendency to admit that critical analyses are inherently biased. As indicated in the introduction to the new historicism (found earlier in this volume), new historicists believe that, as critics describing literary works in terms of shaping historical discourses, they are duty bound to acknowledge that their own analyses are similarly time bound and determined. Meanwhile, recent feminist and gender critics, countering the pose of objectivity struck by formalists and New Critics (see the introductions to deconstruction and reader-response criticism, also found earlier in this volume), have argued that all criticism is "personal" — and that the "objectivity" of formalists and New Critics is in fact shot through with the biased assumptions that were shared by white, heterosexual, intellectually elite white males of the 1950s and 1960s. And reader-response practitioners, especially "subjectivists" at the extreme end of the spectrum (see the introduction to this approach earlier in the volume), have assumed that the meaning of a text is, to a great extent, what the individual reader makes of it.

Fry, who associates his essay with reader-response criticism but who is hardly a subjectivist, never goes that far. Indeed, the above paragraph is not meant to suggest that Fry's expressed personal preference for Wordsworth over Coleridge is made possible by discrete but converging views that *all* views are necessarily biased. Rather, it is meant to demonstrate one of a number of ways in which various theoretical schools and approaches are coming to share common views justified by overlapping, or at least analogous, assumptions.

If one were to insist upon an association between Fry's essay and one of the critical approaches identified in this volume, it might ultimately be easier to align Fry's "Wordsworth and the 'Rime,'" which ultimately is as much about intertextuality (the mutual influence of texts upon texts) with poststructuralist criticism or deconstruction, than with new-historicist, gender, or reader-response theory. Fry's text, after all, is about the ongoing interplay between texts by Coleridge and Wordsworth, Wordsworth and Coleridge. It may be, however, that Fry's approach to the "Rime" owes more to the "antithetical criticism" developed by Harold Bloom — and to the reader-reception theory of Hans Robert Jauss — than to either reader-response criticism or the new historicism, let alone to feminist or gender theory. Bloom incorporated psychoanalytic theory, especially Freud's theory of the Oedipus complex, to suggest that poets in the Western canon are frustrated and made anxious by the achievements of "father figures" who influenced them. In his essay "Coleridge: The Anxiety of Influence," Bloom has written specifically about the "anxiety of influence" Coleridge suffered regarding Wordsworth: "From 1795 on," Bloom writes, "Coleridge knew, loved, envied, was both cheered and darkened by the largest instance of [the] Sublime since [John] Milton himself . . . Wordsworth." During the period when both poets were preparing works (including the "Rime") for the *Lyrical Ballads,* in which they intended to introduce a new type of poetry — and which most scholars credit with inaugurating the Romantic period in English Literature — Coleridge's anxiety might well have become intense.

Synthesizing a number of approaches (while mapping out his own), Fry defines a process of mutual influence — *inter*fluence — that was endemic to and that (re)created their relationship, that involved a poetic exchange the overtones of which were grounded in personal (but also historically determined) differences at a crucial moment in literary history.

Ross C Murfin

WORKS CITED

Bloom, Harold. *The Anxiety of Influence*. New York: Oxford UP, 1973.

————. *A Map of Misreading*. New York: Oxford UP, 1975.

Jauss, Hans Robert. *Aesthetic Experience and Literary Hermeneutics*. Minneapolis: U of Minnesota P, 1982.

————. "Literary History as a Challenge to Literary Theory." *New Directions in Literary History*. Ed. Ralph Cohen. London: Routledge, 1974.

————. *Towards an Aesthetics of Reception*. Trans. Timothy Bahti. Introd. Paul de Man. Brighton: Harvester, 1982.

PAUL H. FRY

Wordsworth in the "Rime"

> He singeth loud his godly hymns
> That he makes in the wood.
> "The Rime of the Ancient Mariner" (1817 l.514–15)

There is a lot of intellectually engaging commentary on the relationship between Wordsworth and Coleridge. Although this literature has frequently been biographical, not just in the fine standard lives of each poet but also in many of the studies pairing them, quite a bit of work has been done, at the other extreme, on the interchange of verbal allusion, most notably in books by Paul Magnuson, Lucy Newlyn, and — rendering allusion finally a matter of ventriloquism — Susan Eilenberg. In addition, there have been studies that are best characterized as dialogues in intellectual history.[1] Of course it oversimplifies to

[1] Of the many biographies, I mention only the most recent distinguished examples in each case: Stephen Gill, *William Wordsworth: A Life* (Oxford: Clarendon, 1989) and Richard Holmes, *Coleridge: Early Visions* (New York: Viking, 1989). Works focusing on verbal allusion are: Mary Jacobus, *Tradition and Experiment in Wordsworth's "Lyrical Ballads"* (Oxford: Clarendon, 1976); Gordon Thomas, "Rueful Woes, Joyous Hap: The Associate Labor of 'The Idiot Boy' and 'Christabel,'" *The Wordsworth Circle* 14–15 (1983–84): 84; Neil Freistat, *The Poem and the Book: Interpreting Collections of Romantic Poetry* (1985) 41–94; Lucy Newlyn, *Coleridge, Wordsworth, and the Language of Allusion* (Oxford: Clarendon, 1986); Paul Magnuson, *Coleridge and Wordsworth: A Lyrical Dialogue* (Princeton: Princeton UP, 1988); and Susan Eilenberg, *Strange Power of Speech: Wordsworth, Coleridge, and Literary Possession* (New York: Oxford UP, 1992). Studies ranging in between these emphases are: H. M. Margoliouth, *Wordsworth and Coleridge*

divide the field in this way, if only because all three choices of emphasis have the same end in view: How did Coleridge and Wordsworth resemble one another and how — and when — did they differ? To study a human relationship is always to perform an exercise in reader-response criticism, and that is what I propose to do in my turn, like my predecessors. However, following only Magnuson and Eilenberg in this respect, I shall use "The Rime of the Ancient Mariner" as a special point of intersection, where the two poets — I shall claim — can be found reading each other.

Let me say right away what I hope to accomplish that is new, and why I find the "Rime" a good text for the purpose. First, I think the "Rime" shows that in late 1797 Wordsworth and Coleridge were already conscious, mutually conscious, of the disagreements that most commentators consider to have surfaced only amid the circumstances surrounding the publication of *Lyrical Ballads* a year later, disagreements that then led, all agree (frequently using the ensuing history of the "Rime" as evidence), to a series of well-documented moments of deepening estrangement: Wordsworth's unforgivably cavalier treatment — and Coleridge's uneasy revisions — of the "Rime," linked to disagreements about the role of the supernatural (entailing a number of weighty metaphysical and literary questions); the tense, rhetorically generous conversations about "the great philosophical poem" that Coleridge wanted Wordsworth to write; the poetic dialogue of 1802 enacted between the drafts of "Dejection" and the first four strophes of the Intimations Ode, with glances back to "Tintern Abbey" by both writers; Wordsworth's pseudo-Coleridgean preface to his Collected Edition of 1815; and Coleridge's long-harbored critique of Wordsworth in the *Biographia Literaria* of 1817 — together with all the equally well known interpersonal frictions of the same period. But these lines of disagreement are already drawn, I shall claim, in the "Rime" itself; and I shall claim further that once one sees them there they show

1795–1834 (Hamden: Archon, 1966); A. S. Byatt, *Wordsworth and Coleridge in Their Time* (London: Nelson, 1970); William Heath, *Wordsworth and Coleridge: A Study of Their Literary Relations in 1801–1802* (Oxford: Clarendon, 1970); Thomas McFarland, *Romanticism and the Forms of Ruin: Wordsworth, Coleridge, and Modalities of Fragmentation* (Princeton: Princeton UP, 1981); Jonathan Wordsworth, *William Wordsworth: The Borders of Vision* (Oxford: Clarendon, 1982); Richard Gravil, "Imagining Wordsworth: 1797 — 1807 — 1817," *Coleridge's Imagination*, ed. Richard Gravil, Lucy Newlyn, Nicholas Roe (Cambridge: Cambridge UP, 1985); Raimonda Modiano, "Coleridge and Wordsworth: The Ethics of Gift Exchange," *The Wordsworth Circle* 20:2 (1989): 113–20; and Gene Ruoff, *Wordsworth and Coleridge: The Making of the Major Lyrics* (New Brunswick: Rutgers UP, 1989).

that even the later intellectual divergence between the two is greater than is commonly believed.

My evidence will be of various sorts, but will hinge most crucially on a perhaps somewhat bold choice among the "reader-response" options. I shall infer the presence of an in itself not unfamiliar dialogue between the poets in text-specific terms, but I shall draw more from subsequent evidence than from past evidence. In contrast with Magnuson, who is able to establish interesting links among the "Rime," Wordsworth's already-existing "Adventures on Salisbury Plain," and his evidently direct response in "The Discharged Soldier" (composed before the "Rime" was finished), I shall make the riskier decision to refer a tissue of allusions to the "Rime" in Wordsworth's 1798 poems prepared for *Lyrical Ballads* back into the text of the "Rime," as though Wordsworth in these poems were saying, "This is what Coleridge evidently thinks I would say, and to some extent he is right, but he misunderstands why I would say it, and I am now going to set him straight." Having elsewhere written in comparable terms linking Wordsworth's *The Idiot Boy* and Coleridge's *Christabel* in what might be called a mutual reading,[2] I shall be especially interested here in the mutual reading that takes place between the "Rime" and a great many Wordsworth poems — including *The Idiot Boy* — written over the next two years.[3]

However, there is one asymmetry in this mutual reading, as it might be called, that should be stressed at the outset. I don't think there is any evidence that Coleridge for his part is saying, at any point, "This is what Wordsworth thinks I would say, but he misunderstands why I would say it, and I am now going to set him straight." The reason for this is no doubt in part psychological. Only those who believe that all was perfect amity and agreement during those first walks across the Quantocks believe that there was as yet no trace of insecurity, hence no compulsive

---

[2] Paul H. Fry, *A Defense of Poetry: Reflections on the Occasion of Writing* (Stanford: Stanford UP, 1995) 101–03.

[3] I leave *Peter Bell* aside simply because it did not appear in *Lyrical Ballads*, but there is little doubt that indeed it is this poem that is Wordsworth's concerted and systematic response to the "Rime." See Margoliouth, *Wordsworth and Coleridge 1795–1834* (29), and Newlyn, *Coleridge, Wordsworth, and the Language of Allusion* (50–51) (*Peter Bell*, she says, is customarily read as an "every-day" retort to the "Rime"). For reasons less easy to justify, I shall have nothing to say about "Hart-Leap Well," which features the blighting of the natural world ensuing upon the shooting of an innocent animal. For pertinent comments, see Jonathan Wordsworth, *William Wordsworth: The Borders of Vision* (137–38).

deference to his friend, on Coleridge's part. But I think it also has to do with the differing nature of the two poets' minds and ideas.

The fact is, Coleridge runs less risk of being misunderstood. He is in one sense the more "difficult" of the two, yet in another sense he leaves relatively little doubt in the competent reader's mind: one needs a good deal of philosophy and theology, together with a taste for aesthetic convolution and a knowledge of his highly conscious changes of opinion, to be certain of what Coleridge is saying; but readers in possession of these prerequisites have in fact formed a broad consensus about his main ideas and local meanings that has remained in place since his own time.[4] The "Rime" itself is only an apparent exception: the wildly divergent readings of this poem, with R. P. Warren and E. E. Bostetter stationed at the Christian and nihilistic extremes, and the fact that it lends itself to so many different reading methods, leave an impression at last that is wonderfully composite, building a cumulative reading of a poem that we all continue to recognize in its self-identity.[5] In the case of Wordsworth, on the other hand, there are relatively few superficial impediments to understanding, yet intelligent readers have always disagreed wildly, and continue to disagree, about the meaning, the purport, even the very raison d'être, of his poetry. If Coleridge's expression is sometimes obscure, Wordsworth's premises are nearly always obscure (so overdetermined or underdetermined that they explain everything but the poetry), and thus it is Wordsworth who is always the prime candidate to be misunderstood. Compare the conflicting readings of "A Slumber Did My Spirit Seal" in their cumulative effect with what I have just said about the conflicting readings of the "Rime." And Wordsworth is misunderstood not least, I shall want to say, by Coleridge, at least in Wordsworth's own opinion. One can read the rest of the 1798 volume, culminating in "Tintern Abbey" with its comment both on the "Rime" and on "Frost at Midnight," as Wordsworth's way of saying, "That is not what I meant. That is not what I meant at all." Not what he meant, certainly, in "Adventures on Salis-

---

[4]Max L. Schulz stresses the degree of underlying agreement among interpreters of Coleridge: *The Poetic Voices of Coleridge* (Detroit: Wayne State UP, 1963) 54. On whether, and why, Coleridge is intelligible, see Frances Ferguson, "Coleridge and the Deluded Reader: 'The Rime of the Ancient Mariner,'" pages 125–26 in this book. For an explanation of why the "Rime" is a standard, but wholly accessible, text for introduction to interpretation courses, see Jerome J. McGann, "The Ancient Mariner: The Meaning of the Meanings," *The Beauty of Inflections: Literary Investigations in Historical Method and Theory* (Oxford: Clarendon, 1988) 135.

[5]For a different approach to this emergent coherence, see McGann, "The Ancient Mariner" (135–72).

bury Plain" and "The Discharged Soldier" and *The Borderers* (with the problematic of the returned expatriate giving the "Rime" its narrative base in all three instances), but not what he meant also and just as interestingly in those moments of the "Rime" when Wordsworth thinks he hears himself saying things that he wouldn't have said, or said for different reasons.

Wordsworth's reading of the "Rime" I shall actually take up here as a kind of afterthought. I shall be mainly concerned to consider the "Rime" as a reading of Wordsworth — both of his oeuvre to date and also of what Coleridge must have deduced from his conversation, especially in view of Coleridge's opinion, expressed in 1796, that Wordsworth was "at least a *Semi*-atheist."[6] Of course, it is not easy to know just what Coleridge meant by this epithet. Most probably he thought that Wordsworth's tentatively formulated pantheism (influenced in part by the odd, "sympathetic" behavior of natural objects reported in Erasmus Darwin's *Zoönomia*) was just too vague and too frankly intuitive to harbor any definite transcendental principle. Between the profession of faith in natural religion and the expression of sympathy with the beings of the natural world there is no reliable distinction, Coleridge seems to have felt; and his feeling in turn seems confirmed when Wordsworth in "Tintern Abbey" calls himself "a worshipper of nature" — a phrase that Wordsworth himself, grown more conventionally pious, later regretted.

Suppose, then, that the "Rime" were to be considered a commentary on Wordsworth's alleged version of natural religion. We can learn that Coleridge had this issue much on his mind by looking no farther than two of his three other contributions to the 1798 *Lyrical Ballads* (setting aside "Lewti: The Indian Love Chant," which appears in the withdrawn print run of some fifty copies). "The Foster-Mother's Tale" (exerpted from a tragedy, *Osorio,* which Coleridge had recently composed with a view to performance in London) describes the educational growth of a boy subject only to the influences of nature, like Wordsworth's 1798 poem called "The Boy of Winander" (eventually part of *The Prelude*), the draft for which was prefaced by a brief attack on pedantic schooling: "most unteachable," Coleridge's boy "knew the names of birds, and mock'd their notes, / And whistled, as he were a bird himself." He planted wildflowers "on the stumps of trees," and was raised by "A Friar, who gathered simples in the wood," presenting

[6]See E. L. Griggs, ed., *Collected Letters of Samuel Taylor Coleridge,* 6 vols. (Oxford: Clarendon, 1956) I, 215–16. See also I, 192–93, for passages attacking the materiality of Priestley's God.

thereby a composite image of the Hermit in the "Rime" and the mossy stump that serves him as an altar. This boy becomes an obscurely amoral young man, like the youth in Wordsworth who has lived among American savages (but whose childhood education is pointedly never mentioned) and who abandons Ruth in the poem of that name (late 1798). The fragment called "The Dungeon" (also from *Osorio*) returns in a seemingly more positive spirit to the Wordsworthian theme of education by the great outdoors, but sees this education as the chastening of an already-existing criminality that is merely superior to the supposed chastisement afforded by prison: "With other ministrations thou, O Nature! / Healest thy wandering and distemper'd child." For the Christian Coleridge, "nature" even at her most appealingly Wordsworthian can do no more than homeopathically cure the original sin with which she herself has infected her "child."[7]

Here I must pause to avoid another sort of misunderstanding. Many important critics, from Bostetter and William Empson on through to Jerome McGann and Richard Matlak, have read the "Rime" as an ironic attack on the trinitarian mysteries to which the Unitarian Coleridge was not yet converted — an approach that has been especially devastating to the "sacramental" emphasis of Warren's reading. On this view, the narrative, which concerns events in themselves perfectly natural, is filtered through the superstitious delusions of a pre-Reformation dotard and has to be understood as a critique, not just of Catholic and — by extension — High Church pieties but also, more broadly, of the belief that any form of received religion can successfully navigate the unsheltered soul though its encounter with the cruelty and immensity of the universe. In arguing that the issue raised by the poem is a religious one, and more particularly a critique of Wordsworth's nature worship, I intend no open or implied disagreement with the main thrust of these readings, which are in fact very close, as I shall show, to what appears to be Wordsworth's reading. What all such readings overlook, however, in sharing what Hans-Georg Gadamer calls the Enlightenment's "superstition against superstition," is that the issue between Coleridge and Wordsworth as *Lyrical Ballads* began to take shape, the issue that divided their tasks and made their collaboration on the "Rime" impossible, was precisely the role of superstition itself in the

---

[7]As Stanley Cavell points out, Coleridge in the *Biographia* criticized Wordsworth for calling the child a "philosopher" in the Intimations Ode (*In Quest of the Ordinary: Lines of Skepticism and Romanticism* [Chicago: U of Chicago P, 1988] 42). "I believe most steadfastly in original Sin," writes Coleridge in March 1798, "that from our mothers' wombs our understandings are darkened" (*Collected Letters* I: 396).

poet's journey toward understanding. It is nearly always for some reason assumed by readers of the *Biographia* account that the two poets
divided up the work arbitrarily, as if by drawing straws. But it was Coleridge and Coleridge alone who was interested in the "delusion" of
"supernatural agency" because he believed, and wanted to prove to
Wordsworth, that "dramatic truth" could be arrived at only through
the conduit of this delusion and by no other means.[8] That form of delusion in which poetry allows us to dwell is for Coleridge, as for Hegel,
the anthropocentric concretization of the metaphysical, but nothing
other than this delusion can reveal the necessary presence of the metaphysical behind the Hartleyan illusion (a form of disbelief within the
theocentric history of thought) that empiricism is a self-sufficient basis,
not just for epistemology but for theology.[9]

At the beginning of the "Rime," the Mariner comes upon a world
that from his point of view requires an infusion of sobriety. Its "merry
din" is founded on the idea that marriage, with its lusty, Burnsian flowering ("Red as a rose") and bold harmony (the loud bassoon rising
above the merry minstrelsy), is an adequate rite of communion. The
Wedding Guest is the one singled out among three companions
because even though they too appear to be guests he in particular is the
"next of kin" — is closest in belief and kind, that is, to the erroneous

---

[8]Note that in the dedicatory epistle (1819) to *Peter Bell*, Wordsworth stresses that
the imagination has no need of the supernatural. See Thomas McFarland, *Romanticism
and the Forms of Ruin: Wordsworth, Coleridge, and the Modalities of Fragmentation*
(Princeton: Princeton UP, 1981) 74. As Lawrence Lipking reminds us in this context,
Coleridge promised to preface the "Rime" with an essay on the supernatural ("The Marginal Gloss," *Critical Inquiry* 3 [1977]: 76).

[9]Of course it was Coleridge himself, not Wordsworth, who was the programmatic
Hartleyan through much of the 1790s, and it was he, too, who believed at one time that
he could prove that every aspect of thought was what we would now call neurophysiolog-
ical. One may suspect, though, that were it not for the enthusiastic theism of part two of
the *Observations on Man*, Coleridge could never have been a Hartleyan even for a
moment; and while the aggressive disavowal of Hartley that culminates in the *Biographia*
cannot yet be said to have begun (any more than the open disagreement with Wordsworth had begun), Coleridge's discovery of Berkeley at the end of 1796 had already
made him a different sort of monist, one who puts matter into mind rather than the other
way around. Wordsworth on the other hand held less programmatic views of the basis
of thought in the senses, views to be found in Locke and others, and never stopped
holding them. For good accounts of this issue, see Walter Jackson Bate, *Coleridge* (New
York: Macmillan, 1968) 32; and James D. Boulger, "Introduction," *Twentieth Century
Interpretations of "The Rime of the Ancient Mariner,"* ed. James D. Boulger (Englewood
Cliffs: Prentice, 1969) 15–16. For the contrary insistence, elaborated in detail, that
Coleridge remains a Hartleyan when writing the "Rime," see Dorothy Waples,
"David Hartley in 'The Rime of the Ancient Mariner,'" *Journal of English and Germanic
Philogy* 35 (1936): 337–51.

faith in natural communion that inspires the marriage.[10] The Mariner is not averse to society, but he finds it "sweeter" to go to church with a goodly company, he will eventually say, than to "the marriage-feast," and therefore the Wedding Guest, whose selection as listener has sometimes perplexed readers, is an obvious choice to be "Turned from the bridegroom's door" and sent home a more soberly reflective and "wiser man": "That moment that his face I see, / I know the man that must hear me" (1817 l.592–93).

One of the two passages we are told that Wordsworth contributed during the walk from Nether Stowey to Dulverton (or, as Wordsworth would have it, via Kilve to Watchet, returning though Dulverton), concerns the Wedding Guest duly mesmerized and listening "like a three-years' child." This is pure Wordsworth, we say at once, with our heads full of "Three years she grew," "two-years' child," "six-years' darling," and so forth; and with this in mind Wordsworth is slipping in his bit of what William Empson in *Some Versions of Pastoral* called "child cult" — the nineteenth-century sentimentalism, from Wordsworth to Lewis Carroll, which we have observed Coleridge subtly repudiating as it were in advance in the two published fragments from *Osorio*. In a way, though, Wordsworth's contributed expression suspends the issue of naiveté between the two poets: the listener in a state approaching the tabula rasa of infancy buttonholed by a dotard speaker joins that speaker in a condition outside of, and apparently inferior to, the ordinary sphere of human intercourse. That was the common project of Wordsworth and Coleridge: to see the ordinary, and rethink the nature of the ordinary, from the standpoint of the marginal — but always with opposite ends in view.

The Mariner immediately accomplishes this movement beyond and beneath the ordinary — but in proleptic fashion, as the process goes as "merrily" as the wedding feast itself — by getting his ship away from what Herman Melville in *Moby-Dick* would later call "the lee shore": "Below the kirk" (evoking low-church Presbyterian pieties that the medieval Mariner does not seem to share, any more than he belongs in the world of the seventeenth-century "bassoon" or "lighthouse"); "below the hill" (natural home of the Wordsworthian shepherd, a land-locked alternative to the Mariner's ocean, as *The Brothers* makes clear); and "Below the lighthouse top," which is allegorically identifiable as the Enlightment materialization of light sources (sun, moon, stars, all

[10]On the contrasting symbolizations of marriage in Wordsworth and Coleridge, see Milton Teichman, "The Marriage Metaphor in the 'Ancient Mariner,'" *Bulletin of the New York Public Library* 73 (1969): 45.

soon to irradiate the poem) that might otherwise be assimilated to ideas of transcendence. The top of a lighthouse is as high as you can go on land; but if you get "below" it, or below the height of a hill, or a steeple, you can go higher.

The coming of wind (l.45) Coleridge had trouble with even in 1798 ("Listen, Stranger!" is too insistent, making the Mariner's hypnotic powers seem less than perfect), and he kept changing the words in later editions: changing the line in the 1800 text (introducing a senseless comparative, "more fierce": yes, there has been a breeze, as the 1817 gloss points out, but it was not even a little fierce), having proposed a different line to Biggs and Cottle in a letter of that year,[11] and settling finally in 1817 on "And now the STORM-BLAST came." We know how important the sequence of wind and calm is for Coleridge, as when the apathetic calm of "Dejection" is dispersed by a gust of stormy imagination. For him the relation is dialectical, with states of death-in-life overtaking sometimes destructive but always exhilarating tempests of thought, and vice versa. The capitalization of 1817 stresses allegory ("and he / Was tyrannous and strong") and points toward the opposite and even more Miltonic allegory of "LIFE-IN-DEATH" at line 193. Here we find Coleridge in 1817 responding to Wordsworth's 1800 response to him, "A Whirl-blast from Behind the Hill" ("The wind sent from behind the hill" in a 1798 manuscript [Butler 283]), which represents a complex copresencing, rather than sequencing, of a hailstorm with the persisting calm of the sheltered bower it passes over. Wordsworth's version of *Stille in Bewegung* (stasis within motion) is an emblem of the mind's self-sufficiency in John Locke's philosophy, with the calmly receptive surface of the sensorium and the active imaginative principle operative together within the single faculty of understanding, shaped and fully naturalized as the spherical surface of a hillside bower. Coleridge, whose Mariner has long since dropped "below the hill," would simply see the calm of such a bower as "dead calm" of mind (the expression is from the 1798 "Frost at Midnight," and in a later version is revised to the more Wordsworthian "deep calm"). Such a calm may be the calm of landlocked normalcy or the calm of a windless ocean, and Coleridge views it as an unalterable state unless it is invigorated by

---

[11]In this same letter (Griggs I: 599), Coleridge also focused on revisions for the 1798 "Withouten wind, withouten tide" (l. 161), suggesting that at this point magic currents were much on his mind (see Martin Wallen, ed., *Coleridge's "Ancient Mariner": An Experimental Edition of Texts and Revisions 1798–1828* [Barrytown: Station Hill, 1993] 28). Again, note the conflict between the strong wind that reaches the ship in 1798 and the loud wind that does not reach the ship in 1800 (Wallen 51).

a strong wind "sent" (as Wordsworth himself had first written) from without, from some originary source outside the mind's immediate sphere and setting.

Driven helplessly southward, the Mariner is henceforth in a position to say that the compass of Wordsworthian tranquility is useless. It scarcely makes sense to say whether one navigates or is driven in such a state. Wordsworth in "Tintern Abbey" scrupulously attributes this confusion to a past condition, both a moment in his own life and a moment of pseudo-Gothic in eighteenth-century nature poetry, when nature "To me was all in all" — lacking as yet the ethical overtone of humanity's still sad music — and when he was "more like a man / Flying from something that he dreads, than one / Who sought the thing he loved." But Coleridge in 1817, lingering in revision over the storm-blast passage, replies sternly to Wordsworth that any orientation confining itself solely to the laws of the natural world must remain subject to this confusion between drivenness and agency: "As who pursued with yell and blow / Still treads the shadow of his foe, / And forward bends his head" (1817 l.46–48). Naturalism, in a word, is necessitarianism, and to get beyond that condition is to enact, with the Mariner, an unprecedented revolution in human consciousness: "We were the first that ever burst / Into that silent sea" (1817 l.105–06).

Without the compass of some external determinant, it is futile to interpret the signs of nature, or the signs clung to by natural man hungry for meaning. The Mariner has shot the Albatross: who knows why, or what it may portend? (Perhaps it was for food, as Empson suggests, the "biscuit-worms" of 1798 having spoiled the provisions.[12] The explanation is as good as any.) The Mariner himself is tempted by sacramental readings, and circumstance sways the crew to believe this or that yet more primitive omen. To this provocation Wordsworth responds at great length, seemingly in this case the more superstitious of the two, in "Nutting" and in the narratives of childhood trespass in the Two-Part *Prelude*, which include two offenses against birds. In these narratives he insists that nature's chastisement of man's environmental violations is unmistakable and infallible: "There is a Spirit in the woods." Once again, however, Wordsworth qualifies a clearly vulnerable argument by stressing that it pertains, like the confused submission of youth to natural law, only to an early phase of human development, a phase in which benevolence and superstition are mutually supportive instincts. He

[12]See Empson, "The Ancient Mariner," 1964, *Argufying,* ed. John Haffenden (Iowa City: U of Iowa P, 1987) 300 ("the darker Albatross mentioned in the anecdote of Shelvock . . . does, I am told, make a tolerable soup that would help to keep off scurvy").

would agree that in natural "breathings" and the like there is a strong affinity with the more openly gothic and horrific visions of his "Salisbury Plain" or of the mouldering gibbet-mast in the Hanged Man episode of the two-part *Prelude*. Coleridge for his part never wavers, however, concerning any phase of human growth, from the theme that links "The Foster-Mother's Tale," "The Dungeon," and the "Rime" together: there is only one state of nature, benign but amoral and lacking in freedom, and curative only to a relative degree of the wounds for which it is responsible.

The attack on Wordsworthian calm persists throughout the second, third, and fourth parts of the "Rime." When the idiot Johnny affirms the ontic identity of the sun and the moon ("The sun did shine so cold") at the end of *The Idiot Boy*, Wordsworth is recuperating the terrifying state of in-difference that prevails, from the Mariner's viewpoint, in a becalmed world:

> All in a hot and copper sky,
> The bloody Sun, at noon,
> Right up above the mast did stand,
> No bigger than the Moon. (111–14)

Wordsworth finding spiritual enlightenment in the unity of all things, qua things, can favor such a state, telling Coleridge in the 1805 *Prelude*, with what must be heavy irony:

> Thou art no slave
> Of that false secondary power by which
> In weakness we create distinctions, then
> Deem that our puny boundaries are things
> Which we perceive, and not which we have made.[13]

So far indeed does Coleridge believe in and value such a faculty (each accuses the other throughout this covertly fierce dialogue of being a slave) that I believe he is thinking rather bitterly of this passage when in the famous discussion of the imagination in the *Biographia Literaria*

---

[13]Although *The Prelude* was written "to Coleridge," there are many signs that Wordsworth often addresses himself; and although no one to my knowledge has gone so far as to say that Wordsworth sometimes criticizes Coleridge while pretending to enlist his agreement, there is a good account of the ways in which the apparent addressee is in fact Wordsworth himself in Eugene L. Selzig, "Coleridge in *The Prelude:* Wordsworth and the Fiction of Alterity," *The Wordsworth Circle* 19:3 (1988): 156–60.

(chapter 13), itself a masterpiece of distinctions made or perceived, he assigns the discriminatory power of writing poetry to "the secondary imagination," confining the primary imagination, to which Wordsworth supposes himself devoted, to the joyous but inarticulate *participation mystique* in the fiat of divine creation.[14]

Ordinarily for Coleridge, the state of Wordsworthian indiscrimination is a horrific nightmare. Without wind or current, nature rots, a mixture of primordial slime and parched aridity. Speech, *pace* Wordsworth, becomes impossible. Or rather, when it comes, aided by an act of autovampirism aptly corresponding to the grotesque person of the approaching female spectre, speech gets blurted out as Coleridge's own textbook example of the feeblest of all rhetorical devices, the synecdoche, or part taken for a whole: "A sail! A sail!"[15] Indeed a repetition in the finite mind, as Coleridge in part defined the primary imagination, this synecdochic speech (which serves no useful purpose, as many commentators have remarked) stands in deliberate contrast to what Coleridge always meant by the symbol.[16] Far from being a "translucence of the special in the individual, or of the general in the special," and so on,[17] synecdoche is an inorganic, dry transparency or false reflection, like the dessicated, barred sails of the death ship itself. The sun has to "peer" through rigging that is like a "dungeon grate" — and also, of course, like the ribs of an emaciated person, corpselike though alive. Synecdoche is the dungeon of perception, language as prison house.

[14]The most important recent revision of the way in which we think about this passage, especially in relation to Wordsworth, is that of Jonathan Wordsworth ("The Infinite I AM: Coleridge and the Ascent of Being," *Coleridge's Imagination,* ed. Richard Gravil, Lucy Newlyn, and Nicholas Roe [Cambridge: Cambridge UP, 1985]). In insisting, though, that the religious function of the primary imagination gives it greater importance than critics focused on the aesthetic have believed, Jonathan Wordsworth somewhat underplays the persisting fact that the secondary imagination alone is capable of producing poetry (see 46 ff.).

[15]The best account of the Mariner's cry as textbook synecdoche is that of Eilenberg, *Strange Power of Speech* (283–85). Eilenberg cites (6n.) the passage from Coleridge's *Miscellaneous Criticism* (ed. T. M. Raysor [London: Constable, 1936] 99) in which Coleridge gives "sail" as an example of synecdoche.

[16]Or nearly always. Coleridge is not always exalted even about the symbol, as in the *Notebooks* (ed. Kathleen Coburn [New York: Bollingen, 1957] II 2998), where he speaks of "the inadequacy of Words to Feeling, of the symbol to the Being" (cited also in this context by Raimonda Modiano, "Words and 'Languageless' Meanings: Limits of Expression in 'The Rime of the Ancient Mariner,'" *Modern Language Quarterly* 38 [1977]: 42).

[17]The famous passage from *The Statesman's Manual* is best known to modern readers from its discussion by Paul de Man in "The Rhetoric of Temporality," *Blindness and Insight: Essays in the Rhetoric of Contemporary Criticism,* 2nd ed. (Minneapolis: U of Minnesota P, 1983) 192.

Here one confronts what seems the most overdetermined figural recurrence in the poem: the skeletal ribs of persons or sea sands, bars or grates (with the barred clouds of "Dejection" and the fireplace grate of "Frost at Midnight" corresponding in important ways) through which nothing organically healthy can see or be seen, the veins of leaves along the Hermit's brook, and the rigging of ultrathin sails that are either slack or blown upon by supernatural agents. In the realm of natural symbol, poetry for Coleridge is language fanned by a current or wind: an aeolian harp, a ship under sail. But there is always the risk — the Wordsworthian risk — that this sort of imagery will lend itself to the disinspirited naturalism that is focussed allegorically in the 1817 "Rime" as Life-in-Death, the opposite of the STORM-BLAST. Allegory, synecdoche, a sail without its ship — that is all poetry is if it lacks what Wordsworth had so derisively called "the false secondary power." Hence a certain remystification is needed: in "Frost at Midnight," the *"stranger"* on the "bars" of the grate, seeming to survive even the last embers, burns like an ignis fatuus without a visible fuel source, and the creative frost itself, most memorably, is "Unhelped by any wind." This is why it is no accident, as Arden Reed has shown most fully, that after his Antarctic adventure the grizzled Mariner produces "rime," or hoarfrost.[18]

From the Mariner's point of view, however, at least at this point in the poem, the most frightening thing about the approach of the ghost ship is that it comes — like the ship that brings plague to Bremen in the later Dracula story — "without a breeze." But the Mariner is himself, as nearly all readers agree, at most but the vessel of understanding. It is one of the most extraordinary effects of Romanticism that Wordsworth and Coleridge together could transform the twin classical figures of the wise and virtuous *senex* and cunning but impotent *senex* into a single dotard and yet imbue that diminished figure, together with the child, the outcast, and the idiot, with the capacity to stumble "unawares" into the presence of radical truth. Here again the stream of Wordsworth and Coleridge runs in a common bed, but with a different source and destination; and it is at this point that one can observe the most complex and interesting interchange of opinion that takes place in the "Rime." It is possible to show, following the figural matrix here emphasized, that whereas Wordsworth subversively and mischievously associates the

---

[18]Reed convincingly elaborates this argument, which hinges on his reminder that, having removed nearly all other archaisms from the poem, Coleridge retained the spelling of "Rime" even in 1817 ("The Mariner Rimed," *Romanticism and Language,* ed. Arden Reed [Ithaca: Cornell UP, 1984] 168).

Coleridgean dungeon of perception with the Mariner, Coleridge in turn links this blindered state to the other *senex* of the poem, the Hermit, and furthermore brilliantly identifies the Hermit with Wordsworth.

The first part of this claim is easily established. The second documented verbal contribution of Wordsworth to the poem is the frightened outburst of the Wedding Guest, who thinks the Mariner a ghost and is made by Wordsworth to recall the sails of the ghost ship: "And thou art long and lank and brown / As is the ribb'd Sea-sand."[19] Wordsworth, who seems even on the first walk to have been subtly out of humor with the poem ("We found that our styles would not assimilate"), might well identify with the Wedding Guest, who has also resembled "a three-years' child" — his other contribution. A member of the wedding, Wordsworth recoils from the living dead and stands for the minstrelsy or spousal verse of mind to the natural world, while retaining that saving naiveté and directness that characterizes both Wordsworth's typical dramatis personae and his then-developing theory of poetic diction, featuring the "real language" of men rooted in rural life and its "best objects." From this dissenting standpoint, at least insofar as Wordsworth is thus able to subvert the mesmerism that conceals it, the Mariner is lost at sea without a sextant, all dried up, possibly not even alive.

Coleridge's comeback is reserved for the moment when the Mariner returns to the everyday, shoreline world of Wordsworth (both poets are then living near the broad Bristol Channel) and is greeted by Wordsworth himself in the person of the Hermit:

> THIS Hermit good lives in that wood
> Which slopes down to the sea.
> How loudly his sweet voice he rears!
> He loves to talk with marineres
> That comes from a far contrée. (518–22)

Here especially is the relevance of the returned sailor in "Adventures on Salisbury Plain" and "The Discharged Soldier." *The Brothers,* a "pastoral" conversation between a country parson and a returned sailor who would rather have remained a shepherd, will be one of Wordsworth's responses to these lines:

[19]McFarland (*Romanticism and the Forms of Ruin* 68) points out that in looking forward to the discharged soldier, the drowned man of Esthwaite, and the leech gatherer, the Mariner is "a projection from the psycho-dramatic center of Wordsworth's fantasy more than from that of Coleridge."

He kneels at morn, and noon and eve —
He hath a cushion plump:
It is the moss that wholly hides
The rotted old oak-stump.

Coleridge gently discredits the piety of the Hermit as the comfortably provincial repose of a person too close to the soil, soil whose very element is organic decay (the "rot" from which the Mariner had at first felt such revulsion).[20] The Hermit literally worships at the altar of nature. Coleridge then ascribes to the Hermit a reaction to the Mariner's ship — linking it to the ghost ship — that resembles the reaction to the Mariner assigned by Wordsworth to the Wedding Guest, adapting the same cluster of images to a sylvan setting. The Hermit's revulsion from the appearance of death cannot now be considered life-affirming, as was the alarm ascribed by Wordsworth to the Wedding Guest, so much as it is simply narrow, a landlocked form of superstition (in contrast with the Mariner's solitary and oceanic form) differing little in kind from that of the Pilot's boy:

The planks look warped! and see those sails,
How thin they are and sere!
I never saw aught like to them,
Unless perchance it were
The skeletons of leaves that lag[21]
My forest-brook along; (533–38)

— and here Coleridge adds an obviously gratuitous touch of horror-Gothic from the eighteenth-century models that both he and Wordsworth saw themselves as having advanced beyond, suggesting once again that Wordsworth cannot be allowed his belief that superstitious anthropomorphism is an adolescent phase through which the nature poet passes en route to a soberer account of universal sympathy. If you

[20]Robert Penn Warren saw that the Hermit's religion is close to the soil: he is "both priest of God and priest of nature ("A Poem of Pure Imagination: An Experimental Reading," 1946, *New and Selected Essays* [New York: Random, 1989] 379). This passage has not gone unobserved by the speculative — from Kenneth Burke deducing vaginal fear from "prayer-above-moss-hiding-rot" (*The Philosophy of Literary Form*, 1941 [New York: Vintage, 1953] 80) to the inference of castration from the stump by Donald Ault in his "Foreward" to Wallen's *Coleridge's 'Ancient Mariner'* (xiii).

[21]In view of Wordsworth's "And thou art long and lank and brown," discussed above, it is notable that "*Brown* skeletons of leaves that lag" was listed as an erratum in 1817 and so printed in 1828 (see Wallen, ed., *Coleridge's 'Ancient Mariner,'* 82).

are going to worship nature, in short, you'll never outgrow the fascina-
tions of the charnel-house:

> When the ivy-tod is heavy with snow,
> And the owlet whoops to the wolf below,
> That eats the she-wolf's young. (539–41)

It is easily overlooked that when the Hermit asks "What manner of man
art thou?" (a question Wordsworth may still be thinking about when in
"Resolution and Independence" [1802] he asks the Leech Gatherer,
"How is it that you live? What is it that you do?"), he becomes the first
person to whom the Mariner feels compelled to tell his tale; and this,
together with the fact that he is also one of three ("I saw a third")
shows him to need the same sort of education that the Wedding Guest
needs.[22] In "Tintern Abbey," Wordsworth will snatch this hermit back,
bestowing upon him, invisible at the heart of the woods, a solitude as
profound as the Mariner's.

Coleridge's point is not at all, obviously, that spiritual man needs to
be weaned away from the love of nature: the Albatross, the sea creatures, and above all the "moral" (adequate to its occasion or not)
would scarcely make any sense in that case. His point is, rather, that
human engagement with the natural world needs to be a dialectical
process if it is not finally to extinguish the spark of mind in the dank
moss of organicity. In order to recognize our autonomy, we need to
betray nature. The more seemingly without meaning the gesture is, the
better: tear off a hazel bough, rob a nest, shoot an albatross. But if we
superstitiously accept the imagined forgiveness of an admonishing environment (in Coleridge's view, the crew in good weather saying it must
have been a good thing to shoot the bird would be like Wordsworth in
The Prelude saying, oh well, at least stealing a rowboat taught me something), then the necessarily radical alienation that is initiated by our
trespass cannot take hold and we can never orient ourselves toward

---

[22]The character Leslie Brisman has dubbed "Porlock" ("Coleridge and the Ancestral
Voices," *Romantic Origins* [Ithaca: Cornell UP]), *passim.* comes closest in existing commentary to the figure I am linking with Wordsworth. With his "genial, natural accents"
(37), Brisman's Porlock must be "made to confront the undisturbed 'one life' that it is his
nature to interrupt" (43). Because "the primacy of the natural voice is Porlock's great
claim" (51), the Ancient Mariner necessarily "goes about seeking out the Porlocks, inter-
rupting marriage feasts for whatever increase in vision his power of voice can impart"
(52). In an excellent reading of the poem, Paul Magnuson points out that the Hermit is
"something of a poet" (*Coleridge's Nightmare Poetry* [Charlottesville: U of Virginia P,
1974] 73).

nature except from within its fundamental state, the state of rotting decay against which our alienation causes us to feel revulsion. The redemptive part of the dialectic, in which an externally induced, aesthetically driven glimmer of redemption[23] makes the Mariner find the sea creatures and the moving moon beautiful, is what Coleridge addresses in the fourth part of the poem. Falling into the sea like lead, the Albatross, which is neither a Dove nor an invisible "Lavrock," has been a material cross to bear, a natural burden. When the ship goes down later, also like lead, one can say that the tenor no longer needs its vehicle, any more than frost, or a ship propelled by spirits, needs wind — or any more than corpses, our natural bodies, can man the ship without the aid of spirits, or our human voices can tell the truth without "strange power of speech." Nature cannot resurrect nature, only transcendental consciousness can. Never mind the empiricist juggling act of what we half create and half perceive: "Ours is her wedding garment," — as Coleridge would write in "Dejection" — "ours her shroud." Even Wordsworth's trademark evocation of calm (most often *horror vacui* to Coleridge), as in his "Night Piece" of early 1798, is finally redeemed by Coleridge under the radiance of numinous agency:

> There was no breeze upon the bay,
>   No wave against the shore.
> The rock shone bright, the kirk no less
>   That stands above the rock:
> The moonlight steep'd in silentness
>   The steady weathercock. (1798 511–16)

The cost is steep. The Mariner is crazed, obsessive, permanently alone — a descendant of the Wandering Jew and an obvious precursor of Conrad's more sinister Kurtz. But the Mariner's solitude can be exaggerated. It is his business to talk to people, after all, and he has simply wanted to redefine the sort of company that it is best to go to church with, not to go there alone. His "woeful agony" can be ascribed in part to the pain of criticizing the attractive and beneficent natural religion of a friend. And as to the inadequacy of the "moral" ("Don't pull poor pussy's tail," wryly paraphrases Empson): well, the point Coleridge has been driving at all along, whatever his means of getting there, has been

[23]Newton P. Stallknecht in 1932 called this process "esthetic love" (*Strange Seas of Thought: Studies in Wordsworth's Philosophy of Man and Nature* [Bloomington: U of Indiana P, 1958] 151).

painfully simple, embarrassingly simple if even Anna Barbauld, who wrote didactic hymns for children, could feel that it was not a moral at all;[24] and Coleridge is speaking, he thinks, however much he may have revered Wordsworth from the beginning, to a three-years' child.

Insofar as one feels the need to choose, I incline to the side of Wordsworth, not Coleridge, hoping only to have prevented the reader from reaching this conclusion in what I have written so far. I cannot here go fully into the reasons why I think Wordsworth saw farther into the penetralium of the mystery than Coleridge — who nevertheless tried harder, as Keats indicates. All I can do is give Wordsworth almost the last word by examining those poems, written for the most part over the first six months of 1798, in which Wordsworth seems to be essaying various sorts of response to the "Rime," both to Coleridge directly and to the portrait of himself that he finds Coleridge to have smuggled into the poem.

In choosing this emphasis, I am very far from denying that the "Rime" was a tremendous inspiration to Wordsworth — that something about it and about its having been written made possible the best, one is tempted to say the most characteristic, poetry he had yet produced. I think it probable, however, that it was in fending off and reconstituting what he took to be Coleridge's misrepresentation of his poetic project that Wordsworth for the first time fully realized himself what that project really was; and if that is the case, then there is nothing inconsistent in my adversarial emphasis with the plain fact that Coleridge had inspired him. This supposition should also lend some credence to what may have raised a measure of suspicion about my procedure on the part of the attentive reader. Mine is largely a post hoc argument, as I have said. The criticism of Wordsworth that I have found in the "Rime" may seem too often to be directed at poetry that Wordsworth has not yet written. I have partly met this objection by supposing an anticipatory strain in Wordsworth's conversation of 1797, on analogy with the documentable fact that in intellectual outlook Keats's letters, for example, are a year or so ahead of his poetry. Thus if we find Coleridge in some degree inventing the Wordsworthian old man or indeed inventing the Wordsworthian idea that nature can be all in all, I think it nevertheless legitimate to infer that these and other such matters had been Wordsworth's topics all along.

---

[24]For the necessary contextualization of Coleridge's celebrated exchange with Anna Barbauld, see Ferguson, "Coleridge and the Deluded Reader" (120–22).

In Coleridge's poem we have found the following six separate admonitions to Wordsworth:

1. A mariner is a more heroic figure than a shepherd, as exploration is worthier than dwelling in place.
2. A merely natural calm is life-in-death, and mere passivity can have no merit apart from a transcendental doctrine of inspiration.
3. Dwelling too exclusively in natural process is a sign of dullness, even dotage, which is also a regression to the ignorance of childhood (exemplars being the Hermit, the three-years' child, and the Pilot's boy).
4. Failure to differentiate properly among objects is a sign of the mind's immersion in the ontic sameness of the natural world.
5. Nature is to some extent a healer, but not a teacher.
6. Nature is not, because it cannot be, a self-sufficient and self-originating entity, either as mind or as world.

I shall now take up Wordsworth's responses to these dicta, drawing exclusively on poems published in the 1798 *Lyrical Ballads* — concluding with remarks about the curious peace Coleridge seems to have made with all of his own objections in his last contribution to *Lyrical Ballads*, "The Nightingale."

"The Thorn," Wordsworth wrote in the 1800 edition, no doubt combating the critics' frequent assumption that the strain of fatuous garrulity in his poems is his own, is narrated by someone resembling

> a Captain of a small trading vessel. . . . Who being past the middle of life, had retired . . . to some country town of which he was not a native, or in which he had not been accustomed to live. Such men having little to do become credulous and talkative from indolence; and from the same cause, and other predisposing causes by which it is probable that such men may have been affected, they are prone to superstition. (Butler 350–51)

Here certainly is the old navigator in a diminished light, the "predisposing causes" left coyly unenumerated by Wordsworth being perhaps the experiences narrated in the "Rime." The issue of superstition is joined immediately, with the strong implication that it is not the Gothic elements of the story (the face in the pool, and so on) that will capture the sensible interlocutor's attention (no Wedding Guest he), but the pathos surrounding the madness of an abandoned unwed mother.

The narrator being out of his element miscasts this lamentable but quotidian event and its aftermath as a kind of inland "Rime:" "There was a thorn," he begins, echoing the Mariner's first words, and then describes the destruction of an innocent being, a child rather than an albatross, followed by the effort of penance in its presence. But all the symbols undermine his intent for them: the thorn itself, gnarled and no higher than "a two years' child," is a candidate to become a natural cross, like the Albatross, and possibly also a crown of thorns, but the gravitational force of the natural world, the mossy element of Coleridge's Hermit (thus child and *senex* are met, as vegetation, in the degree zero of their bodily existence), conspires to level it with all other organic being: the thorn has "no thorny points," it is overgrown with lichens "like a stone," and "heavy tufts of moss" conspire "[t]o bury this poor thorn for ever." This burial, subsiding into the organic mold, the thorn has in common with the equally moss-laden grave, which has all the phosphorescent-seeming colors of Coleridge's slimy sea (which "[b]urnt green and blue and white") — colors that this time from the beginning the retired captain, perhaps in spite of himself, finds to be "lovely": vermilion, olive-green, scarlet, and white.[25]

The pond, which is as small ("Two feet long and three feet wide") as the wide, wide sea was large, constitutes an element of destruction, drowning the child, rather than a medium of absolution that swallows up the Albatross and ship only when they no longer serve as instruments of atonement. There is water, water everywhere in the "Rime," but not a single instance of death by water. I remember thinking, as a youthful reader, how unlikely it was that when shot the wounded Albatross would fall into the ship — and Gustave Doré's illustration made it seem even less likely. Wordsworth in plotting "The Thorn" seems to have felt this as well. However the speaker of "The Thorn" may strain to reconstruct the "Rime," the visionary dreariness of the scene suggests rather that the truth of ontology is not oceanic but mineral. *Sta viator* (Halt, traveler), the admonition of a gravestone, is the occasion of many Wordsworth poems, beginning with the "Lines" left under a yew tree, and this moment has been humanistically revised by Coleridge as the Mariner's interception of the Wedding Guest: but the mountainous domain of shepherds and travellers proves to reveal more about life and death than the fluid element of mariners precisely in revealing less — as the narrator inadvertently admits:

---

[25]Wordsworth got the colors for the thorn from Dorothy Wordsworth's Alfoxden Journal, as James Holt McGavran points out ("Darwin, Coleridge, and 'The Thorn,'" *WC* 25:2 [1994]: 121), but the parallel with Coleridge's colors is still noteworthy. See, e.g., Warren Stevenson, "The Case of the Missing Captain: Power Politics in 'The Rime of the Ancient Mariner,'" *The Wordsworth Circle* 26:1 (1995): 13.

For one day with my telescope,
To view the ocean wide and bright,
When to this country first I came,
Ere I had heard of Martha's name,
I climbed the mountain's height:
A storm came on, and I could see
No object higher than my knee. (1.170–76)

Through the storm-blast — or whirl-blast on the hill — he thinks he sees a jutting crag, but the crag is Martha *Ray*, "sitting on the ground," a beam of light who is also clay.[26]

Insofar as *The Idiot Boy* reflects the "Rime," its hero is the moon, partly because the moon's pale fire reflects the state of joyous indifference that Wordsworth associates with idiocy. "Who's yon," asks the narrator at the moment when the idiot is found, "Beneath the moon, yet shining fair, / As careless as if nothing were"? — syntactically distributing this carelessness equally between moon and boy. If the sun to the becalmed and sweltering Mariner was no bigger than the moon, Johnny himself, for whom the sun did shine so cold, is both son and lunatic, object and focus of his almost equally imbecilic mother's faith (Foy). The horse, which moves sometimes and stands still at others, according to its gentle whim, is Johnny's ship, completely out of his control; it disappears with Johnny, cheered by Betty's joyous face, hence "merrily," beyond a lighthouselike sign of the familiar: "He's at the guide-post — he turns right, / She watches till he's out of sight." The awful monotony of sameness Coleridge dreads at the point when the sun resembles the moon ("Water, water, every where") is for Wordsworth, with "the moon in heaven," the distribution throughout the landscape of the undifferentiated idiocy with which he associates the truth of being, elusive only because it is the object of the frantic Betty's quest rather than the revelation of quietude: "'Twas Johnny, Johnny, every where." When Johnny is finally in view, he seems as insubstantial, as little himself, to Betty as the returning Mariner seemed to the Hermit and his companions: "Why stand you thus Good Betty Foy? / It is no goblin, 'tis no ghost." Something similar has happened, but in a carefully inverted context and with amused forbearance. The disagreement concerns the ontology of the poetic: whereas the Mariner

---

[26]For other remarks connecting the "Rime" and "The Thorn," see Susan J. Wolfson, "The Language of Interpretation in Romantic Poetry: 'A Strong Working of the Mind,'" *Romanticism and Language,* ed. Arden Reed (Ithaca: Cornell UP, 1984) 23 ff.; and Stevenson, "The Case of the Missing Captain" (13).

in a state of undifferentiated calm is deprived of speech except for a lone synecdoche, Johnny, whose burring all along has been more authentically the language of nature even than the real language of men, can finally speak, out of the undifferentiated element in which he moves, the language of radical metaphor: "The cocks did crow to-whoo, to-whoo, / And the sun did shine so cold."

"Anecdote for Fathers" and "We Are Seven" teach this same lesson to adult victims of the false secondary power. In asking a child to choose between locales, whether Kilve (evoking the walk that engendered the "Rime" as Wordsworth remembered it) or Liswyn farm, the speaker forces him to discriminate meretriciously, and thereby teaches him what Plato called poetry and Wordsworth chooses for a subtitle, "The Art of Lying." That the boy both is and is not on the site of the Mariner's return (he is not on "Kilve by the green sea"), and at least claims to prefer another site, is proven by his repudiation of the "weathercock" by means of which Coleridge in the "Rime" had attempted to make his peace on his own terms with Wordsworthian states of numinous calm: "The moonlight steeped in silentness / The steady weathercock." "We Are Seven," the poem that called forth the note to Isabella Fenwick reminiscing about the composition of the "Rime," dispels the gloom of what Coleridge calls "life-in-death" by refusing to distinguish between life and death.[27] From the standpoint of a "simple child," none of the "Rime"'s scrupulous distinctions among modes of being alive, being dead, and being both at once can affect the simple animism of believing that there is only one state of being. Objects wherever they may be — here, there, above- or below-ground, but never partly here, partly "in heaven" — are unified indissolubly by their state of common existence, whether playing or lying still, in the churchyard of process.

Thus "We murder to dissect." It is commonplace that "Expostulation and Reply" and "The Tables Turned" were written to admonish the future essayist William Hazlitt during his visit to Wordsworth and Coleridge. But why Hazlitt, or Hazlitt exclusively? I hope that my argument will have shown how precisely the lines are drawn, albeit as caricature in each case, between Wordsworth and Coleridge in these two poems. Wordsworth casts himself as the Hermit, on "an old grey

---

[27]In 1836 Wordsworth told Henry Crabb Robinson that Coleridge had written the first four lines of "We Are Seven." I would suggest only that even with such evidence in hand one must appeal to the asymmetry of motive alleged above. See Mark L. Reed, "Wordsworth, Coleridge, and the 'Plan' of the Lyrical Ballads," *University of Toronto Quarterly* 34 (1965): 250.

stone," inveighing against the idea that the only teachers are "science" and "art," grand abstractions which are made curiously to resemble the crew on the Mariner's ship: "the spirit breath'd / From dead men to their kind" — that is, perhaps, from dead men to dead men. These poems are Wordsworth's corrective to the notion that the Wedding Guest, who also "sat on a stone,"[28] must be "sadder and wiser." There is "more of wisdom" in the linnet's voice or that of the throstle ("no mean preacher") than in any iterable, booklike tale about the death of a bird. Anticipating Keats's critique of Coleridge and his "irritable reaching after fact" while also anticipating the concept of negative capability, Wordsworth sets forth his own doctrine of "wise passiveness."

Perhaps strangest of all, Coleridge seems to have taken all of Wordsworth's counterassertions to heart, and accepted them, in the poem he composed last for *Lyrical Ballads*, "The Nightingale" (April 1798). In an opening setting of untroubled, beatific calm, a penseroso scene, there is "nothing melancholy" about the nightingale's song, which is, and seems sufficiently to be, the "merry . . . love-chant" from which the Mariner had barred the Wedding Guest. There is a sardonic reflection on persons of sensibility whose idea of nature comes from books — "youths and maidens most poetical, / Who lose the deepening twilights of the spring / In ball-rooms and hot theatres," and "Full of meek sympathy must heave their sighs / O'er Philomela's pity-pleading strains." But Wordsworth and Dorothy and Coleridge together, he is at pains to say, "have learnt / A different lore," the teaching of nature that he is now eager to share with his "dear babe," whose restlessness, like the Idiot Boy's, is soothed by the moon. The concession seems total, and while it is possible to point to passages that, on various grounds, only Coleridge could have written, they do not materially alter the poem's theme and motive, which appear to be a peace offering. The only difference in this moment, a difference however that amounts to a guarantee that the rift must reopen, is Coleridge's curious compulsion (visible also in the "Friends, whom I never more may meet again" of "This Lime-Tree Bower My Prison") to exile himself from paradise: "Once more, farewell, / Sweet nightingale! Once more, my friends! farewell." And perhaps, after all, looking forward to more visionary speech whatever social loss may be entailed, the parting voice is still the Mariner's.

<hr />

[28]For comments on this parallel, see Peter Larkin, "*Lyrical Ballads:* Wordsworth's Book of Questions," *WC* 20:2 (1989): 107.

WORKS CITED

Coleridge, Samuel Taylor. *Biographia Literaria*. Ed. James Engell and Walter Jackson Bate. 2 vols. Vol. 7 of *The Collected Works of Samuel Taylor Coleridge*. Princeton: Princeton UP, 1983.

———. *Collected Letters of Samuel Taylor Coleridge*. Ed. Earl Leslie Griggs. 6 vols. Oxford: Clarendon, 1956–71.

———. *The Complete Poetical Works of Samuel Taylor Coleridge*. Ed. Ernest Hartley Coleridge. 2 vols. Oxford: Clarendon, 1975.

de Man, Paul. *Blindness and Insight: Essays into the Rhetoric of Contemporary Criticism*. Minneapolis: U of Minnesota P, 1983.

Empson, William. *Argufying*. Ed. John Haffenden. Iowa City: U of Iowa P, 1987.

———. *Some Versions of Pastoral*. London: Chatto, 1935.

Ferguson, Frances. "Coleridge and the Deluded Reader: 'The Rime of the Ancient Mariner.'" *Georgia Review* 31 (1977): 617–35. Reprinted in this book on pages 113–30.

Reed, Arden. "The Mariner Rimed." *Romanticism and Language*. Ed. Arden Reed. Ithaca: Cornell UP, 1984, 168–201.

Wordsworth, William. *"Lyrical Ballads," and Other Poems, 1797–1800*. Ed. James Butler and Karen Green. Ithaca: Cornell UP, 1992.

Glossary of Critical
and Theoretical Terms

Most terms have been glossed parenthetically where they first appear in the text. Mainly, the glossary lists terms that are too complex to define in a phrase or a sentence or two. A few of the terms listed are discussed at greater length elsewhere (feminist criticism, for instance); these terms are defined succinctly and a page reference to the longer discussion is provided.

AFFECTIVE FALLACY First used by William K. Wimsatt and Monroe C. Beardsley to refer to what they regarded as the erroneous practice of interpreting texts according to the psychological responses of readers. "The Affective Fallacy," they wrote in a 1946 essay later republished in *The Verbal Icon* (1954), "is a confusion between the poem and its *results* (what it *is* and what it *does*). . . . begins by trying to derive the standards of criticism from the psychological effects of a poem and ends in impressionism and relativism." The affective fallacy, like the intentional fallacy (confusing the meaning of a work with the author's expressly intended meaning), was one of the main tenets of the New Criticism, or formalism. The affective fallacy has recently been contested by reader-response critics, who have deliberately dedicated their efforts to describing the way individual readers and "interpretive communities" go about "making sense" of texts.

See also: Authorial Intention, Formalism, Reader-Response Criticism.

AUTHORIAL INTENTION Defined narrowly, an author's intention in writing a work, as expressed in letters, diaries, interviews, and conversations. Defined more broadly, "intentionality" involves unexpressed motivations, designs, and purposes, some of which may have remained unconscious.

The debate over whether critics should try to discern an author's intentions (conscious or otherwise) is an old one. William K. Wimsatt and Monroe C. Beardsley, in an essay first published in the 1940s, coined the term "intentional fallacy" to refer to the practice of basing interpretations on the expressed or implied intentions of authors, a practice they judged to be erroneous. As proponents of the New Criticism, or formalism, they argued that a work of literature is an object in itself and should be studied as such. They believed that it is sometimes helpful to learn what an author intended, but the critic's real purpose is to show what is actually in the text, not what an author intended to put there.

See also: Affective Fallacy, Formalism.

BASE *See* Marxist Criticism.

BINARY OPPOSITIONS *See* Oppositions.

BLANKS *See* Gaps.

CANON Since the fourth century, used to refer to those books of the Bible that the Christian church accepts as being Holy Scripture. The term has come to be applied more generally to those literary works given special status or "privileged," by a culture. Works we tend to think of as "classics" or the "Great Books" produced by Western culture — texts that are found in every anthology of American, British, and world literature — would be among those that constitute the canon.

Recently, Marxist, feminist, minority, and postcolonial critics have argued that, for political reasons, many excellent works never enter the canon. Canonized works, they claim, are those that reflect — and respect — the culture's dominant ideology or perform some socially acceptable or even necessary form of "cultural work." Attempts have been made to broaden or redefine the canon by discovering valuable texts, or versions of texts, that were repressed or ignored for political reasons. These have been published both in traditional and in nontraditional anthologies. The most outspoken critics of the canon, especially radical critics practicing cultural criticism, have called into question the whole concept of canon or "canonicity." Privileging no form of artistic expression that reflects and revises the culture, these critics treat cartoons, comics, and soap operas with the same cogency and respect they accord novels, poems, and plays.

See also: Cultural Criticism, Feminist Criticism, Ideology, Marxist Criticism.

CONFLICTS, CONTRADICTIONS *See* Gaps.

CULTURAL CRITICISM A critical approach that is sometimes referred to as "cultural studies" or "cultural critique." Practitioners of cultural criticism oppose "high" definitions of culture and take seriously popular cultural forms. Grounded in a variety of European influences, cultural criticism nonetheless gained institutional force in England, in 1964, with the founding of the Centre for Contemporary Cultural Studies at Birmingham University. Broadly interdisciplinary in its scope and approach, cultural criticism views the text as the locus and catalyst of a complex network of political and economic discourses. Cultural critics share with Marxist critics an interest in the ideological contexts of cultural forms.

DECONSTRUCTION A poststructuralist approach to literature that is strongly influenced by the writings of the French philosopher Jacques Derrida. Deconstruction, partly in response to structuralism and formalism, posits the undecidability of meaning for all texts. In fact, as the deconstructionist critic J. Hillis Miller points out, "deconstruction is not a dismantling of the structure of a text but a demonstration that it has already dismantled itself." *See* "What Is Deconstruction?" pp. 261–78.

DIALECTIC Originally developed by Greek philosophers, mainly Socrates and Plato, as a form and method of logical argumentation; the term later came to denote a philosophical notion of evolution. The German philosopher G. W. F. Hegel described dialectic as a process whereby a thesis, when countered by an antithesis, leads to the synthesis of a new idea. Karl Marx and Friedrich Engels, adapting Hegel's idealist theory, used the phrase "dialectical materialism" to discuss the way in which a revolutionary class war might lead to the synthesis of a new social economic order. The American Marxist critic Fredric Jameson has coined the phrase "dialectical criticism" to refer to a Marxist critical approach that synthesizes structuralist and poststructuralist methodologies.
See also: Marxist Criticism, Poststructuralism, Structuralism.

DIALOGIC *See* Discourse.

DISCOURSE Used specifically, can refer to (1) spoken or written discussion of a subject or area of knowledge; (2) the words in, or text of, a narrative as opposed to its story line; or (3) a "strand" within a given narrative that argues a certain point or defends a given value system.

More generally, "discourse" refers to the language in which a subject or area of knowledge is discussed or a certain kind of business is transacted. Human knowledge is collected and structured in discourses. Theology and medicine are defined by their discourses, as are politics, sexuality, and literary criticism.

A society is generally made up of a number of different discourses or "discourse communities," one or more of which may be dominant or serve the dominant ideology. Each discourse has its own vocabulary, concepts, and rules, the knowledge of which constitutes power. The psychoanalyst and psychoanalytic critic Jacques Lacan has treated the unconscious as a form of discourse, the patterns of which are repeated in literature. Cultural critics, following Mikhail Bakhtin, use the word "dialogic" to discuss the dialogue *between* discourses that takes place within language or, more specifically, a literary text.
See also: Cultural Criticism, Ideology, Narrative, Psychoanalytic Criticism.

FEMINIST CRITICISM An aspect of the feminist movement whose primary goals include critiquing masculine-dominated language and literature by showing how they reflect a masculine ideology; writing the history of unknown or undervalued women writers, thereby earning them their rightful place in the literary canon; and helping to create a climate in which women's creativity may be fully realized and appreciated.

FIGURE *See* Metaphor, Metonymy, Symbol.

FORMALISM Also referred to as the New Criticism, formalism reached its height during the 1940s and 1950s, but it is still practiced today. Formalists treat a work of literary art as if it were a self-contained, self-referential object. Rather than basing their interpretations of a text on the reader's response, the author's stated intentions, or parallels between the text and historical contexts (such as the author's life), formalists concentrate on the relationships *within* the text that give it its own distinctive character or form. Special attention is paid to repetition, particularly of images or symbols, but also of sound effects and rhythms in poetry.

Because of the importance placed on close analysis and the stress on the text as a carefully crafted, orderly object containing observable formal patterns, formalism has often been seen as an attack on Romanticism and impressionism, particularly impressionistic criticism. It has sometimes even been called an "objective" approach to literature. Formalists are more likely than certain other critics to believe and say that the meaning of a text can be known objectively. For instance, reader-response critics see meaning as a function either of each reader's experience or of the norms that govern a particular "interpretive community," and deconstructors argue that texts mean opposite things at the same time.

Formalism was originally based on essays written during the 1920s and 1930s by T. S. Eliot, I. A. Richards, and William Empson. It was significantly developed later by a group of American poets and critics, including R. P. Blackmur, Cleanth Brooks, John Crowe Ransom, Allen Tate, Robert Penn Warren, and William K. Wimsatt. Although we associate formalism with certain principles and terms (such as the "affective fallacy" and the "intentional fallacy" as defined by Wimsatt and Monroe C. Beardsley), formalists were trying to make a cultural statement rather than establish a critical dogma. Generally southern, religious, and culturally conservative, they advocated the inherent value of literary works (particularly of literary works regarded as beautiful art objects) because they were sick of the growing ugliness of modern life and contemporary events. Some recent theorists even suggest that the rising popularity of formalism after World War II was a feature of American isolationism, the formalist tendency to isolate literature from biography and history being a manifestation of the American fatigue with wider involvements.

See also: Affective Fallacy, Authorial Intention, Deconstruction, Reader-Response Criticism, Symbol.

GAPS When used by reader-response critics familiar with the theories of Wolfgang Iser, refers to "blanks" in texts that must be filled in by readers. A gap may be said to exist whenever and wherever a reader perceives something to be missing between words, sentences, paragraphs, stanzas, or chapters. Readers respond to gaps actively and creatively, explaining apparent inconsistencies in point of view, accounting for jumps in chronology, speculatively supplying information missing from plots, and resolving problems or issues left ambiguous or "indeterminate" in the text.

Reader-response critics sometimes speak as if a gap actually exists in a text; a gap is, of course, to some extent a product of readers' perceptions. Different readers may find gaps in different texts, and different gaps in the same text. Furthermore, they may fill these gaps in different ways, which is why, a reader-response critic might argue, works are interpreted in different ways.

Although the concept of the gap has been used mainly by reader-response critics, it has also been used by critics taking other theoretical approaches. Practitioners of deconstruction might use "gap" when speaking of the radical contradictoriness of a text. Marxists have used the term to speak of everything from the gap that opens up between economic base and cultural superstructure to the two kinds of conflicts or contradictions to be found in literary texts. The first of these, they would argue, results from the fact that texts reflect ideology, within which certain subjects cannot be covered, things that cannot be said, contradictory views that cannot be recognized as contradictory. The second kind of conflict, contradiction, or gap within a text results from the fact that works don't just reflect ideology: they are also fictions that, consciously or unconsciously, distance themselves from the same ideology.

See also: Deconstruction, Ideology, Marxist Criticism, Reader-Response Criticism.

GENDER CRITICISM Developing out of feminist criticism in the mid-1980s, this fluid and inclusive movement by its nature defies neat definition. Its practitioners include, but are not limited to, self-identified feminists, gay and lesbian critics, queer and performance theorists, and poststructuralists interested in deconstructing oppositions such as masculine/feminine, heterosexual/homosexual. This diverse group of critics shares an interest in interrogating categories of gender and sexuality and exploring the relationships between them, though it does not necessarily share any central assumptions about the nature of these categories. For example, some gender critics insist that all gender identities are cultural constructions, but others have maintained a belief in essential gender identity. Often gender critics are more interested in examining gender issues through a literary text than a literary text through gender issues.

GENRE A French word referring to a kind or type of literature. Individual works within a genre may exhibit a distinctive form, be governed by certain conventions, or represent characteristic subjects. Tragedy, epic, and romance are all genres.

Perhaps inevitably, the term *genre* is used loosely. Lyric poetry is a genre, but so are characteristic *types* of the lyric, such as the sonnet, the ode, and the elegy. Fiction is a genre, as are detective fiction and science fiction. The list of genres grows constantly as critics establish new lines of connection between individual works and discern new categories of works with common characteristics. Moreover, some writers form hybrid genres by combining the characteristics of several in a single work. Knowledge of genres helps critics to understand and explain what is conventional and unconventional, borrowed and original, in a work.

HEGEMONY Given intellectual currency by the Italian communist Antonio Gramsci, the word (a translation of *egemonia*) refers to the pervasive system of assumptions, meanings, and values — the web of ideologies, in other words — that shapes the way things look, what they mean, and therefore what reality *is* for the majority of people within a given culture.

See also: Ideology, Marxist Criticism.

IDEOLOGY A set of beliefs underlying the customs, habits, or practices common to a given social group. To members of that group, the beliefs seem obviously true, natural, and even universally applicable. They may seem just as obviously arbitrary, idiosyncratic, and even false to outsiders or members of another group who adhere to another ideology. Within a society, several ideologies may coexist, or one or more may be dominant.

Ideologies may be forcefully imposed or willingly subscribed to. Their component beliefs may be held consciously or unconsciously. In either case, they come to form what Johanna M. Smith has called "the unexamined ground of our experience." Ideology governs our perceptions, judgments, and prejudices — our sense of what is acceptable, normal, and deviant. Ideology may cause a revolution; it may also allow discrimination and even exploitation.

Ideologies are of special interest to sociologically oriented critics of literature because of the way in which authors reflect or resist prevailing views in their texts. Some Marxist critics have argued that literary texts reflect and reproduce the ideologies that produced them; most, however, have shown how ideologies are riven with contradictions that works of literature manage to expose and widen. Still other Marxists have focused on the way in which texts themselves are characterized by gaps, conflicts, and contradictions between their ideological and anti-ideological functions.

Feminist critics have addressed the question of ideology by seeking to expose (and thereby call into question) the patriarchal ideology mirrored or inscribed in works written by men — even men who have sought to counter sexism and break down sexual stereotypes. New historicists have been interested in demonstrating the ideological underpinnings not only of literary representations but also of our interpretations of them. Fredric Jameson, an American Marxist critic, argues that all thought is ideological, but that ideological thought that knows itself as such stands the chance of seeing through and transcending ideology.

See also: Cultural Criticism, Feminist Criticism, Marxist Criticism, New Historicism.

IMAGINARY ORDER One of the three essential orders of the psychoanalytic field (*see* Real and Symbolic Order), it is most closely associated with the senses (sight, sound, touch, taste, and smell). The infant, who by comparison to other animals is born premature and thus is wholly dependent on others for a prolonged period, enters the Imaginary order when it begins to experience a unity of body parts and motor control that is empowering. This usually occurs between six and eighteen months, and is called by Lacan the "mirror stage" or "mirror phase," in which the child anticipates mastery of its body. It does so by identifying with the *image* of wholeness (that is, seeing its own image in the mirror, experiencing its mother as a whole body, and so on). This sense of oneness, and also difference from others (especially the mother or primary caretaker), is established through an image or a vision of harmony that is both a mirroring and a "mirage of maturation" or false sense of individuality and independence. The Imaginary is a metaphor for unity, is related to the visual order, and is always part of human subjectivity. Because the subject is fundamentally separate from others and also internally divided (conscious/unconscious), the apparent coherence of the Imaginary, its fullness and grandiosity, is always false, a *mis*recognition that the ego (or "me") tries to deny by imagining itself as coherent and empowered. The Imaginary operates in conjunction with the Real and the Symbolic and is not a "stage" of development equivalent to Freud's "pre-oedipal stage," nor is it prelinguistic.

See also: Psychoanalytic Criticism, Real, Symbolic Order.

IMPLIED READER A phrase used by some reader-response critics in place of the phrase "the reader." Whereas "the reader" could refer to any idiosyncratic individual who happens to have read or to be reading the text, "the implied reader" is *the* reader intended, even created, by the text. Other reader-response critics seeking to describe this more generally conceived reader have spoken of the "informed reader" or the "narratee," who is "the necessary counterpart of a given narrator."

See also: Reader-Response Criticism.

INTENTIONAL FALLACY *See* Authorial Intention.

INTENTIONALITY *See* Authorial Intention.

INTERTEXTUALITY The condition of interconnectedness among texts. Every author has been influenced by others, and every work contains explicit and implicit references to other works. Writers may consciously or unconsciously echo a predecessor or precursor; they may also consciously or unconsciously disguise their indebtedness, making intertextual relationships difficult for the critic to trace.

Reacting against the formalist tendency to view each work as a freestanding object, some poststructuralist critics suggested that the meaning of a work emerges only intertextually, that is, within the context provided by other works. But there has been a reaction, too, against this type of intertextual criticism. Some new historicist critics suggest that literary history is itself too narrow a context and that works should be interpreted in light of a larger set of cultural contexts.

There is, however, a broader definition of intertextuality, one that refers to the relationship between works of literature and a wide range of narratives and discourses that we don't usually consider literary. Thus defined, intertextuality could be used by a new historicist to refer to the significant interconnectedness between a literary text and nonliterary discussions of or discourses about contemporary culture. Or it could be used by a poststructuralist to suggest that a work can be recognized and read only within a vast field of signs and tropes that is *like* a text and that makes any single text self-contradictory and "undecidable."

See also: Discourse, Formalism, Narrative, New Historicism, Poststructuralism, Trope.

MARXIST CRITICISM An approach that treats literary texts as material products, describing them in broadly historical terms. In Marxist criticism, the text is viewed in terms of its production and consumption, as a product *of* work that does identifiable cultural work of its own. Following Karl Marx, the founder of communism, Marxist critics have used the terms *base* to refer to economic reality and *superstructure* to refer to the corresponding or "homologous" infrastructure consisting of politics, law, philosophy, religion, and the arts. Also following Marx, they have used the word *ideology* to refer to that set of cultural beliefs that literary works at once reproduce, resist, and revise. *See* "What Is Marxist Criticism?" pp. 131–45.

METAPHOR The representation of one thing by another related or similar thing. The image (or activity or concept) used to represent or "figure"

something else is known as the "vehicle" of the metaphor; the thing represented is called the "tenor." In other words, the vehicle is what we substitute
for the tenor. The relationship between vehicle and tenor can provide much
additional meaning. Thus, instead of saying, "Last night I read a book," we
might say, "Last night I plowed through a book." "Plowed through" (or the
activity of plowing) is the vehicle of our metaphor; "read" (or the act of reading) is the tenor, the thing being figured. The increment in meaning through
metaphor is fairly obvious. Our audience knows not only *that* we read but also
how we read, because to read a book in the way that a plow rips through earth
is surely to read in a relentless, unreflective way. Note that in the sentence
above, a new metaphor — "rips through" — has been used to explain an old
one. This serves (which is a metaphor) as an example of just how thick (another
metaphor) language is with metaphors!

Metaphor is a kind of "trope" (literally, a "turning," that is, a figure of
speech that alters or "turns" the meaning of a word or phrase). Other tropes
include allegory, conceit, metonymy, personification, simile, symbol, and synecdoche. Traditionally, metaphor and symbol have been viewed as the principal
tropes; minor tropes have been categorized as *types* of these two major ones.
Similes, for instance, are usually defined as simple metaphors that usually
employ *like* or *as* and state the tenor outright, as in "My love is like a red, red
rose." Synecdoche involves a vehicle that is a *part* of the tenor, as in "I see a
sail" meaning "I see a boat." Metonymy is viewed as a metaphor involving two
terms commonly if arbitrarily associated with (but not fundamentally or intrinsically related to) each other. Recently, however, deconstructors such as Paul de
Man and J. Hillis Miller have questioned the "privilege" granted to metaphor
and the metaphor/metonymy distinction or "opposition." They have suggested that all metaphors are really metonyms and that all figuration is arbitrary.

See also: Deconstruction, Metonymy, Oppositions, Symbol.

METONYMY The representation of one thing by another that is commonly and often physically associated with it. To refer to a writer's handwriting
as his or her "hand" is to use a metonymic "figure" or "trope." The image or
thing used to represent something else is known as the "vehicle" of the
metonym; the thing represented is called the "tenor."

Like other tropes (such as metaphor), metonymy involves the replacement
of one word or phrase by another. Liquor may be referred to as "the bottle," a
monarch as "the crown." Narrowly defined, the vehicle of a metonym is arbitrarily, not intrinsically, associated with the tenor. In other words, the bottle just
happens to be what liquor is stored in and poured from in our culture. The
hand may be involved in the production of handwriting, but so are the brain
and the pen. There is no special, intrinsic likeness between a crown and a
monarch; it's just that crowns traditionally sit on monarchs' heads and not on
the heads of university professors. More broadly, *metonym* and *metonymy* have
been used by recent critics to refer to a wide range of figures and tropes. Deconstructors have questioned the distinction between metaphor and metonymy.

See also: Deconstruction, Metaphor, Trope.

NARRATIVE A story or a telling of a story, or an account of a situation
or of events. A novel and a biography of a novelist are both narratives, as are
Freud's case histories.

Some critics use the word "narrative" even more generally; Brook Thomas, a new historicist, has critiqued "narratives of human history that neglect the role human labor has played."

NEW CRITICISM *See* Formalism.

NEW HISTORICISM First practiced and articulated in the late 1970s and early 1980s in the work of critics such as Stephen Greenblatt — who named this movement in contemporary critical theory — and Louis Montrose, its practitioners share certain convictions, primarily that literary critics need to develop a high degree of historical consciousness and that literature should not be viewed apart from other human creations, artistic or otherwise. They share a belief in referentiality — a belief that literature refers to and is referred to by things outside itself — that is fainter in the works of formalist, poststructuralist, and even reader-response critics. Discarding old distinctions between literature, history, and the social sciences, new historicists agree with Greenblatt that the "central concerns" of criticism "should prevent it from permanently sealing off one type of discourse from another, or decisively separating works of art from the minds and lives of their creators and their audiences."

See also: "What Is the New Historicism?" pp. 168–82; Authorial Intention, Deconstruction, Formalism, Ideology, Poststructuralism, Psychoanalytic Criticism.

OPPOSITIONS A concept highly relevant to linguistics, inasmuch as linguists maintain that words (such as *black* and *death*) have meaning not in themselves but in relation to other words (*white* and *life*). Jacques Derrida, a poststructuralist philosopher of language, has suggested that in the West we think in terms of these "binary oppositions" or dichotomies, which on examination turn out to be evaluative hierarchies. In other words, each opposition — beginning/end, presence/absence, or consciousness/unconsciousness — contains one term that our culture views as superior and one term that we view as negative or inferior.

Derrida has "deconstructed" a number of these binary oppositions, including two — speech/writing and signifier/signified — that he believes to be central to linguistics in particular and Western culture in general. He has concurrently critiqued the "law" of noncontradiction, which is fundamental to Western logic. He and other deconstructors have argued that a text can contain opposed strands of discourse and, therefore, mean opposite things: reason *and* passion, life *and* death, hope *and* despair, black *and* white. Traditionally, criticism has involved choosing between opposed or contradictory meanings and arguing that one is present in the text and the other absent.

French feminists have adopted the ideas of Derrida and other deconstructors, showing not only that we think in terms of such binary oppositions as male/female, reason/emotion, and active/passive, but that we also associate reason and activity with masculinity and emotion and passivity with femininity. Because of this, they have concluded that language is "phallocentric," or masculine-dominated.

See also: Deconstruction, Discourse, Feminist Criticism, Poststructuralism.

PHALLUS The symbolic value of the penis that organizes libidinal development and which Freud saw as a stage in the process of human subjectivity. Lacan viewed the Phallus as the representative of a fraudulent power (male over female) whose "Law" is a principle of psychic division (conscious/unconscious) and sexual difference (masculine/feminine). The Symbolic order (*see* Symbolic Order) is ruled by the Phallus, which of itself has no inherent meaning *apart from* the power and meaning given to it by individual cultures and societies, and represented by the name of the father as lawgiver and namer.

POSTSTRUCTURALISM The general attempt to contest and subvert structuralism initiated by deconstructors and certain other critics associated with psychoanalytic, Marxist, and feminist theory. Structuralists, using linguistics as a model and employing semiotic (sign) theory, posit the possibility of knowing a text systematically and revealing the "grammar" behind its form and meaning. Poststructuralists argue against the possibility of such knowledge and description. They counter that texts can be shown to contradict not only structuralist accounts of them but also themselves. In making their adversarial claims, they rely on close readings of texts and on the work of theorists such as Jacques Derrida and Jacques Lacan.

Poststructuralists have suggested that structuralism rests on distinctions between "signifier" and "signified" (signs and the things they point toward), "self" and "language" (or "text"), texts and other texts, and text and world that are overly simplistic, if not patently inaccurate. Poststructuralists have shown how all signifieds are also signifiers, and they have treated texts as "intertexts." They have viewed the world as if it *were* a text (we desire a certain car because it *symbolizes* achievement) and the self as the subject, as well as the user, of language; for example, we may shape and speak through language, but it also shapes and speaks through us.

See also: Deconstruction, Feminist Criticism, Intertextuality, Psychoanalytic Criticism, Semiotics, Structuralism.

PSYCHOANALYTIC CRITICISM Grounded in the psychoanalytic theories of Sigmund Freud, it is one of the oldest critical methodologies still in use. Freud's view that works of literature, like dreams, express secret, unconscious desires led to criticism and interpreted literary works as manifestations of the authors' neuroses. More recently, psychoanalytic critics have come to see literary works as skillfully crafted artifacts that may appeal to *our* neuroses by tapping into our repressed wishes and fantasies. Other forms of psychological criticism that diverge from Freud, although they ultimately derive from his insights, include those based on the theories of Carl Jung and Jacques Lacan. *See* "What Is Psychoanalytic Criticism?" pp. 220–33.

READER-RESPONSE CRITICISM An approach to literature that, as its name implies, considers the way readers respond to texts, as they read. Stanley Fish describes the method by saying that it substitutes for one question, "What does this sentence mean?" a more operational question, "What does this sentence do?" Reader-response criticism shares with deconstruction a strong textual orientation and a reluctance to define a single meaning for a work. Along with psychoanalytic criticism, it shares an interest in the dynamics of mental response to textual cues. *See* "What Is Reader-Response Criticism?" pp. 97–109.

REAL One of the three orders of subjectivity (*see* Imaginary Order and Symbolic Order), the Real is the intractable and substantial world that resists and exceeds interpretation. The Real cannot be imagined, symbolized, or known directly. It constantly eludes our efforts to name it (death, gravity, the physicality of objects are examples of the Real), and thus challenges both the Imaginary and the Symbolic orders. The Real is fundamentally "Other," the mark of the divide between conscious and unconscious, and is signaled in language by gaps, slips, speechlessness, and the sense of the uncanny. The Real is not what we call "reality." It is the stumbling block of the Imaginary (which thinks it can "imagine" anything, including the Real) and of the Symbolic, which tries to bring the Real under its laws (the Real exposes the "phallacy" of the Law of the Phallus). The Real is frightening; we try to tame it with laws and language and call it "reality."

    See also: Imaginary Order, Psychoanalytic Criticism, Symbolic Order.

SEMIOLOGY, SEMIOTIC *See* Semiotics.

SEMIOTICS The study of signs and sign systems and the way meaning is derived from them. Structuralist anthropologists, psychoanalysts, and literary critics developed semiotics during the decades following 1950, but much of the pioneering work had been done at the turn of the century by the founder of modern linguistics, Ferdinand de Saussure, and the American philosopher Charles Sanders Peirce.

    Semiotics is based on several important distinctions, including the distinction between "signifier" and "signified" (the sign and what it points toward) and the distinction between "langue" and "parole." *Langue* (French for "tongue," as in "native tongue," meaning language) refers to the entire system within which individual utterances or usages of language have meaning; *parole* (French for "word") refers to the particular utterances or usages. A principal tenet of semiotics is that signs, like words, are not significant in themselves, but instead have meaning only in relation to other signs and the entire system of signs, or langue.

    The affinity between semiotics and structuralist literary criticism derives from this emphasis placed on langue, or system. Structuralist critics, after all were reacting against formalists and their procedure of focusing on individual words as if meanings didn't depend on anything external to the text.

    Poststructuralists have used semiotics but questioned some of its underlying assumptions, including the opposition between signifier and signified. The feminist poststructuralist Julia Kristeva for instance, has used the word *semiotic* to describe feminine language, a highly figurative, fluid form of discourse that she sets in opposition to rigid, symbolic masculine language.

    See also: Deconstruction, Feminist Criticism, Formalism, Oppositions, Poststructuralism, Structuralism, Symbol.

SIMILE *See* Metaphor.

SOCIOHISTORICAL CRITICISM *See* New Historicism.

STRUCTURALISM A science of humankind whose proponents attempted to show that all elements of human culture, including literature, may be understood as parts of a system of signs. Structuralism, according to Robert Scholes, was a reaction to "'modernist' alienation and despair."

    Using Ferdinand de Saussure's linguistic theory, European structuralists such as Roman Jakobson, Claude Lévi-Strauss, and Roland Barthes (before his shift toward poststructuralism) attempted to develop a "semiology" or "semiotics" (science of signs). Barthes, among others, sought to recover literature and even language from the isolation in which they had been studied and to show that the laws that govern them govern all signs, from road signs to articles of clothing.

Particularly useful to structuralists were two of Saussure's concepts: the idea of "phoneme" in language and the idea that phonemes exist in two kinds of relationships: "synchronic" and "diachronic." A phoneme is the smallest consistently significant unit in language; thus, both "a" and "an" are phonemes, but "n" is not. A diachronic relationship is that which a phoneme has with those that have preceded it in time and those that will follow it. These "horizontal" relationships produce what we might call discourse or narrative and what Saussure called "parole." The synchronic relationship is the "vertical" one that a word has in a given instant with the entire system of language ("langue") in which it may generate meaning. "An" means what it means in English because those of us who speak the language are using it in the same way at a given time.

Following Saussure, Lévi-Strauss studied hundreds of myths, breaking them into their smallest meaningful units, which he called "mythemes." Removing each from its diachronic relations with other mythemes in a single myth (such as the myth of Oedipus and his mother), he vertically aligned those mythemes that he found to be homologous (structurally correspondent). He then studied the relationships within as well as between vertically aligned columns, in an attempt to understand scientifically, through ratios and proportions, those thoughts and processes that humankind has shared, both at one particular time and across time. One could say, then, that structuralists followed Saussure in preferring to think about the overriding langue or language of myth, in which each mytheme and mytheme-constituted myth fits meaningfully, rather than about isolated individual paroles or narratives. Structuralists followed Saussure's lead in believing what the poststructuralist Jacques Derrida later decided he could not subscribe to — that sign systems must be understood in terms of binary oppositions. In analyzing myths and texts to find basic structures, structuralists tended to find that opposite terms modulate until they are finally resolved or reconciled by some intermediary third term. Thus, a structuralist reading of *Paradise Lost* would show that the war between God and the bad angels becomes a rift between God and sinful, fallen man, the rift then being healed by the Son of God, the mediating third term.

See also: Deconstruction, Discourse, Narrative, Poststructuralism, Semiotics.

SUPERSTRUCTURE *See* Marxist Criticism.

SYMBOL A thing, image, or action that, although it is of interest in its own right, stands for or suggests something larger and more complex — often an idea or a range of interrelated ideas, attitudes, and practices.

Within a given culture, some things are understood to be symbols: the flag of the United States is an obvious example. More subtle cultural symbols might be the river as a symbol of time and the journey as a symbol of life and its manifold experiences.

Instead of appropriating symbols generally used and understood within their culture, writers often create symbols by setting up, in their works, a complex but identifiable web of associations. As a result, one object, image, or action suggests others, and often, ultimately, a range of ideas.

A symbol may thus be defined as a metaphor in which the "vehicle," the thing, image, or action used to represent something else, represents many related things (or "tenors") or is broadly suggestive. The urn in Keats's "Ode on a Grecian Urn" suggests many interrelated concepts, including art, truth, beauty, and timelessness.

Symbols have been of particular interest to formalists, who study how meanings emerge from the complex, patterned relationships between images in a work, and psychoanalytic critics, who are interested in how individual authors and the larger culture both disguise and reveal unconscious fears and desires through symbols. Recently, French feminists have also focused on the symbolic. They have suggested that, as wide-ranging as it seems, symbolic language is ultimately rigid and restrictive. They favor semiotic language and writing, which, they contend, is at once more rhythmic, unifying, and feminine.

See also: Feminist Criticism, Metaphor, Psychoanalytic Criticism, Trope.

SYMBOLIC ORDER One of the three orders of subjectivity (*see* Imaginary Order and Real), it is the realm of law, language, and society; it is the repository of generally held cultural beliefs. Its symbolic system is language, whose agent is the father or lawgiver, the one who has the power of naming. The human subject is commanded into this preestablished order by language (a process that begins long before a child can speak) and must submit to its orders of communication (grammar, syntax, and so on). Entrance into the Symbolic order determines subjectivity according to a primary law of referentiality that takes the male sign (phallus, *see* Phallus) as its ordering principle. Lacan states that both sexes submit to the Law of the Phallus (the law of order, language, and differentiation) but that their individual relation to the law determines whether they see themselves as — and are seen by others to be — either "masculine" or "feminine." The Symbolic institutes repression (of the Imaginary), thus creating the unconscious, which itself is structured like the language of the symbolic. The unconscious, a timeless realm, cannot be known directly, but it can be understood by a kind of translation that takes place in language — psychoanalysis is the "talking cure." The Symbolic is not a "stage" of development (as is Freud's "oedipal stage") nor is it set in place once and for all in human life. We constantly negotiate its threshold (in sleep, in drunkenness) and can "fall out" of it altogether in psychosis.

See also: Imaginary Order, Psychoanalytic Criticism, Real.

SYNECDOCHE *See* Metaphor, Metonymy.

TENOR *See* Metaphor, Metonymy, Symbol.

TROPE A figure, as in "figure of speech." Literally a "turning," that is, a turning or twisting of a word or phrase to make it mean something else. Principal tropes include metaphor, metonymy, personification, simile, and synecdoche.

See also: Metaphor, Metonymy.

VEHICLE *See* Metaphor, Metonymy, Symbol.

About the Contributors

THE VOLUME EDITOR

Paul H. Fry is William Lampson Professor of English and Master of Ezra Stiles College at Yale University. His numerous scholarly articles and books on Romantic poetry and literary theory include *The Poet's Calling in the English Ode* (1980), *The Reach of Criticism: Method and Perception in Literary Theory* (1983), *William Empson: Prophet against Sacrifice* (1991), and *A Defense of Poetry: Reflections on the Occasion of Writing* (1995). He is currently at work on a study of William Wordsworth.

THE CRITICS

Susan Eilenberg is an associate professor of English at the State University of New York — Buffalo. A frequent reviewer of scholarly work on Romantic literature, she is the author of *Strange Power of Speech: Wordsworth, Coleridge, and Literary Possession* (1992).

Frances Ferguson is professor of English and the humanities and director of the Center for Research on Culture and Literature at Johns Hopkins University. She is the author of numerous articles on literature of the eighteenth century and the Romantic period and of *Wordsworth: Language as Counter-Spirit* (1977) and *Solitude and the Sublime:*

Romanticism and the Aesthetics of Individuation (1993). Her study of the rise of the importance of pornography in the past two centuries, *Pornography: The Theory* is forthcoming.

Raimonda Modiano is Lockwood Professor of Humanities at the University of Washington. She is the author of numerous scholarly articles and reviews about Romanticism and is the coeditor of two volumes of Coleridge's *Marginalia* (1984, 1992), as well as the author of *Coleridge and the Concept of Nature* (1985). She is currently at work on *Rites of Violence: Sacrifice, Gift Economy and Literary Exchange in Coleridge and Wordsworth*.

David Simpson is Professor and G.B. Needham Fellow in English at the University of California, Davis. His most recent books are *The Academic Postmodern and the Rule of Literature: A Report on Half Knowledge* (1995) and *Romanticism, Nationalism and the Revolt Against Theory* (1993). He is currently at work on a study titled *Situatedness: or, Why We Keep Saying Where We're Coming From*.

Anne Williams is a professor of English at the University of Georgia. She is the author of *Prophetic Strain: The Greater Lyric in the Eighteenth Century* (1984) and *Art of Darkness: A Poetics of Gothic* (1995). At present chair of the English department, she is writing a Gothic novel and a study of Horace Walpole's fascination with Italian opera.

THE SERIES EDITOR

Ross C Murfin, general editor of the Case Studies in Contemporary Criticism and volume editor of Joseph Conrad's *Heart of Darkness* and Nathaniel Hawthorne's *The Scarlet Letter* in the series, is provost and vice president for academic affairs at Southern Methodist University. He has taught at the University of Miami, Yale University, and the University of Virginia and has published scholarly studies of Joseph Conrad, Thomas Hardy, and D. H. Lawrence.